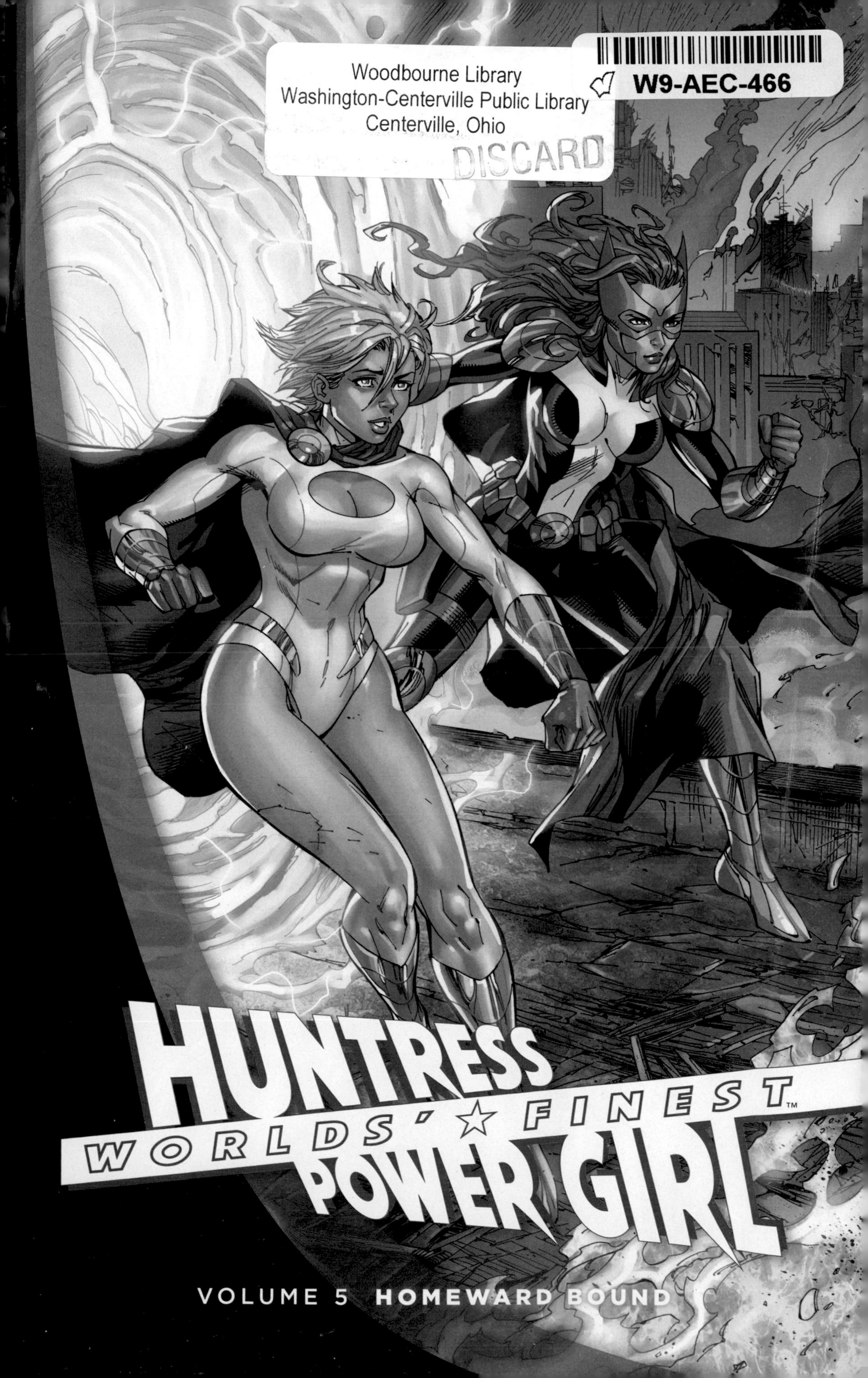
HUNTRESS
WORLDS' FINEST™
POWER GIRL
VOLUME 5 HOMEWARD BOUND

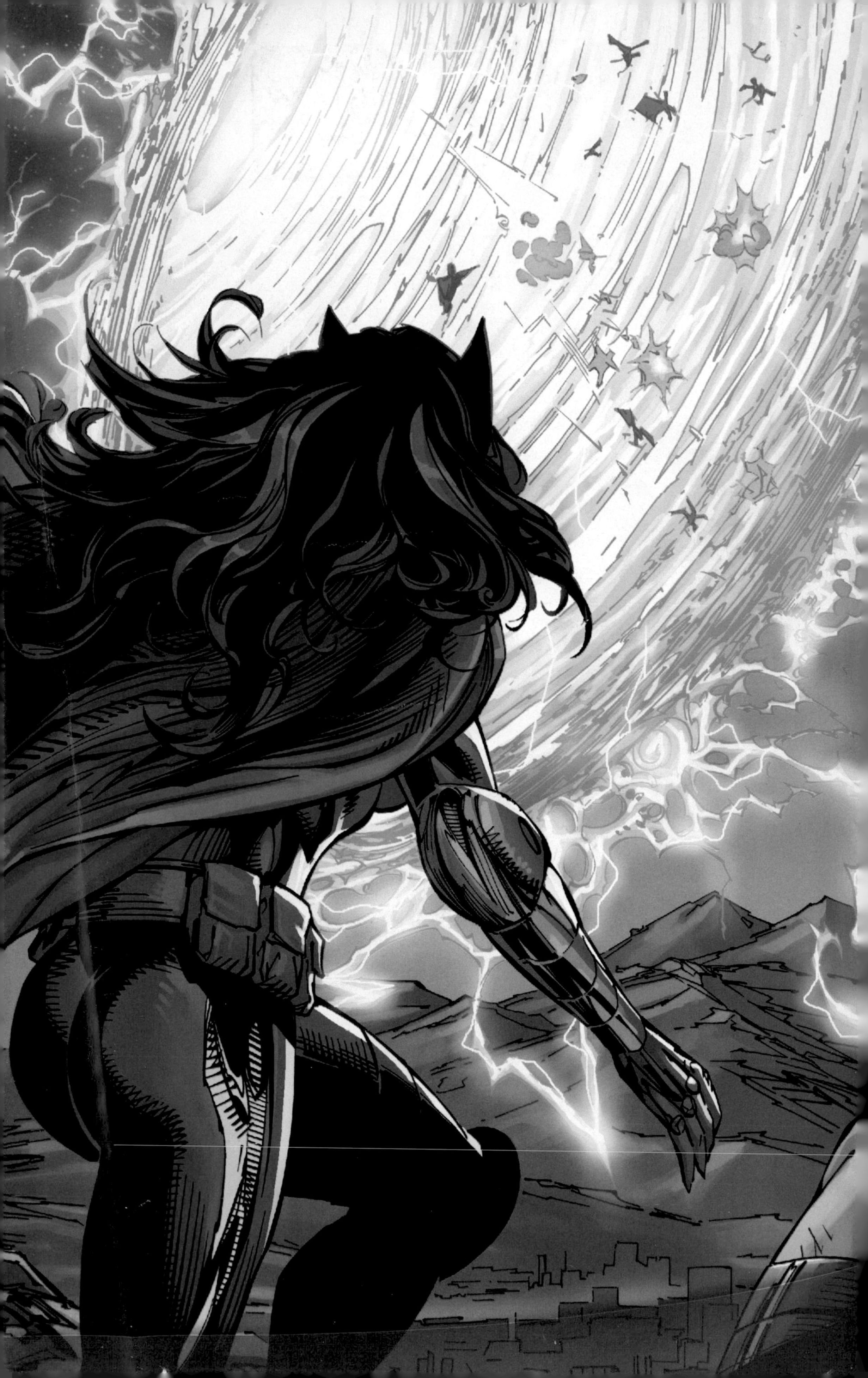

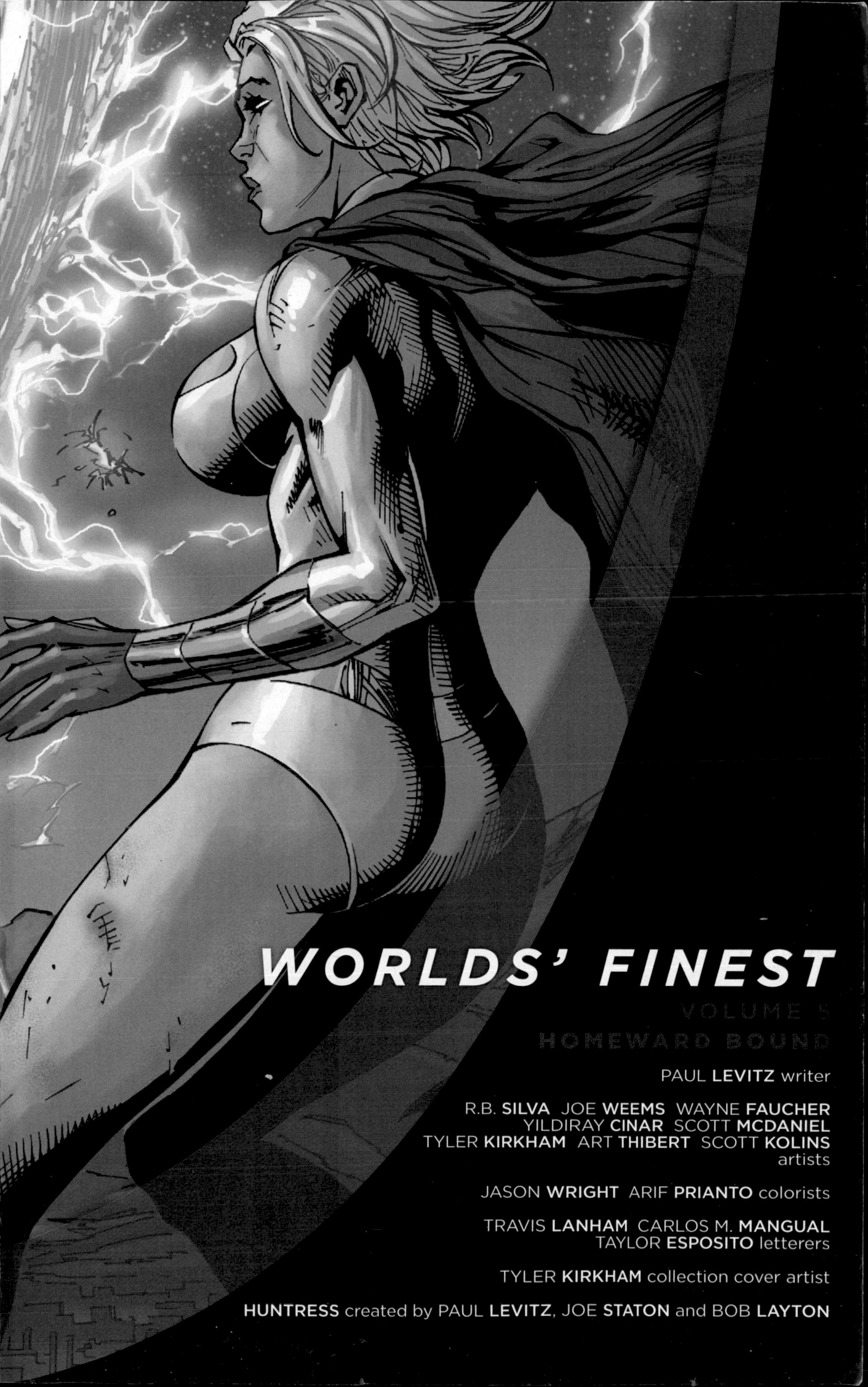

WORLDS' FINEST

VOLUME 5
HOMEWARD BOUND

PAUL **LEVITZ** writer

R.B. **SILVA** JOE **WEEMS** WAYNE **FAUCHER**
YILDIRAY **CINAR** SCOTT **MCDANIEL**
TYLER **KIRKHAM** ART **THIBERT** SCOTT **KOLINS**
artists

JASON **WRIGHT** ARIF **PRIANTO** colorists

TRAVIS **LANHAM** CARLOS M. **MANGUAL**
TAYLOR **ESPOSITO** letterers

TYLER **KIRKHAM** collection cover artist

HUNTRESS created by PAUL **LEVITZ**, JOE **STATON** and BOB **LAYTON**

EDDIE BERGANZA MIKE COTTON Editors – Original Series ANTHONY MARQUES Assistant Editor – Original Series
PAUL SANTOS Editor ROBBIN BROSTERMAN Design Director – Books ROBBIE BIEDERMAN Publication Design

BOB HARRAS Senior VP – Editor-in-Chief, DC Comics

DIANE NELSON President DAN DIDIO and JIM LEE Co-Publishers
GEOFF JOHNS Chief Creative Officer AMIT DESAI Senior VP – Marketing and Franchise Management
AMY GENKINS Senior VP – Business and Legal Affairs NAIRI GARDINER Senior VP – Finance
JEFF BOISON VP – Publishing Planning MARK CHIARELLO VP – Art Direction and Design
JOHN CUNNINGHAM VP – Marketing TERRI CUNNINGHAM VP – Editorial Administration
LARRY GANEM VP – Talent Relations and Services ALISON GILL Senior VP – Manufacturing and Operations
HANK KANALZ Senior VP – Vertigo and Integrated Publishing JAY KOGAN VP – Business and Legal Affairs, Publishing
JACK MAHAN VP – Business Affairs, Talent NICK NAPOLITANO VP – Manufacturing Administration
SUE POHJA VP – Book Sales FRED RUIZ VP – Manufacturing Operations
COURTNEY SIMMONS Senior VP – Publicity BOB WAYNE Senior VP – Sales

WORLDS' FINEST VOLUME 5: HOMEWARD BOUND

DC Comics, 4000 Warner Blvd., Burbank, CA 91522
A Warner Bros. Entertainment Company.
Printed by RR Donnelley, Owensville, MO, USA. 5/1/15. First Printing.
ISBN: 978-1-4012-5420-9

Library of Congress Cataloging-in-Publication Data

Levitz, Paul, author.
Worlds' Finest. Volume 5 / Paul Levitz, writer ; R.B. Silva, artist.
pages cm
ISBN 978-1-4012-5420-9 (paperback)
1. Graphic novels. I. Silva, R. B., 1985- illustrator. II. Title.
PN6728.W7L54 2014
741.5'973—dc23

2014026902

SUSTAINABLE
FORESTRY
INITIATIVE

Certified Chain of Custody
20% Certified Forest Content,
80% Certified Sourcing
www.sfiprogram.org
SFI-01042
APPLIES TO TEXT STOCK ONLY

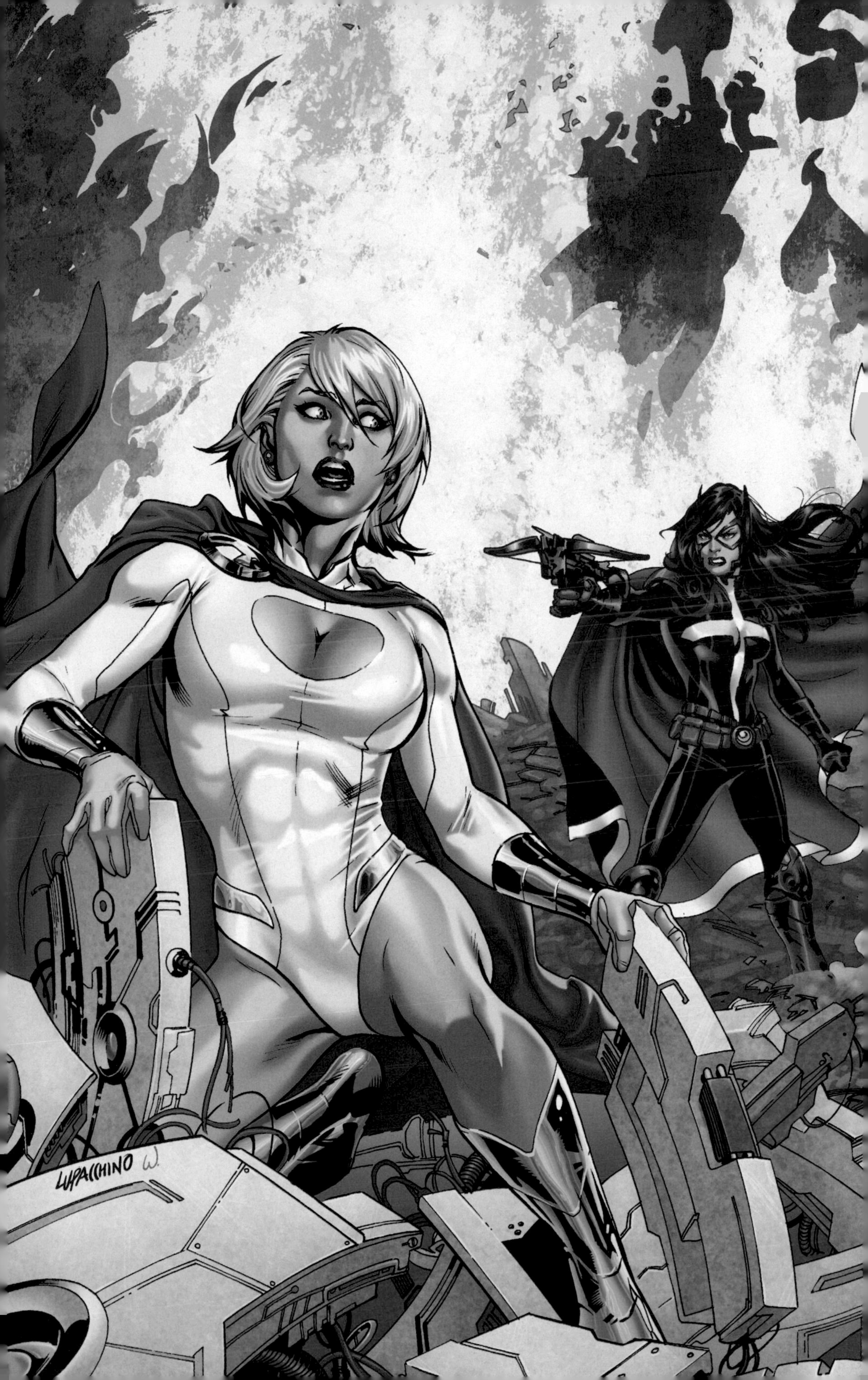
LUPACCHINO W.

NOW AND THEN

PAUL LEVITZ writer **SCOTT MCDANIEL** breakdowns **R.B. SILVA** **YILDIRAY CINAR** pencillers

JOE WEEMS **WAYNE FAUCHER** **YILDIRAY CINAR** inkers **JASON WRIGHT** colorist **TRAVIS LANHAM** letterer

cover by **EMANUELA LUPACCHINO** and **JASON WRIGHT**

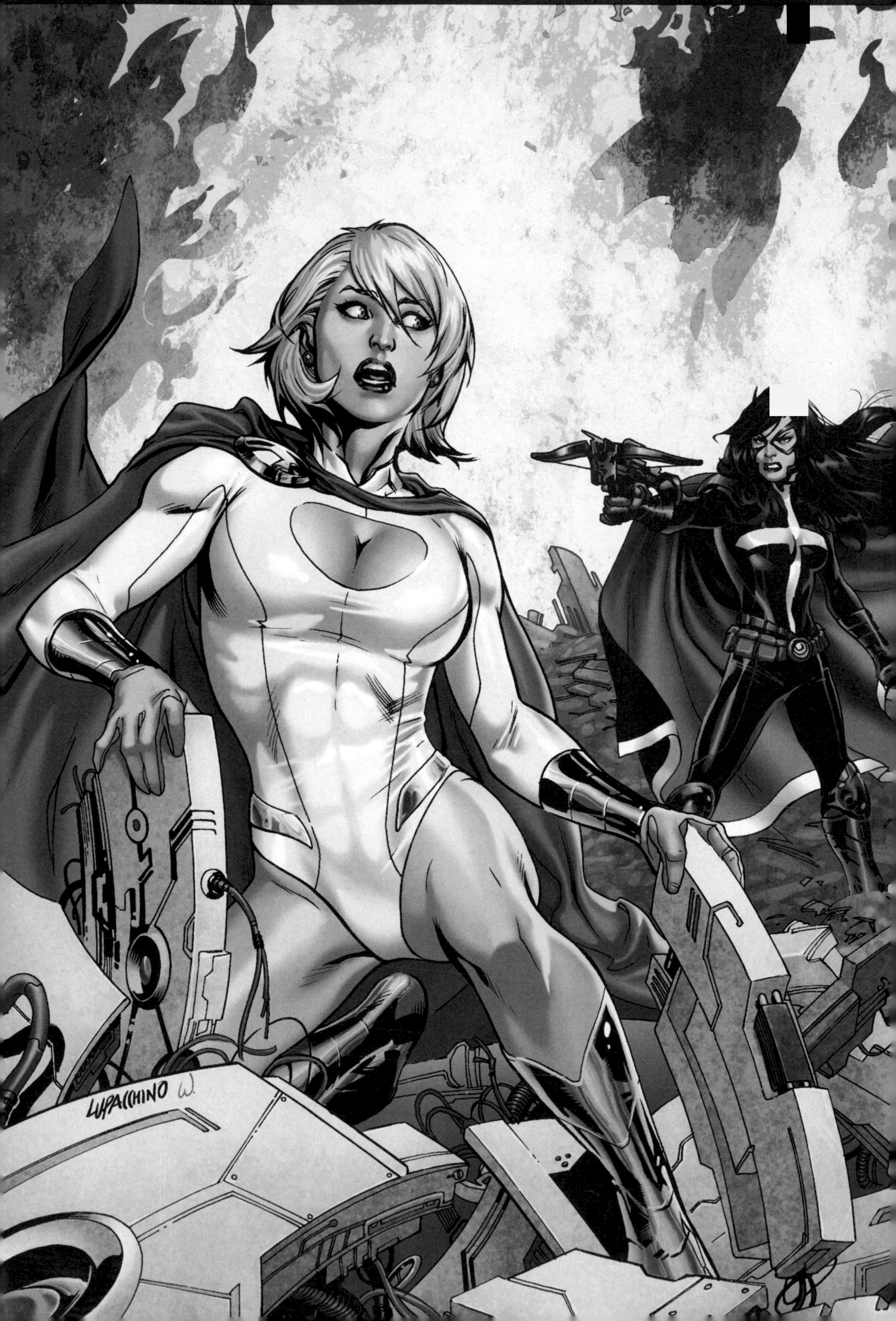
LUPACCHINO W.

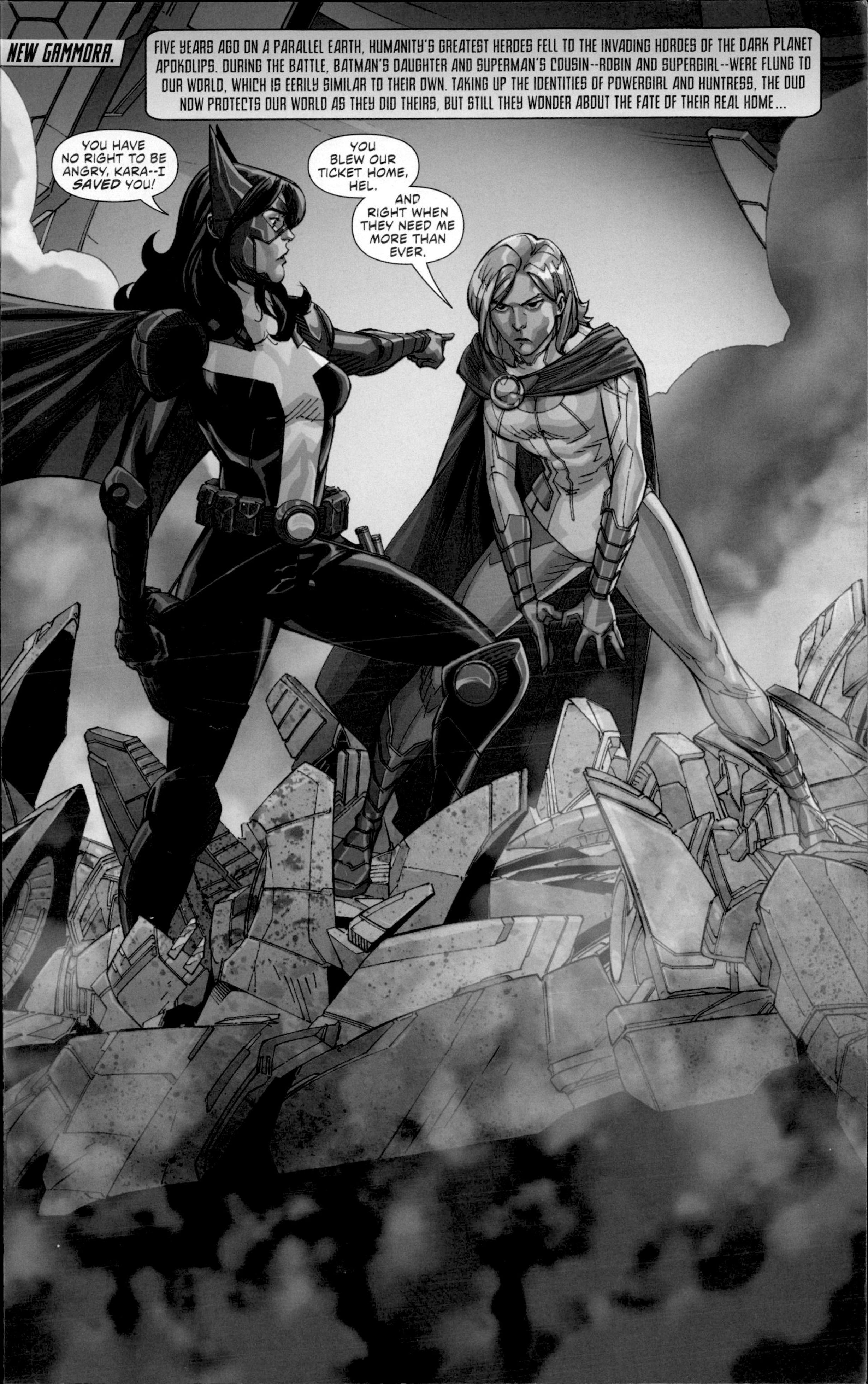
NEW GAMMORA.
FIVE YEARS AGO ON A PARALLEL EARTH, HUMANITY'S GREATEST HEROES FELL TO THE INVADING HORDES OF THE DARK PLANET APOKOLIPS. DURING THE BATTLE, BATMAN'S DAUGHTER AND SUPERMAN'S COUSIN--ROBIN AND SUPERGIRL--WERE FLUNG TO OUR WORLD, WHICH IS EERILY SIMILAR TO THEIR OWN. TAKING UP THE IDENTITIES OF POWERGIRL AND HUNTRESS, THE DUO NOW PROTECTS OUR WORLD AS THEY DID THEIRS, BUT STILL THEY WONDER ABOUT THE FATE OF THEIR REAL HOME...
YOU HAVE NO RIGHT TO BE ANGRY, KARA--I SAVED YOU!
YOU BLEW OUR TICKET HOME, HEL.
AND RIGHT WHEN THEY NEED ME MORE THAN EVER.

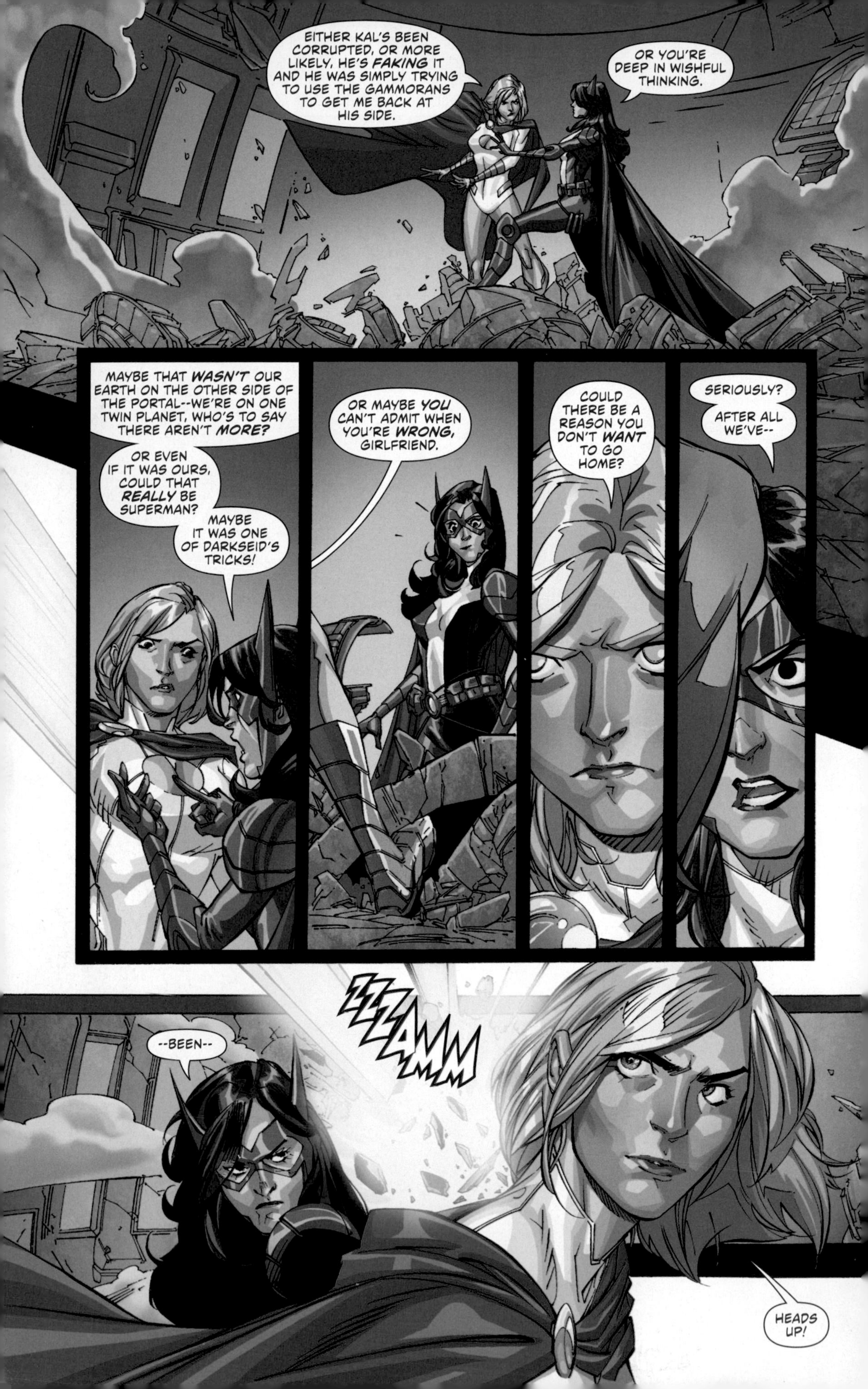
EITHER KAL'S BEEN CORRUPTED, OR MORE LIKELY, HE'S FAKING IT AND HE WAS SIMPLY TRYING TO USE THE GAMMORANS TO GET ME BACK AT HIS SIDE.
OR YOU'RE DEEP IN WISHFUL THINKING.
MAYBE THAT WASN'T OUR EARTH ON THE OTHER SIDE OF THE PORTAL--WE'RE ON ONE TWIN PLANET, WHO'S TO SAY THERE AREN'T MORE?
OR EVEN IF IT WAS OURS, COULD THAT REALLY BE SUPERMAN?
MAYBE IT WAS ONE OF DARKSEID'S TRICKS!
OR MAYBE YOU CAN'T ADMIT WHEN YOU'RE WRONG, GIRLFRIEND.
COULD THERE BE A REASON YOU DON'T WANT TO GO HOME?
SERIOUSLY?
AFTER ALL WE'VE--
--BEEN--
ZZZAMMM
HEADS UP!

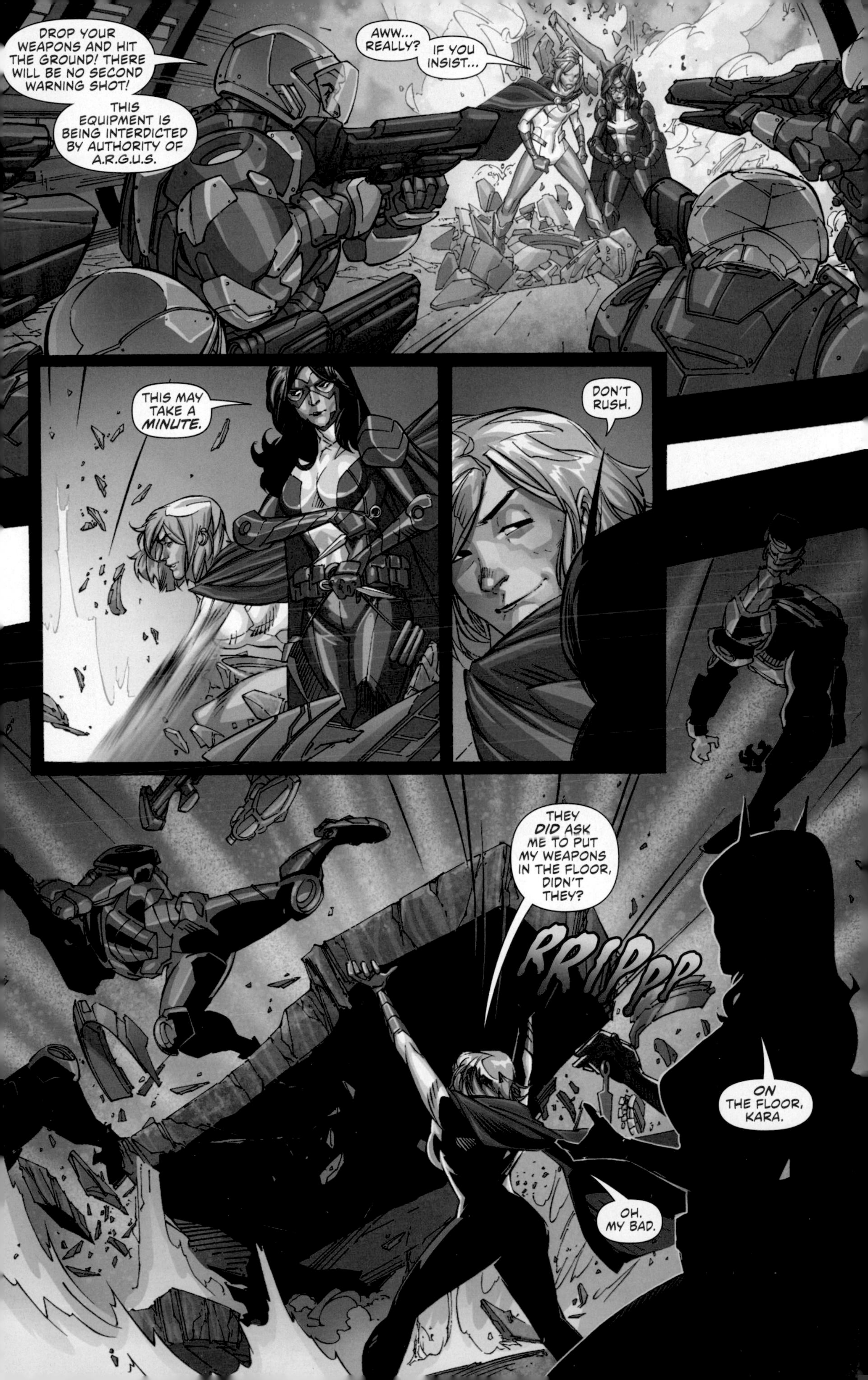
DROP YOUR WEAPONS AND HIT THE GROUND! THERE WILL BE NO SECOND WARNING SHOT!
THIS EQUIPMENT IS BEING INTERDICTED BY AUTHORITY OF A.R.G.U.S.
AWW... REALLY?
IF YOU INSIST...
THIS MAY TAKE A MINUTE.
DON'T RUSH.
THEY DID ASK ME TO PUT MY WEAPONS IN THE FLOOR, DIDN'T THEY?
RRIPPP
ON THE FLOOR, KARA.
OH. MY BAD.

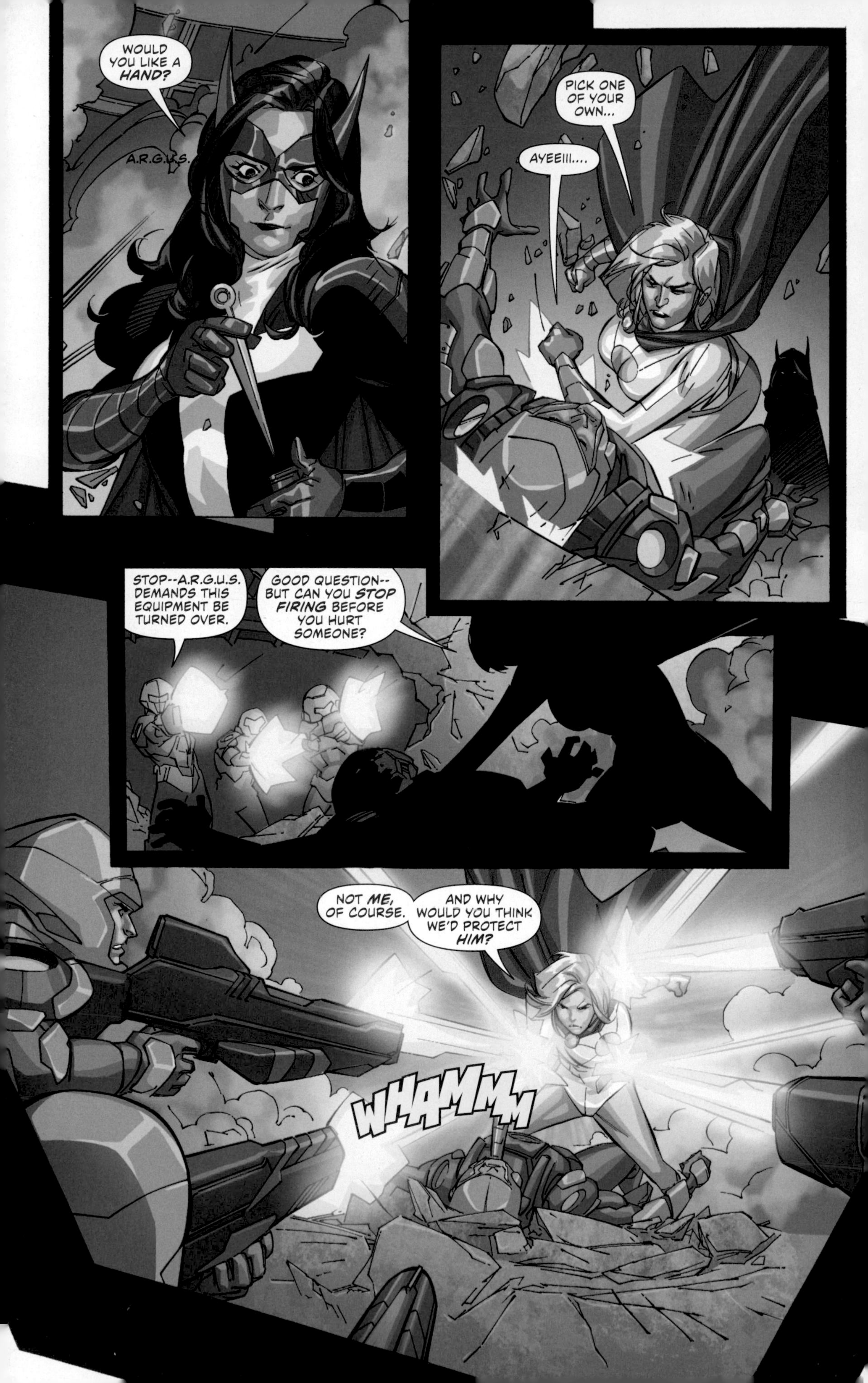

WOULD YOU LIKE A HAND?
A.R.G.U.S.
PICK ONE OF YOUR OWN...
AYEEIII....
STOP--A.R.G.U.S. DEMANDS THIS EQUIPMENT BE TURNED OVER.
GOOD QUESTION--BUT CAN YOU STOP FIRING BEFORE YOU HURT SOMEONE?
NOT ME, OF COURSE.
AND WHY WOULD YOU THINK WE'D PROTECT HIM?
WHAMMM

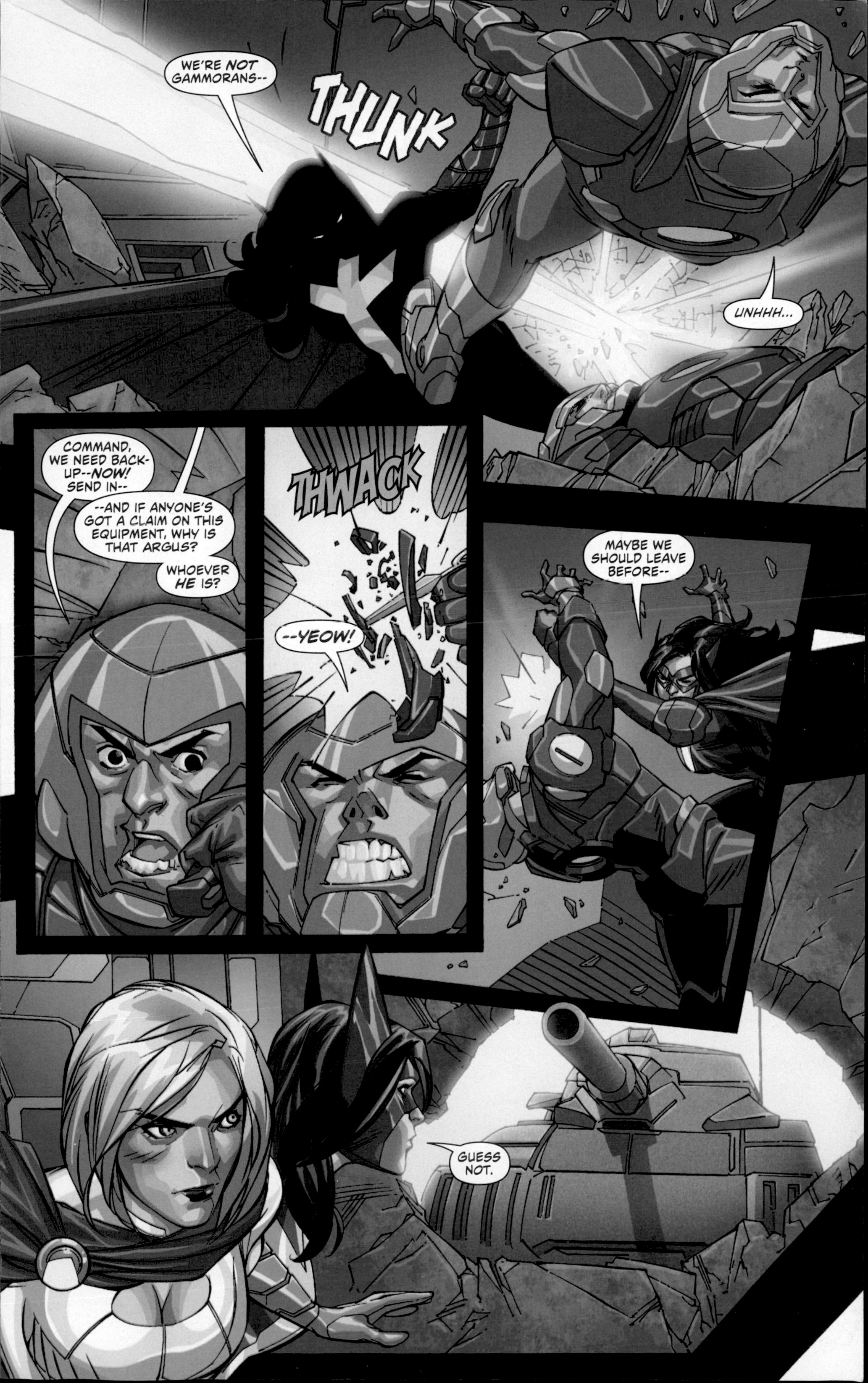
WE'RE NOT GAMMORANS--
THUNK
UNHHH...
COMMAND, WE NEED BACK-UP--NOW! SEND IN--
--AND IF ANYONE'S GOT A CLAIM ON THIS EQUIPMENT, WHY IS THAT ARGUS?
WHOEVER HE IS?
THWACK
--YEOW!
MAYBE WE SHOULD LEAVE BEFORE--
GUESS NOT.

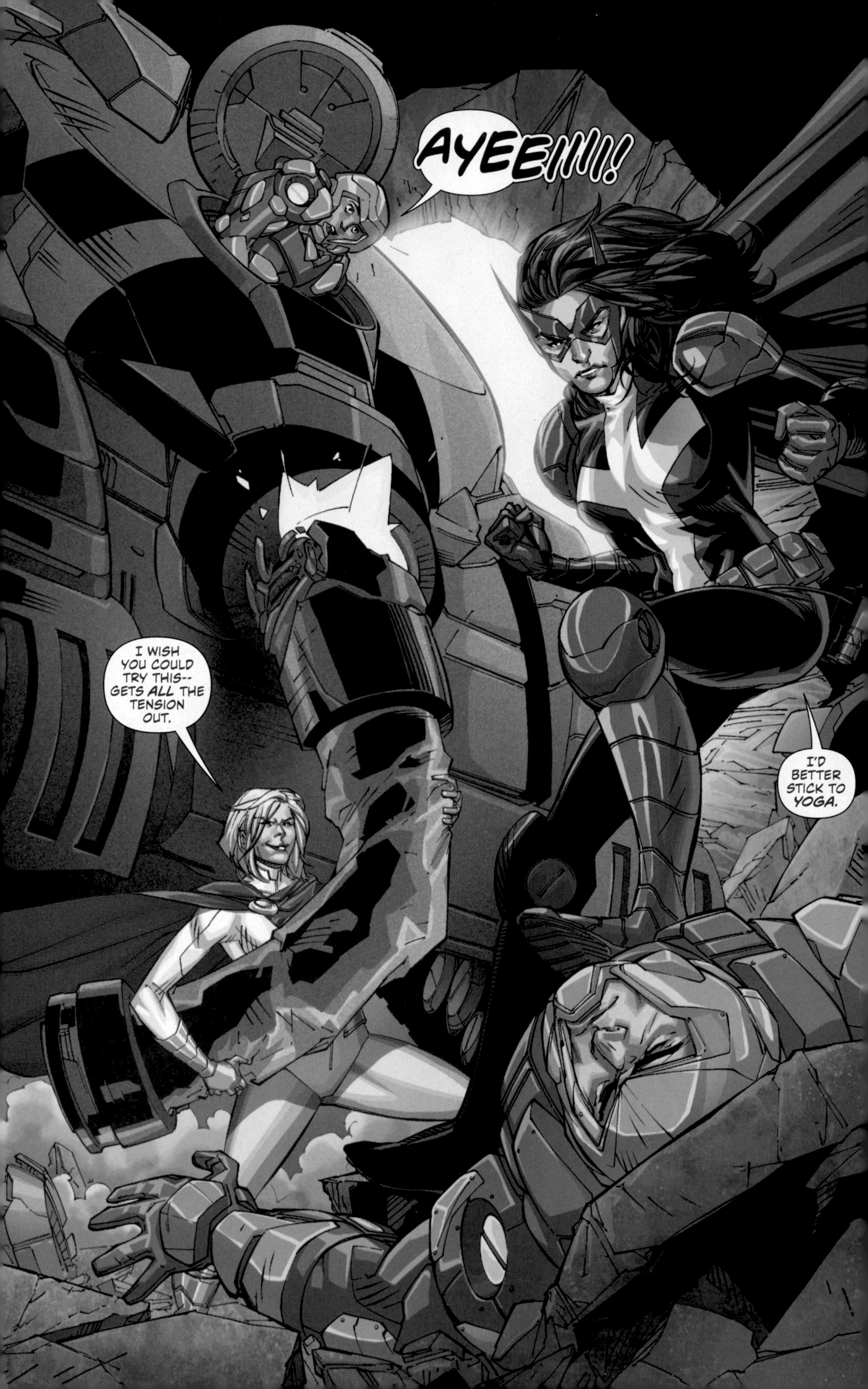
AYEEIIIII!
I WISH YOU COULD TRY THIS-- GETS ALL THE TENSION OUT.
I'D BETTER STICK TO YOGA.

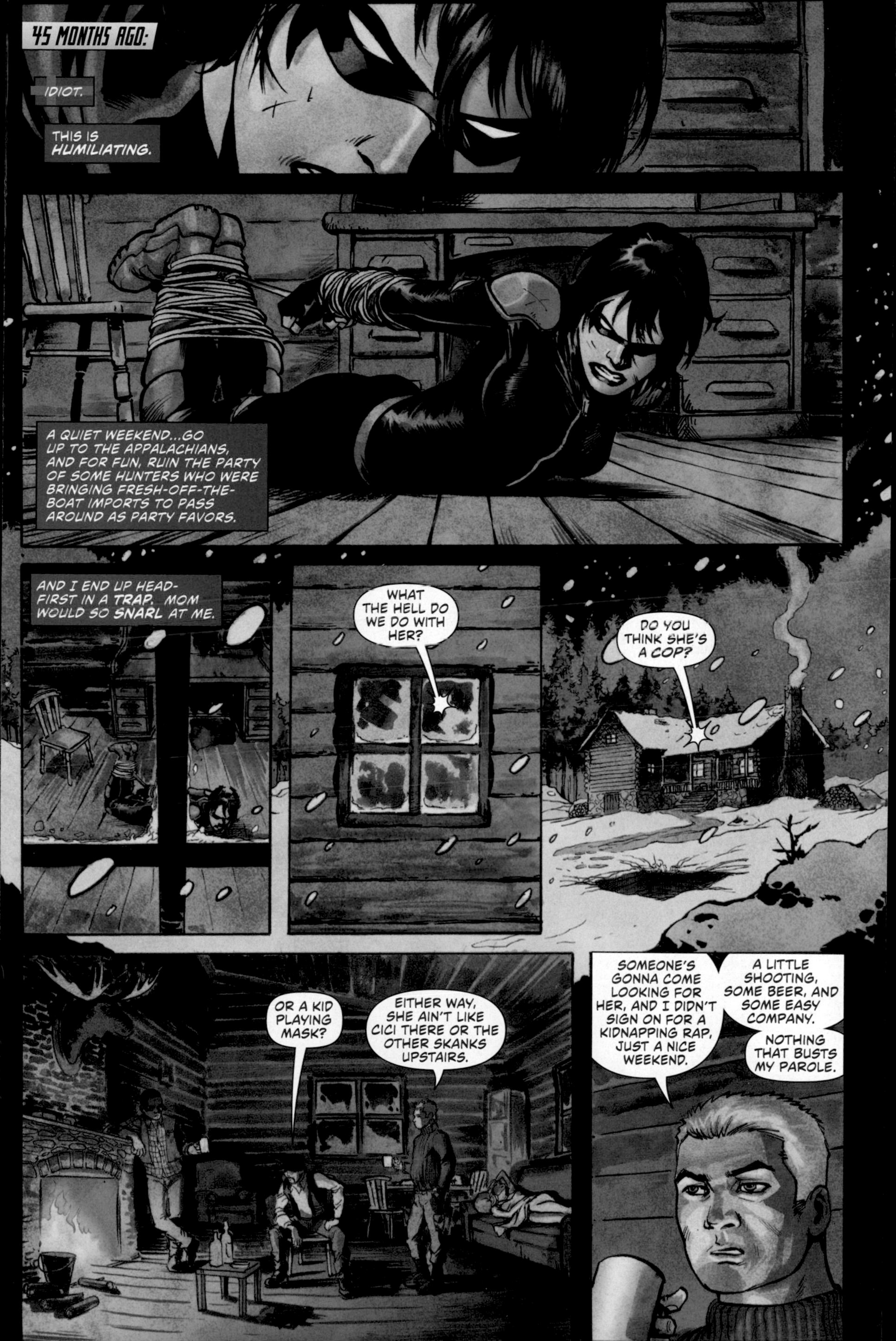
45 MONTHS AGO:
IDIOT.
THIS IS HUMILIATING.
A QUIET WEEKEND...GO UP TO THE APPALACHIANS, AND FOR FUN, RUIN THE PARTY OF SOME HUNTERS WHO WERE BRINGING FRESH-OFF-THE-BOAT IMPORTS TO PASS AROUND AS PARTY FAVORS.
AND I END UP HEAD-FIRST IN A TRAP. MOM WOULD SO SNARL AT ME.
WHAT THE HELL DO WE DO WITH HER?
DO YOU THINK SHE'S A COP?
OR A KID PLAYING MASK?
EITHER WAY, SHE AIN'T LIKE CICI THERE OR THE OTHER SKANKS UPSTAIRS.
SOMEONE'S GONNA COME LOOKING FOR HER, AND I DIDN'T SIGN ON FOR A KIDNAPPING RAP, JUST A NICE WEEKEND.
A LITTLE SHOOTING, SOME BEER, AND SOME EASY COMPANY.
NOTHING THAT BUSTS MY PAROLE.

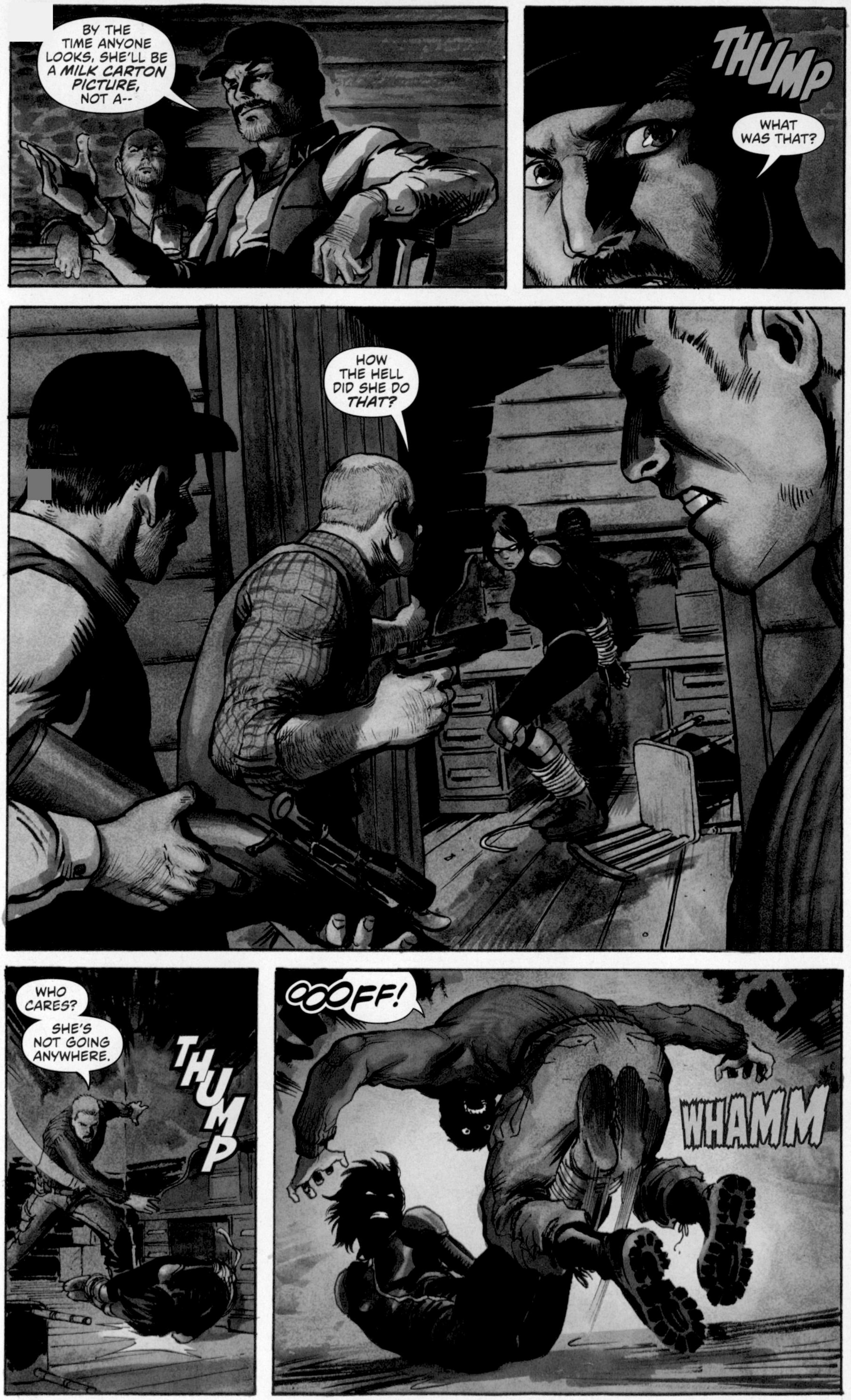
BY THE TIME ANYONE LOOKS, SHE'LL BE A *MILK CARTON PICTURE,* NOT A--
THUMP
WHAT WAS THAT?
HOW THE HELL DID SHE DO *THAT?*
WHO CARES?
SHE'S NOT GOING ANYWHERE.
THUMP
OOOFF!
WHAMM

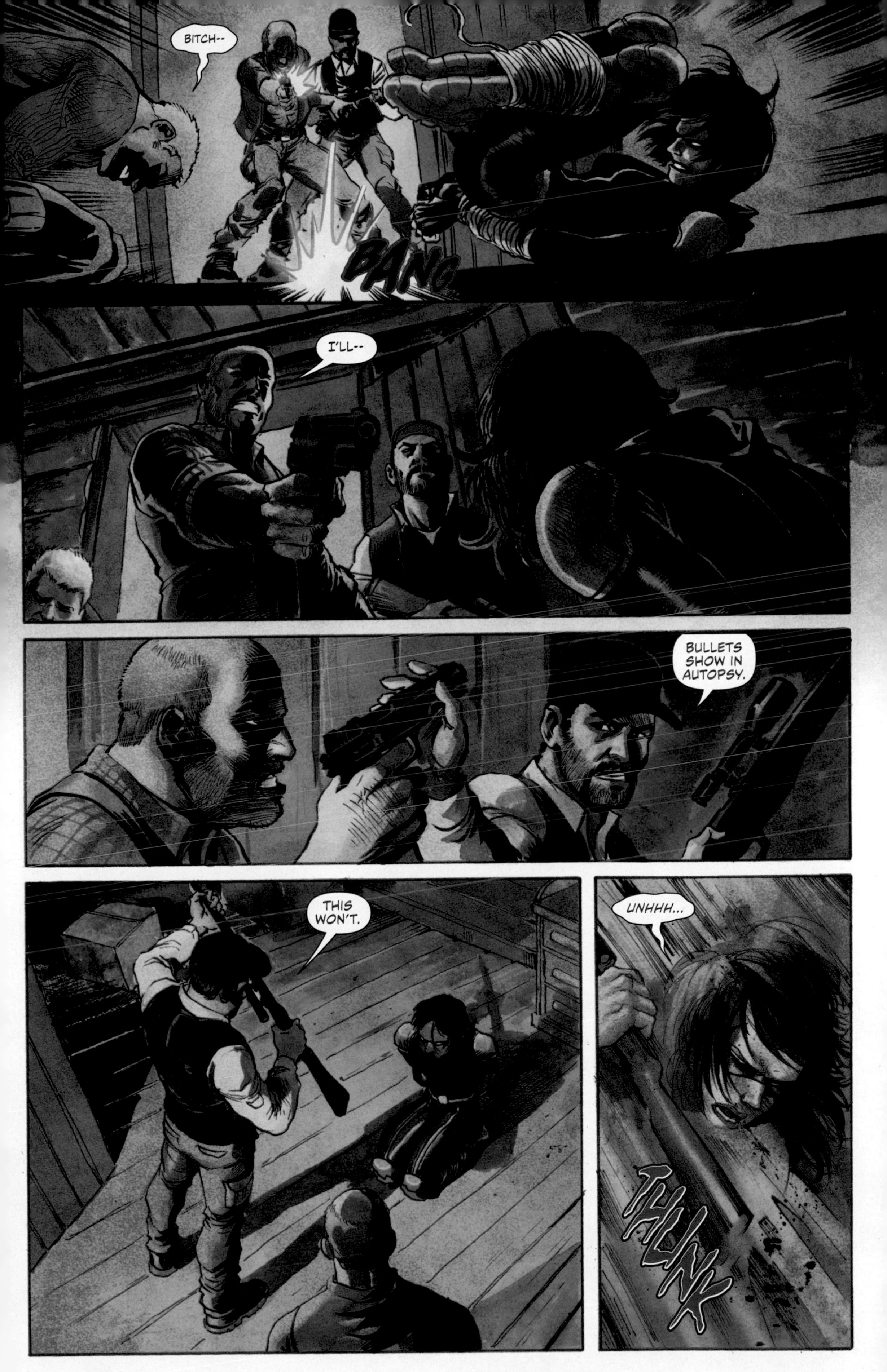
BITCH--
BANG
I'LL--
BULLETS SHOW IN AUTOPSY.
THIS WON'T.
UNHHH...
THUNK

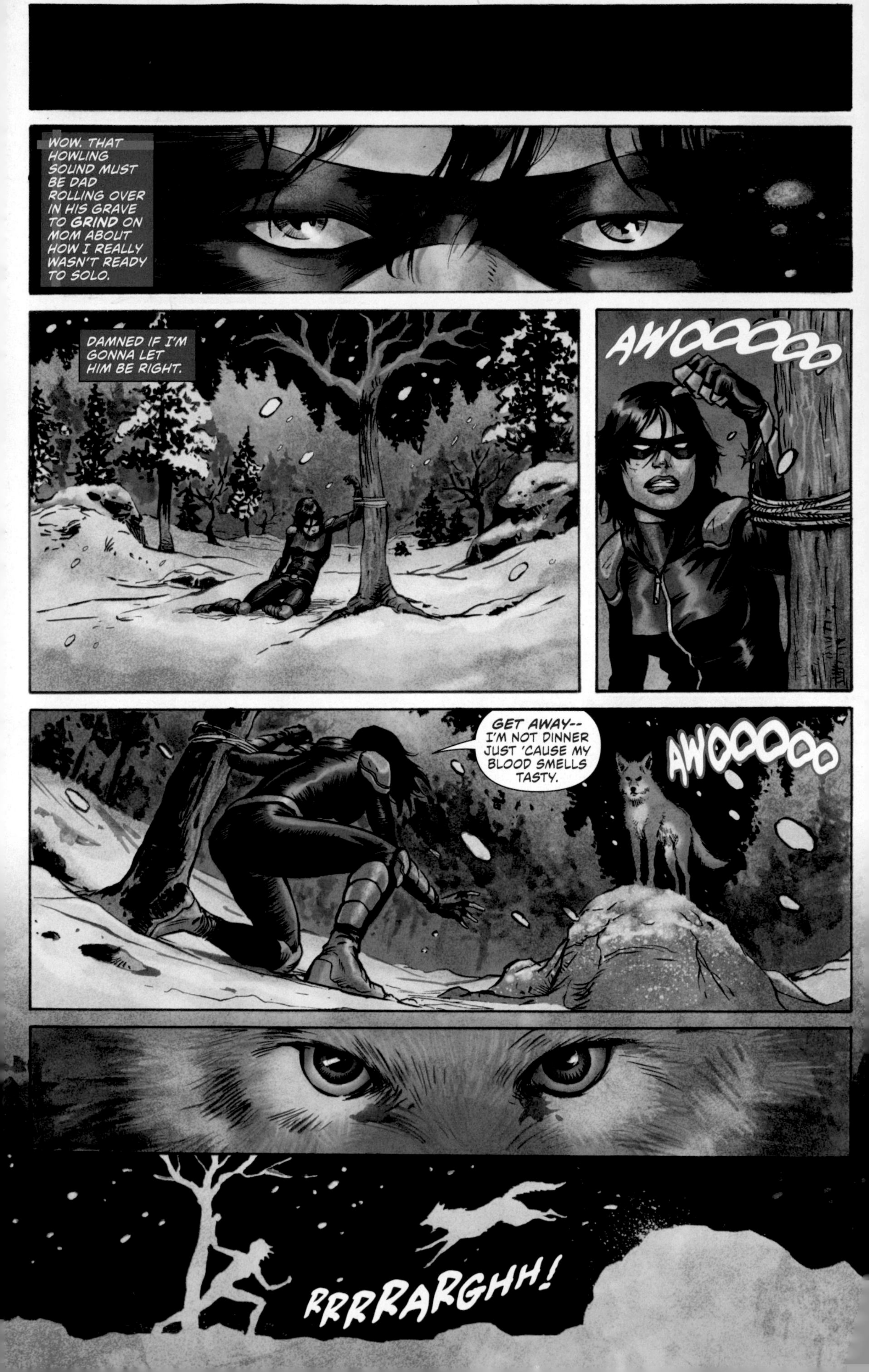
WOW. THAT HOWLING SOUND MUST BE DAD ROLLING OVER IN HIS GRAVE TO GRIND ON MOM ABOUT HOW I REALLY WASN'T READY TO SOLO.
DAMNED IF I'M GONNA LET HIM BE RIGHT.
AWOOOOOO
GET AWAY-- I'M NOT DINNER JUST 'CAUSE MY BLOOD SMELLS TASTY.
AWOOOOO
RRRRARGHH!

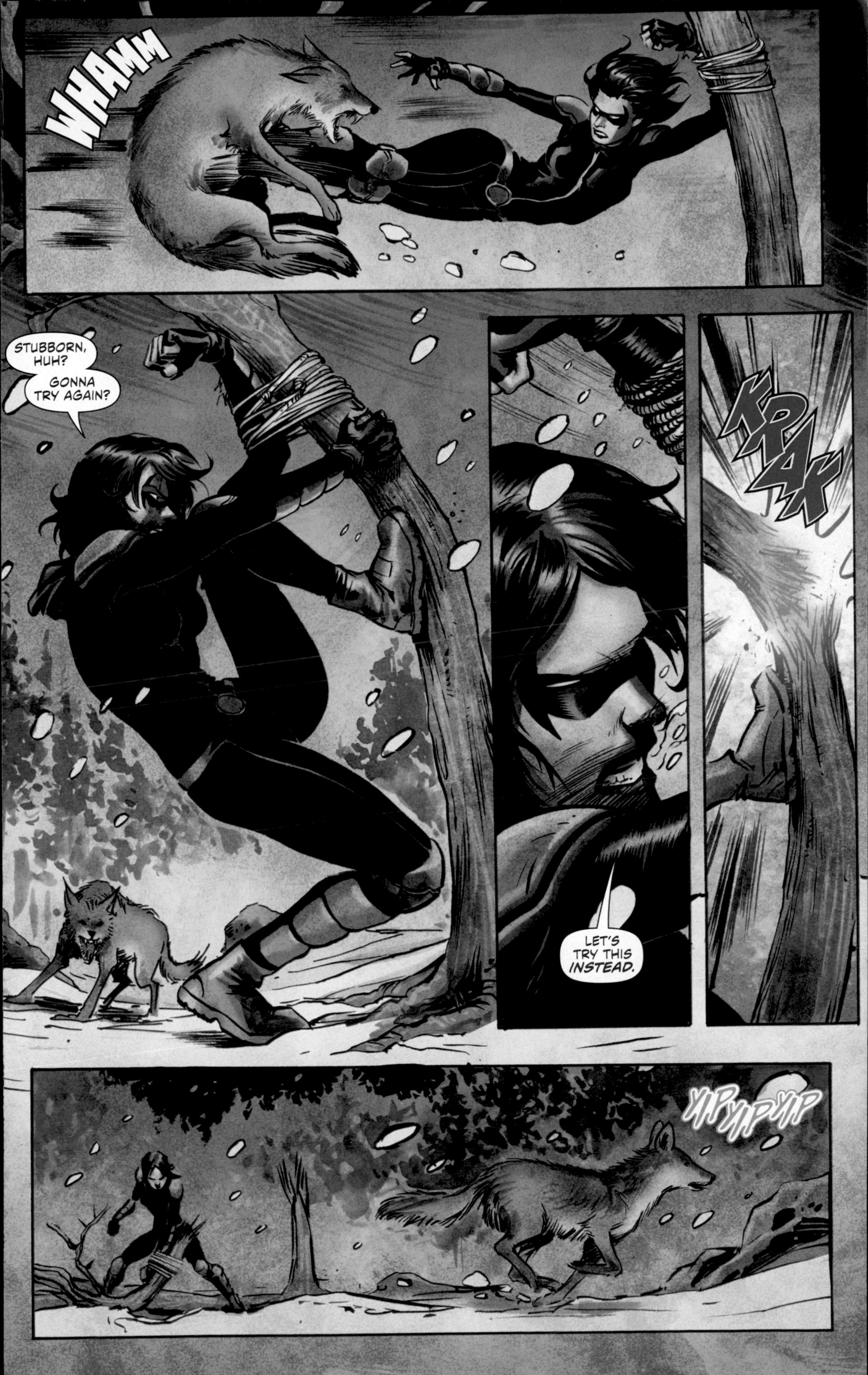
WHAMM
STUBBORN, HUH? GONNA TRY AGAIN?
KRAK
LET'S TRY THIS *INSTEAD.*
YIPYIPYIP

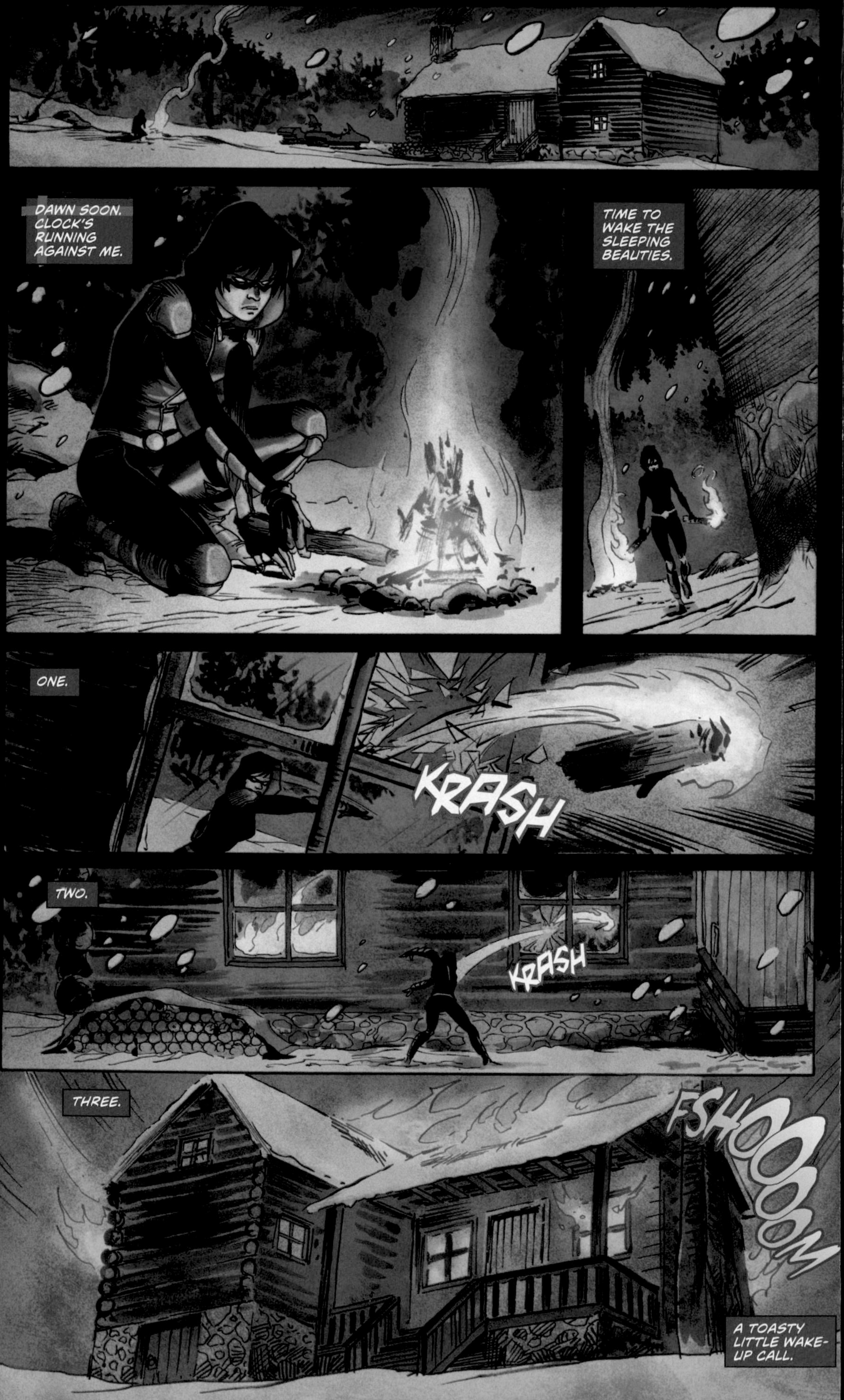
DAWN SOON. CLOCK'S RUNNING AGAINST ME.
TIME TO WAKE THE SLEEPING BEAUTIES.
ONE.
KRASH
TWO.
KRASH
THREE.
FSHOOOOOM
A TOASTY LITTLE WAKE-UP CALL.

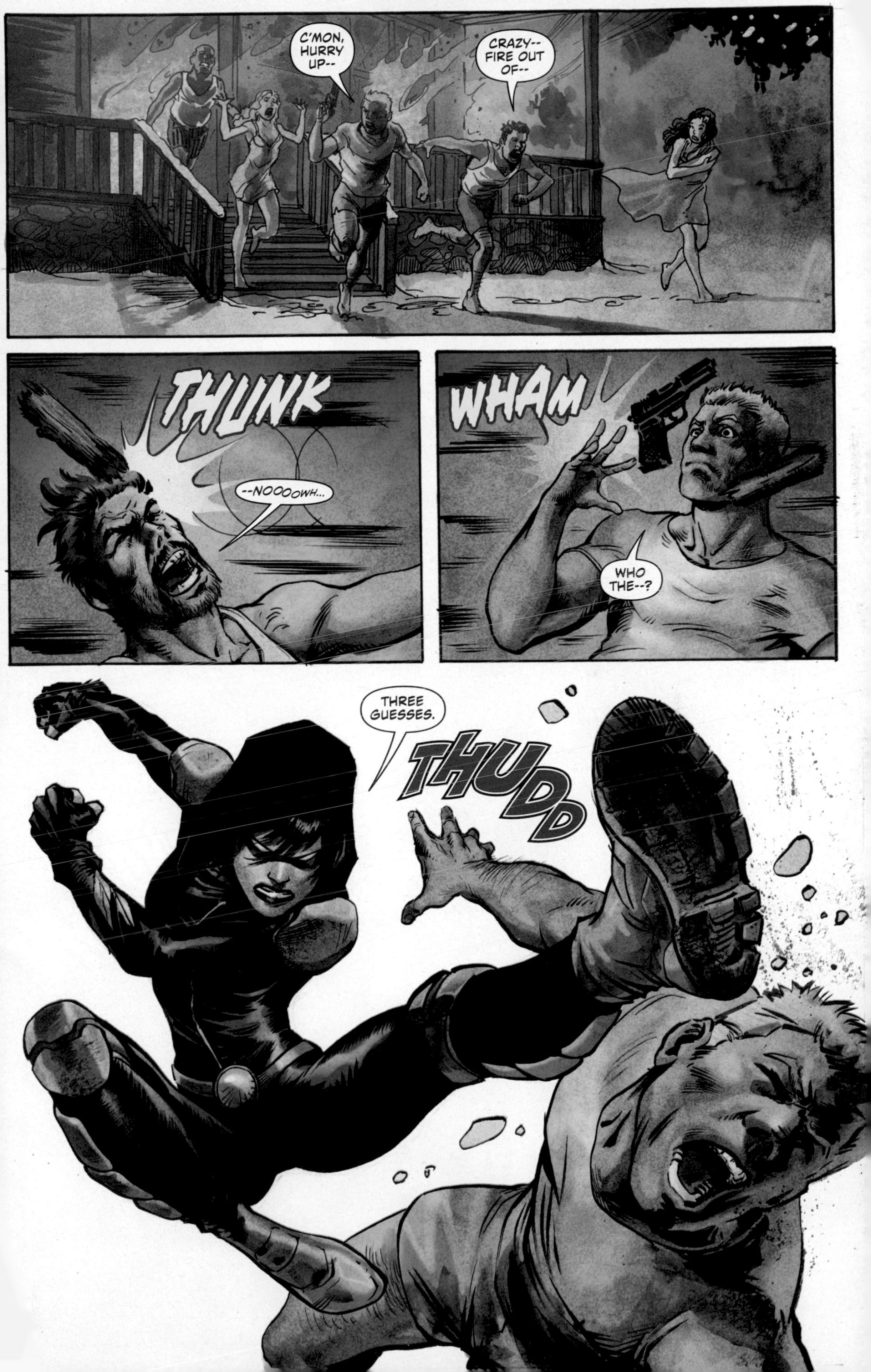
C'MON, HURRY UP--
CRAZY-- FIRE OUT OF--
THUNK
--NOOOOWH...
WHAM
WHO THE--?
THREE GUESSES.
THUDD

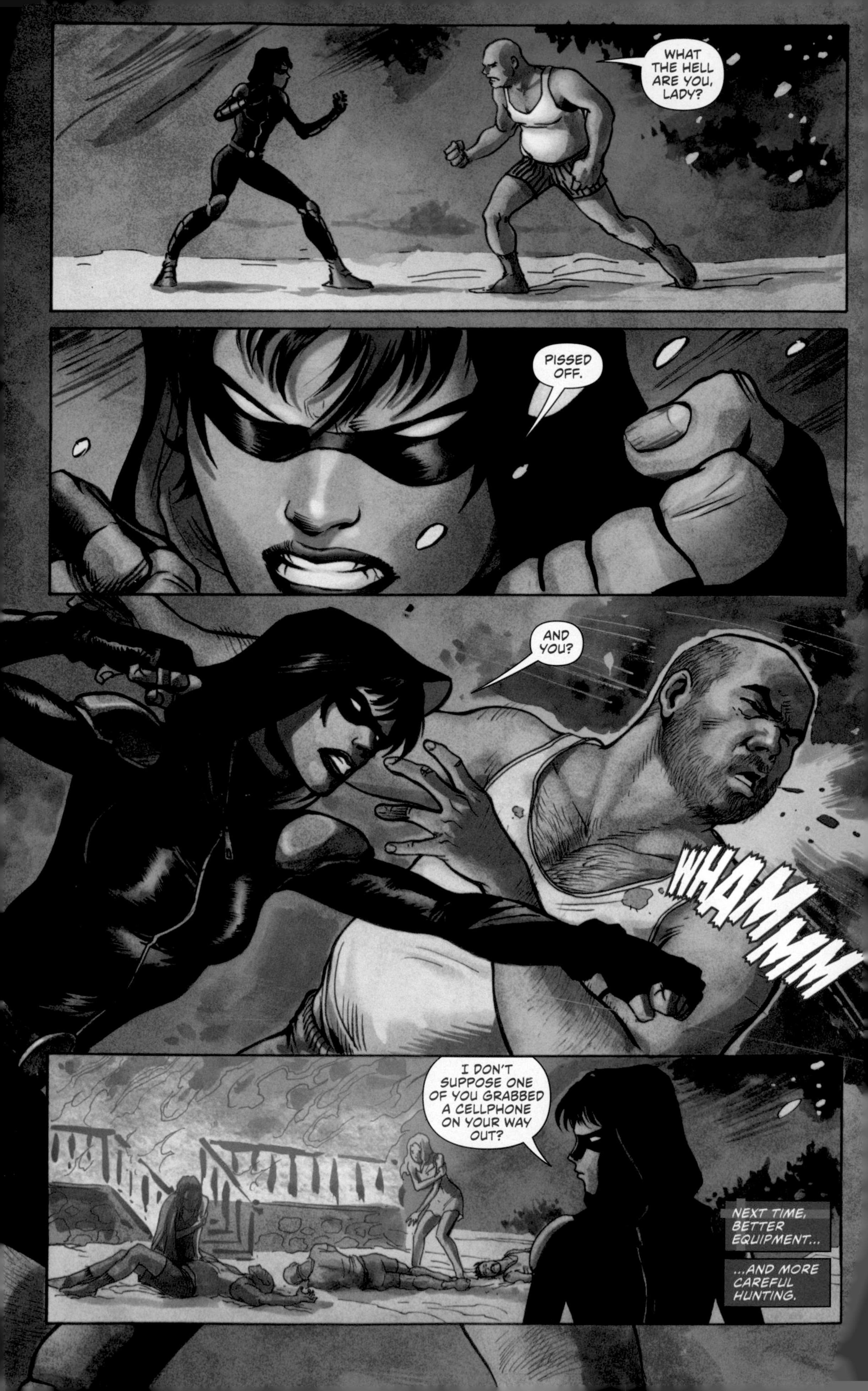
WHAT THE HELL ARE YOU, LADY?
PISSED OFF.
AND YOU?
WHAMMM
I DON'T SUPPOSE ONE OF YOU GRABBED A CELLPHONE ON YOUR WAY OUT?
NEXT TIME, BETTER EQUIPMENT...
...AND MORE CAREFUL HUNTING.

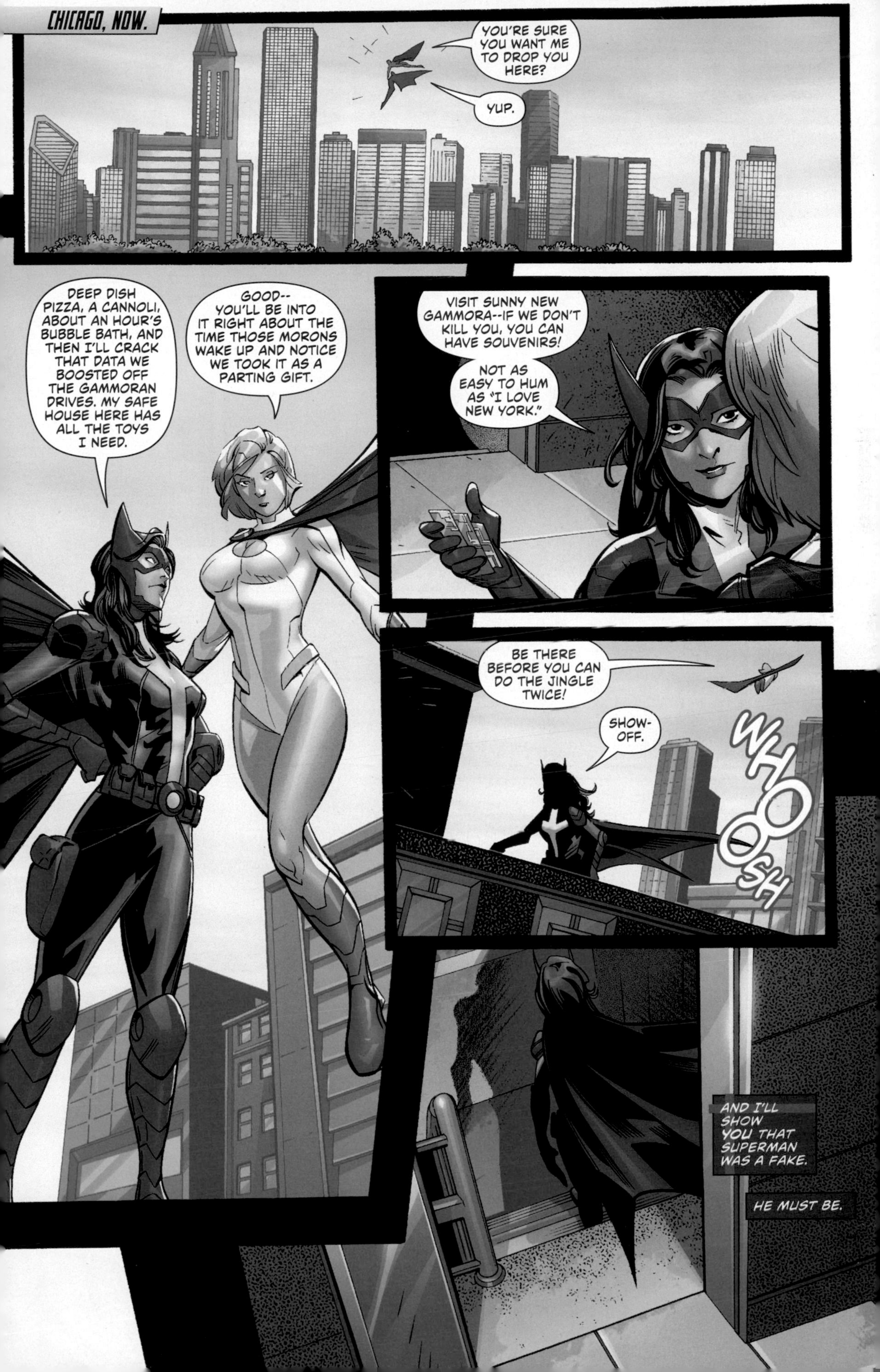
CHICAGO, NOW.
YOU'RE SURE YOU WANT ME TO DROP YOU HERE?
YUP.
DEEP DISH PIZZA, A CANNOLI, ABOUT AN HOUR'S BUBBLE BATH, AND THEN I'LL CRACK THAT DATA WE BOOSTED OFF THE GAMMORAN DRIVES. MY SAFE HOUSE HERE HAS ALL THE TOYS I NEED.
GOOD-- YOU'LL BE INTO IT RIGHT ABOUT THE TIME THOSE MORONS WAKE UP AND NOTICE WE TOOK IT AS A PARTING GIFT.
VISIT SUNNY NEW GAMMORA--IF WE DON'T KILL YOU, YOU CAN HAVE SOUVENIRS!
NOT AS EASY TO HUM AS "I LOVE NEW YORK."
BE THERE BEFORE YOU CAN DO THE JINGLE TWICE!
SHOW-OFF.
WHOOOSH
AND I'LL SHOW YOU THAT SUPERMAN WAS A FAKE.
HE MUST BE.

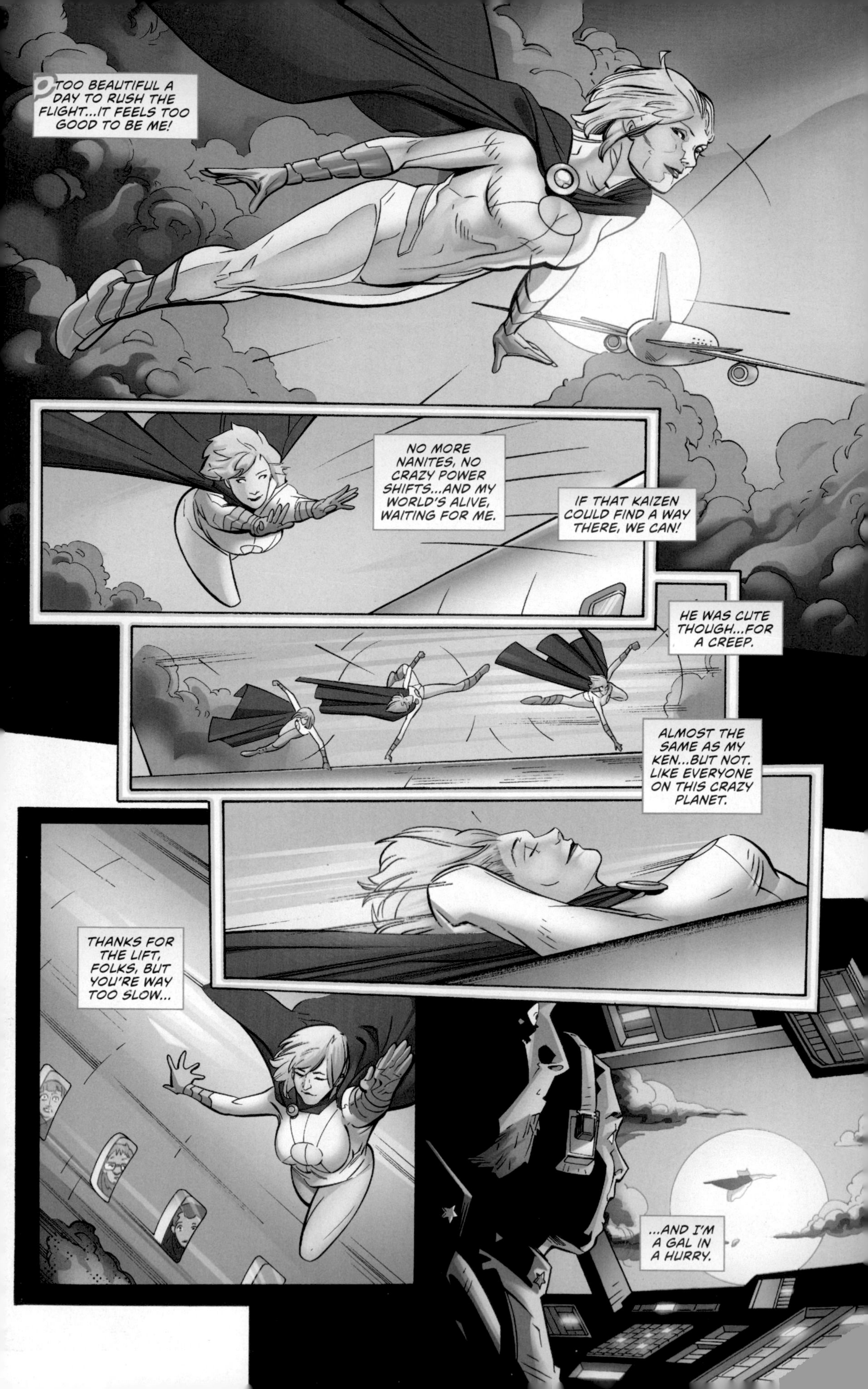
TOO BEAUTIFUL A DAY TO RUSH THE FLIGHT...IT FEELS TOO GOOD TO BE ME!
NO MORE NANITES, NO CRAZY POWER SHIFTS...AND MY WORLD'S ALIVE, WAITING FOR ME.
IF THAT KAIZEN COULD FIND A WAY THERE, WE CAN!
HE WAS CUTE THOUGH...FOR A CREEP.
ALMOST THE SAME AS MY KEN...BUT NOT. LIKE EVERYONE ON THIS CRAZY PLANET.
THANKS FOR THE LIFT, FOLKS, BUT YOU'RE WAY TOO SLOW...
...AND I'M A GAL IN A HURRY.

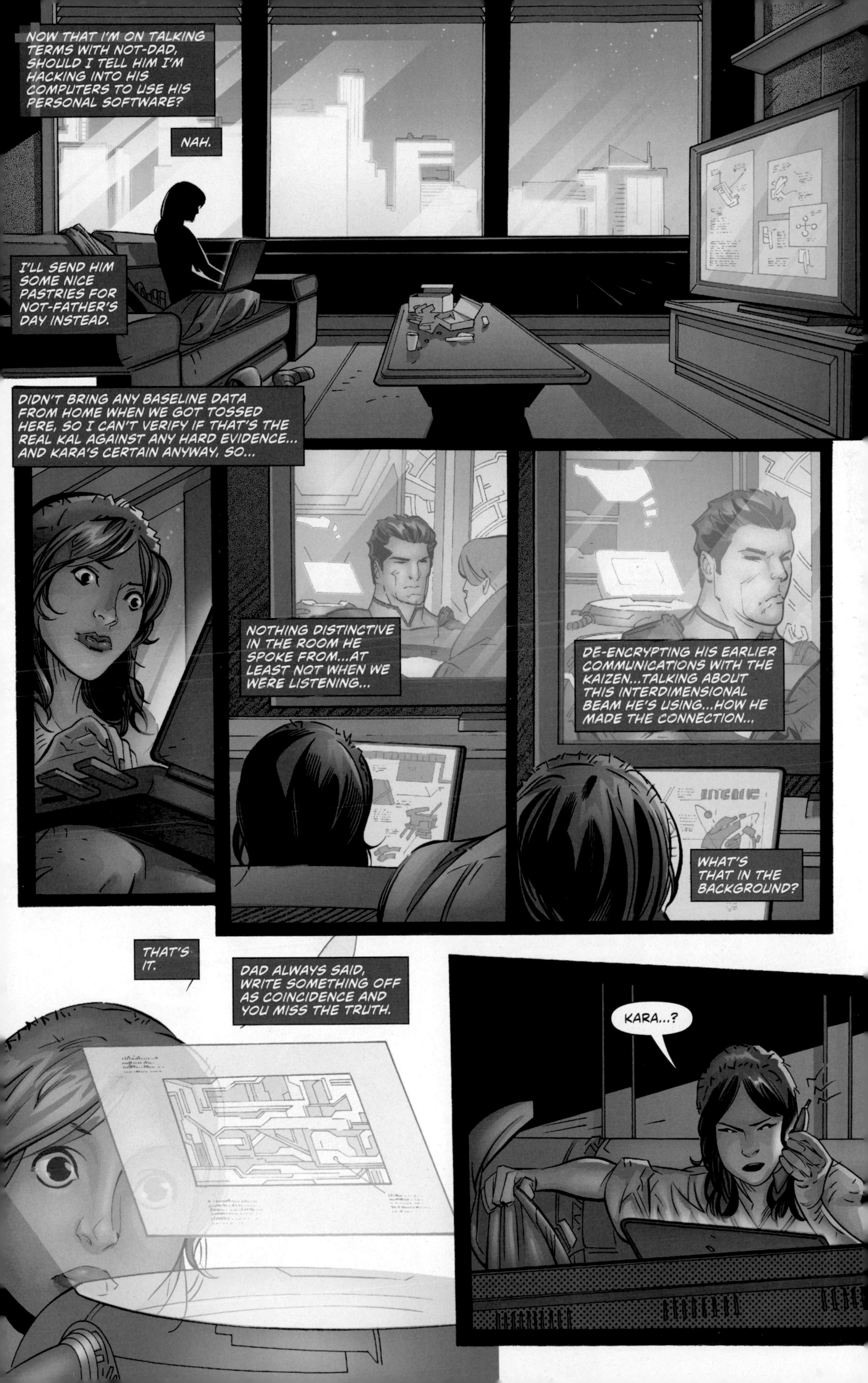
NOW THAT I'M ON TALKING TERMS WITH NOT-DAD, SHOULD I TELL HIM I'M HACKING INTO HIS COMPUTERS TO USE HIS PERSONAL SOFTWARE?
NAH.
I'LL SEND HIM SOME NICE PASTRIES FOR NOT-FATHER'S DAY INSTEAD.
DIDN'T BRING ANY BASELINE DATA FROM HOME WHEN WE GOT TOSSED HERE, SO I CAN'T VERIFY IF THAT'S THE REAL KAL AGAINST ANY HARD EVIDENCE... AND KARA'S CERTAIN ANYWAY, SO...
NOTHING DISTINCTIVE IN THE ROOM HE SPOKE FROM...AT LEAST NOT WHEN WE WERE LISTENING...
DE-ENCRYPTING HIS EARLIER COMMUNICATIONS WITH THE KAIZEN...TALKING ABOUT THIS INTERDIMENSIONAL BEAM HE'S USING...HOW HE MADE THE CONNECTION...
WHAT'S THAT IN THE BACKGROUND?
THAT'S IT.
DAD ALWAYS SAID, WRITE SOMETHING OFF AS COINCIDENCE AND YOU MISS THE TRUTH.
KARA...?

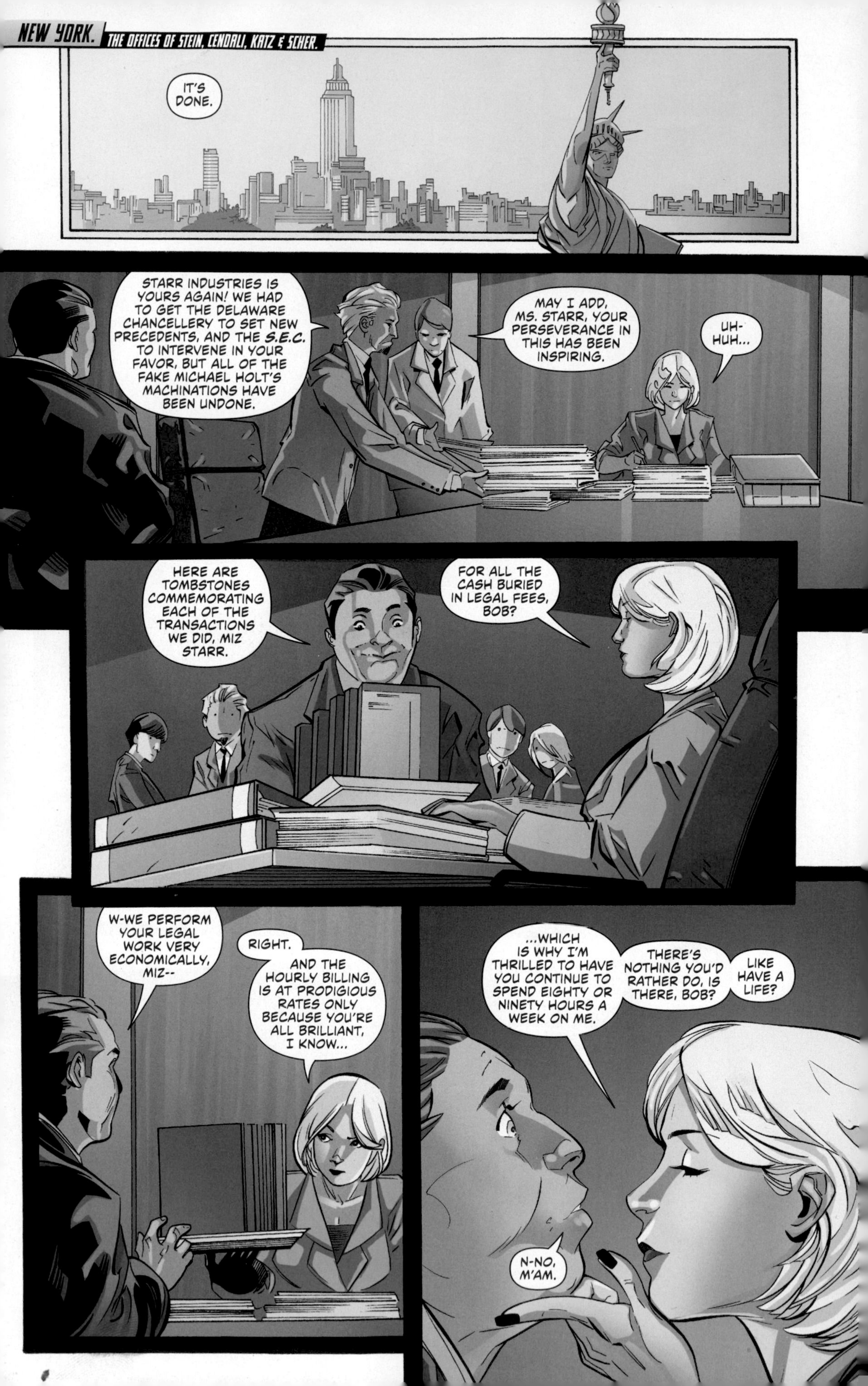
NEW YORK.
THE OFFICES OF STEIN, CENDALI, KATZ & SCHER.
IT'S DONE.
STARR INDUSTRIES IS YOURS AGAIN! WE HAD TO GET THE DELAWARE CHANCELLERY TO SET NEW PRECEDENTS, AND THE S.E.C. TO INTERVENE IN YOUR FAVOR, BUT ALL OF THE FAKE MICHAEL HOLT'S MACHINATIONS HAVE BEEN UNDONE.
MAY I ADD, MS. STARR, YOUR PERSEVERANCE IN THIS HAS BEEN INSPIRING.
UH-HUH...
HERE ARE TOMBSTONES COMMEMORATING EACH OF THE TRANSACTIONS WE DID, MIZ STARR.
FOR ALL THE CASH BURIED IN LEGAL FEES, BOB?
W-WE PERFORM YOUR LEGAL WORK VERY ECONOMICALLY, MIZ--
RIGHT.
AND THE HOURLY BILLING IS AT PRODIGIOUS RATES ONLY BECAUSE YOU'RE ALL BRILLIANT, I KNOW...
...WHICH IS WHY I'M THRILLED TO HAVE YOU CONTINUE TO SPEND EIGHTY OR NINETY HOURS A WEEK ON ME.
THERE'S NOTHING YOU'D RATHER DO, IS THERE, BOB?
LIKE HAVE A LIFE?
N-NO, M'AM.

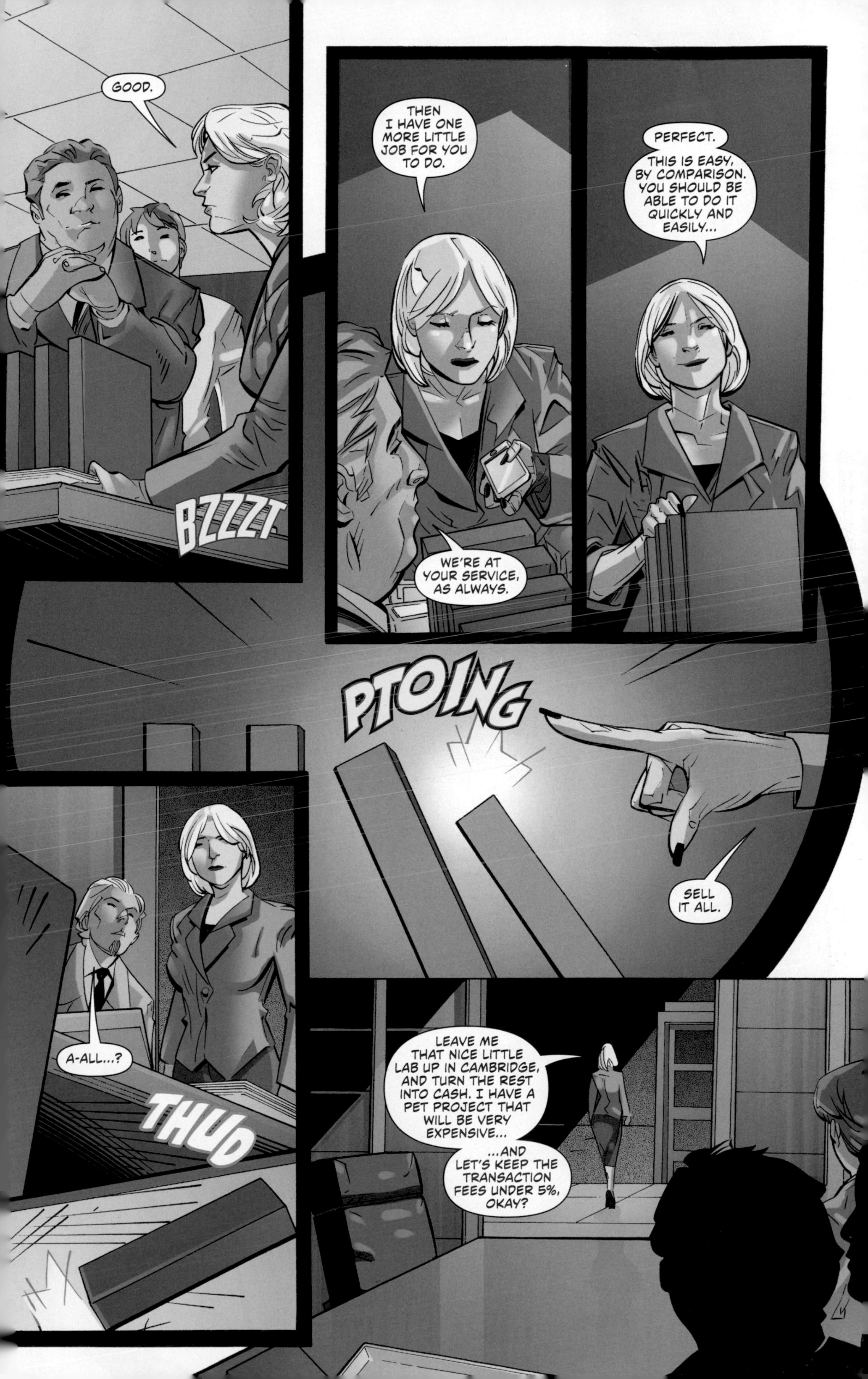
GOOD.
BZZZT.
THEN I HAVE ONE MORE LITTLE JOB FOR YOU TO DO.
WE'RE AT YOUR SERVICE, AS ALWAYS.
PERFECT.
THIS IS EASY, BY COMPARISON. YOU SHOULD BE ABLE TO DO IT QUICKLY AND EASILY...
PTOING
SELL IT ALL.
A-ALL...?
THUD
LEAVE ME THAT NICE LITTLE LAB UP IN CAMBRIDGE, AND TURN THE REST INTO CASH. I HAVE A PET PROJECT THAT WILL BE VERY EXPENSIVE...
...AND LET'S KEEP THE TRANSACTION FEES UNDER 5%, OKAY?

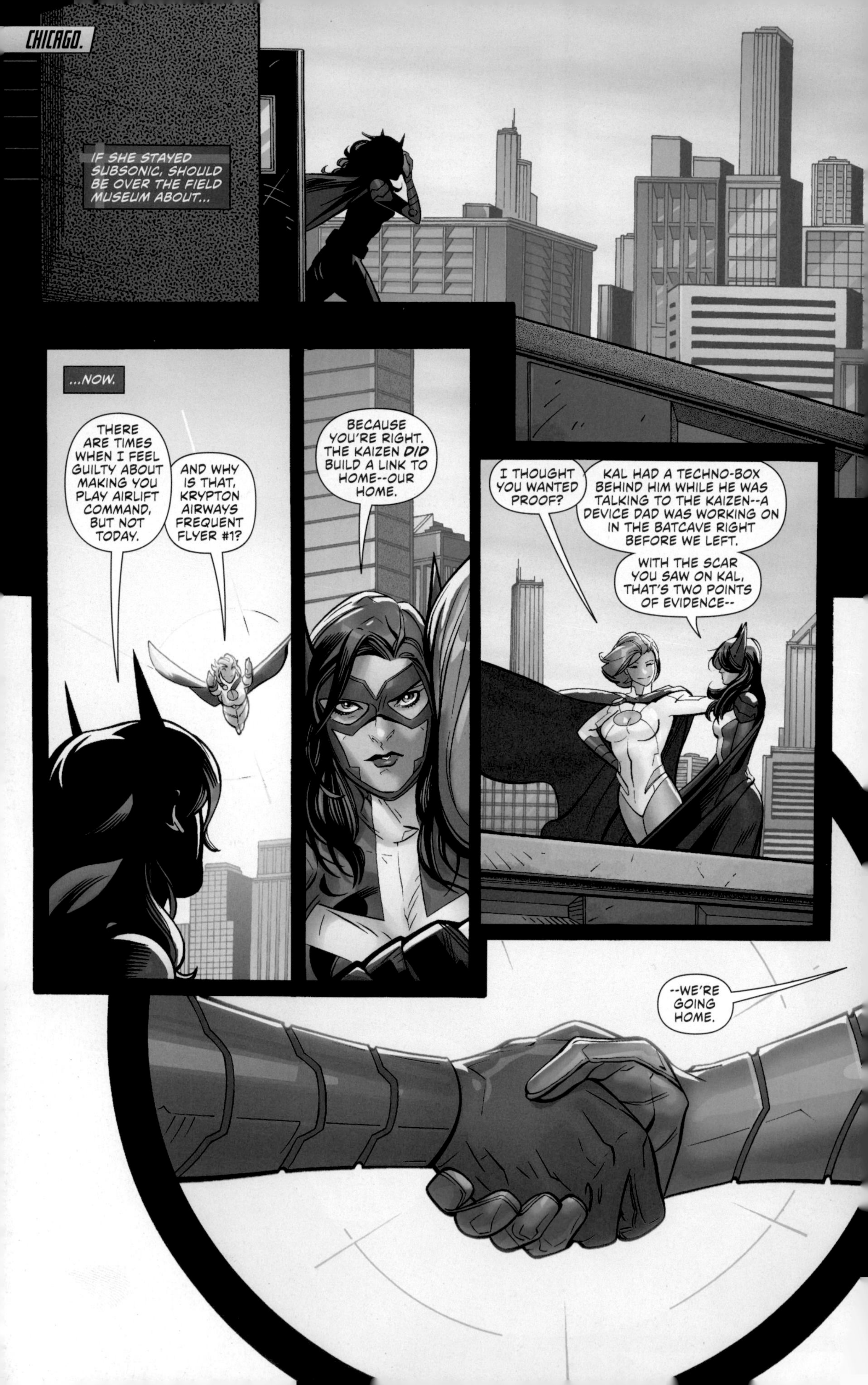
CHICAGO.
IF SHE STAYED SUBSONIC, SHOULD BE OVER THE FIELD MUSEUM ABOUT...
...NOW.
THERE ARE TIMES WHEN I FEEL GUILTY ABOUT MAKING YOU PLAY AIRLIFT COMMAND, BUT NOT TODAY.
AND WHY IS THAT, KRYPTON AIRWAYS FREQUENT FLYER #1?
BECAUSE YOU'RE RIGHT. THE KAIZEN DID BUILD A LINK TO HOME--OUR HOME.
I THOUGHT YOU WANTED PROOF?
KAL HAD A TECHNO-BOX BEHIND HIM WHILE HE WAS TALKING TO THE KAIZEN--A DEVICE DAD WAS WORKING ON IN THE BATCAVE RIGHT BEFORE WE LEFT.
WITH THE SCAR YOU SAW ON KAL, THAT'S TWO POINTS OF EVIDENCE--
--WE'RE GOING HOME.

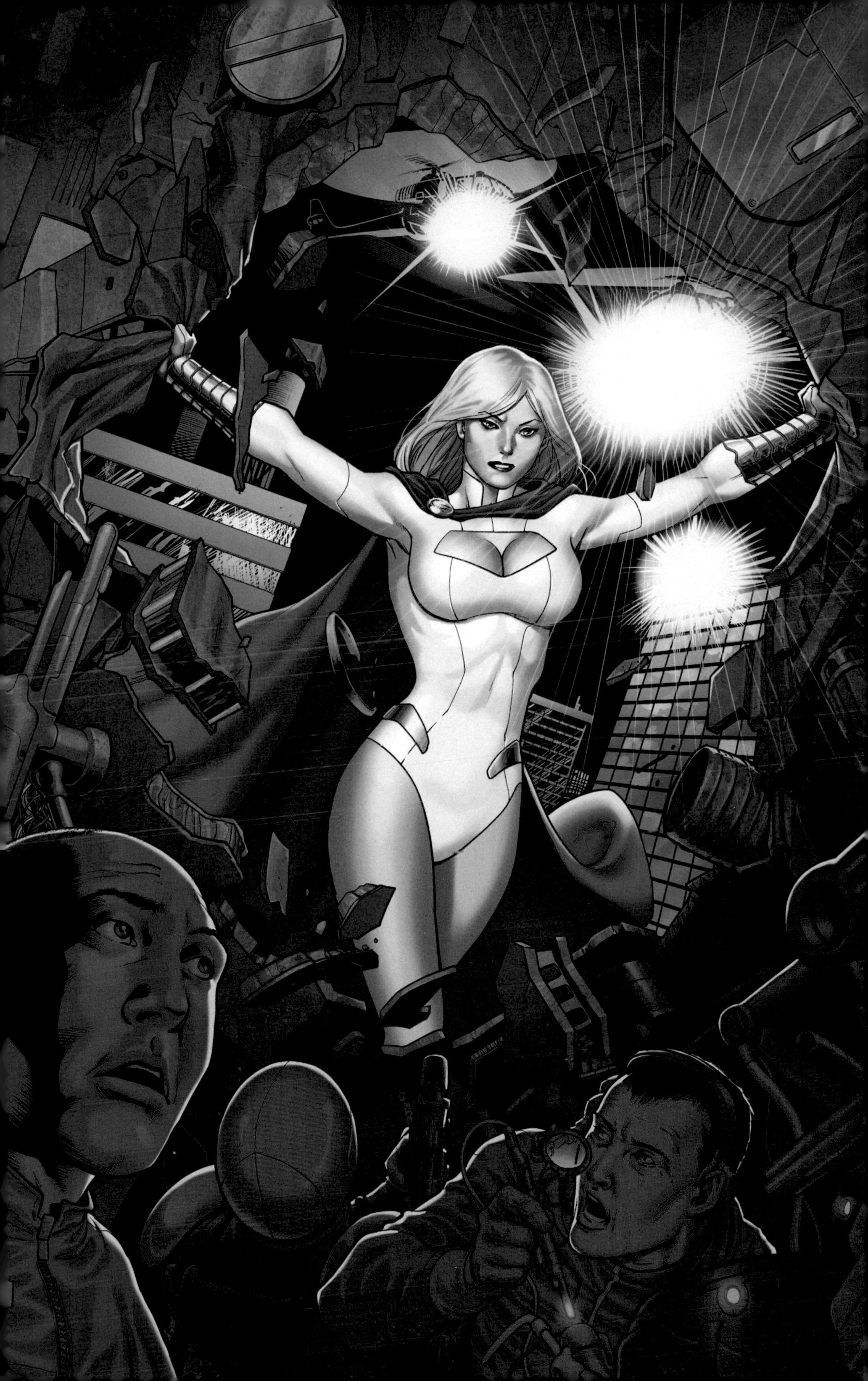

I MUST BE GOING PART 1

PAUL LEVITZ writer **R.B. SILVA YILDIRAY CINAR** pencillers **JOE WEEMS YILDIRAY CINAR** inkers **JASON WRIGHT** colorist **CARLOS M. MANGUAL** letterer cover by **BARRY KITSON** and **JASON WRIGHT**

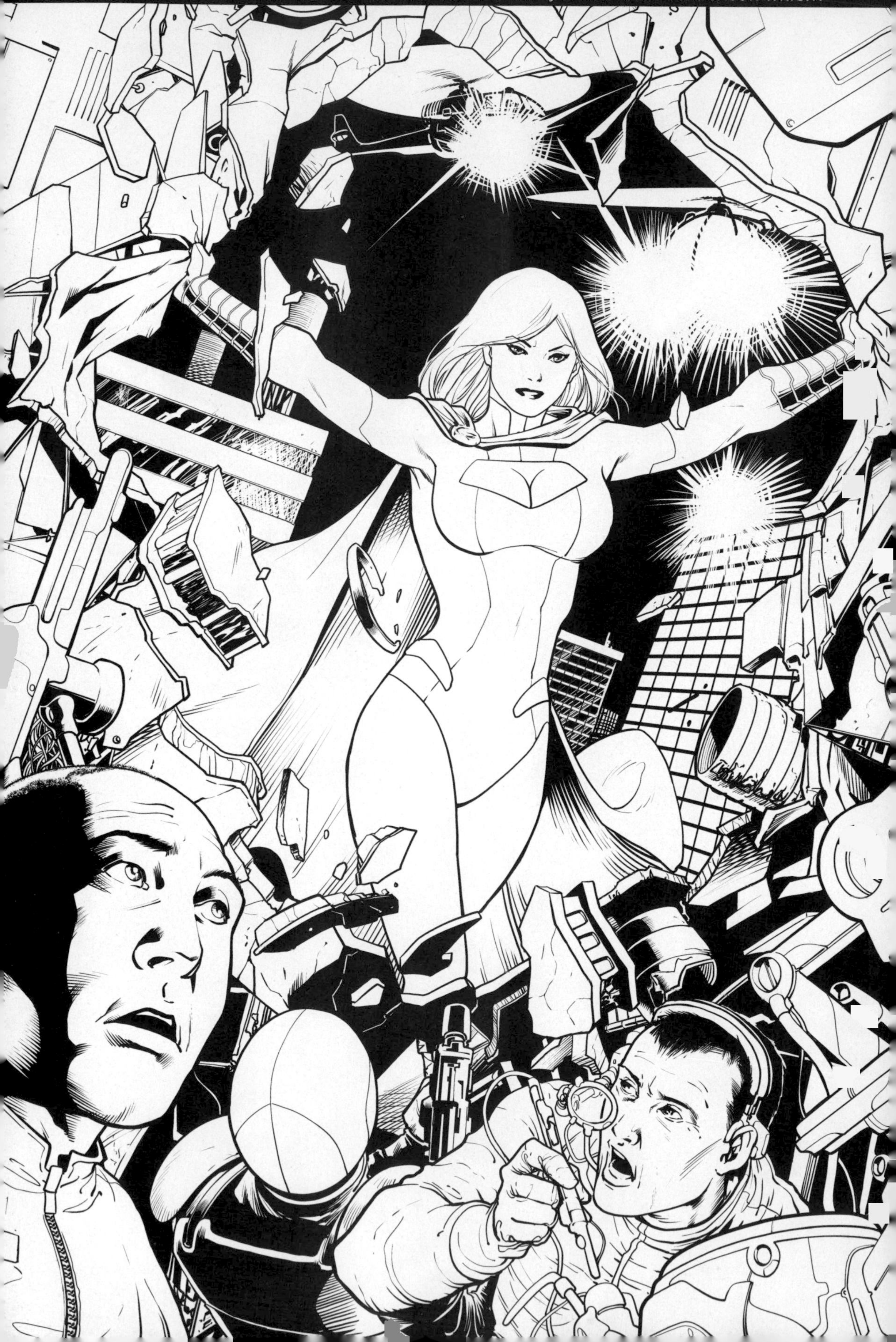

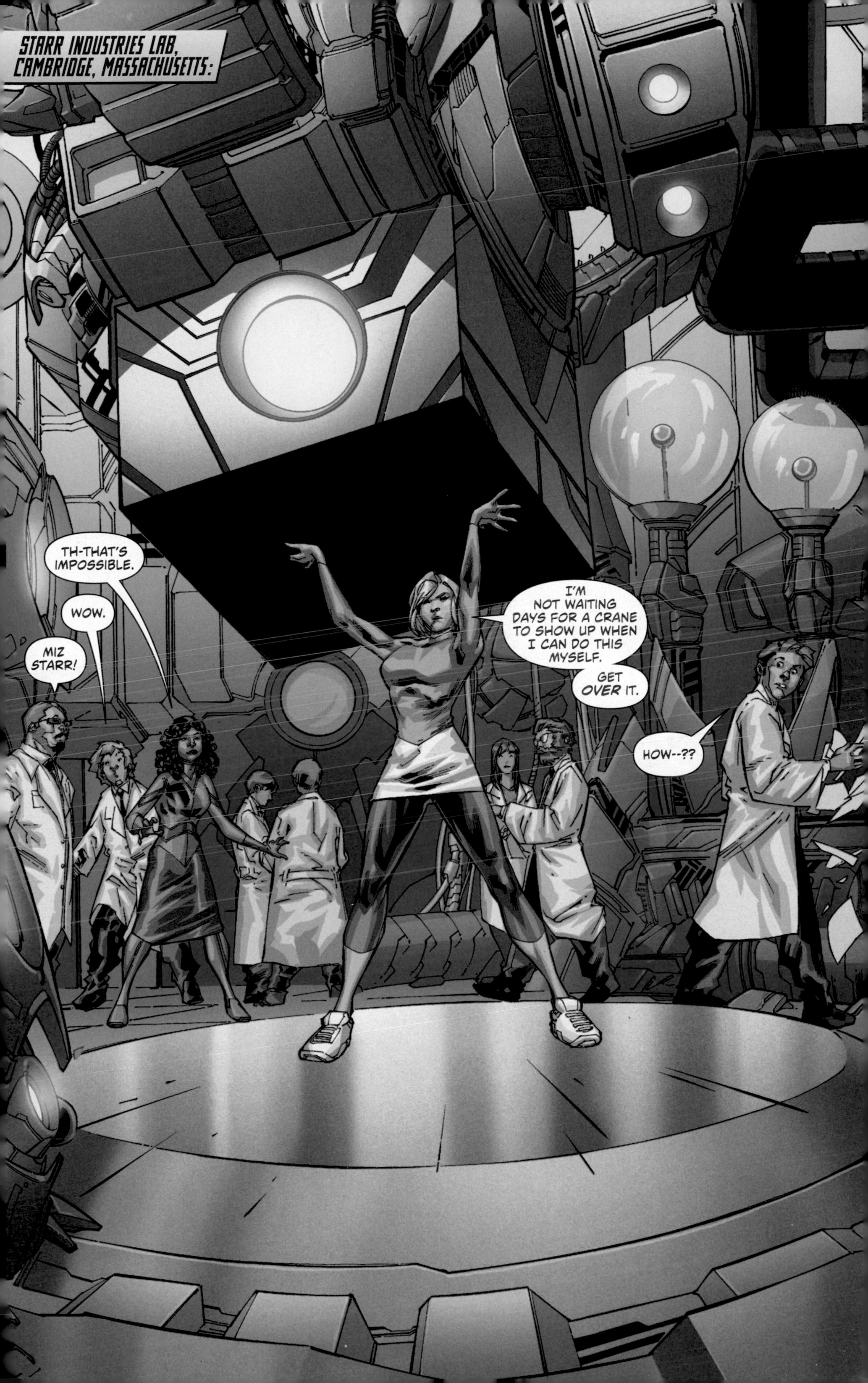
STARR INDUSTRIES LAB, CAMBRIDGE, MASSACHUSETTS:
TH-THAT'S IMPOSSIBLE.
WOW.
MIZ STARR!
I'M NOT WAITING DAYS FOR A CRANE TO SHOW UP WHEN I CAN DO THIS MYSELF.
GET OVER IT.
HOW--??

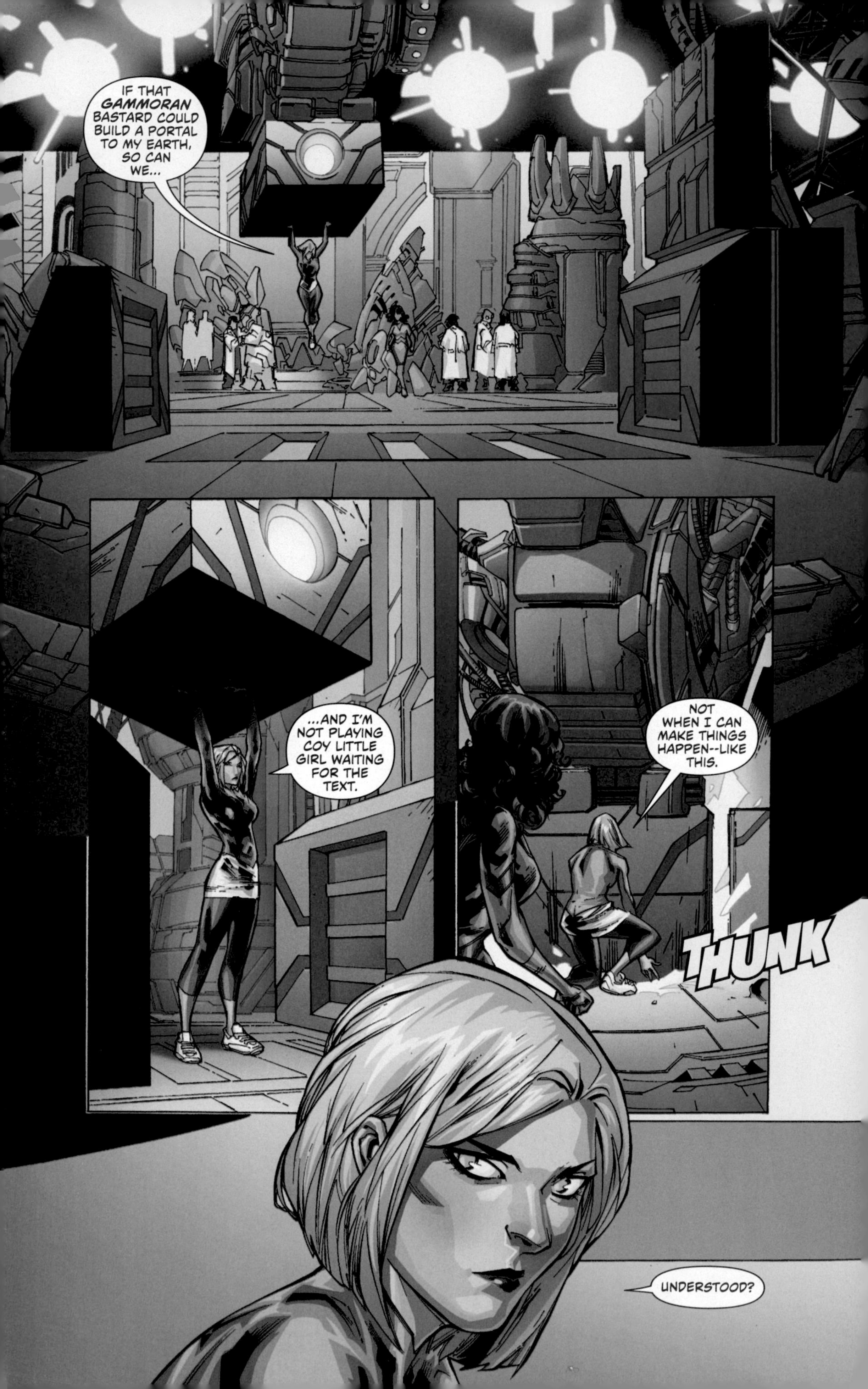
IF THAT GAMMORAN BASTARD COULD BUILD A PORTAL TO MY EARTH, SO CAN WE...
...AND I'M NOT PLAYING COY LITTLE GIRL WAITING FOR THE TEXT.
NOT WHEN I CAN MAKE THINGS HAPPEN--LIKE THIS.
THUNK
UNDERSTOOD?

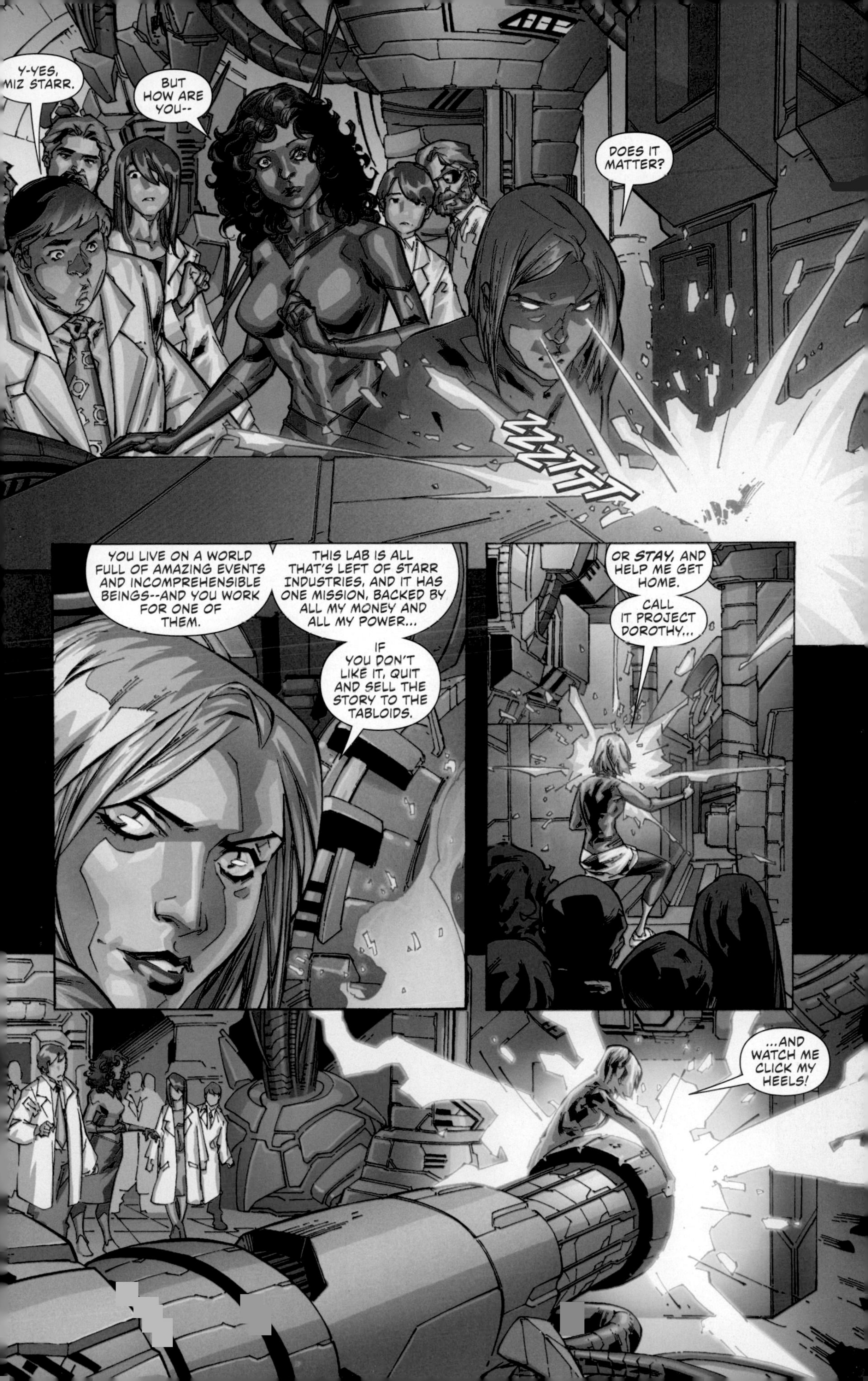
Y-YES, MIZ STARR.
BUT HOW ARE YOU--
DOES IT MATTER?
ZZZTTT
YOU LIVE ON A WORLD FULL OF AMAZING EVENTS AND INCOMPREHENSIBLE BEINGS--AND YOU WORK FOR ONE OF THEM.
THIS LAB IS ALL THAT'S LEFT OF STARR INDUSTRIES, AND IT HAS ONE MISSION, BACKED BY ALL MY MONEY AND ALL MY POWER...
IF YOU DON'T LIKE IT, QUIT AND SELL THE STORY TO THE TABLOIDS.
OR STAY, AND HELP ME GET HOME.
CALL IT PROJECT DOROTHY...
...AND WATCH ME CLICK MY HEELS!

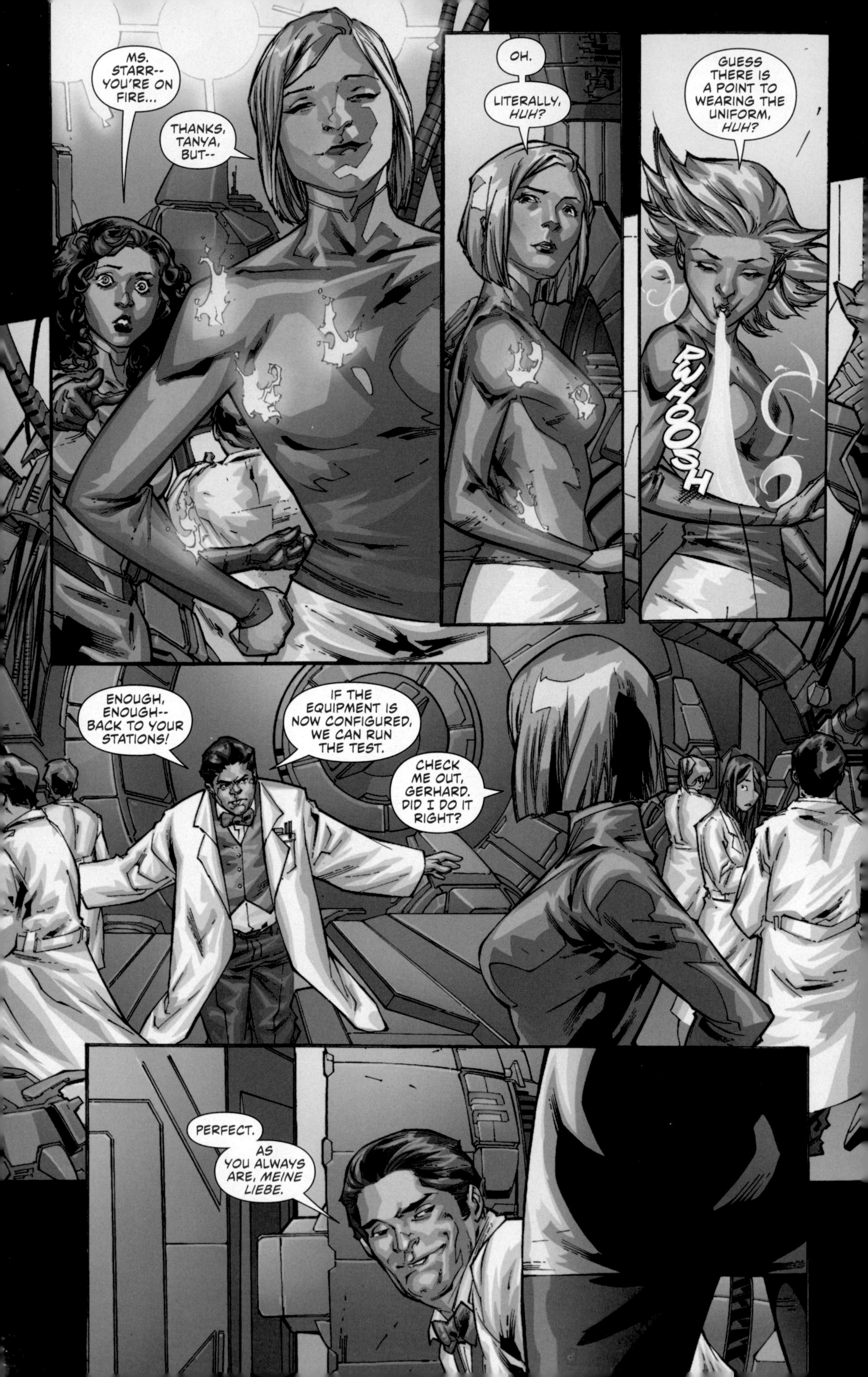
MS. STARR-- YOU'RE ON FIRE...
THANKS, TANYA, BUT--
OH.
LITERALLY, HUH?
GUESS THERE IS A POINT TO WEARING THE UNIFORM, HUH?
PWHOOSH
ENOUGH, ENOUGH-- BACK TO YOUR STATIONS!
IF THE EQUIPMENT IS NOW CONFIGURED, WE CAN RUN THE TEST.
CHECK ME OUT, GERHARD. DID I DO IT RIGHT?
PERFECT.
AS YOU ALWAYS ARE, MEINE LIEBE.

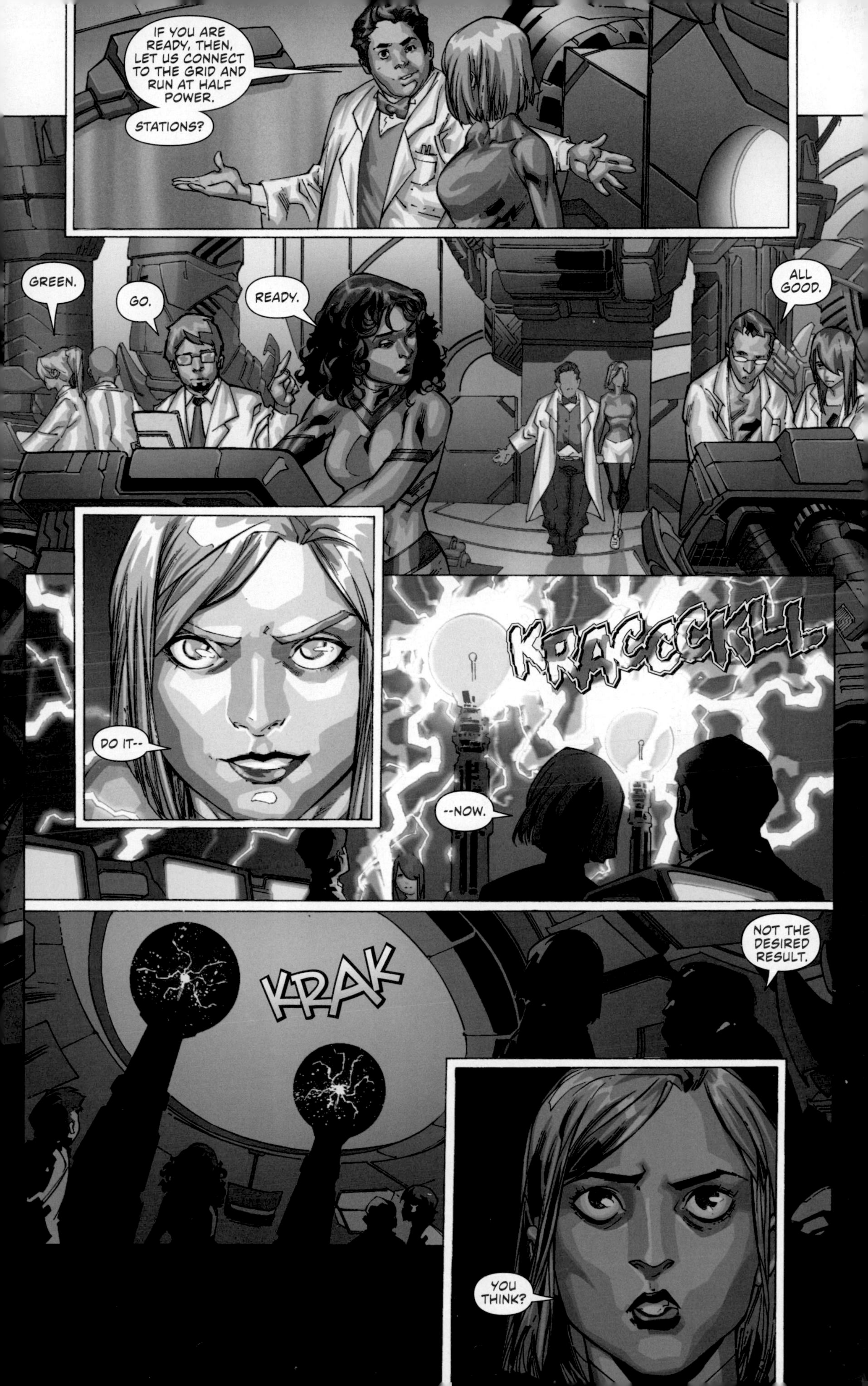
IF YOU ARE READY, THEN, LET US CONNECT TO THE GRID AND RUN AT HALF POWER.
STATIONS?
GREEN.
GO.
READY.
ALL GOOD.
DO IT--
KRACCCKLL
--NOW.
KRAK
NOT THE DESIRED RESULT.
YOU THINK?

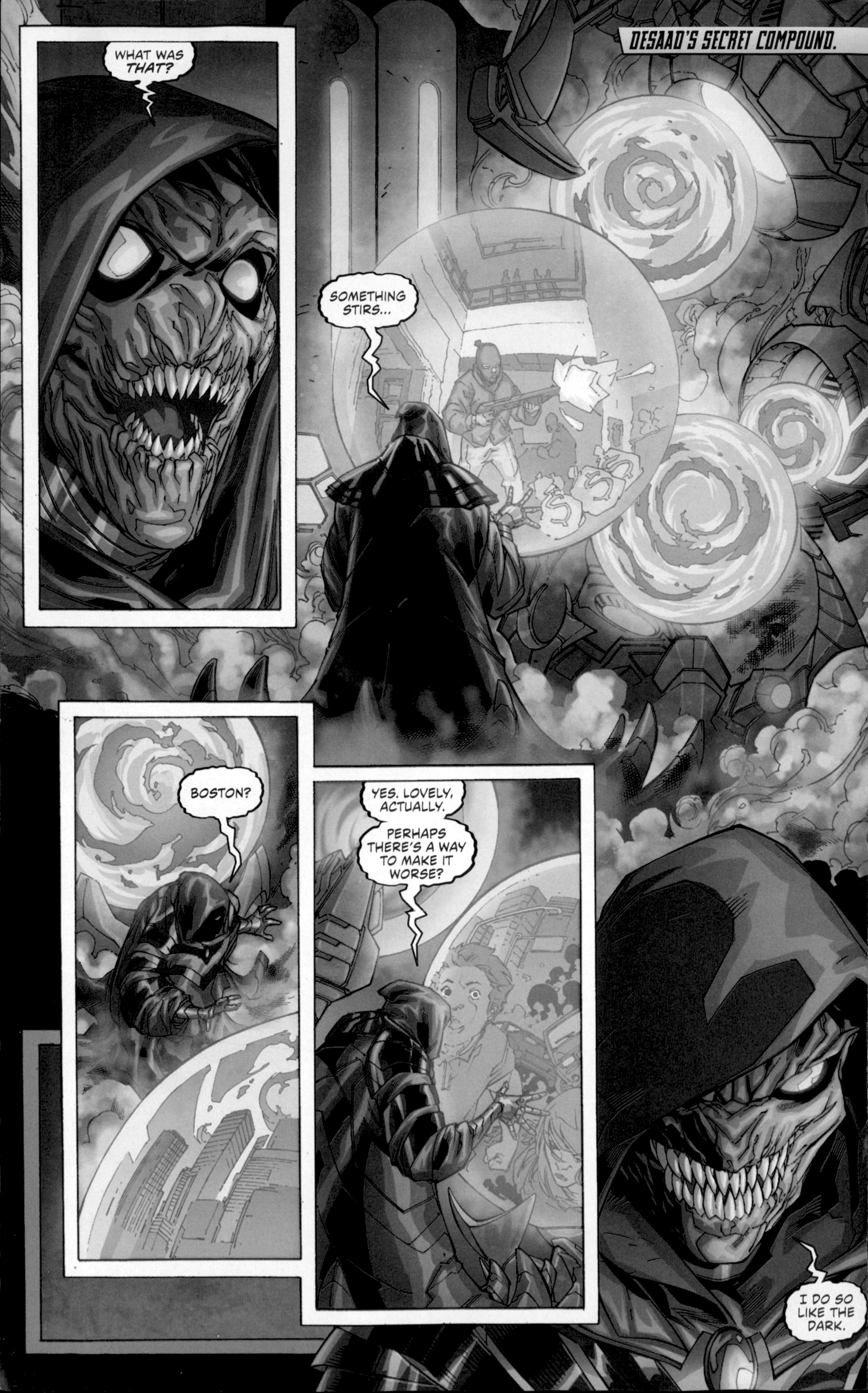
DESAAD'S SECRET COMPOUND.
WHAT WAS THAT?
SOMETHING STIRS...
BOSTON?
YES. LOVELY, ACTUALLY.
PERHAPS THERE'S A WAY TO MAKE IT WORSE?
I DO SO LIKE THE DARK.

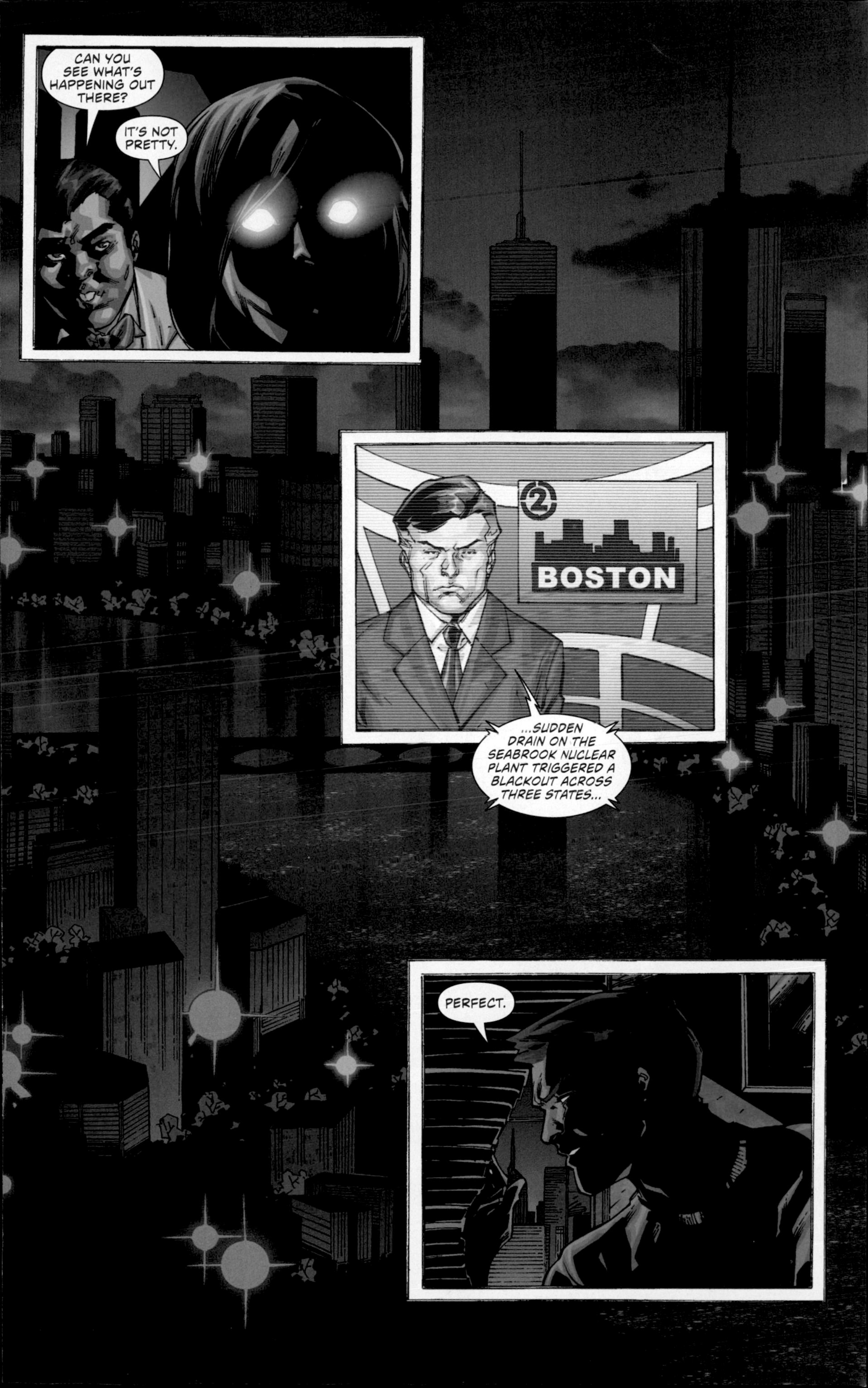
CAN YOU SEE WHAT'S HAPPENING OUT THERE?
IT'S NOT PRETTY.
BOSTON
...SUDDEN DRAIN ON THE SEABROOK NUCLEAR PLANT TRIGGERED A BLACKOUT ACROSS THREE STATES...
PERFECT.

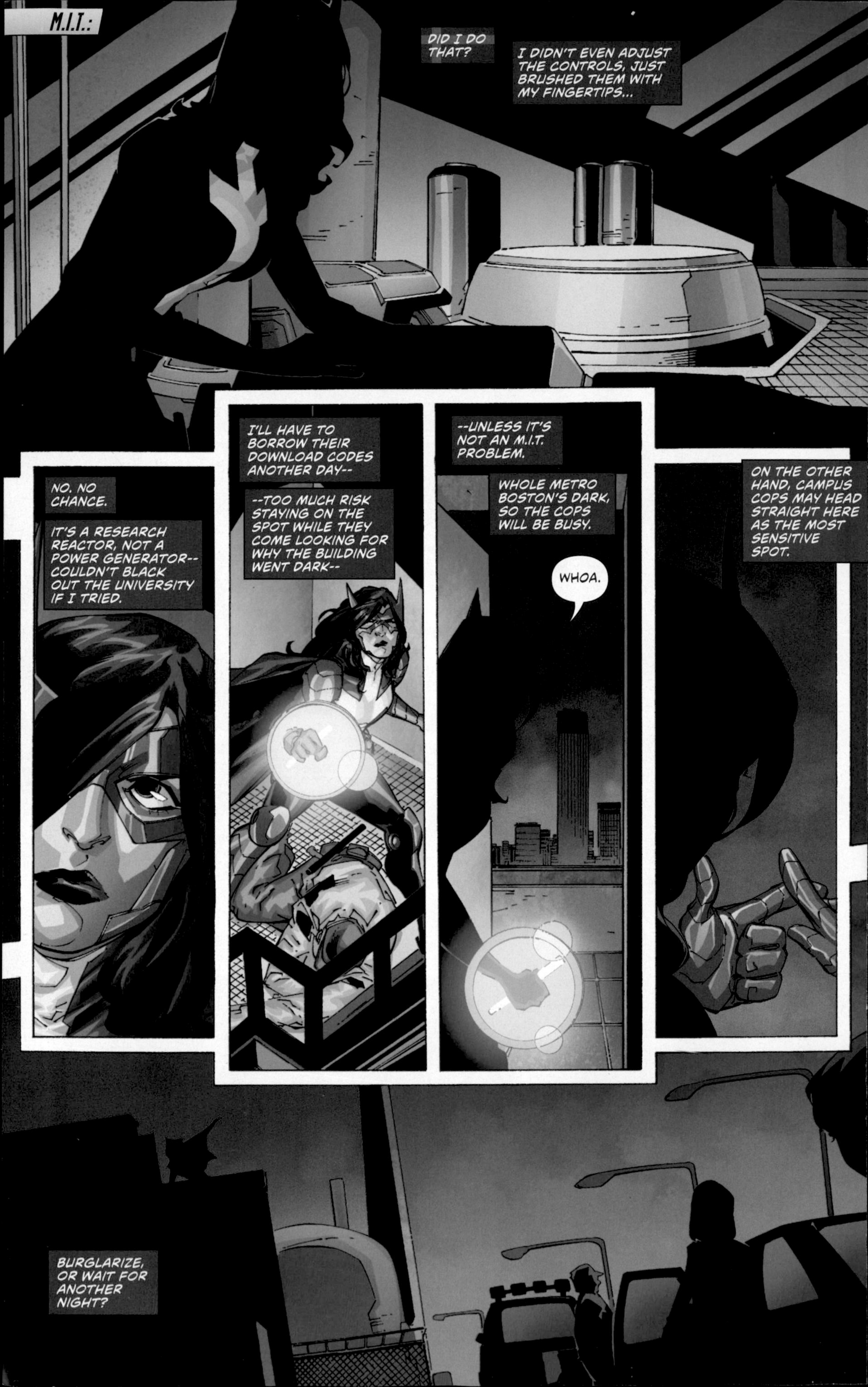
M.I.T.:
DID I DO THAT?
I DIDN'T EVEN ADJUST THE CONTROLS, JUST BRUSHED THEM WITH MY FINGERTIPS...
NO. NO CHANCE.
IT'S A RESEARCH REACTOR, NOT A POWER GENERATOR-- COULDN'T BLACK OUT THE UNIVERSITY IF I TRIED.
I'LL HAVE TO BORROW THEIR DOWNLOAD CODES ANOTHER DAY--
--TOO MUCH RISK STAYING ON THE SPOT WHILE THEY COME LOOKING FOR WHY THE BUILDING WENT DARK--
--UNLESS IT'S NOT AN M.I.T. PROBLEM.
WHOLE METRO BOSTON'S DARK, SO THE COPS WILL BE BUSY.
WHOA.
ON THE OTHER HAND, CAMPUS COPS MAY HEAD STRAIGHT HERE AS THE MOST SENSITIVE SPOT.
BURGLARIZE, OR WAIT FOR ANOTHER NIGHT?

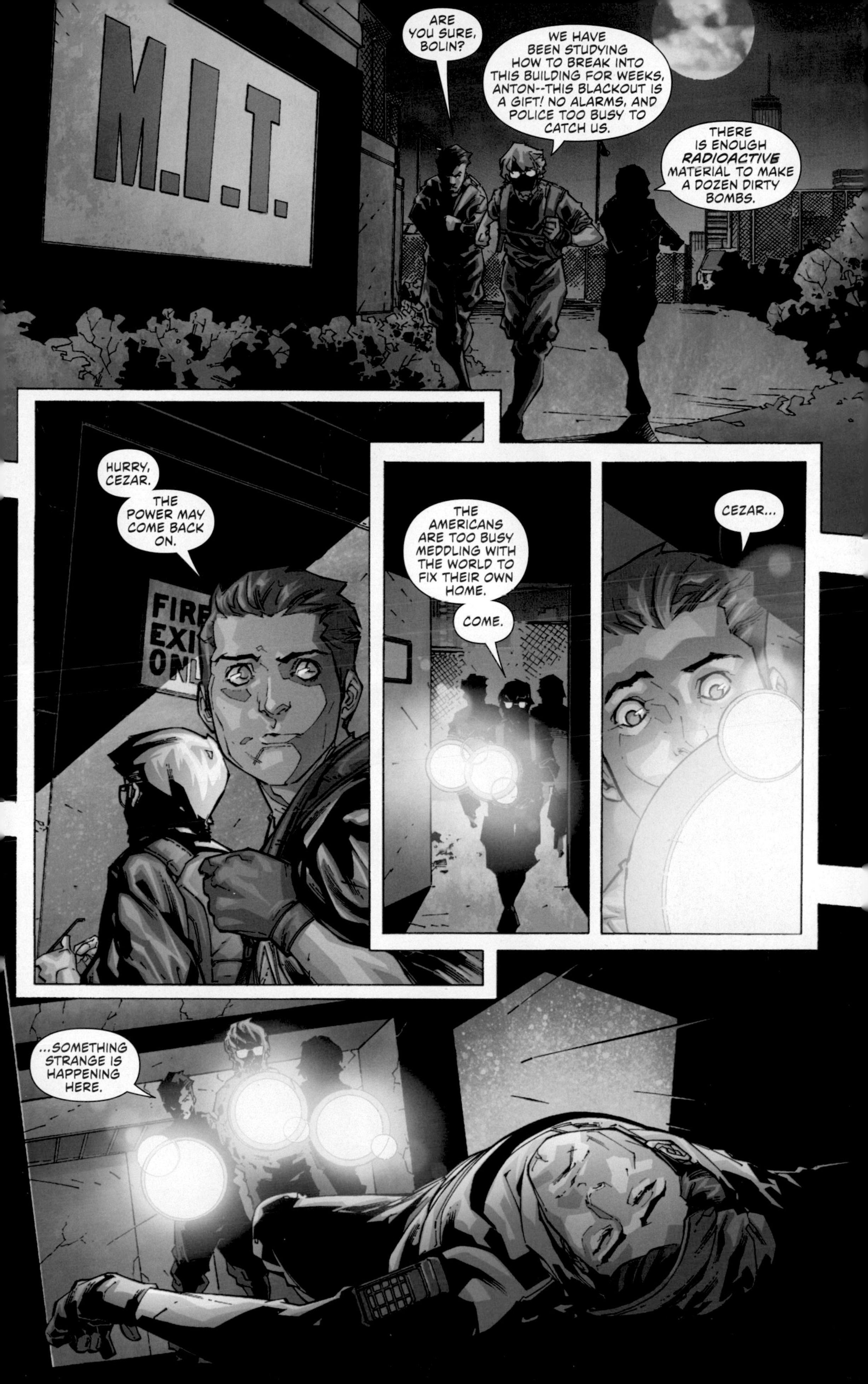
M.I.T.
ARE YOU SURE, BOLIN?
WE HAVE BEEN STUDYING HOW TO BREAK INTO THIS BUILDING FOR WEEKS, ANTON--THIS BLACKOUT IS A GIFT! NO ALARMS, AND POLICE TOO BUSY TO CATCH US.
THERE IS ENOUGH RADIOACTIVE MATERIAL TO MAKE A DOZEN DIRTY BOMBS.
HURRY, CEZAR.
THE POWER MAY COME BACK ON.
FIRE EXIT ONLY
THE AMERICANS ARE TOO BUSY MEDDLING WITH THE WORLD TO FIX THEIR OWN HOME.
COME.
CEZAR...
...SOMETHING STRANGE IS HAPPENING HERE.

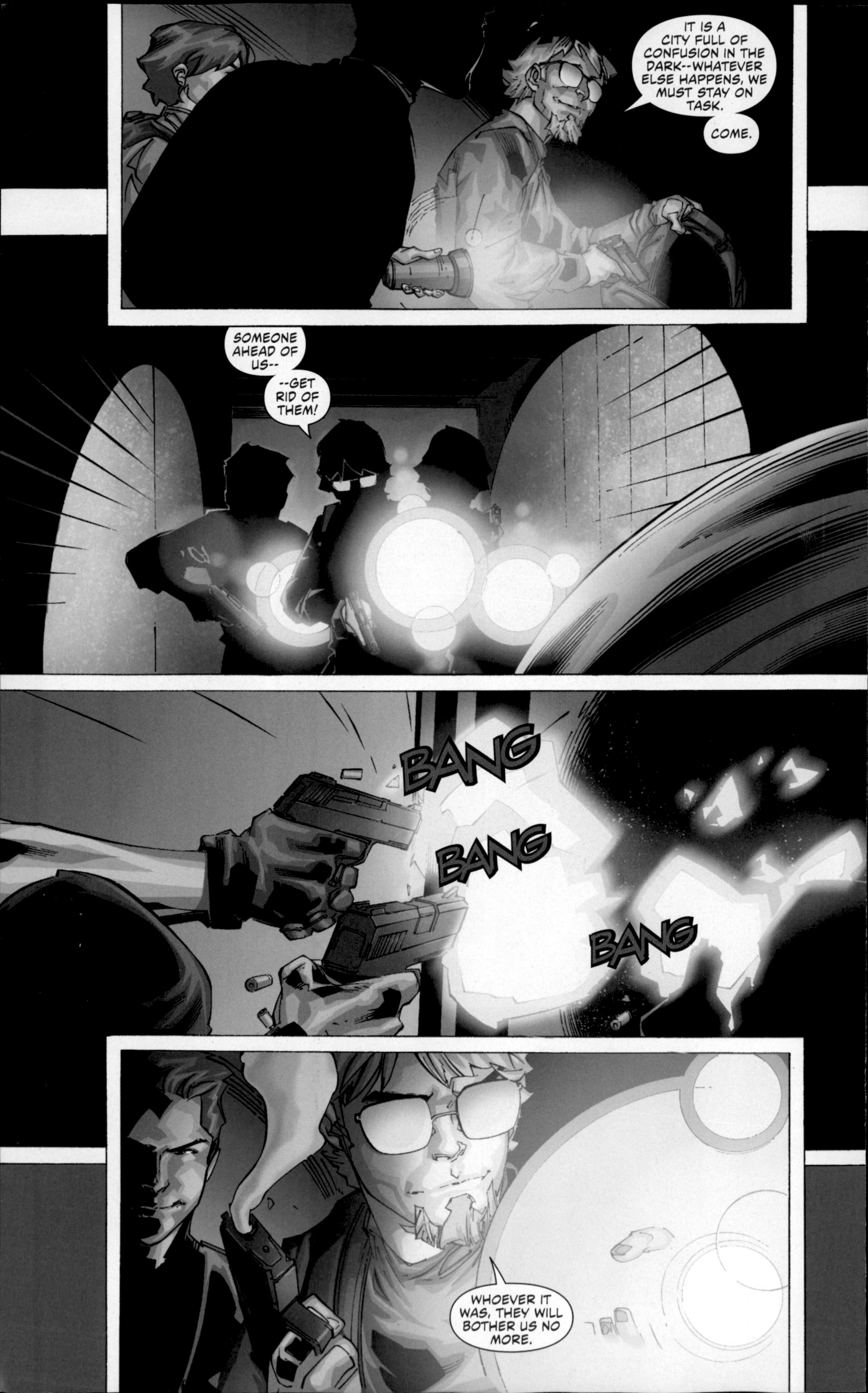
IT IS A CITY FULL OF CONFUSION IN THE DARK--WHATEVER ELSE HAPPENS, WE MUST STAY ON TASK.
COME.
SOMEONE AHEAD OF US--
--GET RID OF THEM!
BANG
BANG
BANG
WHOEVER IT WAS, THEY WILL BOTHER US NO MORE.

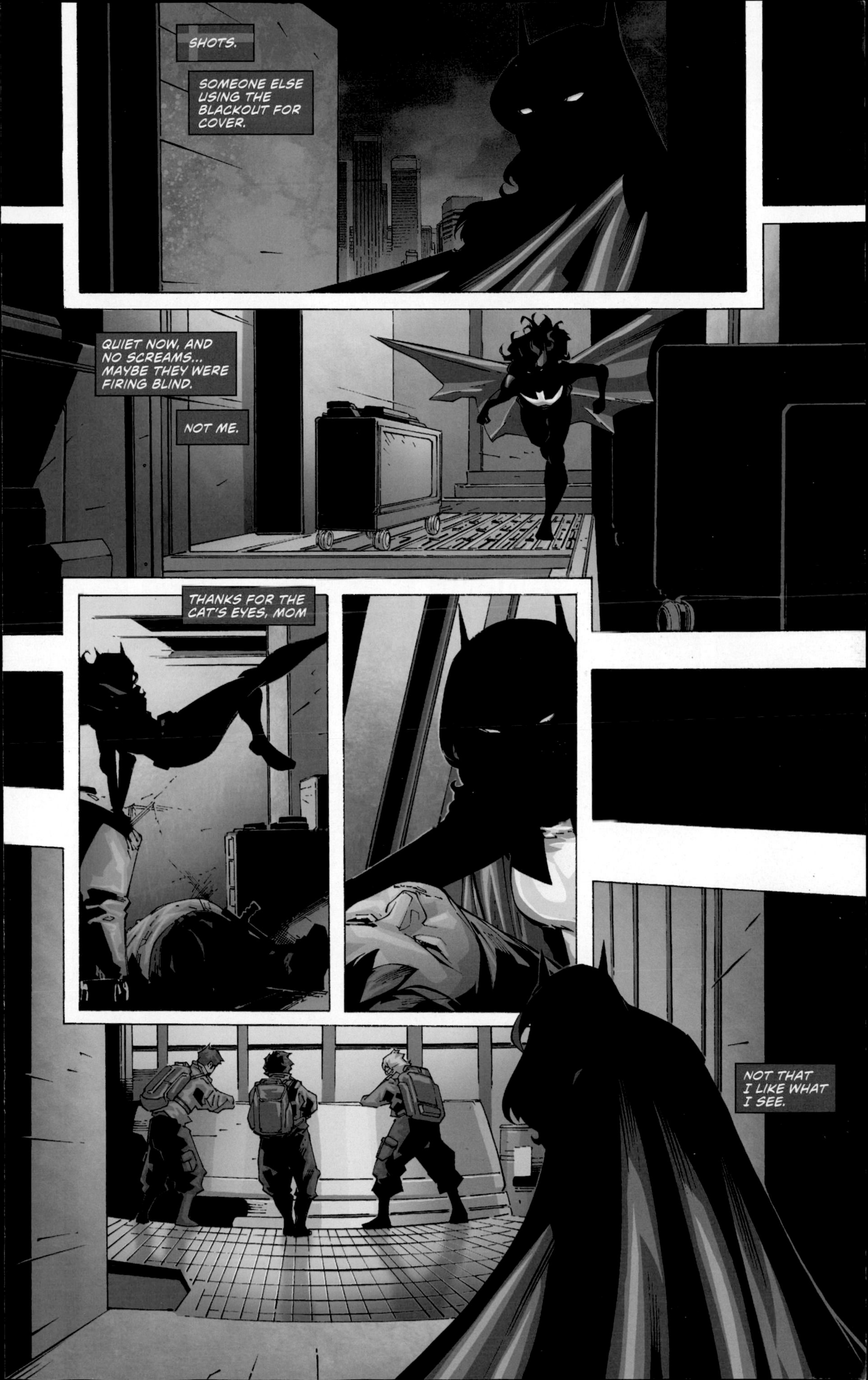
SHOTS.
SOMEONE ELSE USING THE BLACKOUT FOR COVER.
QUIET NOW, AND NO SCREAMS... MAYBE THEY WERE FIRING BLIND.
NOT ME.
THANKS FOR THE CAT'S EYES, MOM
NOT THAT I LIKE WHAT I SEE.

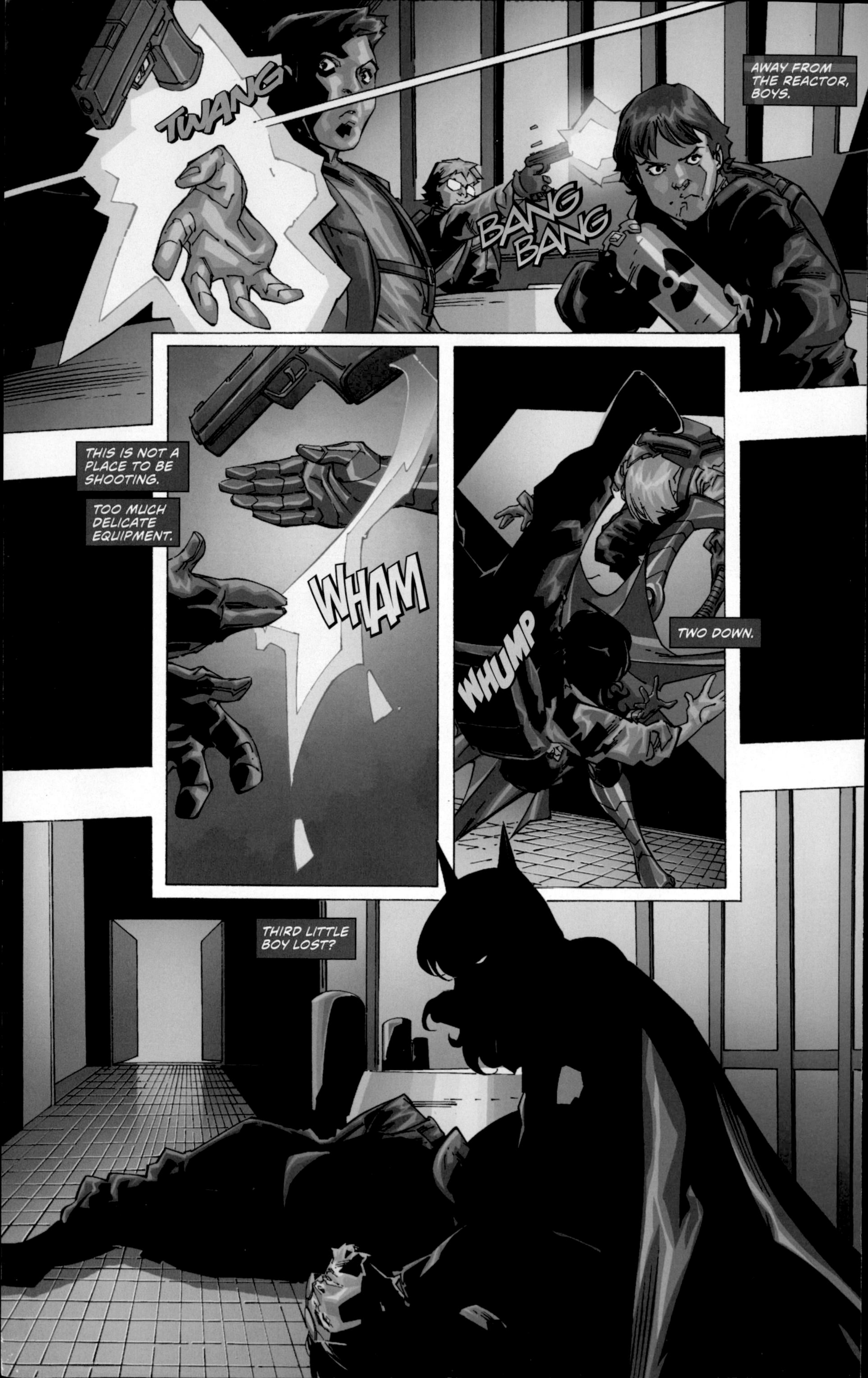
TWANG
AWAY FROM THE REACTOR, BOYS.
BANG BANG
THIS IS NOT A PLACE TO BE SHOOTING.
TOO MUCH DELICATE EQUIPMENT.
WHAM
WHUMP
TWO DOWN.
THIRD LITTLE BOY LOST?

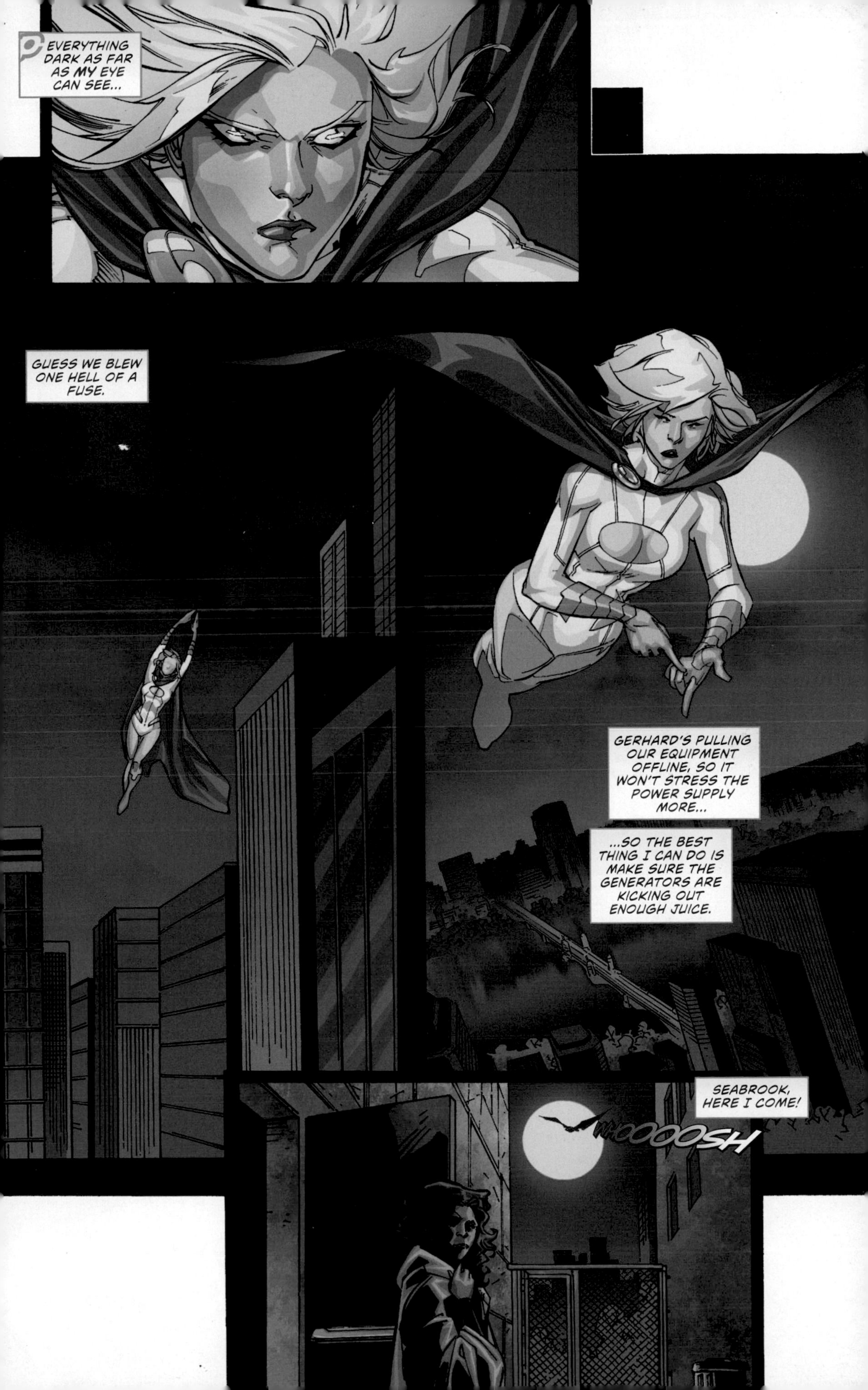
EVERYTHING DARK AS FAR AS MY EYE CAN SEE...
GUESS WE BLEW ONE HELL OF A FUSE.
GERHARD'S PULLING OUR EQUIPMENT OFFLINE, SO IT WON'T STRESS THE POWER SUPPLY MORE...
...SO THE BEST THING I CAN DO IS MAKE SURE THE GENERATORS ARE KICKING OUT ENOUGH JUICE.
SEABROOK, HERE I COME!
WHOOOOOSH

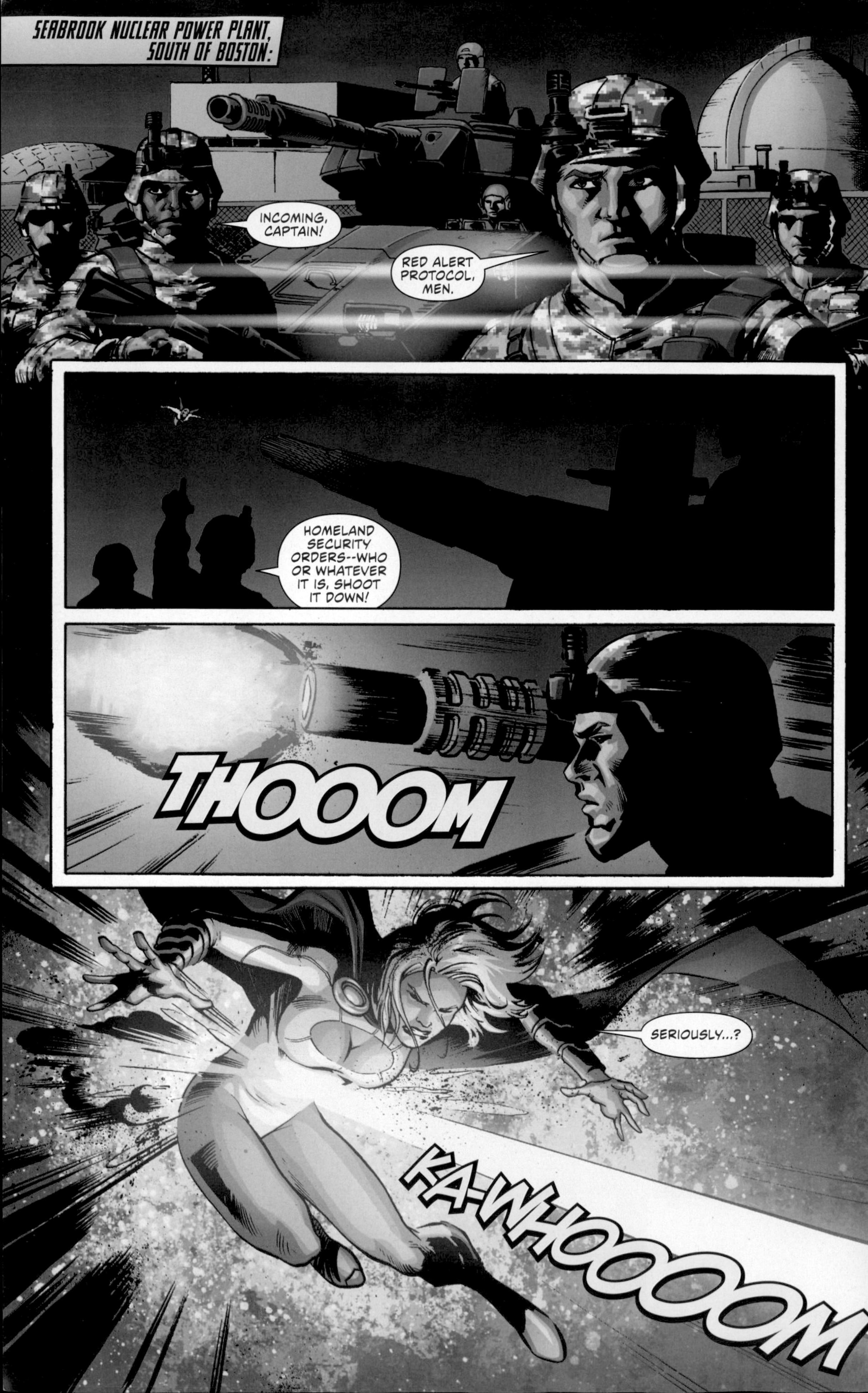
SEABROOK NUCLEAR POWER PLANT, SOUTH OF BOSTON:
INCOMING, CAPTAIN!
RED ALERT PROTOCOL, MEN.
HOMELAND SECURITY ORDERS--WHO OR WHATEVER IT IS, SHOOT IT DOWN!
THOOOM
SERIOUSLY...?
KA-WHOOOOOM

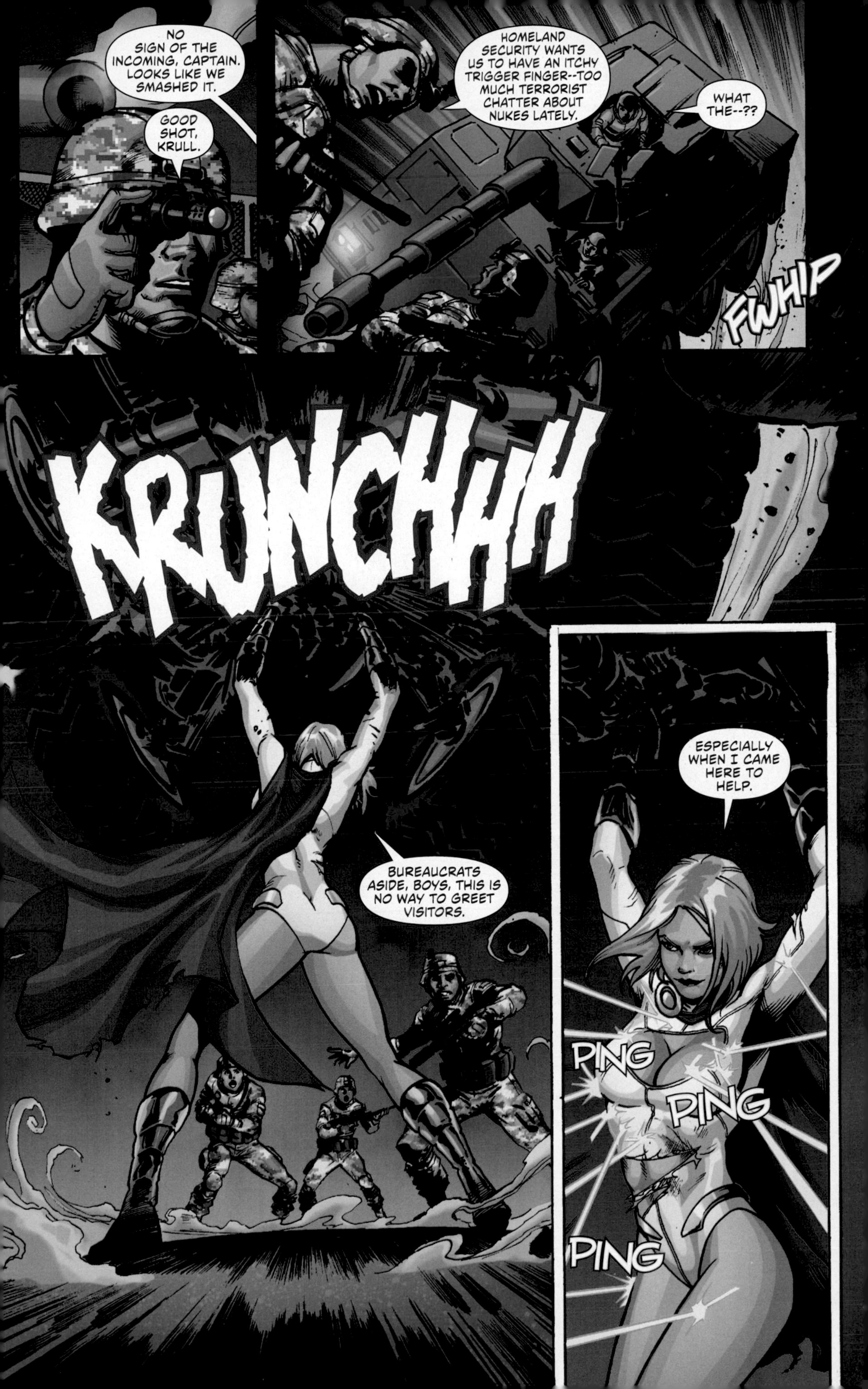
NO SIGN OF THE INCOMING, CAPTAIN. LOOKS LIKE WE SMASHED IT.
GOOD SHOT, KRULL.
HOMELAND SECURITY WANTS US TO HAVE AN ITCHY TRIGGER FINGER--TOO MUCH TERRORIST CHATTER ABOUT NUKES LATELY.
WHAT THE--??
FWHIP
KRUNCHHH
BUREAUCRATS ASIDE, BOYS, THIS IS NO WAY TO GREET VISITORS.
ESPECIALLY WHEN I CAME HERE TO HELP.
PING
PING
PING

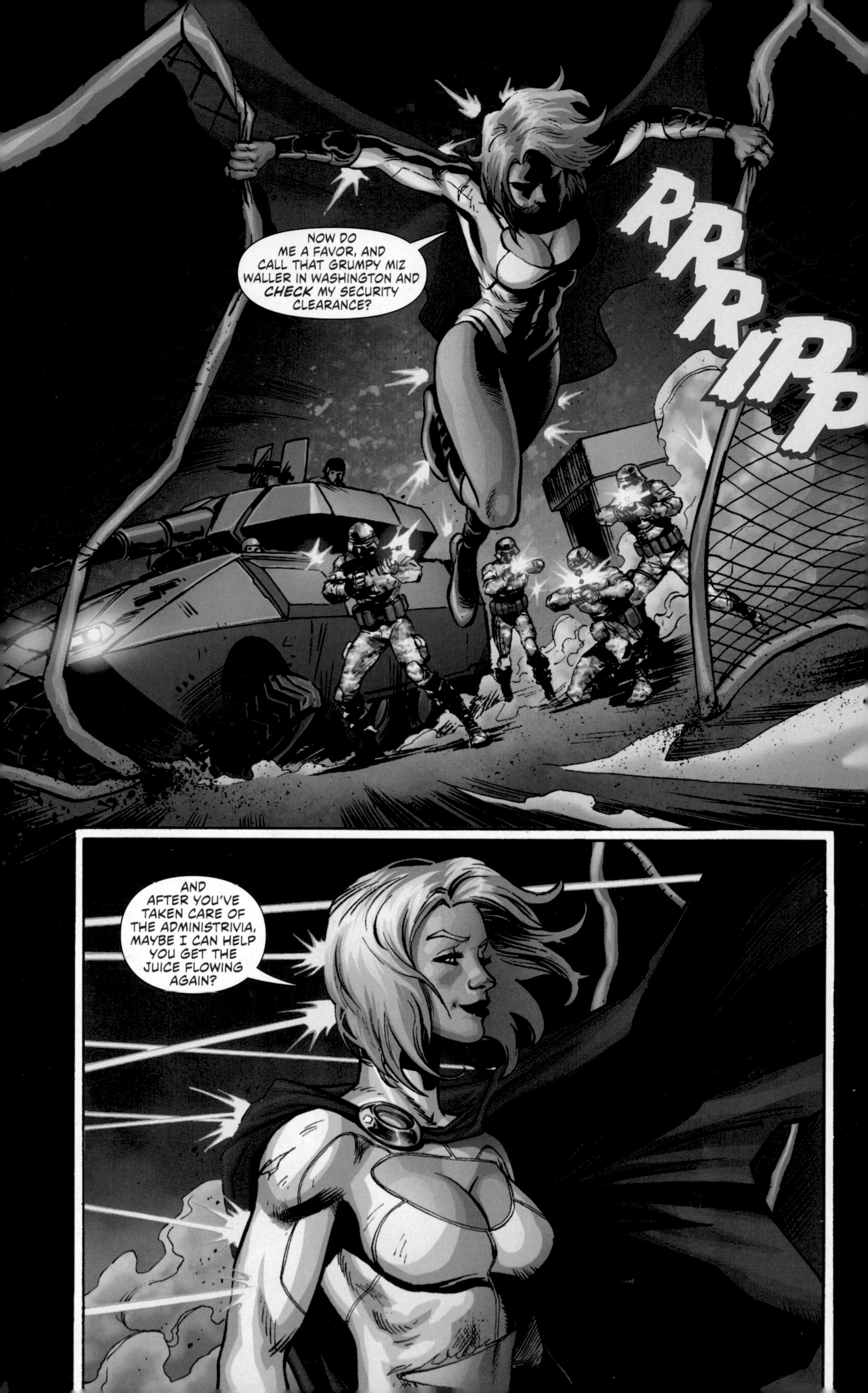
NOW DO ME A FAVOR, AND CALL THAT GRUMPY MIZ WALLER IN WASHINGTON AND CHECK MY SECURITY CLEARANCE?
RRRIPP
AND AFTER YOU'VE TAKEN CARE OF THE ADMINISTRIVIA, MAYBE I CAN HELP YOU GET THE JUICE FLOWING AGAIN?

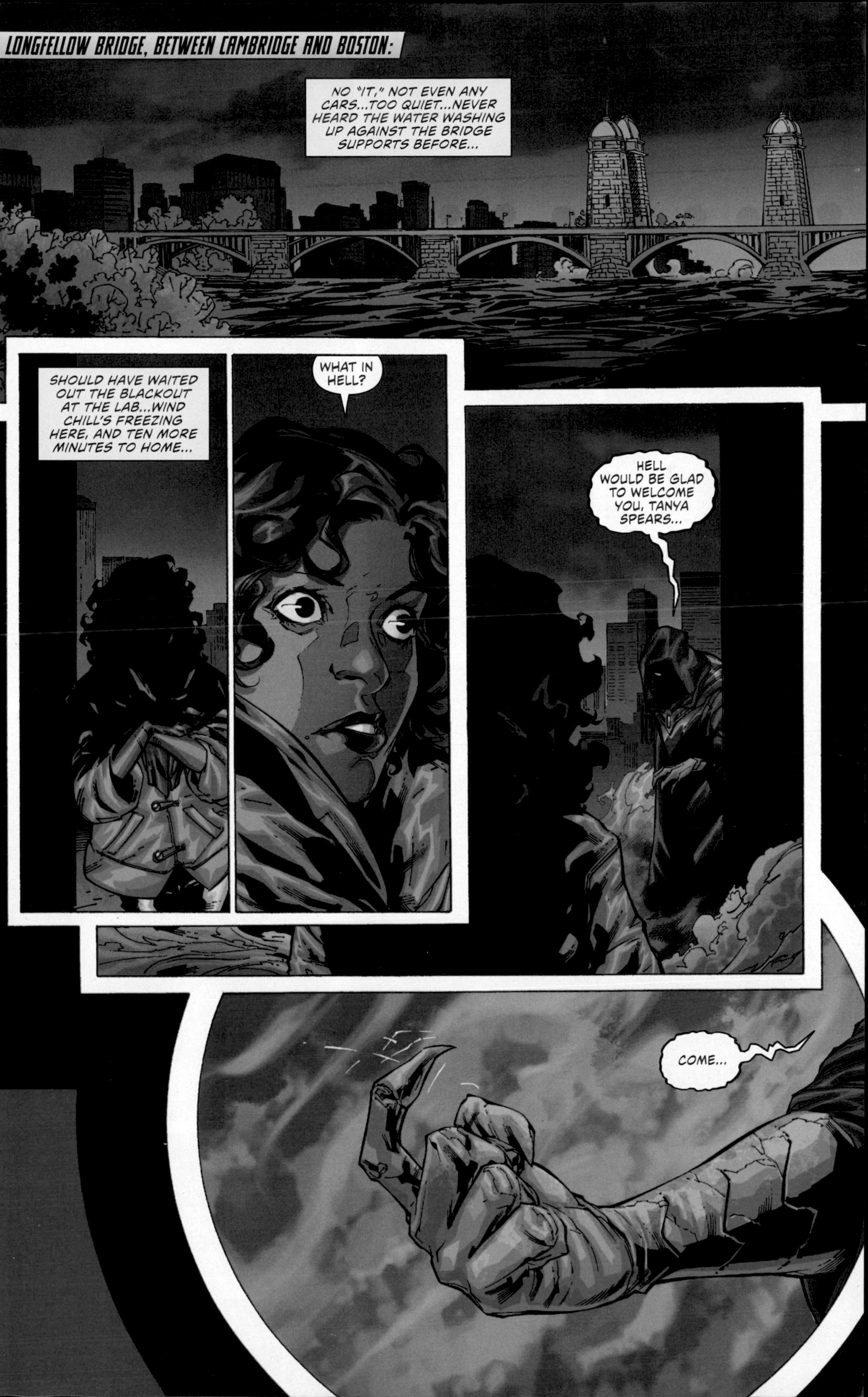
LONGFELLOW BRIDGE, BETWEEN CAMBRIDGE AND BOSTON:
NO "IT," NOT EVEN ANY CARS...TOO QUIET...NEVER HEARD THE WATER WASHING UP AGAINST THE BRIDGE SUPPORTS BEFORE...
SHOULD HAVE WAITED OUT THE BLACKOUT AT THE LAB...WIND CHILL'S FREEZING HERE, AND TEN MORE MINUTES TO HOME...
WHAT IN HELL?
HELL WOULD BE GLAD TO WELCOME YOU, TANYA SPEARS...
COME...

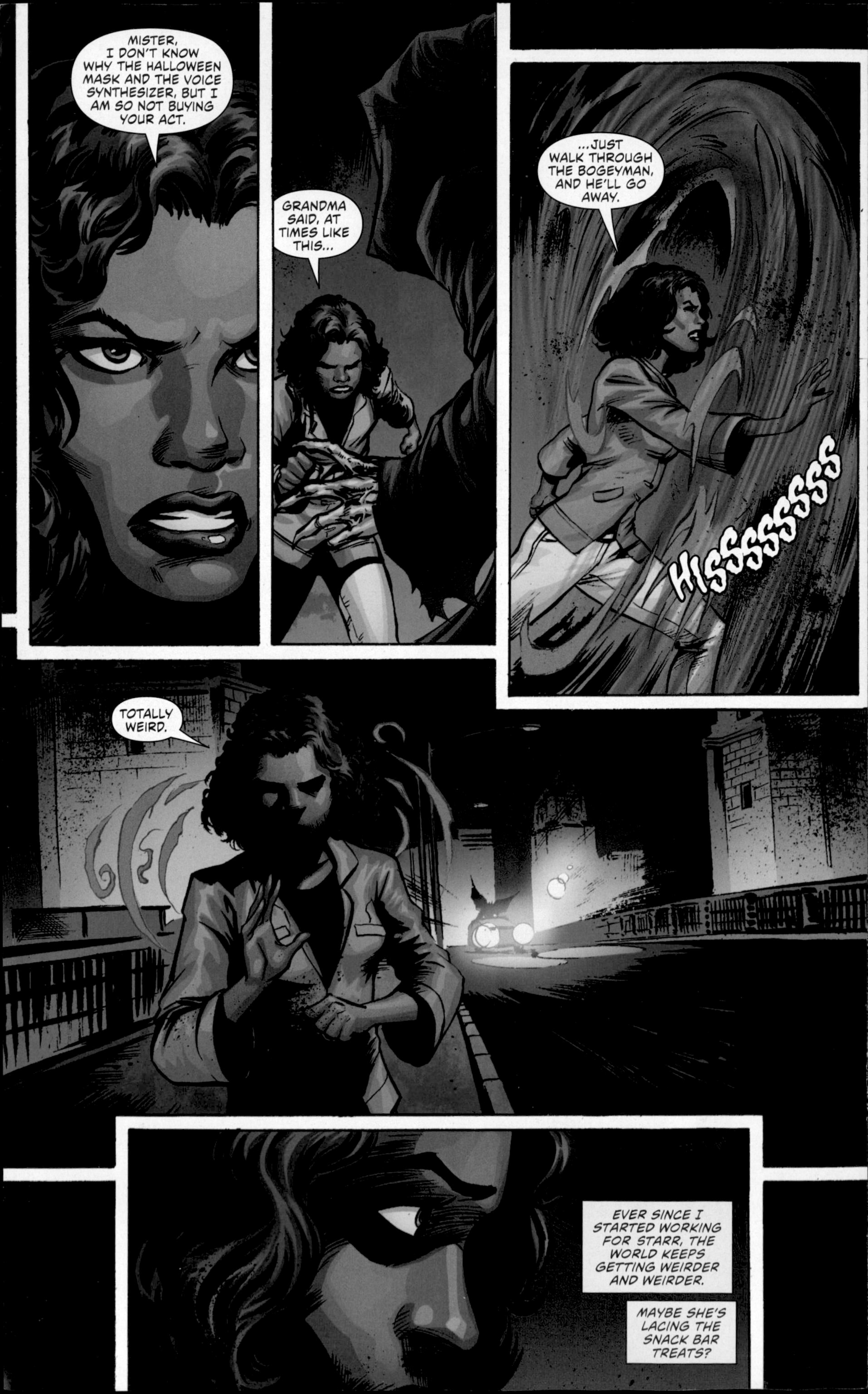
MISTER, I DON'T KNOW WHY THE HALLOWEEN MASK AND THE VOICE SYNTHESIZER, BUT I AM SO NOT BUYING YOUR ACT.
GRANDMA SAID, AT TIMES LIKE THIS...
...JUST WALK THROUGH THE BOGEYMAN, AND HE'LL GO AWAY.
HISSSSSSSS
TOTALLY WEIRD.
EVER SINCE I STARTED WORKING FOR STARR, THE WORLD KEEPS GETTING WEIRDER AND WEIRDER.
MAYBE SHE'S LACING THE SNACK BAR TREATS?

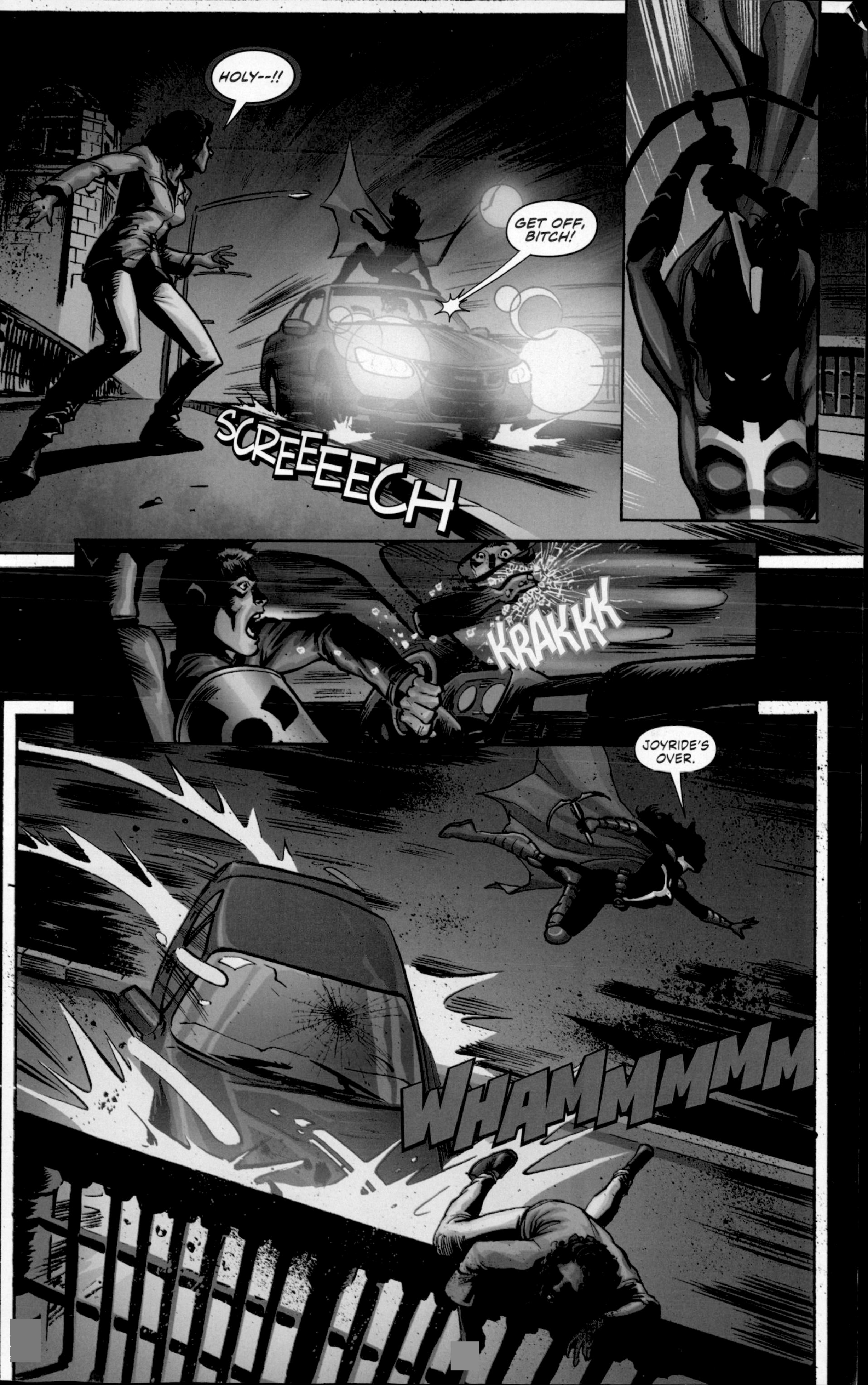
HOLY--!!
GET OFF, BITCH!
SCREEEEECH
KRAKKK
JOYRIDE'S OVER.
WHAMMMMMM

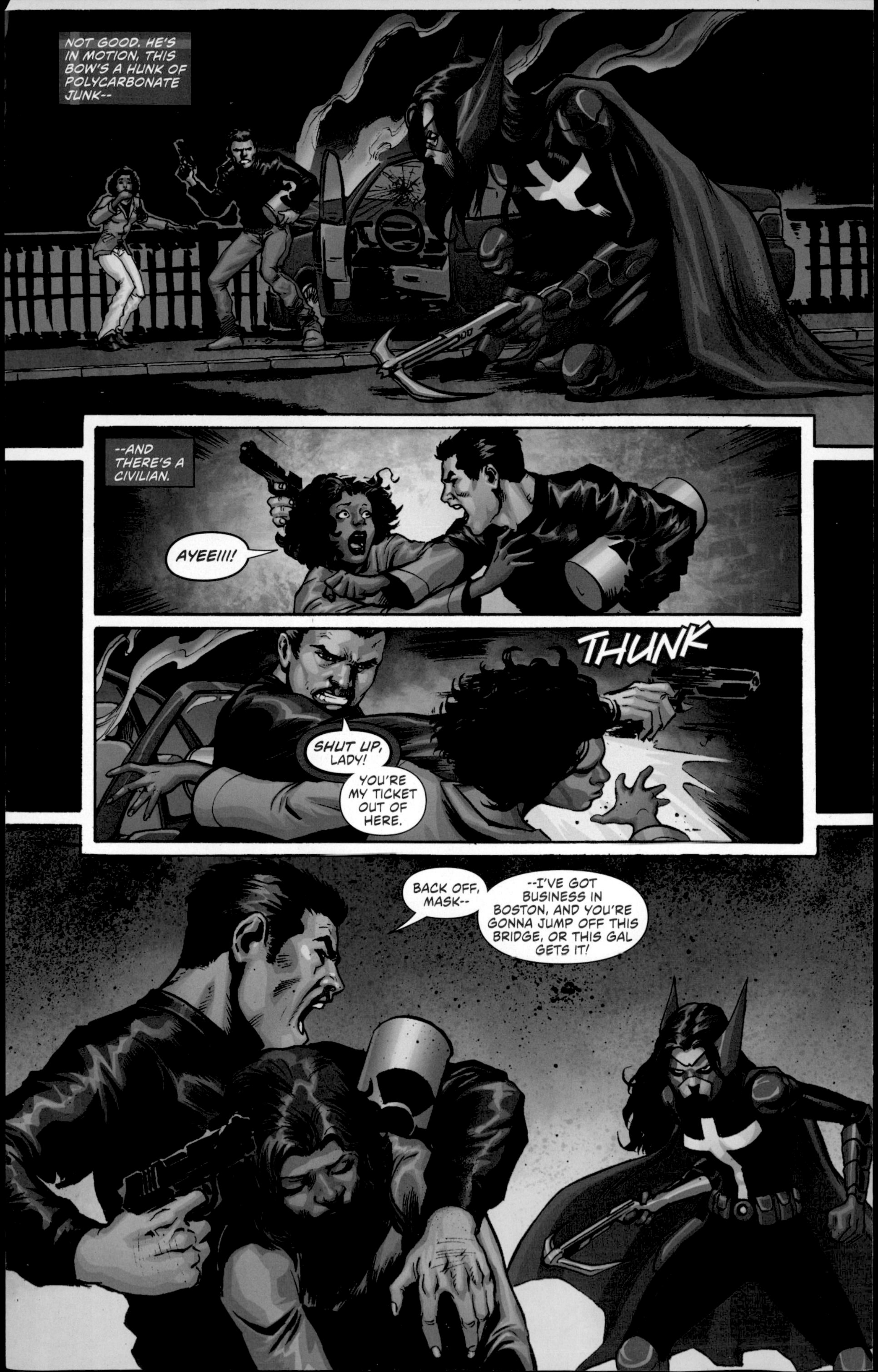
NOT GOOD. HE'S IN MOTION, THIS BOW'S A HUNK OF POLYCARBONATE JUNK--
--AND THERE'S A CIVILIAN.
AYEEIII!
THUNK
SHUT UP, LADY!
YOU'RE MY TICKET OUT OF HERE.
BACK OFF, MASK--
--I'VE GOT BUSINESS IN BOSTON, AND YOU'RE GONNA JUMP OFF THIS BRIDGE, OR THIS GAL GETS IT!

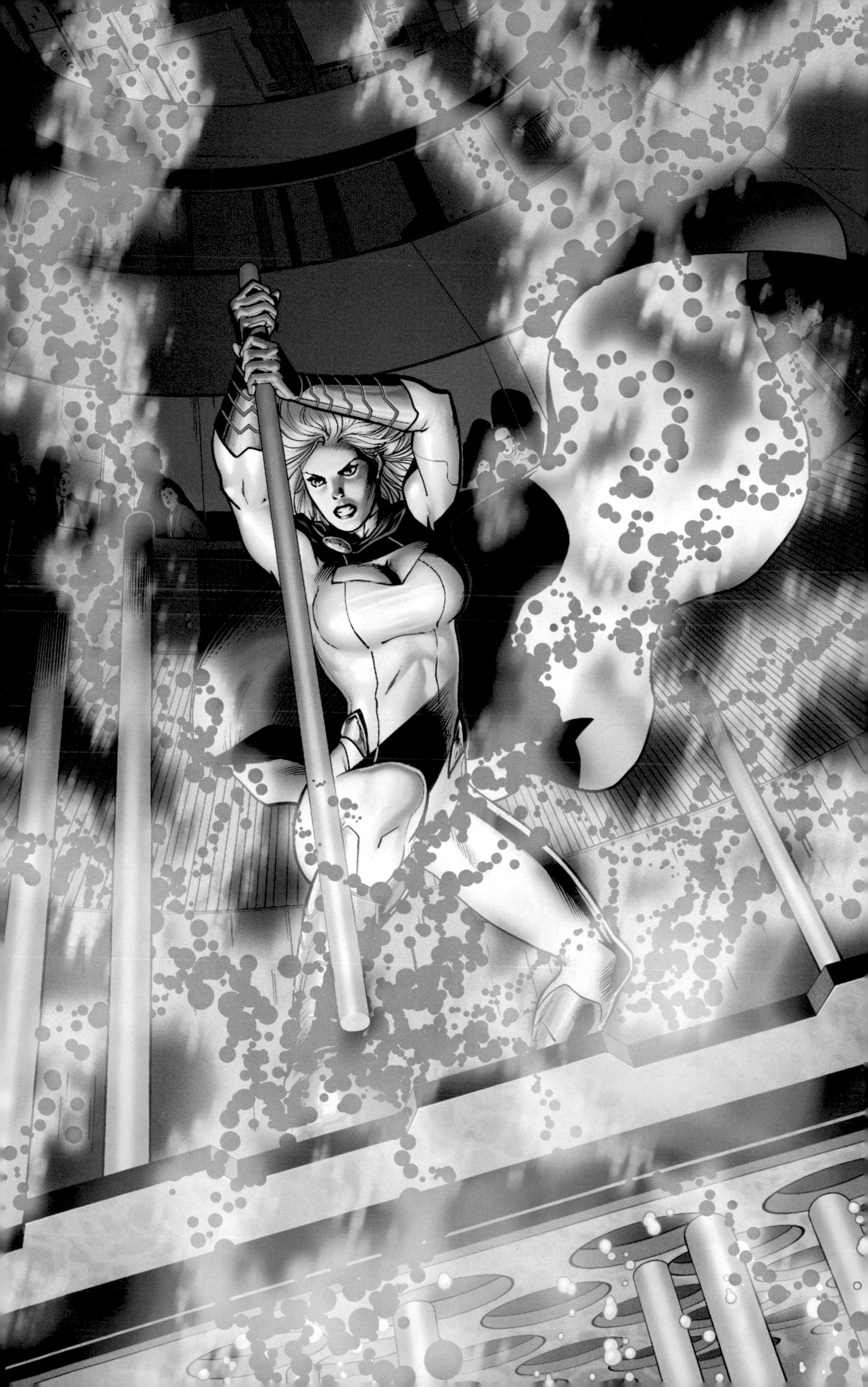

I MUST BE GOING PART 2

PAUL LEVITZ writer **SCOTT MCDANIEL** artist **JASON WRIGHT** colorist **TAYLOR ESPOSITO** letterer

cover by **BARRY KITSON** and **JASON WRIGHT**

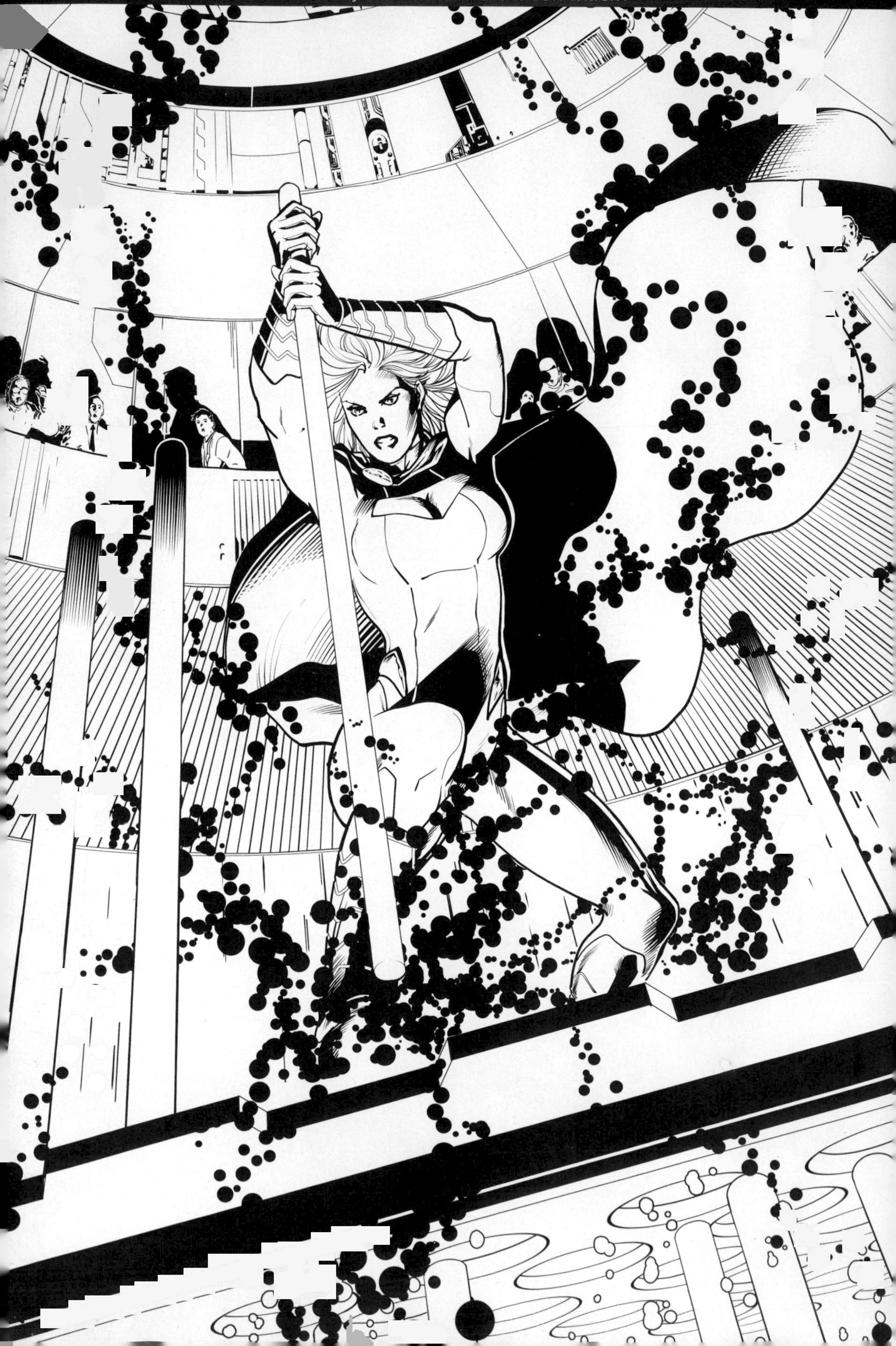

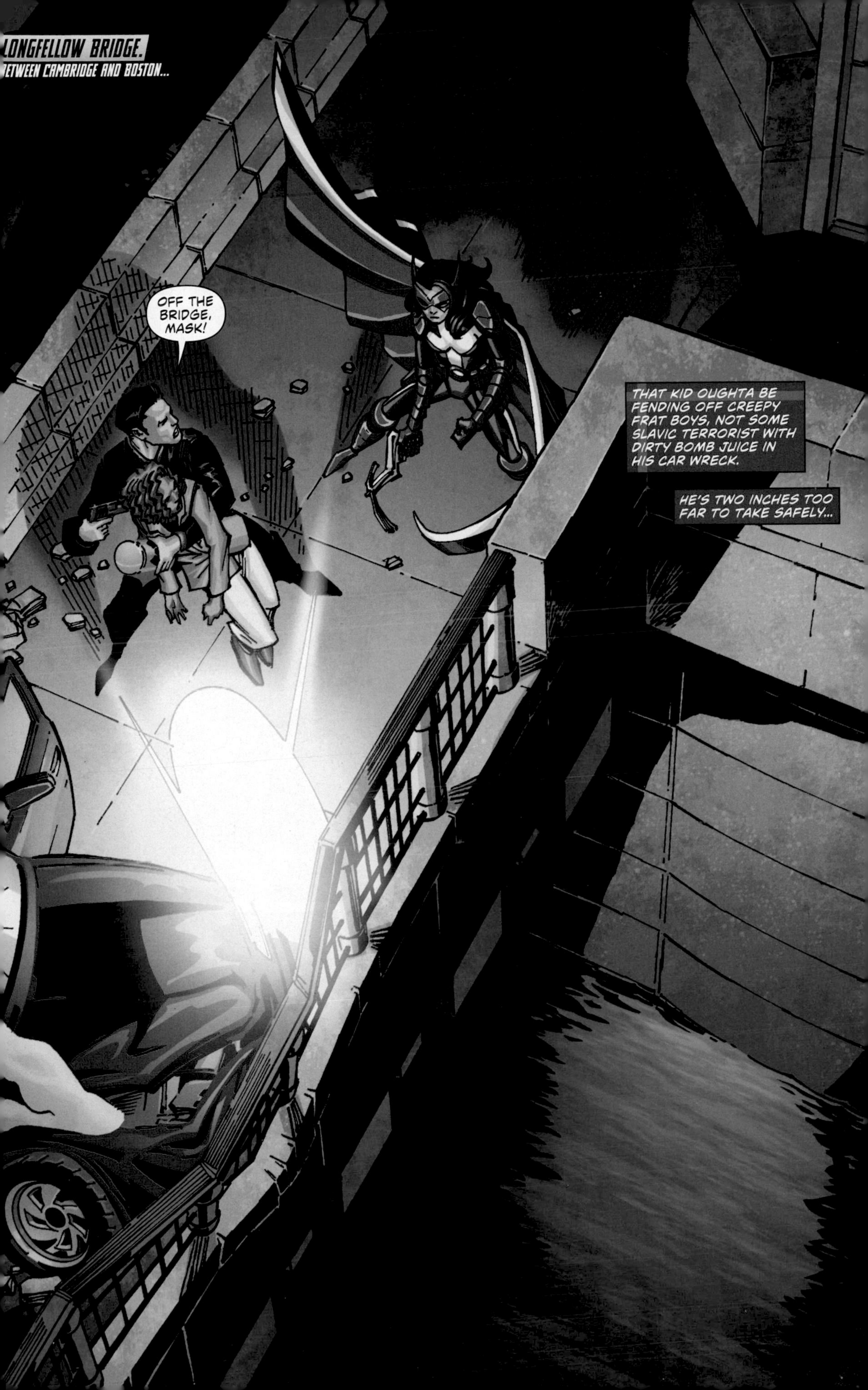
LONGFELLOW BRIDGE.
BETWEEN CAMBRIDGE AND BOSTON...
OFF THE BRIDGE, MASK!
THAT KID OUGHTA BE FENDING OFF CREEPY FRAT BOYS, NOT SOME SLAVIC TERRORIST WITH DIRTY BOMB JUICE IN HIS CAR WRECK.
HE'S TWO INCHES TOO FAR TO TAKE SAFELY...

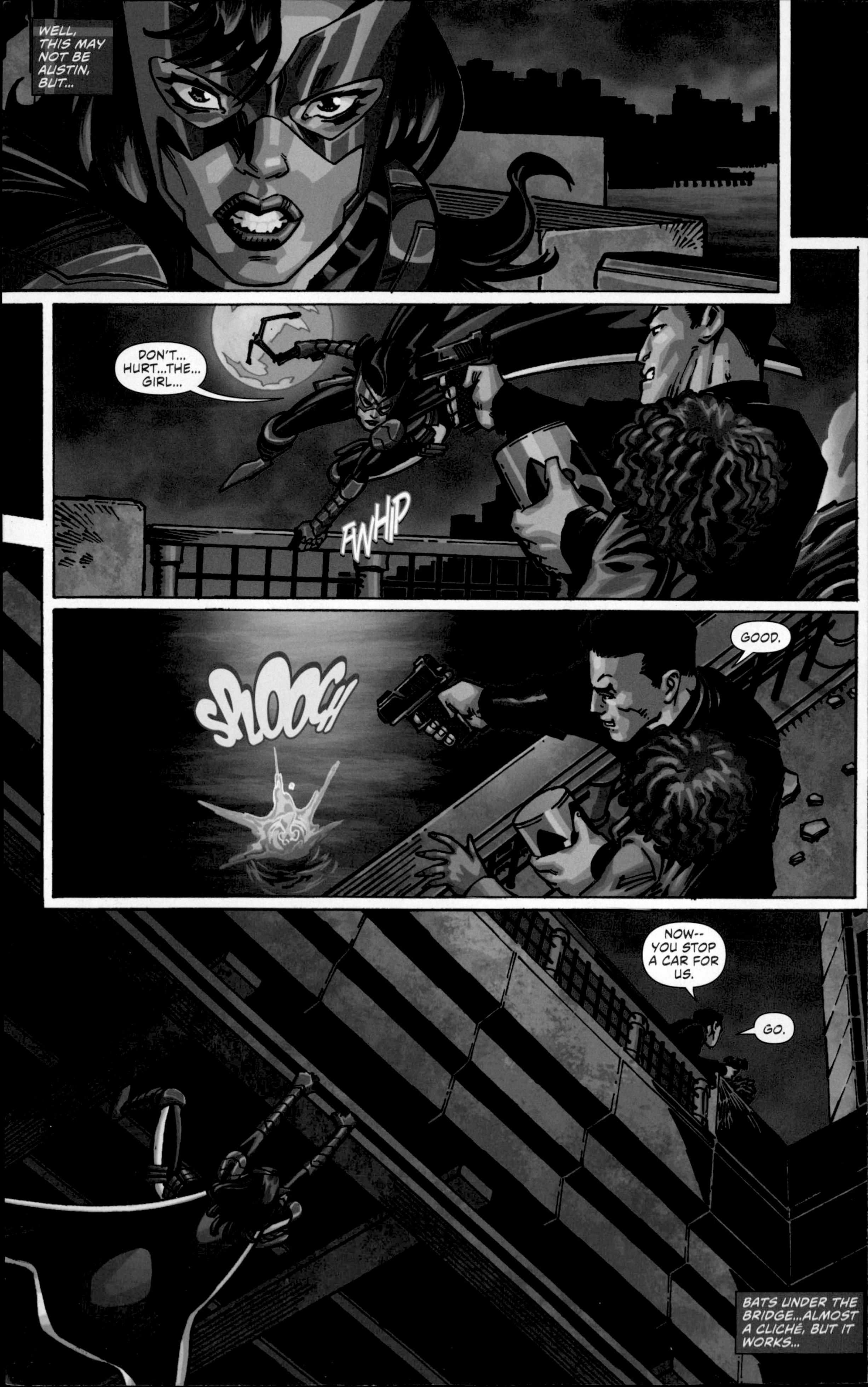
WELL, THIS MAY NOT BE AUSTIN, BUT...
DON'T... HURT...THE... GIRL...
FWHIP
GOOD.
SHOOOM
NOW-- YOU STOP A CAR FOR US.
GO.
BATS UNDER THE BRIDGE...ALMOST A CLICHÉ, BUT IT WORKS...

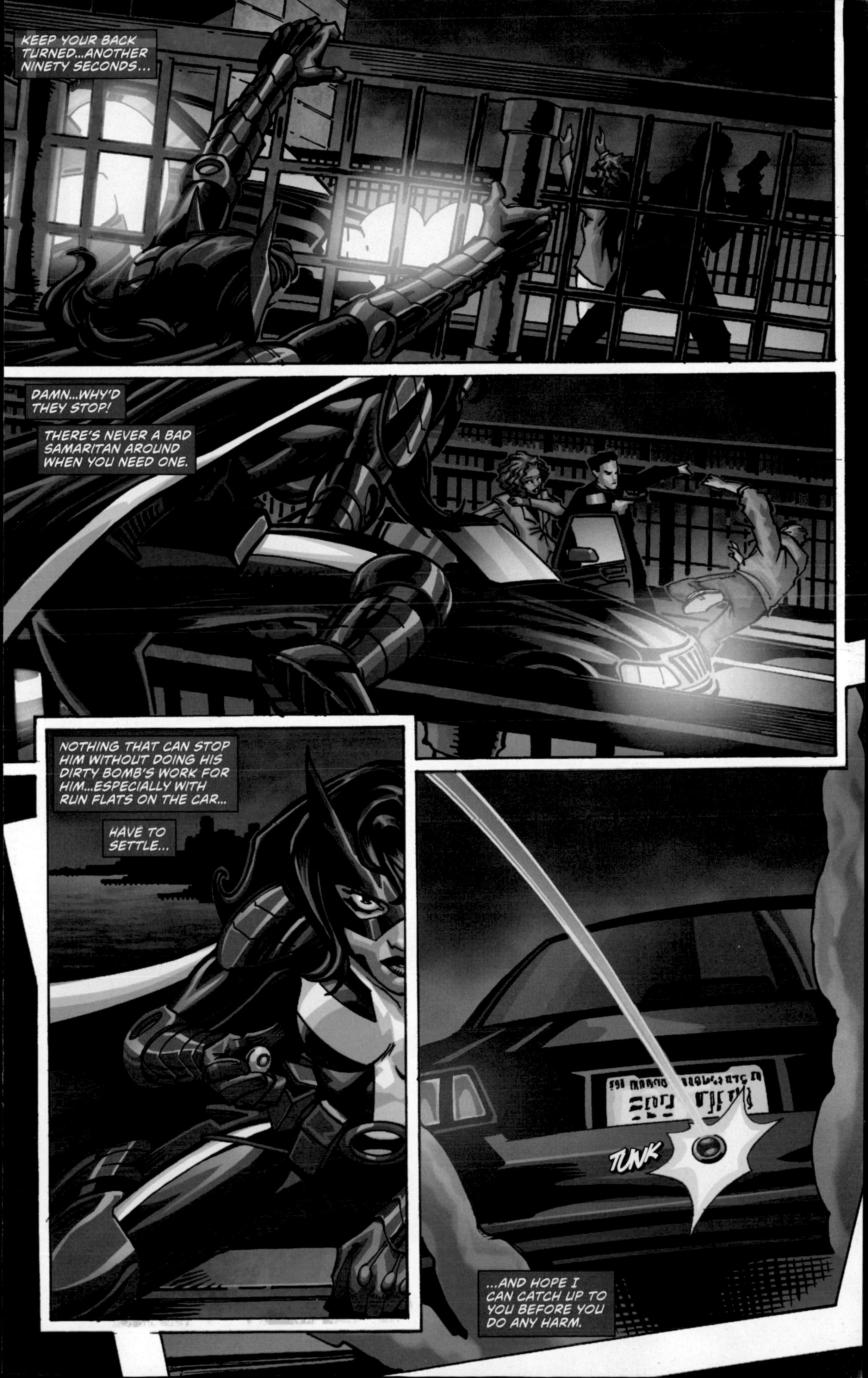
KEEP YOUR BACK TURNED...ANOTHER NINETY SECONDS...
DAMN...WHY'D THEY STOP!
THERE'S NEVER A BAD SAMARITAN AROUND WHEN YOU NEED ONE.
NOTHING THAT CAN STOP HIM WITHOUT DOING HIS DIRTY BOMB'S WORK FOR HIM...ESPECIALLY WITH RUN FLATS ON THE CAR...
HAVE TO SETTLE...
TUNK
...AND HOPE I CAN CATCH UP TO YOU BEFORE YOU DO ANY HARM.

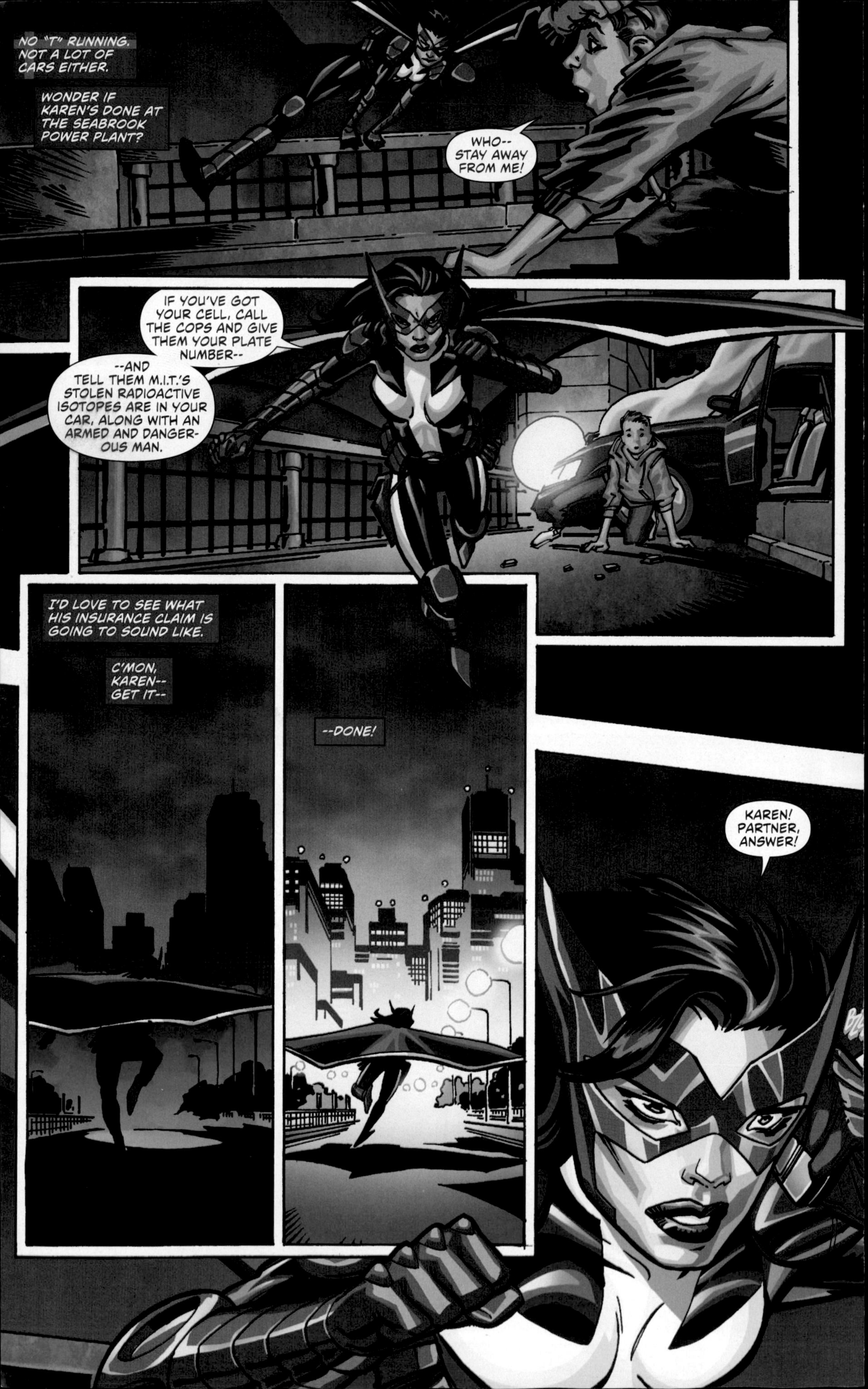
NO "T" RUNNING. NOT A LOT OF CARS EITHER.
WONDER IF KAREN'S DONE AT THE SEABROOK POWER PLANT?
WHO-- STAY AWAY FROM ME!
IF YOU'VE GOT YOUR CELL, CALL THE COPS AND GIVE THEM YOUR PLATE NUMBER--
--AND TELL THEM M.I.T.'S STOLEN RADIOACTIVE ISOTOPES ARE IN YOUR CAR, ALONG WITH AN ARMED AND DANGEROUS MAN.
I'D LOVE TO SEE WHAT HIS INSURANCE CLAIM IS GOING TO SOUND LIKE.
C'MON, KAREN-- GET IT--
--DONE!
KAREN! PARTNER, ANSWER!

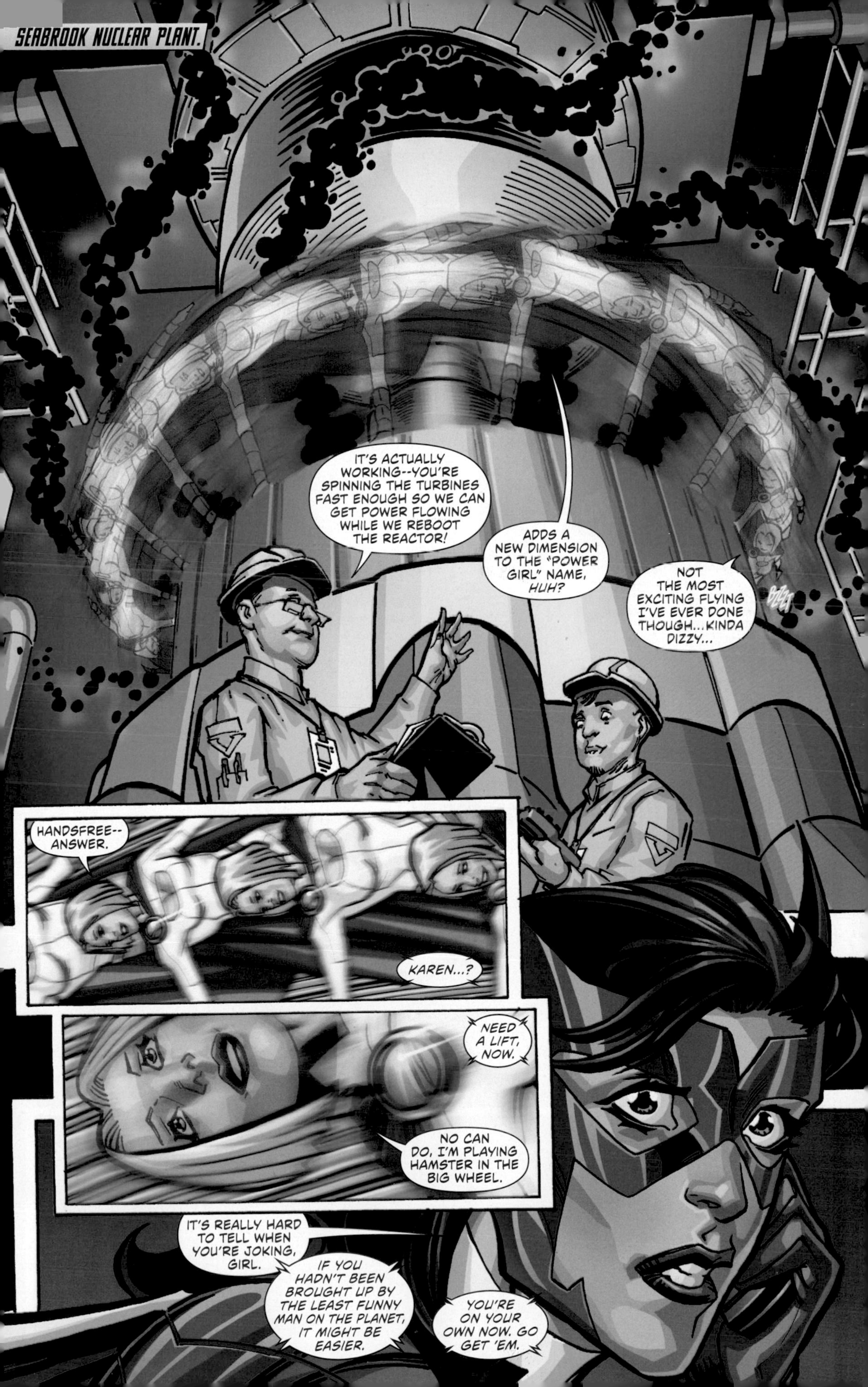
SEABROOK NUCLEAR PLANT.
IT'S ACTUALLY WORKING--YOU'RE SPINNING THE TURBINES FAST ENOUGH SO WE CAN GET POWER FLOWING WHILE WE REBOOT THE REACTOR!
ADDS A NEW DIMENSION TO THE "POWER GIRL" NAME, HUH?
NOT THE MOST EXCITING FLYING I'VE EVER DONE THOUGH...KINDA DIZZY...
HANDSFREE--ANSWER.
KAREN...?
NEED A LIFT, NOW.
NO CAN DO. I'M PLAYING HAMSTER IN THE BIG WHEEL.
IT'S REALLY HARD TO TELL WHEN YOU'RE JOKING, GIRL.
IF YOU HADN'T BEEN BROUGHT UP BY THE LEAST FUNNY MAN ON THE PLANET, IT MIGHT BE EASIER.
YOU'RE ON YOUR OWN NOW. GO GET 'EM.

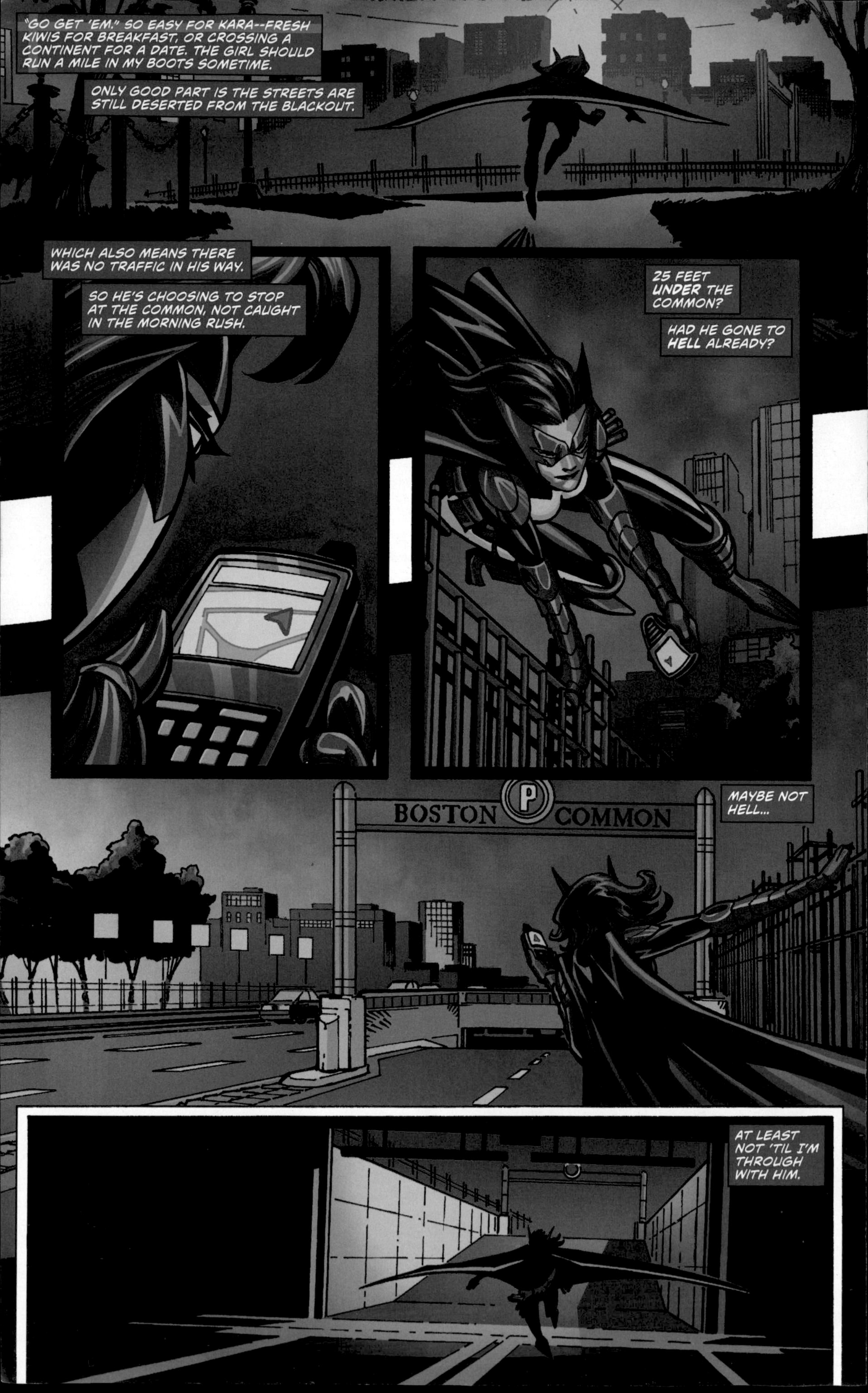
"GO GET 'EM." SO EASY FOR KARA--FRESH KIWIS FOR BREAKFAST, OR CROSSING A CONTINENT FOR A DATE. THE GIRL SHOULD RUN A MILE IN MY BOOTS SOMETIME.
ONLY GOOD PART IS THE STREETS ARE STILL DESERTED FROM THE BLACKOUT.
WHICH ALSO MEANS THERE WAS NO TRAFFIC IN HIS WAY.
SO HE'S CHOOSING TO STOP AT THE COMMON, NOT CAUGHT IN THE MORNING RUSH.
25 FEET UNDER THE COMMON?
HAD HE GONE TO HELL ALREADY?
BOSTON P COMMON
MAYBE NOT HELL...
AT LEAST NOT 'TIL I'M THROUGH WITH HIM.

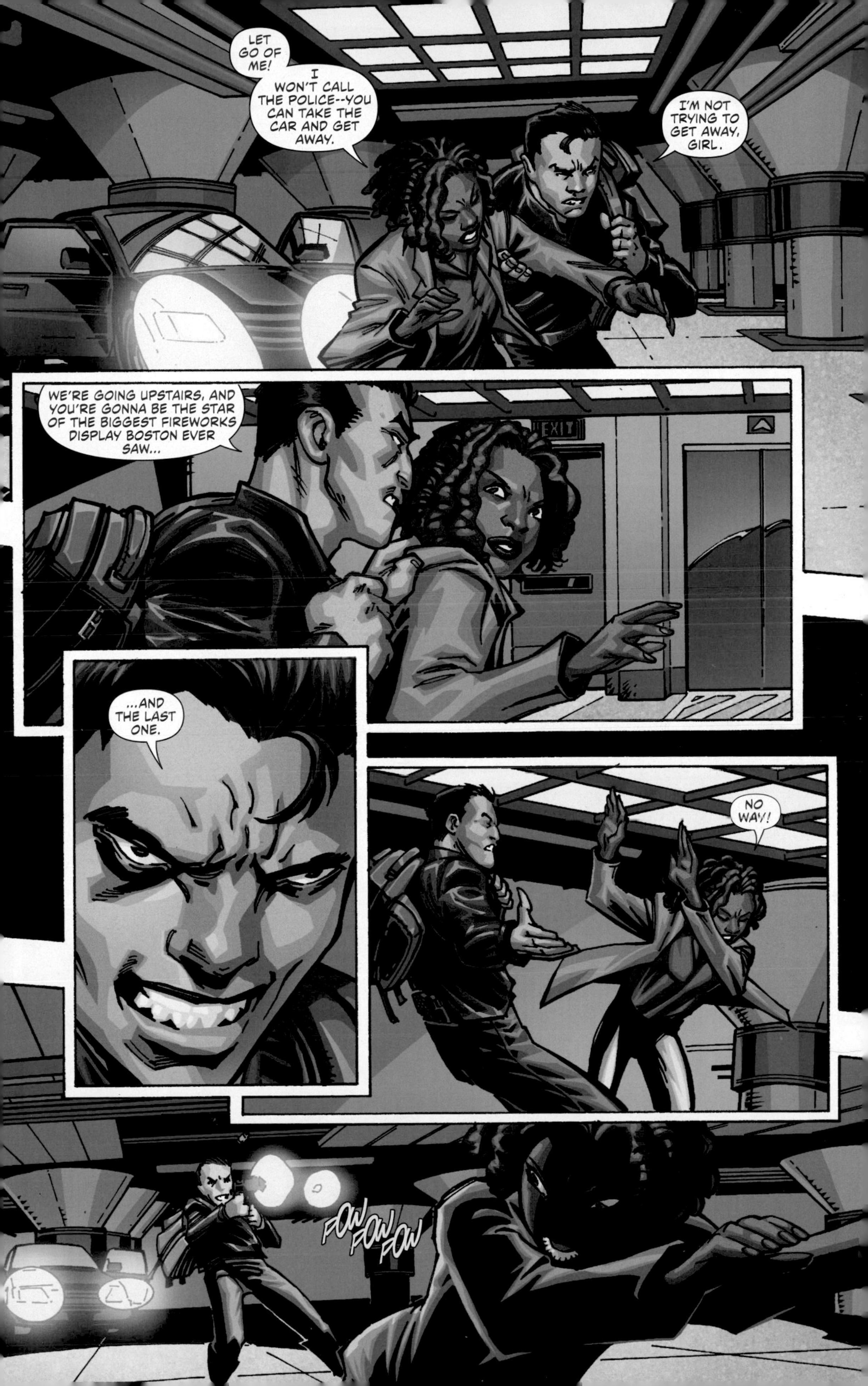
LET GO OF ME!
I WON'T CALL THE POLICE--YOU CAN TAKE THE CAR AND GET AWAY.
I'M NOT TRYING TO GET AWAY, GIRL.
WE'RE GOING UPSTAIRS, AND YOU'RE GONNA BE THE STAR OF THE BIGGEST FIREWORKS DISPLAY BOSTON EVER SAW...
EXIT
...AND THE LAST ONE.
NO WAY!
POW POW POW

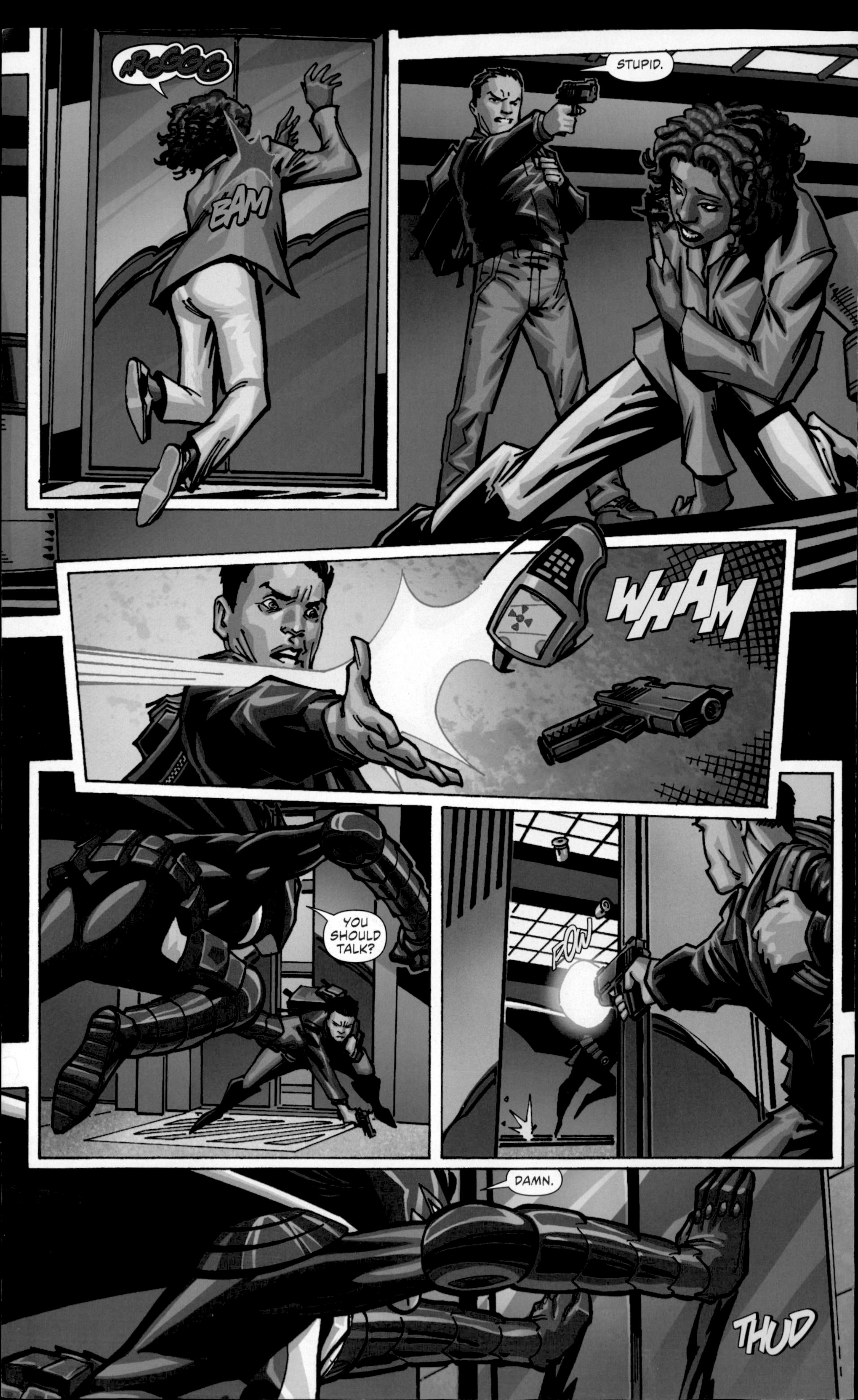
ARGGGG
BAM
STUPID.
WHAM
YOU SHOULD TALK?
POW
DAMN.
THUD

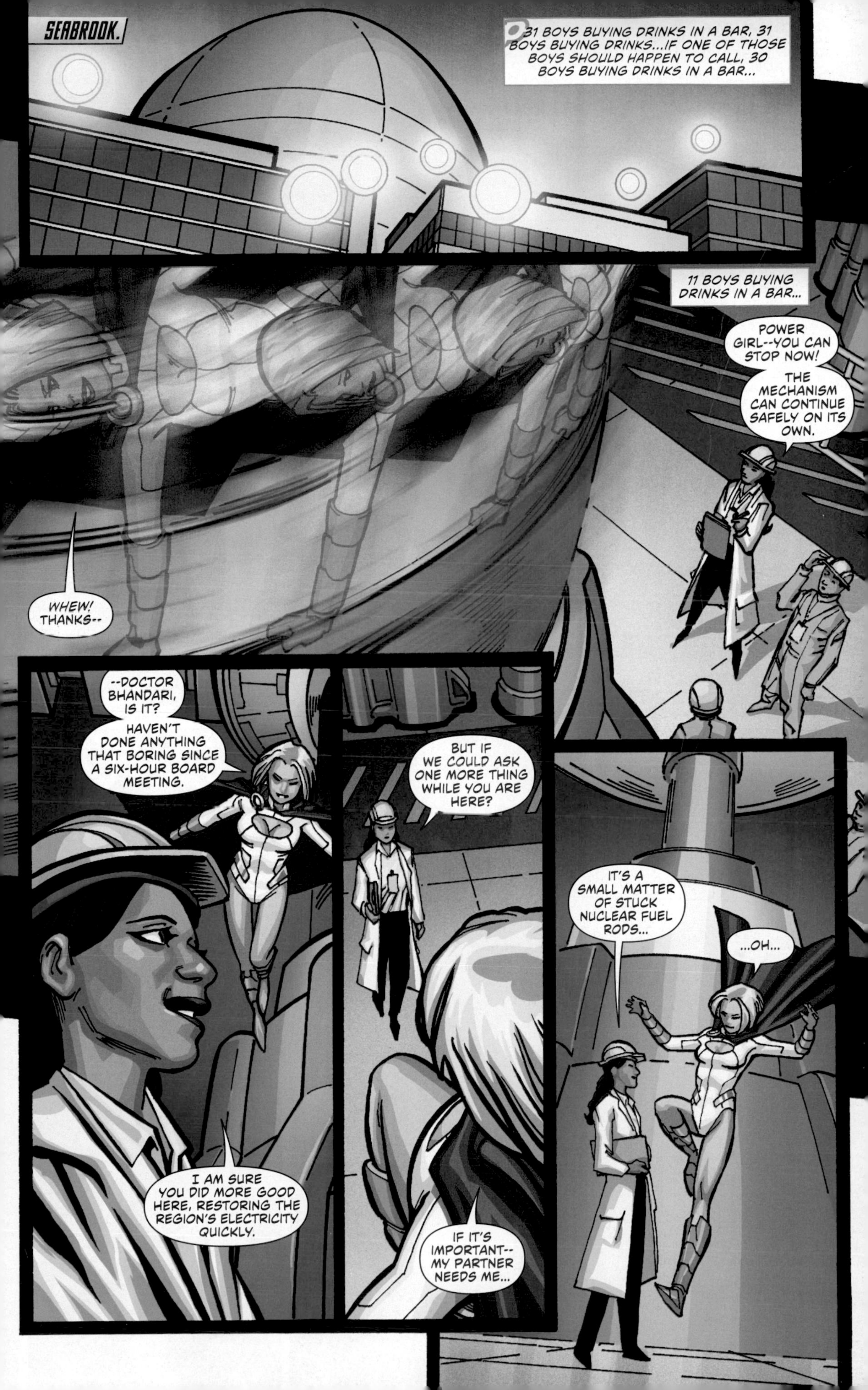
SEABROOK.
31 BOYS BUYING DRINKS IN A BAR, 31 BOYS BUYING DRINKS...IF ONE OF THOSE BOYS SHOULD HAPPEN TO CALL, 30 BOYS BUYING DRINKS IN A BAR...
11 BOYS BUYING DRINKS IN A BAR...
POWER GIRL--YOU CAN STOP NOW!
THE MECHANISM CAN CONTINUE SAFELY ON ITS OWN.
WHEW! THANKS--
--DOCTOR BHANDARI, IS IT?
HAVEN'T DONE ANYTHING THAT BORING SINCE A SIX-HOUR BOARD MEETING.
I AM SURE YOU DID MORE GOOD HERE, RESTORING THE REGION'S ELECTRICITY QUICKLY.
BUT IF WE COULD ASK ONE MORE THING WHILE YOU ARE HERE?
IF IT'S IMPORTANT--MY PARTNER NEEDS ME...
IT'S A SMALL MATTER OF STUCK NUCLEAR FUEL RODS...
...OH...

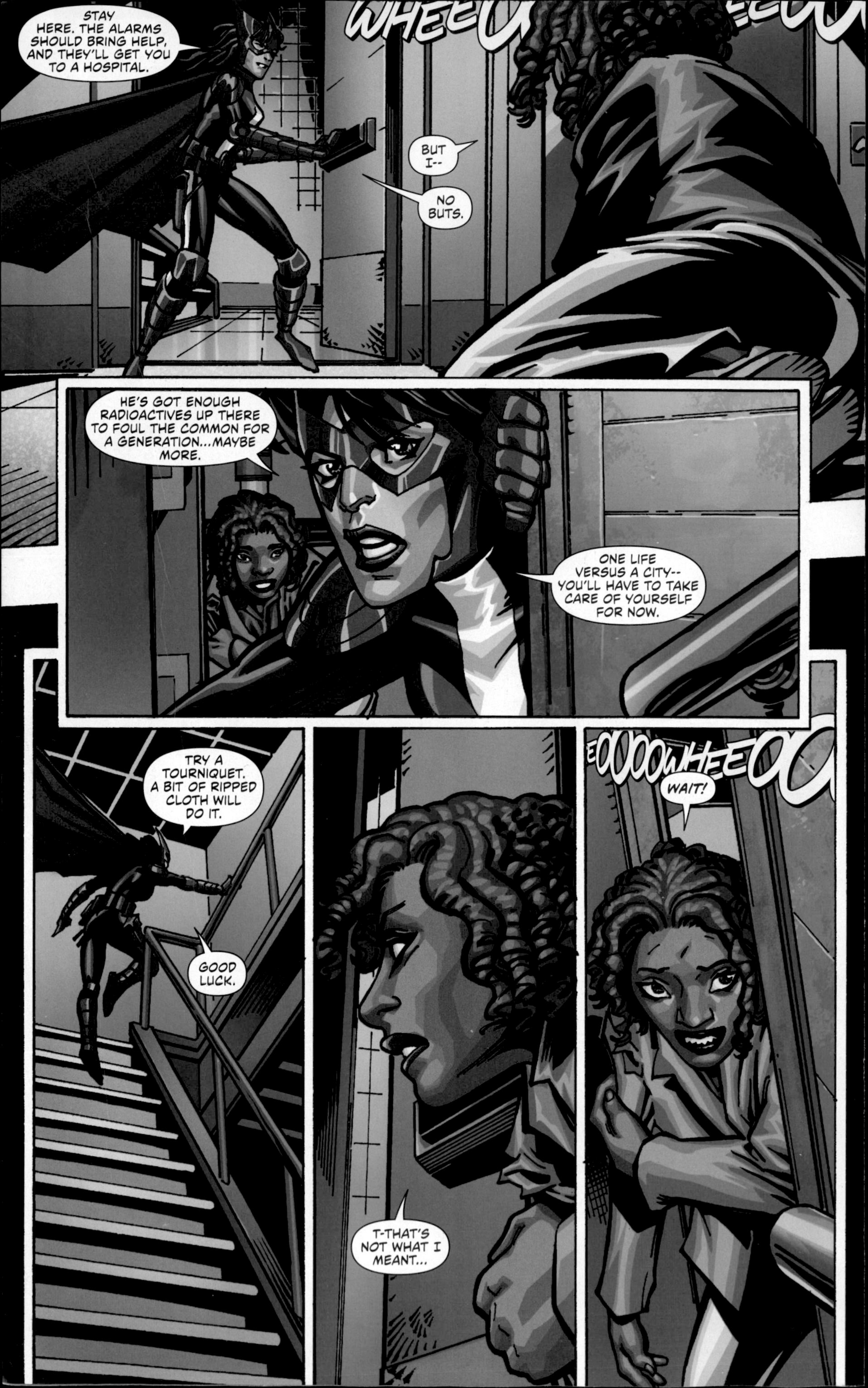
WHEEOO
EEOO
STAY HERE. THE ALARMS SHOULD BRING HELP, AND THEY'LL GET YOU TO A HOSPITAL.
BUT I--
NO BUTS.
HE'S GOT ENOUGH RADIOACTIVES UP THERE TO FOUL THE COMMON FOR A GENERATION...MAYBE MORE.
ONE LIFE VERSUS A CITY-- YOU'LL HAVE TO TAKE CARE OF YOURSELF FOR NOW.
TRY A TOURNIQUET. A BIT OF RIPPED CLOTH WILL DO IT.
GOOD LUCK.
T-THAT'S NOT WHAT I MEANT...
EOOOOWHEEOO
WAIT!

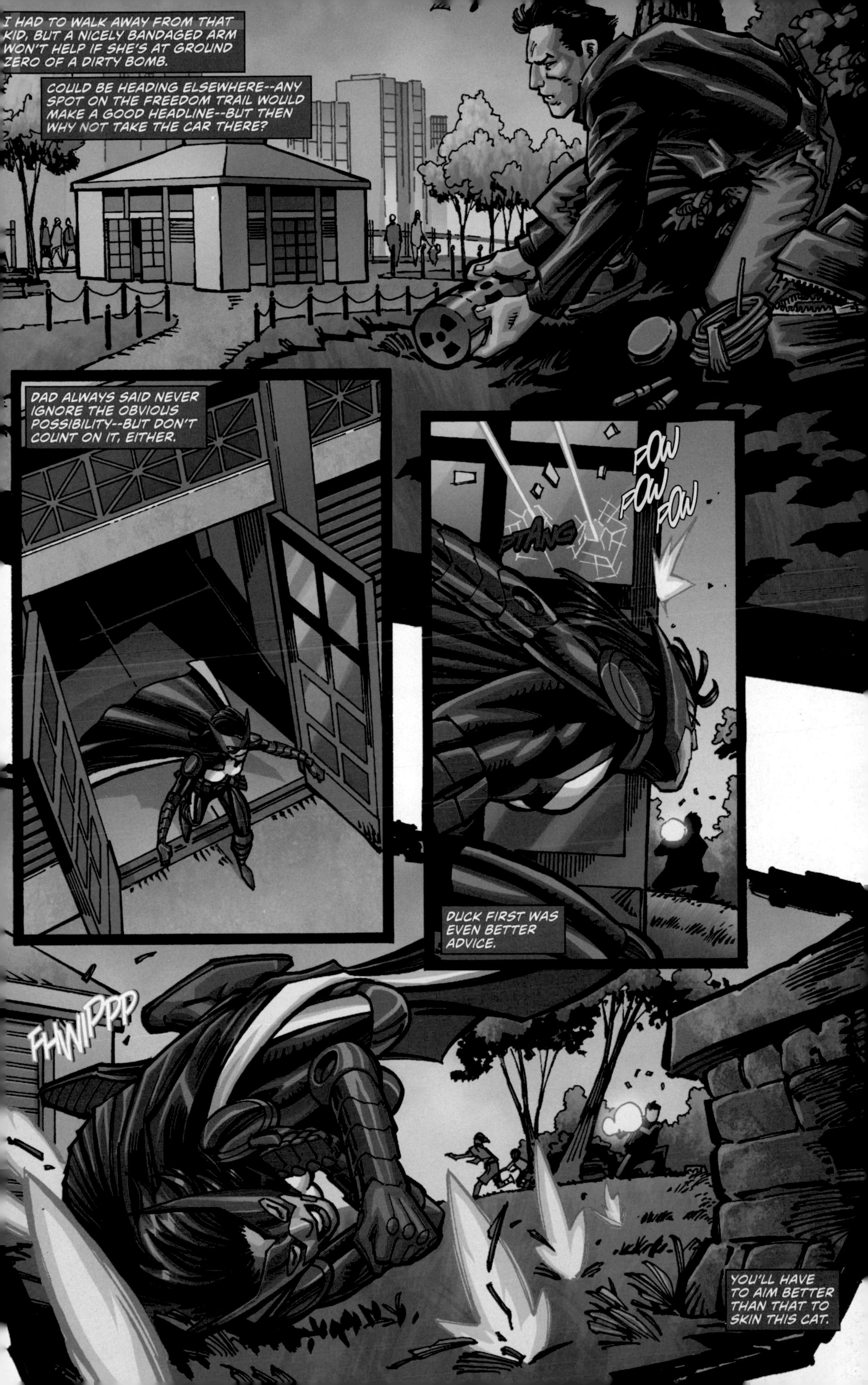
I HAD TO WALK AWAY FROM THAT KID, BUT A NICELY BANDAGED ARM WON'T HELP IF SHE'S AT GROUND ZERO OF A DIRTY BOMB.
COULD BE HEADING ELSEWHERE--ANY SPOT ON THE FREEDOM TRAIL WOULD MAKE A GOOD HEADLINE--BUT THEN WHY NOT TAKE THE CAR THERE?
DAD ALWAYS SAID NEVER IGNORE THE OBVIOUS POSSIBILITY--BUT DON'T COUNT ON IT, EITHER.
POW
POW
POW
PTANG
DUCK FIRST WAS EVEN BETTER ADVICE.
FHWIPPP
YOU'LL HAVE TO AIM BETTER THAN THAT TO SKIN THIS CAT.

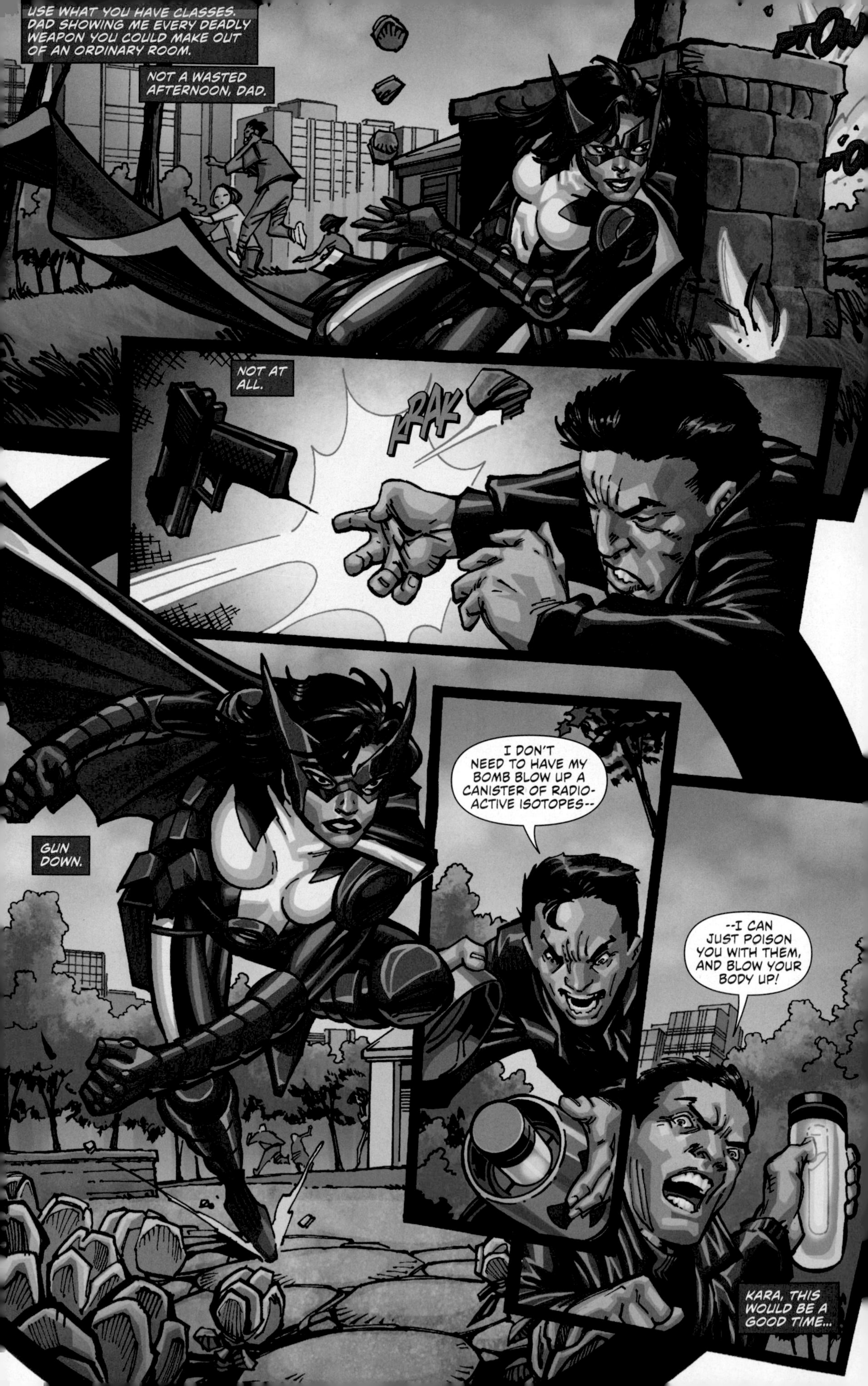
USE WHAT YOU HAVE CLASSES. DAD SHOWING ME EVERY DEADLY WEAPON YOU COULD MAKE OUT OF AN ORDINARY ROOM.
NOT A WASTED AFTERNOON, DAD.
FTOW
FTOW
NOT AT ALL.
KRAK
GUN DOWN.
I DON'T NEED TO HAVE MY BOMB BLOW UP A CANISTER OF RADIO-ACTIVE ISOTOPES--
--I CAN JUST POISON YOU WITH THEM, AND BLOW YOUR BODY UP!
KARA, THIS WOULD BE A GOOD TIME...

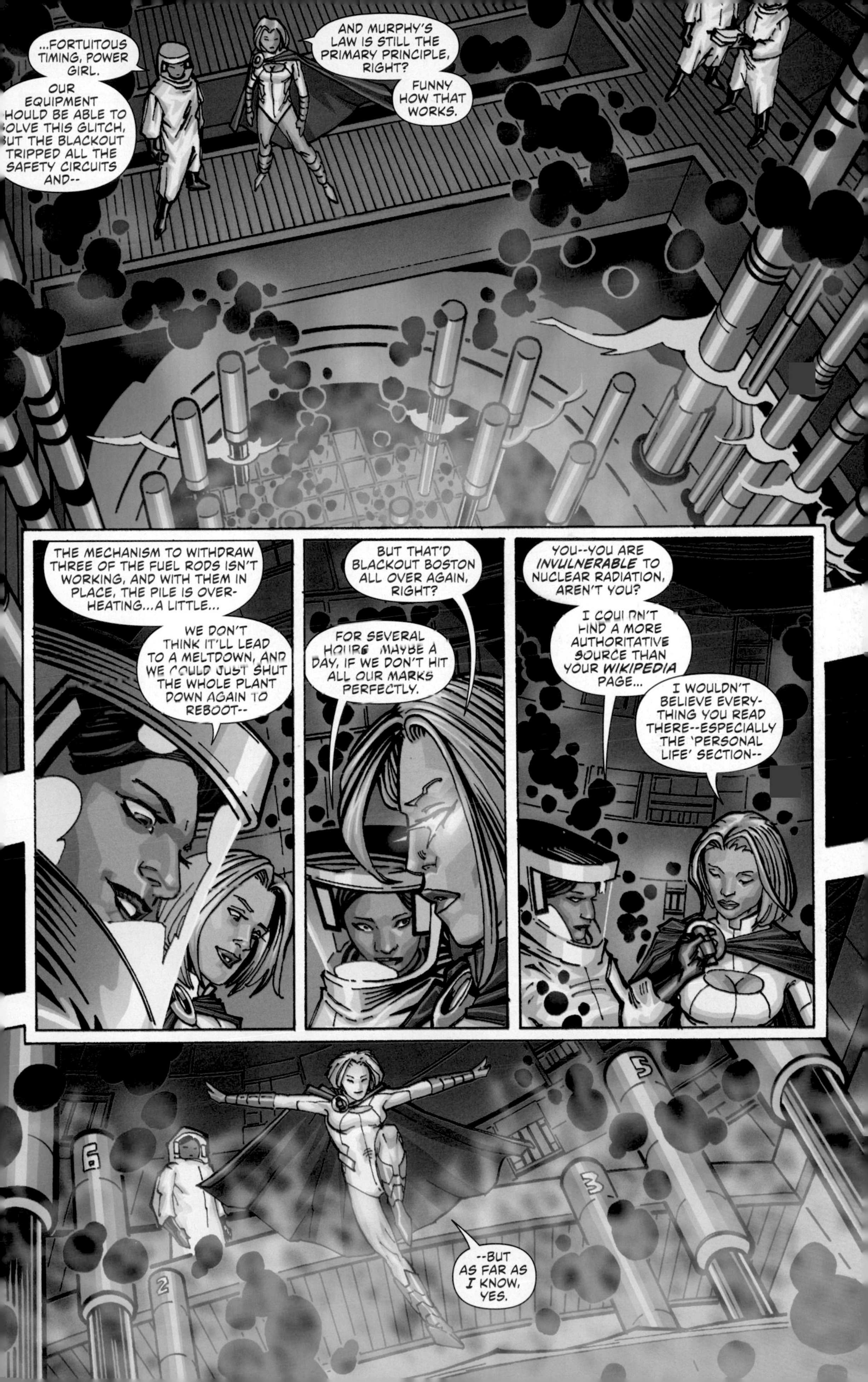
...FORTUITOUS TIMING, POWER GIRL.
OUR EQUIPMENT HOULD BE ABLE TO OLVE THIS GLITCH, UT THE BLACKOUT TRIPPED ALL THE SAFETY CIRCUITS AND--
AND MURPHY'S LAW IS STILL THE PRIMARY PRINCIPLE, RIGHT?
FUNNY HOW THAT WORKS.
THE MECHANISM TO WITHDRAW THREE OF THE FUEL RODS ISN'T WORKING, AND WITH THEM IN PLACE, THE PILE IS OVER-HEATING...A LITTLE...
WE DON'T THINK IT'LL LEAD TO A MELTDOWN, AND WE COULD JUST SHUT THE WHOLE PLANT DOWN AGAIN TO REBOOT--
BUT THAT'D BLACKOUT BOSTON ALL OVER AGAIN, RIGHT?
FOR SEVERAL HOURS, MAYBE A DAY, IF WE DON'T HIT ALL OUR MARKS PERFECTLY.
YOU--YOU ARE *INVULNERABLE* TO NUCLEAR RADIATION, AREN'T YOU?
I COULDN'T FIND A MORE AUTHORITATIVE SOURCE THAN YOUR *WIKIPEDIA* PAGE...
I WOULDN'T BELIEVE EVERY-THING YOU READ THERE--ESPECIALLY THE 'PERSONAL LIFE' SECTION--
5
6
3
2
--BUT AS FAR AS *I* KNOW, YES.

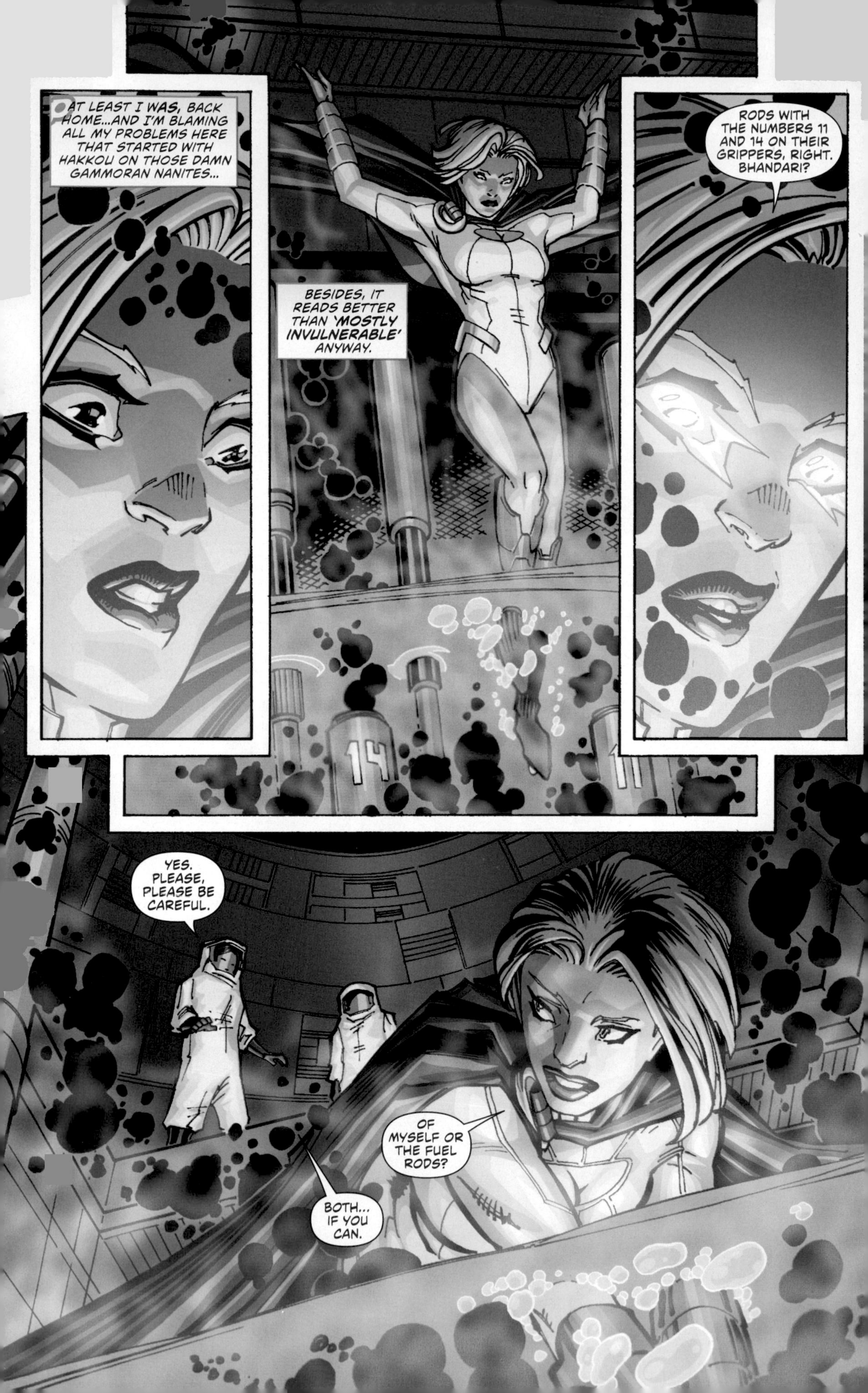
AT LEAST I WAS, BACK HOME...AND I'M BLAMING ALL MY PROBLEMS HERE THAT STARTED WITH HAKKOU ON THOSE DAMN GAMMORAN NANITES...
BESIDES, IT READS BETTER THAN 'MOSTLY INVULNERABLE' ANYWAY.
RODS WITH THE NUMBERS 11 AND 14 ON THEIR GRIPPERS, RIGHT. BHANDARI?
14
11
YES. PLEASE, PLEASE BE CAREFUL.
OF MYSELF OR THE FUEL RODS?
BOTH... IF YOU CAN.

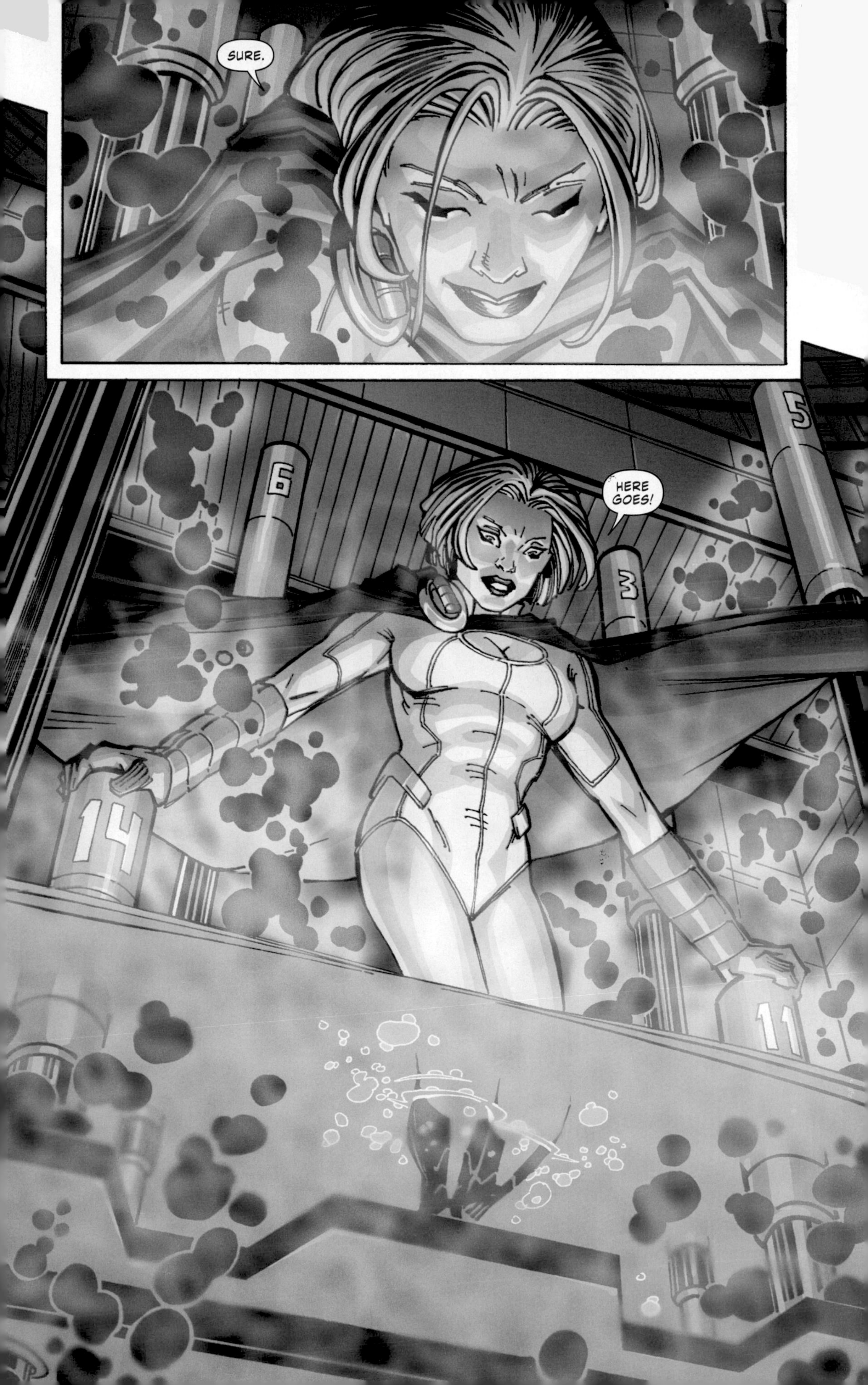
SURE.
HERE GOES!

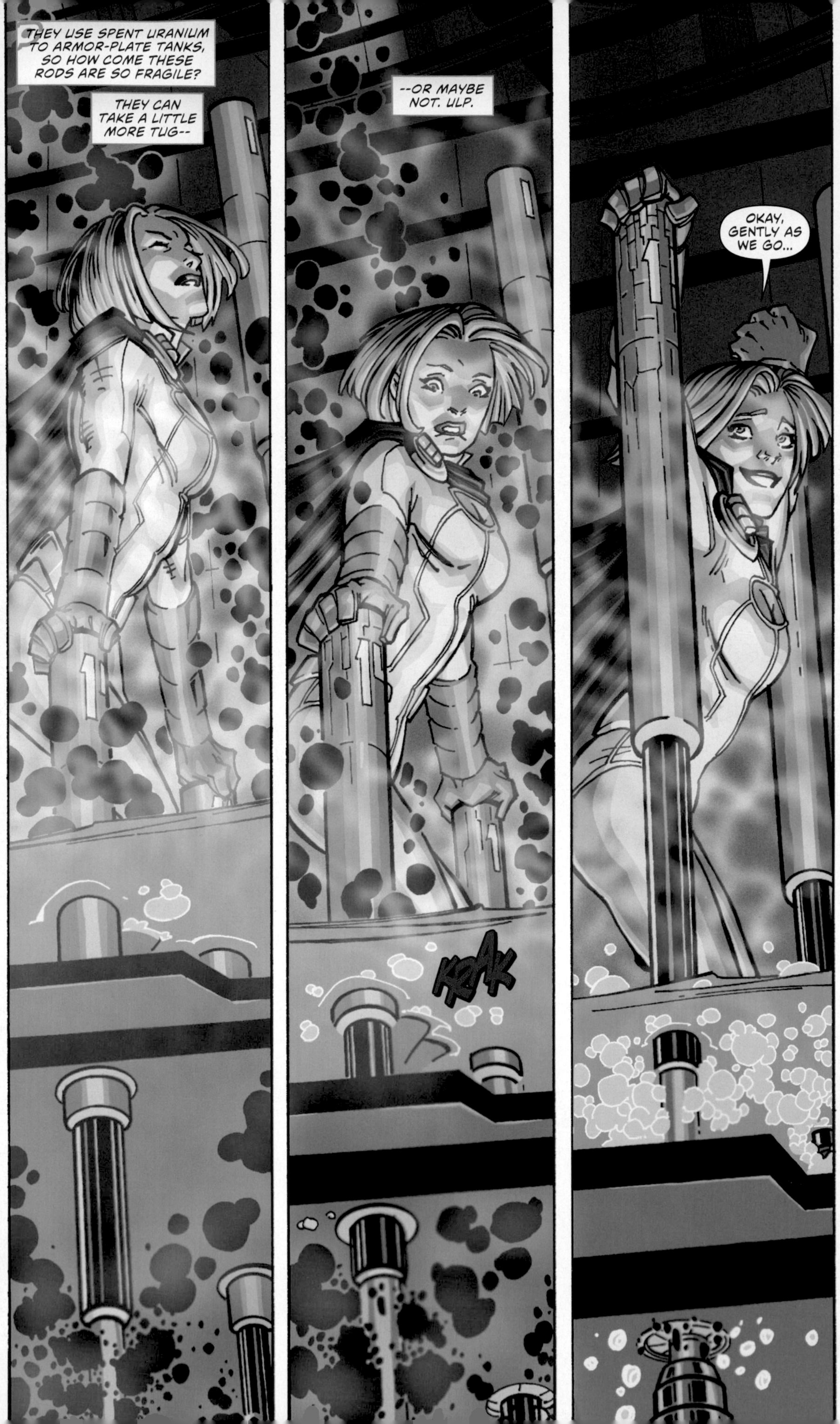
THEY USE SPENT URANIUM TO ARMOR-PLATE TANKS, SO HOW COME THESE RODS ARE SO FRAGILE?
THEY CAN TAKE A LITTLE MORE TUG--
--OR MAYBE NOT. ULP.
KRAK
OKAY, GENTLY AS WE GO...

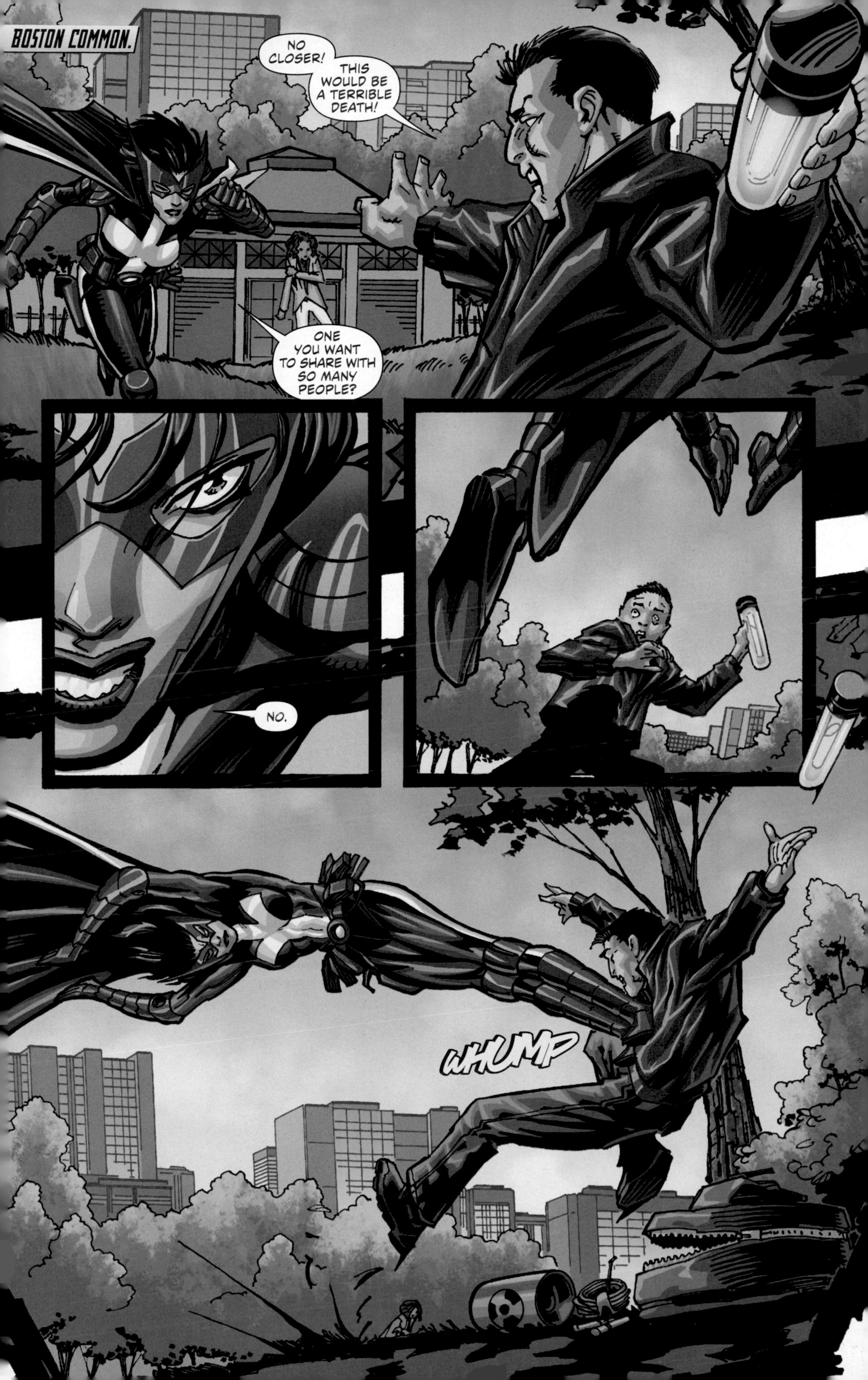
BOSTON COMMON.
NO CLOSER!
THIS WOULD BE A TERRIBLE DEATH!
ONE YOU WANT TO SHARE WITH SO MANY PEOPLE?
NO.
WHUMP

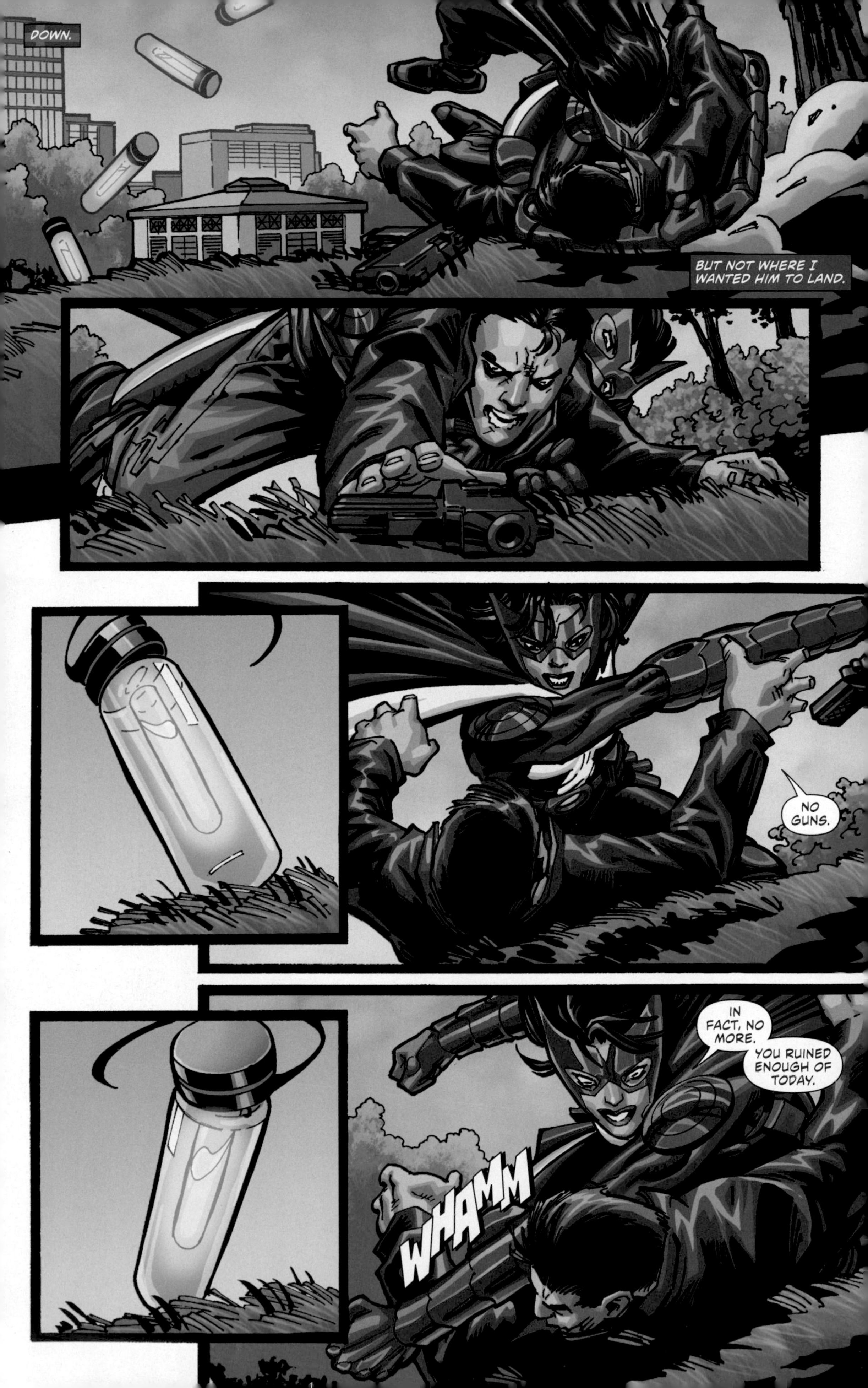
DOWN.
BUT NOT WHERE I WANTED HIM TO LAND.
NO GUNS.
IN FACT, NO MORE.
YOU RUINED ENOUGH OF TODAY.
WHAMM

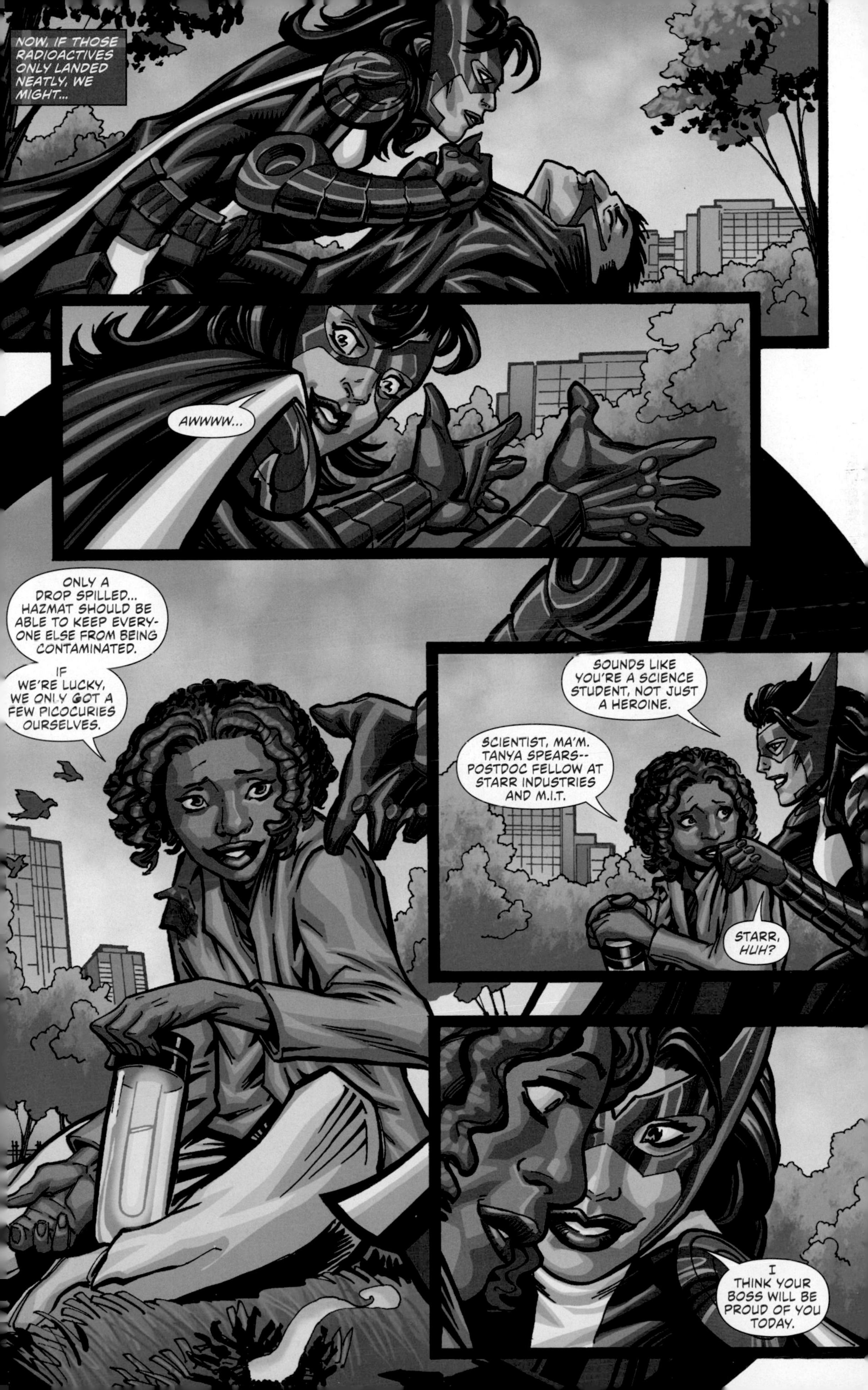
NOW, IF THOSE RADIOACTIVES ONLY LANDED NEATLY, WE MIGHT...
AWWWW...
ONLY A DROP SPILLED... HAZMAT SHOULD BE ABLE TO KEEP EVERY-ONE ELSE FROM BEING CONTAMINATED.
IF WE'RE LUCKY, WE ONLY GOT A FEW PICOCURIES OURSELVES.
SOUNDS LIKE YOU'RE A SCIENCE STUDENT, NOT JUST A HEROINE.
SCIENTIST, MA'M. TANYA SPEARS-- POSTDOC FELLOW AT STARR INDUSTRIES AND M.I.T.
STARR, HUH?
I THINK YOUR BOSS WILL BE PROUD OF YOU TODAY.

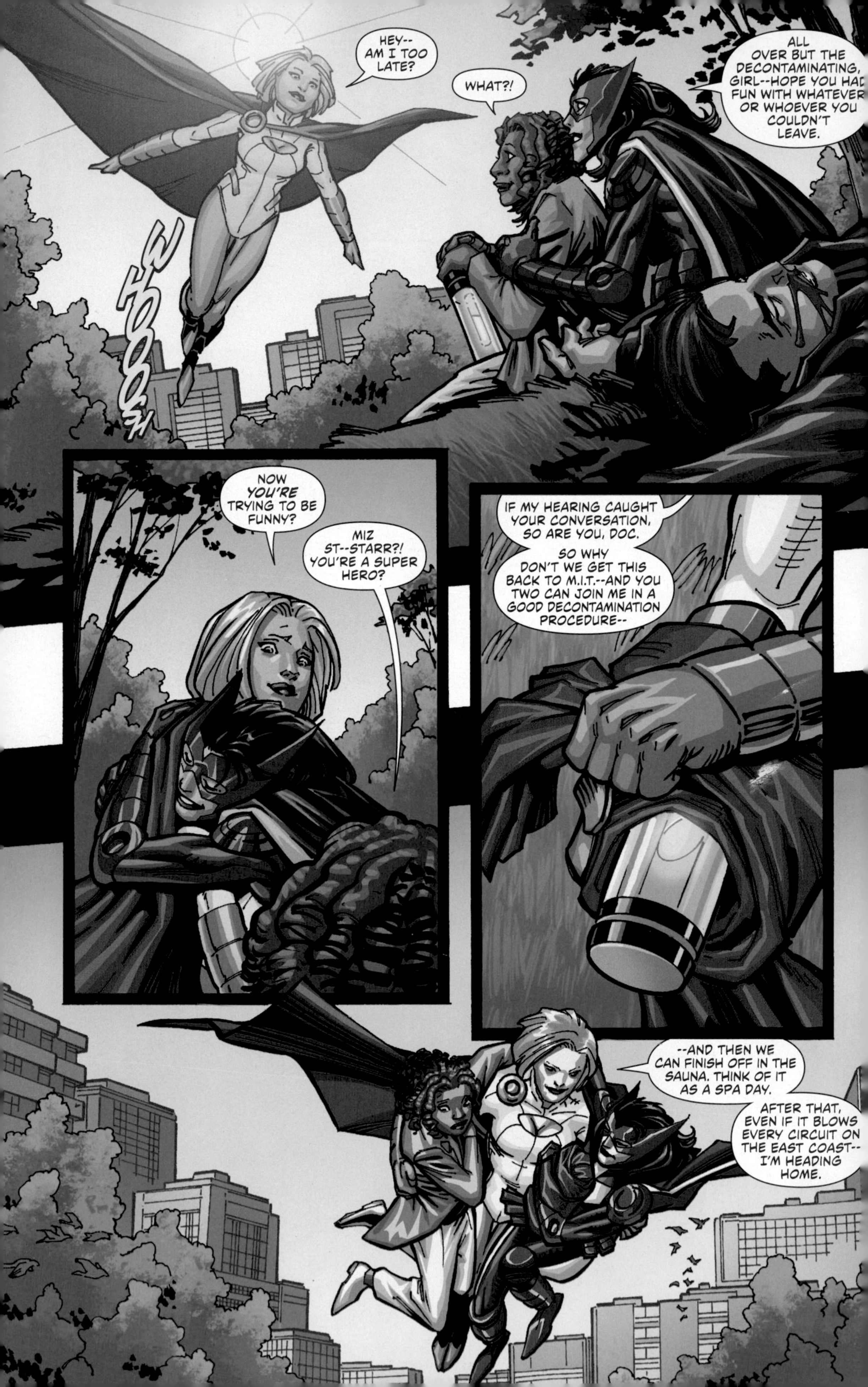
HEY-- AM I TOO LATE?
WHAT?!
ALL OVER BUT THE DECONTAMINATING, GIRL--HOPE YOU HAD FUN WITH WHATEVER OR WHOEVER YOU COULDN'T LEAVE.
WHOOOSH
NOW *YOU'RE* TRYING TO BE FUNNY?
MIZ ST--STARR?! YOU'RE A SUPER HERO?
IF MY HEARING CAUGHT YOUR CONVERSATION, SO ARE YOU, DOC.
SO WHY DON'T WE GET THIS BACK TO M.I.T.--AND YOU TWO CAN JOIN ME IN A GOOD DECONTAMINATION PROCEDURE--
--AND THEN WE CAN FINISH OFF IN THE SAUNA. THINK OF IT AS A SPA DAY.
AFTER THAT, EVEN IF IT BLOWS EVERY CIRCUIT ON THE EAST COAST-- I'M HEADING HOME.

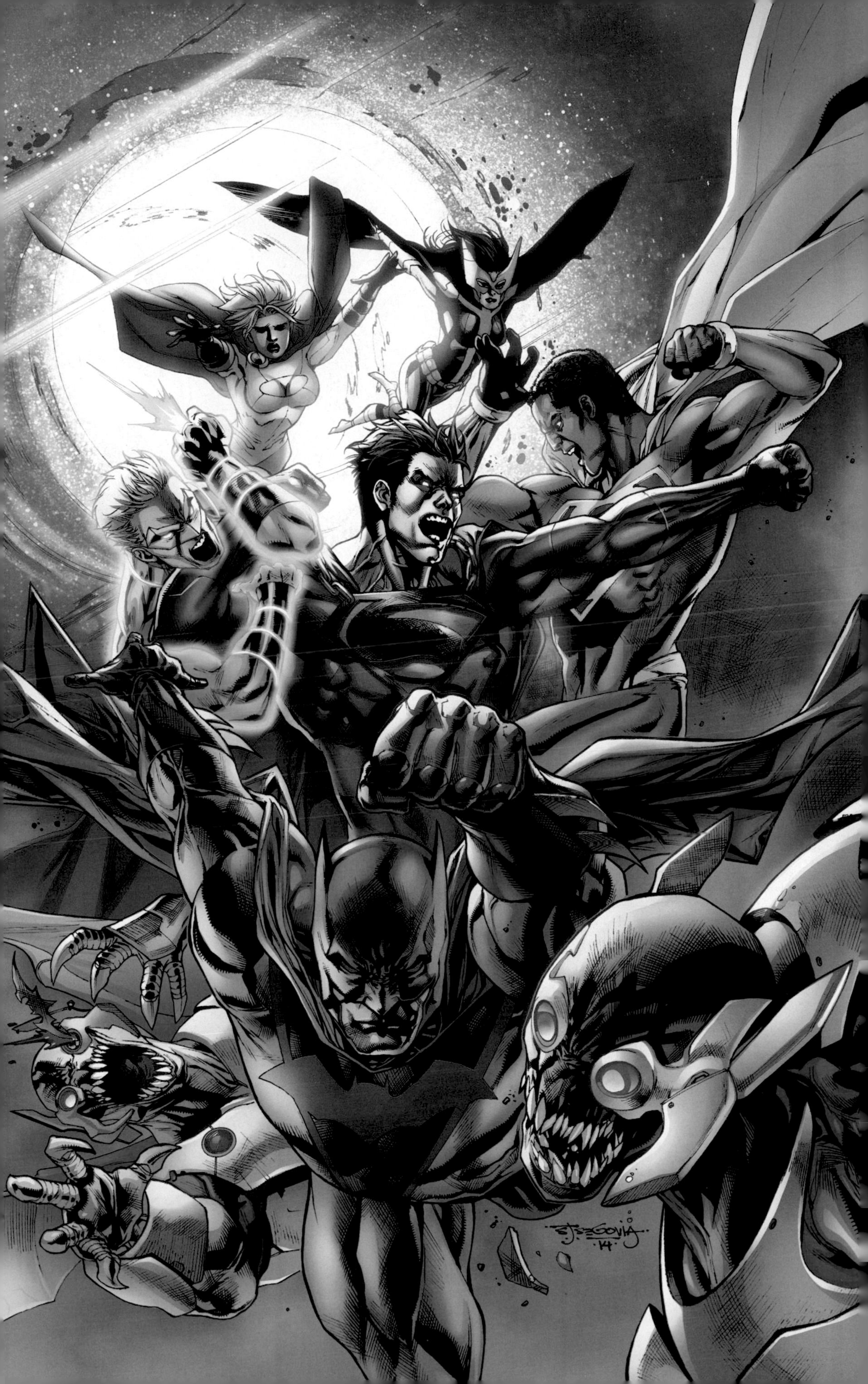

FAREWELLS

PAUL LEVITZ writer **TYLER KIRKHAM** penciller **JOE WEEMS ART THIBERT** inkers
ARIF PRIANTO colorist **TAYLOR ESPOSITO** letterer cover by **STEPHEN SEGOVIA** and **MICHAEL ATIYEH**

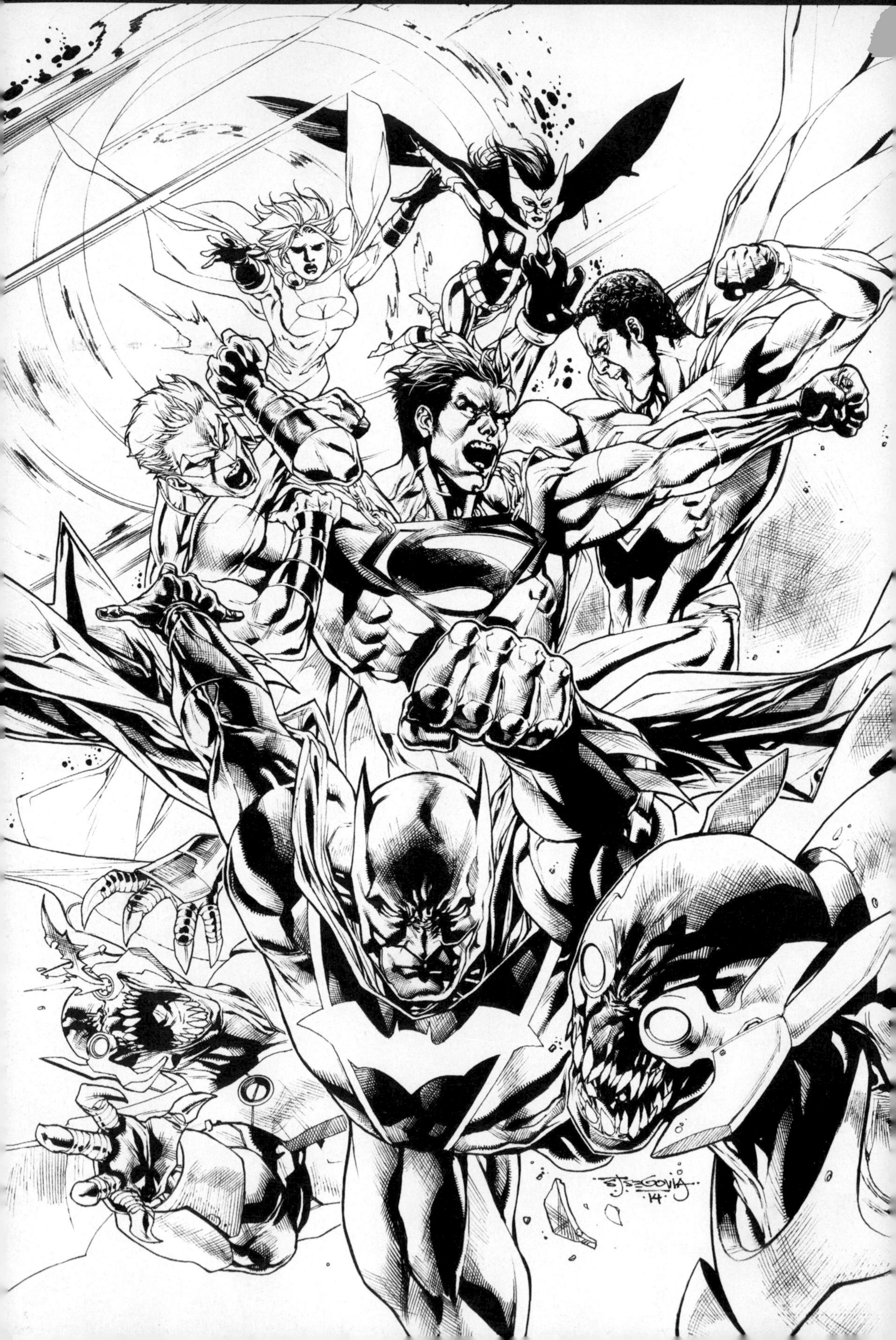

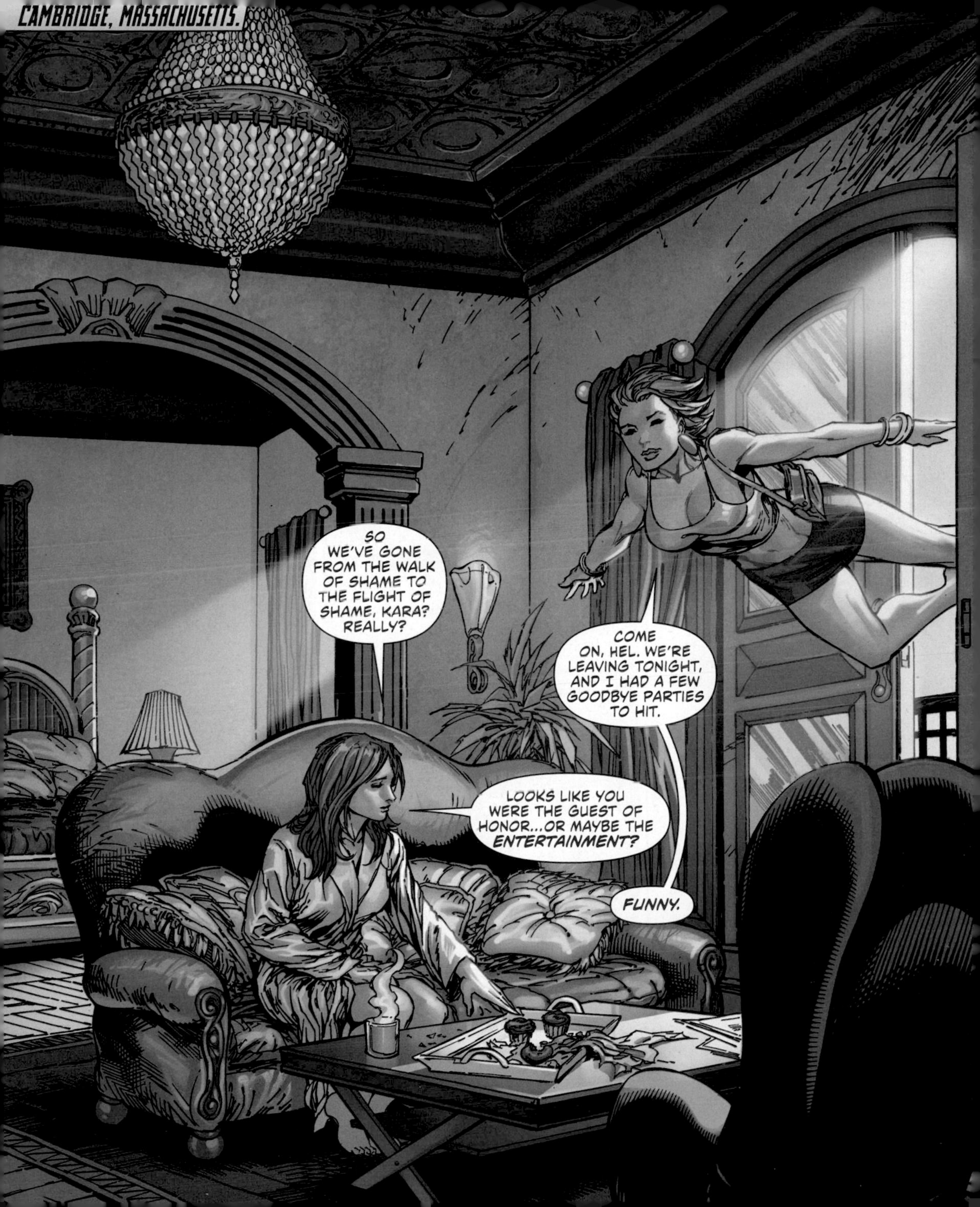
CAMBRIDGE, MASSACHUSETTS.
SO WE'VE GONE FROM THE WALK OF SHAME TO THE FLIGHT OF SHAME, KARA? REALLY?
COME ON, HEL. WE'RE LEAVING TONIGHT, AND I HAD A FEW GOODBYE PARTIES TO HIT.
LOOKS LIKE YOU WERE THE GUEST OF HONOR...OR MAYBE THE *ENTERTAINMENT*?
FUNNY.

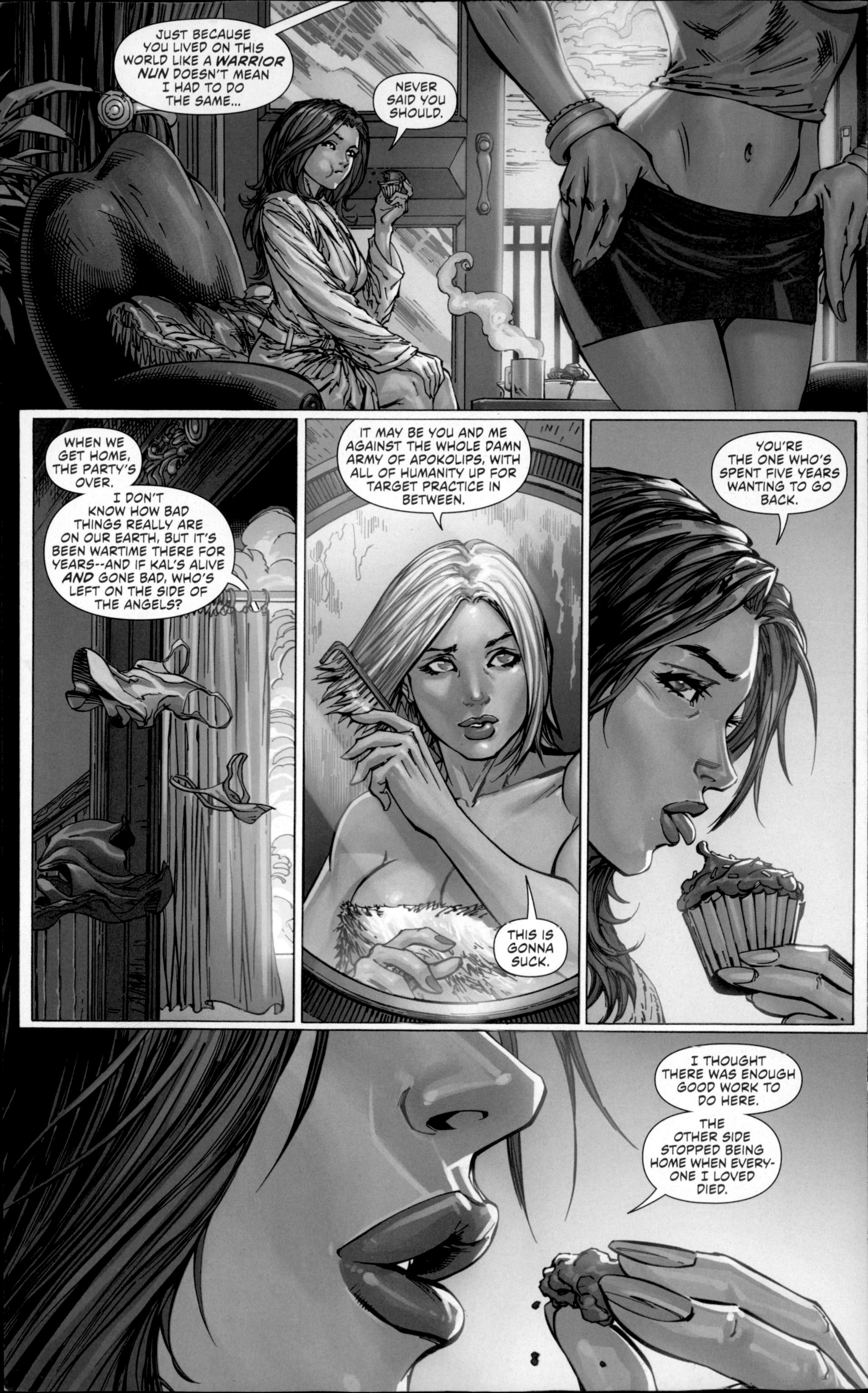
JUST BECAUSE YOU LIVED ON THIS WORLD LIKE A WARRIOR NUN DOESN'T MEAN I HAD TO DO THE SAME...
NEVER SAID YOU SHOULD.
WHEN WE GET HOME, THE PARTY'S OVER.
I DON'T KNOW HOW BAD THINGS REALLY ARE ON OUR EARTH, BUT IT'S BEEN WARTIME THERE FOR YEARS--AND IF KAL'S ALIVE AND GONE BAD, WHO'S LEFT ON THE SIDE OF THE ANGELS?
IT MAY BE YOU AND ME AGAINST THE WHOLE DAMN ARMY OF APOKOLIPS, WITH ALL OF HUMANITY UP FOR TARGET PRACTICE IN BETWEEN.
THIS IS GONNA SUCK.
YOU'RE THE ONE WHO'S SPENT FIVE YEARS WANTING TO GO BACK.
I THOUGHT THERE WAS ENOUGH GOOD WORK TO DO HERE.
THE OTHER SIDE STOPPED BEING HOME WHEN EVERY-ONE I LOVED DIED.

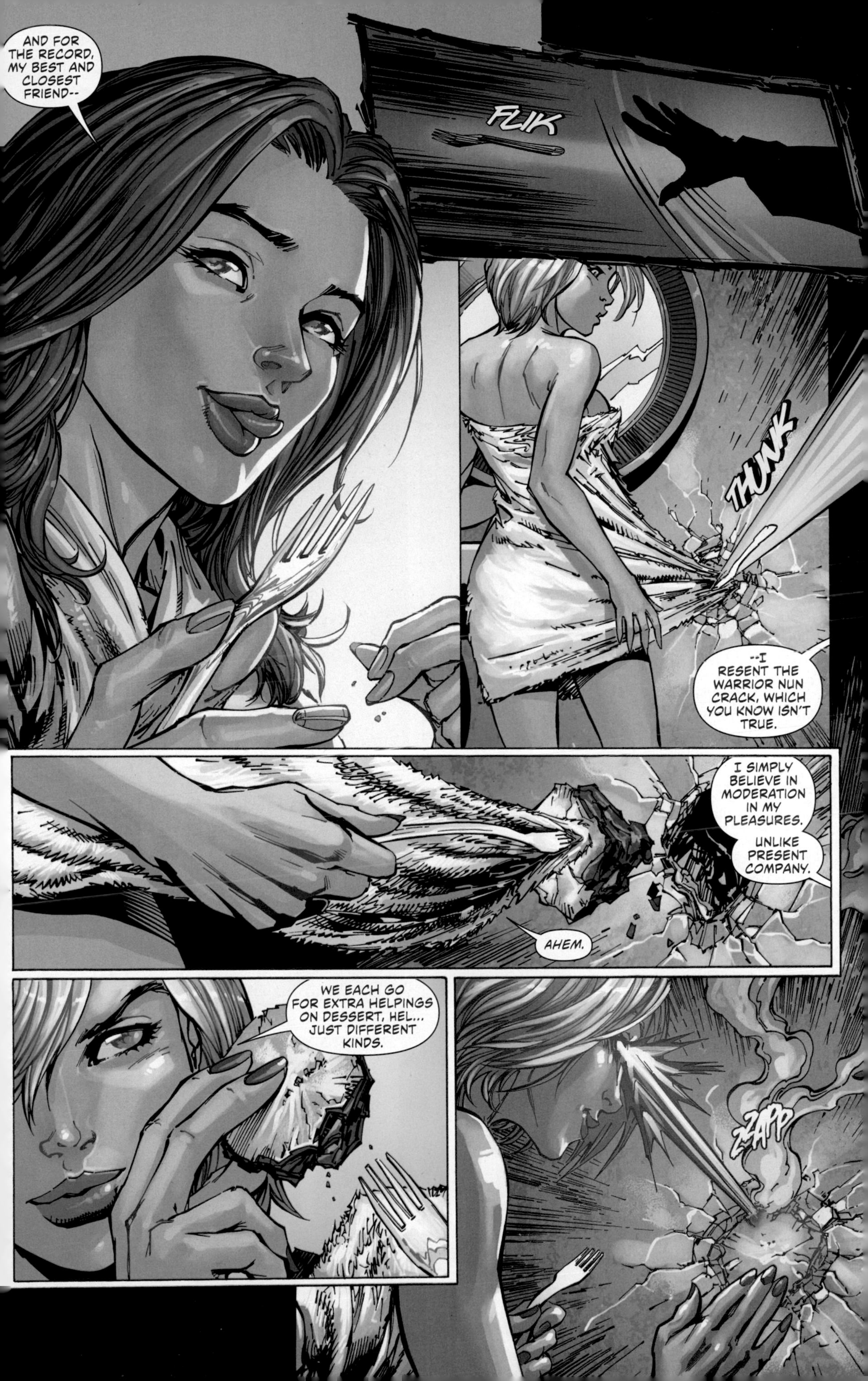
AND FOR THE RECORD, MY BEST AND CLOSEST FRIEND--
FLIK
THUNK
--I RESENT THE WARRIOR NUN CRACK, WHICH YOU KNOW ISN'T TRUE.
I SIMPLY BELIEVE IN MODERATION IN MY PLEASURES.
UNLIKE PRESENT COMPANY.
AHEM.
WE EACH GO FOR EXTRA HELPINGS ON DESSERT, HEL... JUST DIFFERENT KINDS.
ZZAPP

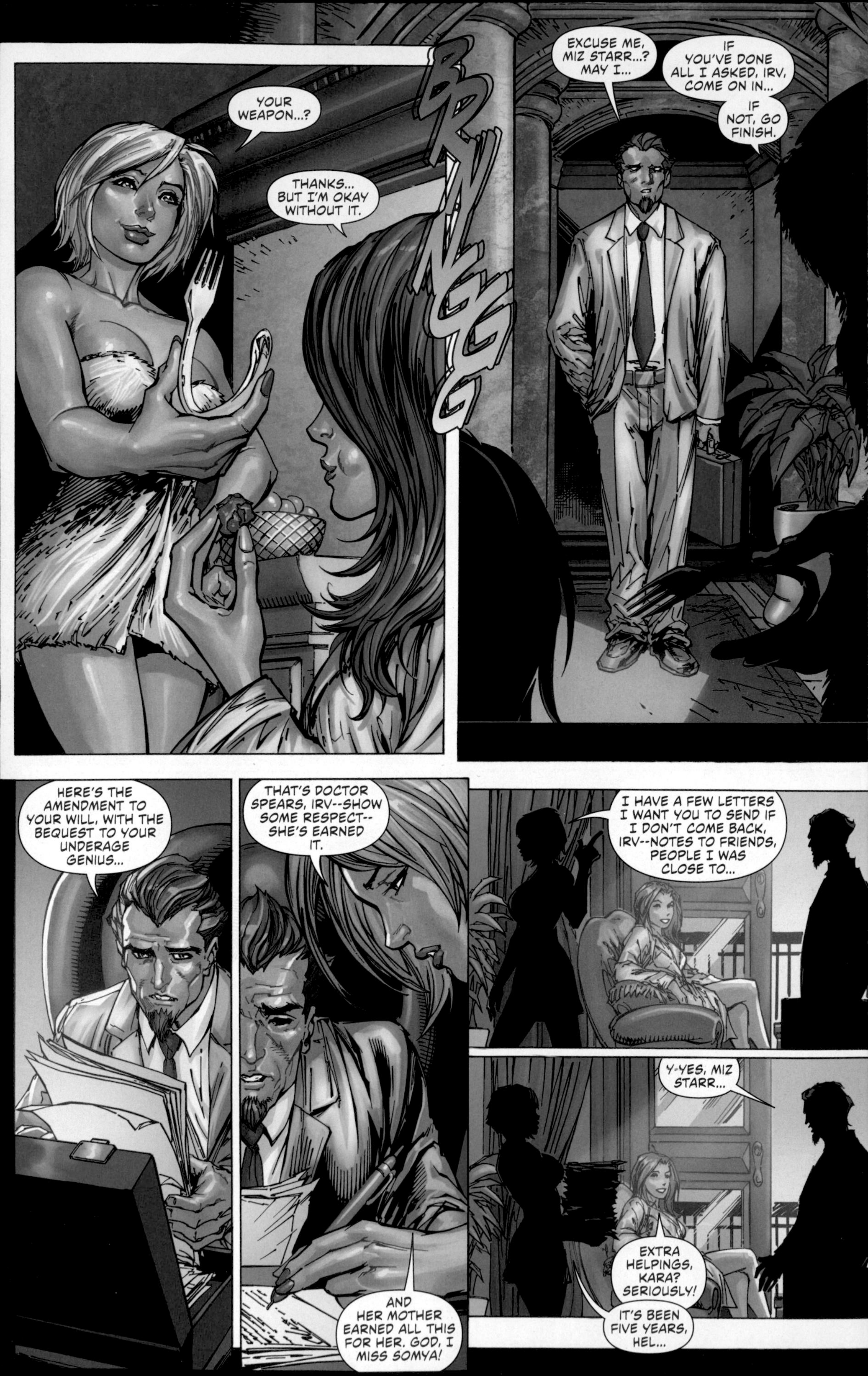
YOUR WEAPON...?
THANKS... BUT I'M OKAY WITHOUT IT.
BRRNNGG
EXCUSE ME, MIZ STARR...? MAY I...
IF YOU'VE DONE ALL I ASKED, IRV, COME ON IN...
IF NOT, GO FINISH.
HERE'S THE AMENDMENT TO YOUR WILL, WITH THE BEQUEST TO YOUR UNDERAGE GENIUS...
THAT'S DOCTOR SPEARS, IRV--SHOW SOME RESPECT--SHE'S EARNED IT.
AND HER MOTHER EARNED ALL THIS FOR HER. GOD, I MISS SOMYA!
I HAVE A FEW LETTERS I WANT YOU TO SEND IF I DON'T COME BACK, IRV--NOTES TO FRIENDS, PEOPLE I WAS CLOSE TO...
Y-YES, MIZ STARR...
EXTRA HELPINGS, KARA? SERIOUSLY!
IT'S BEEN FIVE YEARS, HEL...

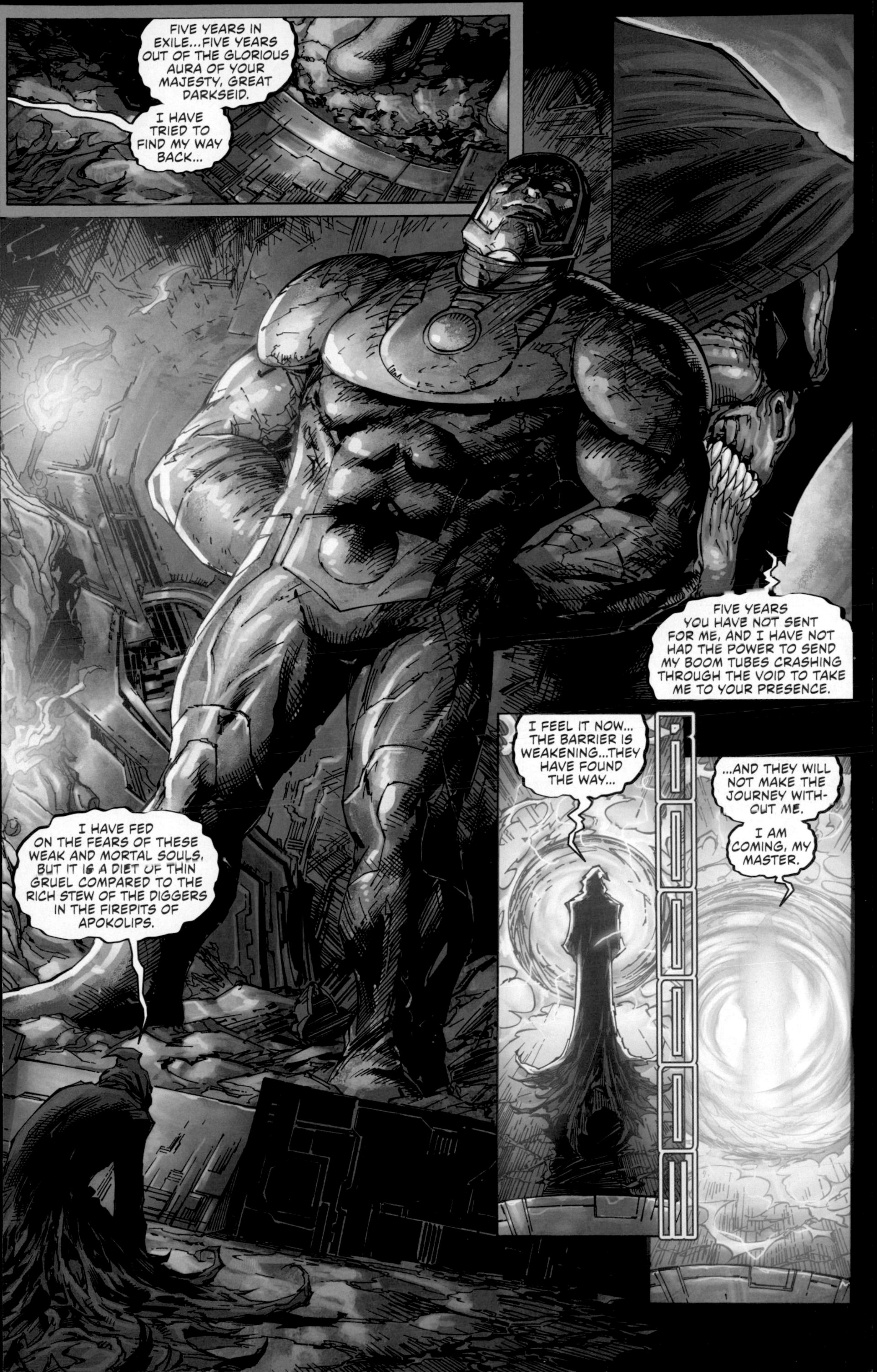
FIVE YEARS IN EXILE...FIVE YEARS OUT OF THE GLORIOUS AURA OF YOUR MAJESTY, GREAT DARKSEID.
I HAVE TRIED TO FIND MY WAY BACK...
FIVE YEARS YOU HAVE NOT SENT FOR ME, AND I HAVE NOT HAD THE POWER TO SEND MY BOOM TUBES CRASHING THROUGH THE VOID TO TAKE ME TO YOUR PRESENCE.
I HAVE FED ON THE FEARS OF THESE WEAK AND MORTAL SOULS, BUT IT IS A DIET OF THIN GRUEL COMPARED TO THE RICH STEW OF THE DIGGERS IN THE FIREPITS OF APOKOLIPS.
I FEEL IT NOW... THE BARRIER IS WEAKENING...THEY HAVE FOUND THE WAY...
...AND THEY WILL NOT MAKE THE JOURNEY WITH-OUT ME.
I AM COMING, MY MASTER.

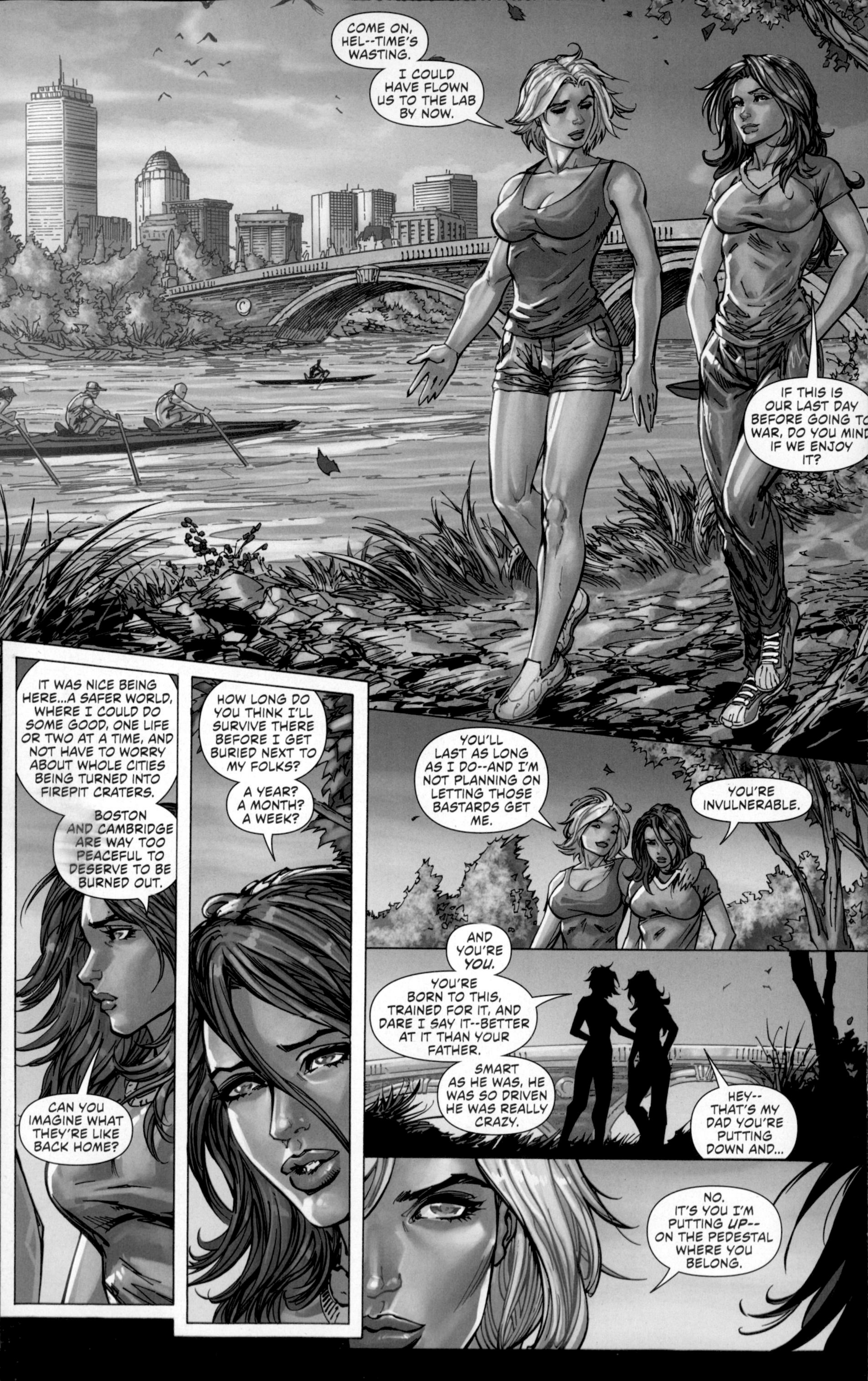
COME ON, HEL--TIME'S WASTING.
I COULD HAVE FLOWN US TO THE LAB BY NOW.
IF THIS IS OUR LAST DAY BEFORE GOING TO WAR, DO YOU MIND IF WE ENJOY IT?
IT WAS NICE BEING HERE...A SAFER WORLD, WHERE I COULD DO SOME GOOD, ONE LIFE OR TWO AT A TIME, AND NOT HAVE TO WORRY ABOUT WHOLE CITIES BEING TURNED INTO FIREPIT CRATERS.
BOSTON AND CAMBRIDGE ARE WAY TOO PEACEFUL TO DESERVE TO BE BURNED OUT.
CAN YOU IMAGINE WHAT THEY'RE LIKE BACK HOME?
HOW LONG DO YOU THINK I'LL SURVIVE THERE BEFORE I GET BURIED NEXT TO MY FOLKS?
A YEAR? A MONTH? A WEEK?
YOU'LL LAST AS LONG AS I DO--AND I'M NOT PLANNING ON LETTING THOSE BASTARDS GET ME.
YOU'RE INVULNERABLE.
AND YOU'RE YOU.
YOU'RE BORN TO THIS, TRAINED FOR IT, AND DARE I SAY IT--BETTER AT IT THAN YOUR FATHER.
SMART AS HE WAS, HE WAS SO DRIVEN HE WAS REALLY CRAZY.
HEY--THAT'S MY DAD YOU'RE PUTTING DOWN AND...
NO. IT'S YOU I'M PUTTING UP--ON THE PEDESTAL WHERE YOU BELONG.

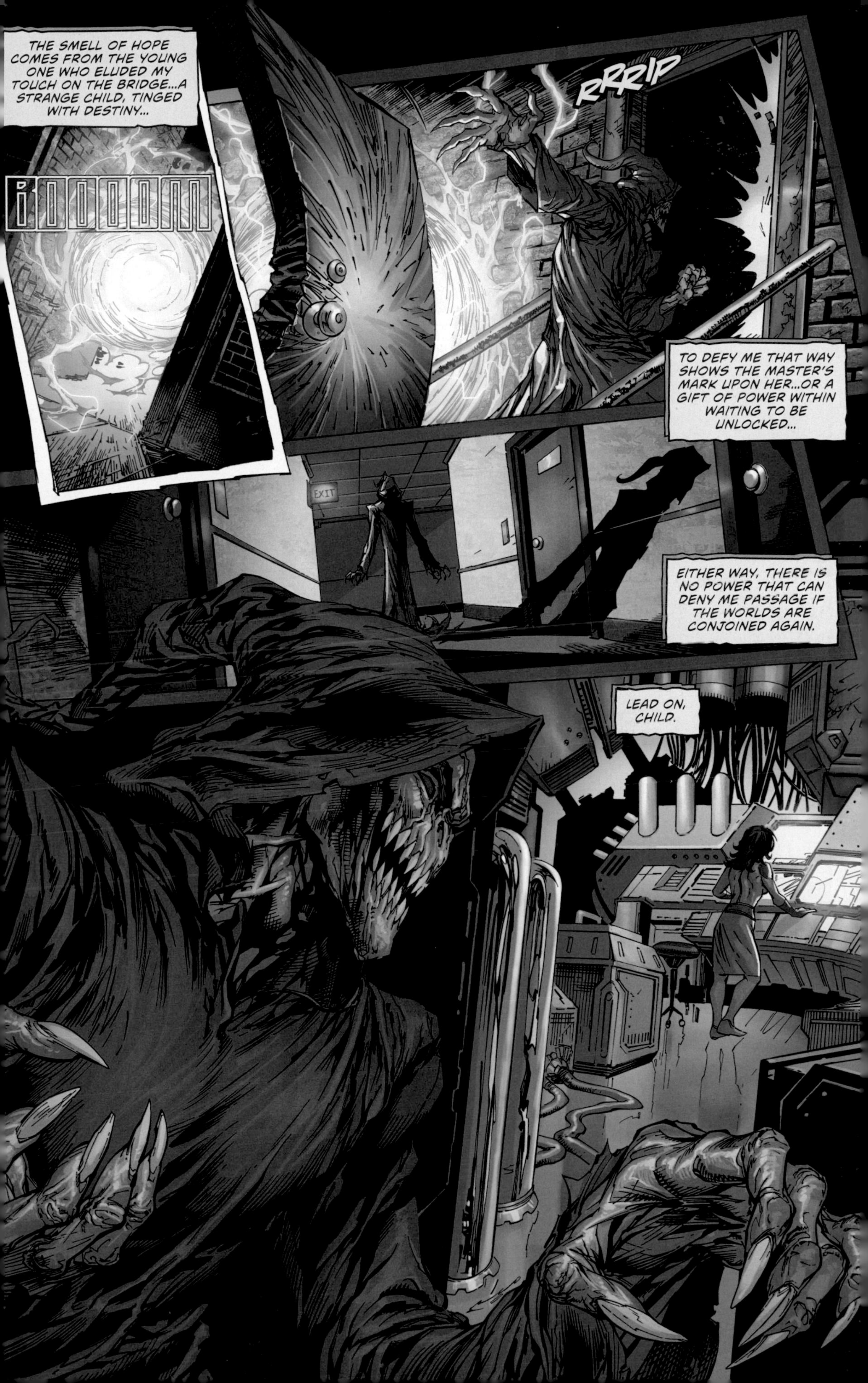
THE SMELL OF HOPE COMES FROM THE YOUNG ONE WHO ELUDED MY TOUCH ON THE BRIDGE...A STRANGE CHILD, TINGED WITH DESTINY...
BOOOOOM
RRRIP
TO DEFY ME THAT WAY SHOWS THE MASTER'S MARK UPON HER...OR A GIFT OF POWER WITHIN WAITING TO BE UNLOCKED...
EXIT
EITHER WAY, THERE IS NO POWER THAT CAN DENY ME PASSAGE IF THE WORLDS ARE CONJOINED AGAIN.
LEAD ON, CHILD.

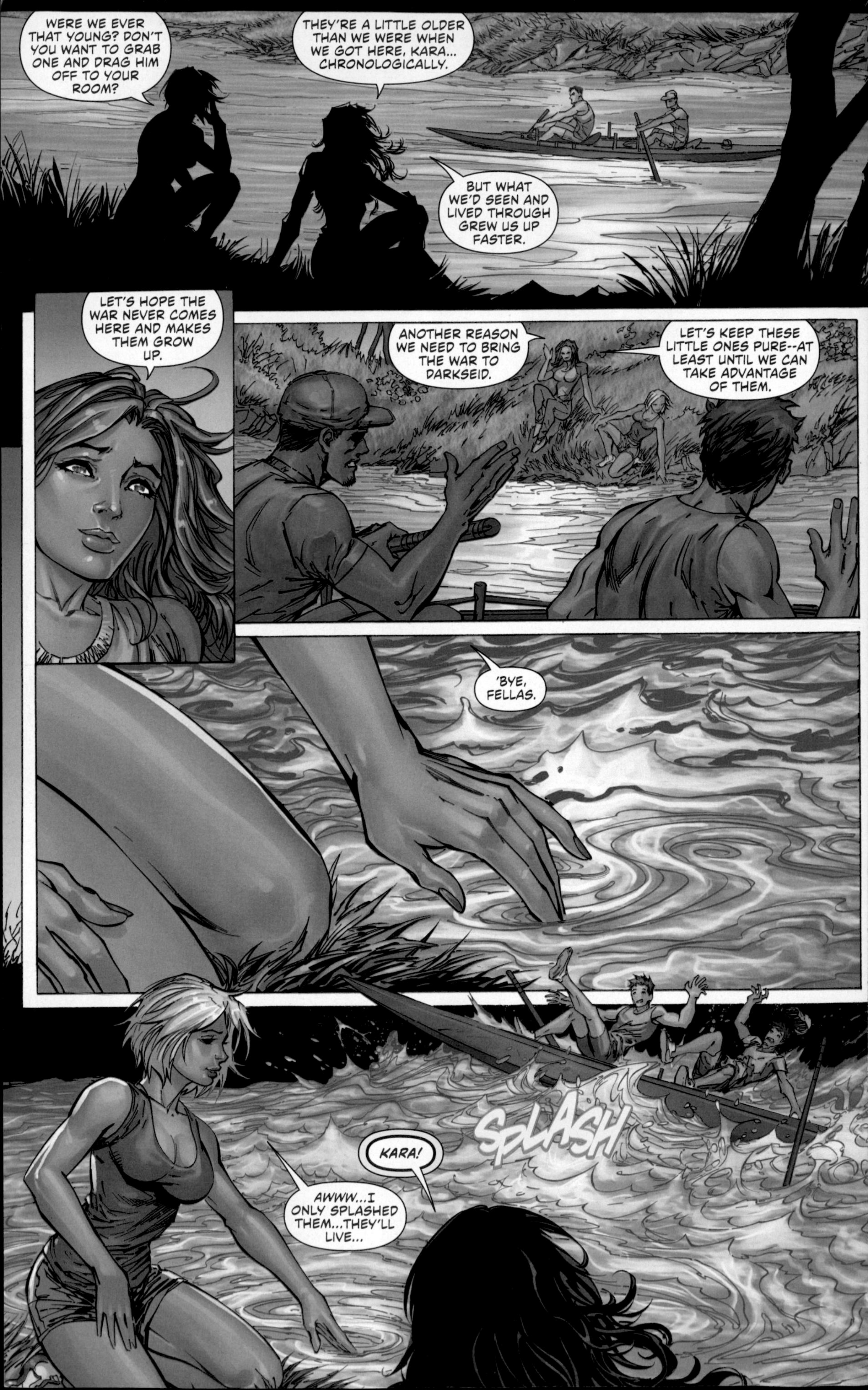
WERE WE EVER THAT YOUNG? DON'T YOU WANT TO GRAB ONE AND DRAG HIM OFF TO YOUR ROOM?
THEY'RE A LITTLE OLDER THAN WE WERE WHEN WE GOT HERE, KARA... CHRONOLOGICALLY.
BUT WHAT WE'D SEEN AND LIVED THROUGH GREW US UP FASTER.
LET'S HOPE THE WAR NEVER COMES HERE AND MAKES THEM GROW UP.
ANOTHER REASON WE NEED TO BRING THE WAR TO DARKSEID.
LET'S KEEP THESE LITTLE ONES PURE--AT LEAST UNTIL WE CAN TAKE ADVANTAGE OF THEM.
'BYE, FELLAS.
SPLASH
KARA!
AWWW...I ONLY SPLASHED THEM...THEY'LL LIVE...

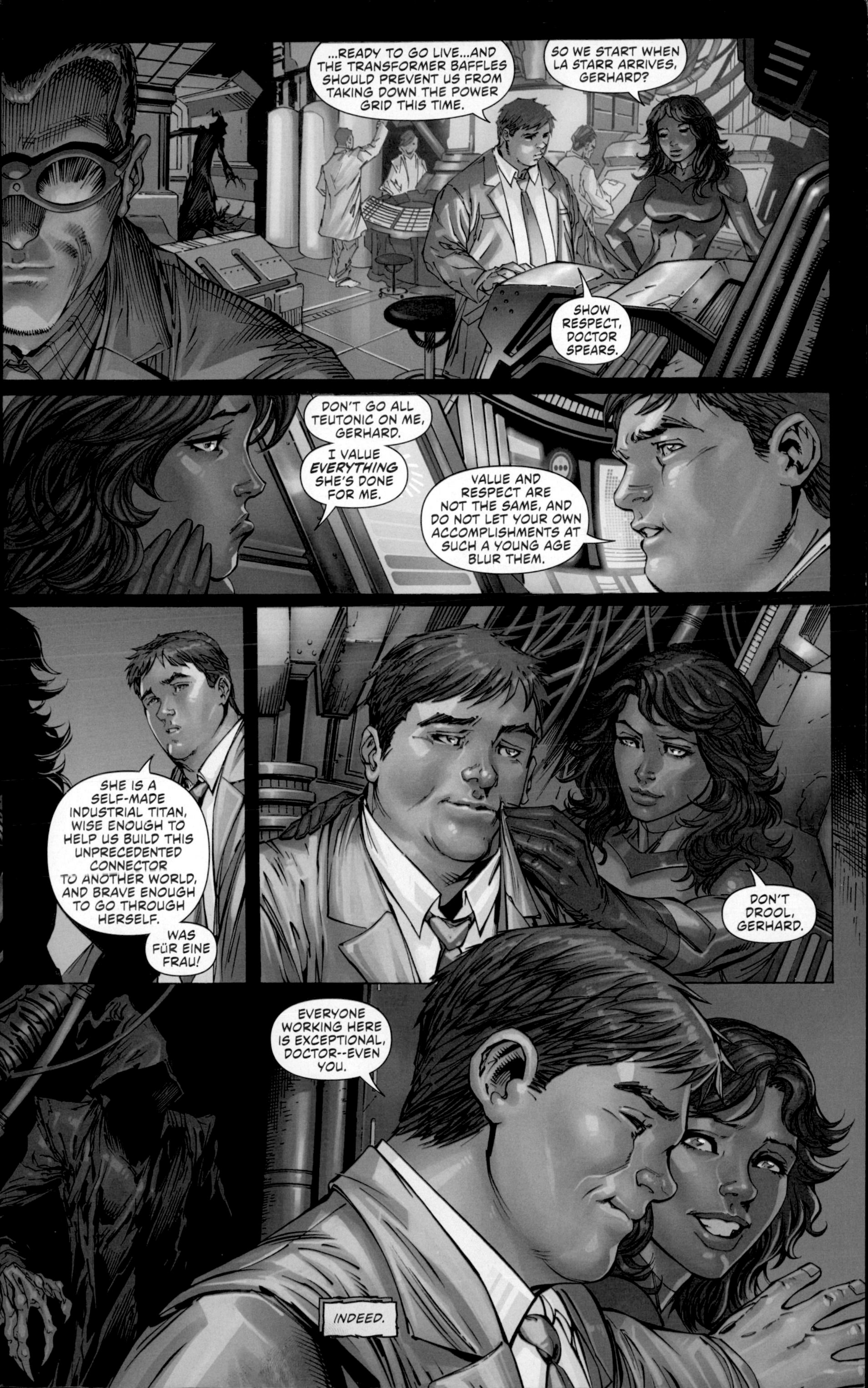
...READY TO GO LIVE...AND THE TRANSFORMER BAFFLES SHOULD PREVENT US FROM TAKING DOWN THE POWER GRID THIS TIME.
SO WE START WHEN LA STARR ARRIVES, GERHARD?
SHOW RESPECT, DOCTOR SPEARS.
DON'T GO ALL TEUTONIC ON ME, GERHARD.
I VALUE *EVERYTHING* SHE'S DONE FOR ME.
VALUE AND RESPECT ARE NOT THE SAME, AND DO NOT LET YOUR OWN ACCOMPLISHMENTS AT SUCH A YOUNG AGE BLUR THEM.
SHE IS A SELF-MADE INDUSTRIAL TITAN, WISE ENOUGH TO HELP US BUILD THIS UNPRECEDENTED CONNECTOR TO ANOTHER WORLD, AND BRAVE ENOUGH TO GO THROUGH HERSELF.
WAS FÜR EINE FRAU!
DON'T DROOL, GERHARD.
EVERYONE WORKING HERE IS EXCEPTIONAL, DOCTOR--EVEN YOU.
INDEED.

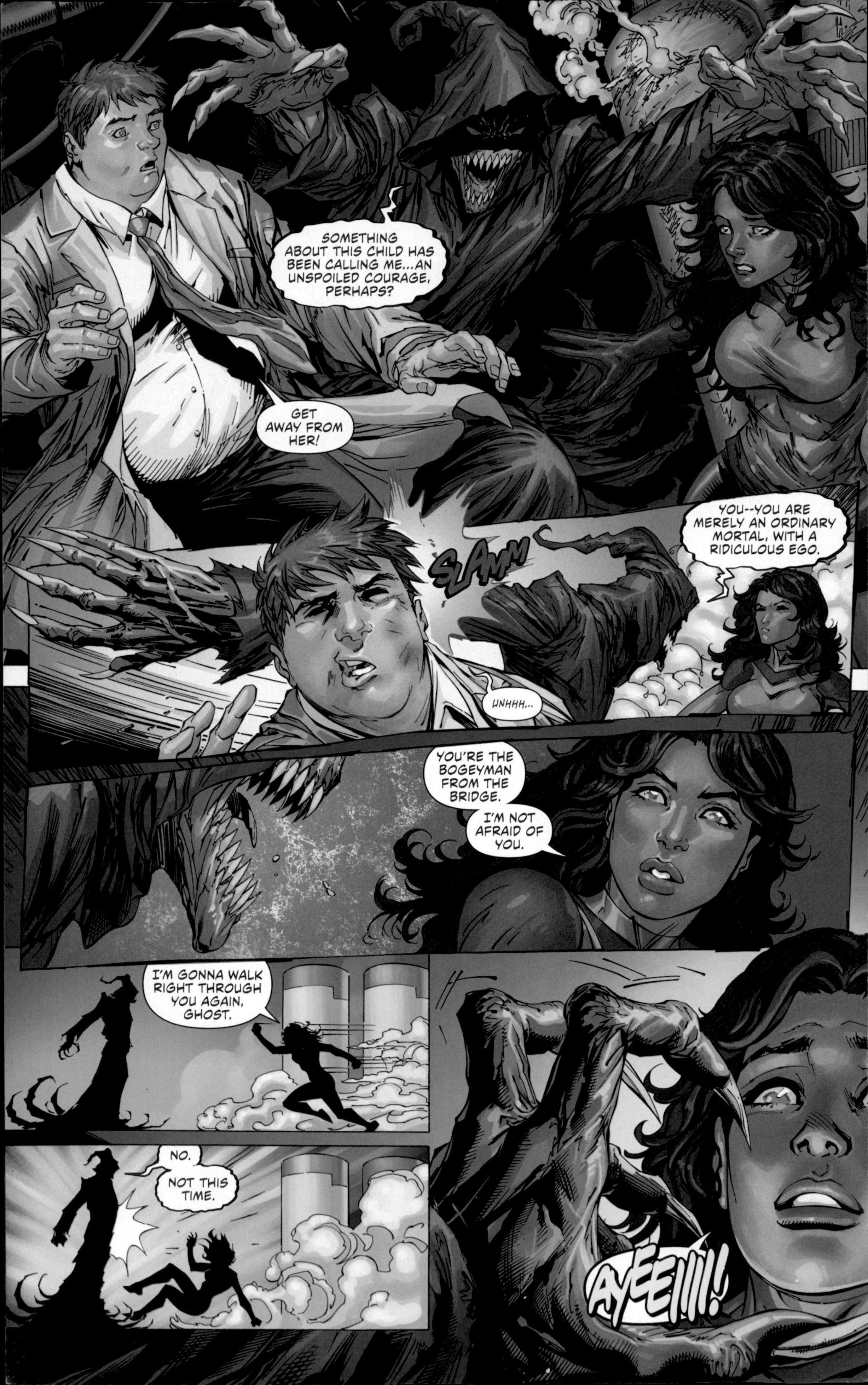
SOMETHING ABOUT THIS CHILD HAS BEEN CALLING ME...AN UNSPOILED COURAGE, PERHAPS?
GET AWAY FROM HER!
SLAMM
YOU--YOU ARE MERELY AN ORDINARY MORTAL, WITH A RIDICULOUS EGO.
UNHHH...
YOU'RE THE BOGEYMAN FROM THE BRIDGE.
I'M NOT AFRAID OF YOU.
I'M GONNA WALK RIGHT THROUGH YOU AGAIN, GHOST.
NO.
NOT THIS TIME.
AYEEIIIII!

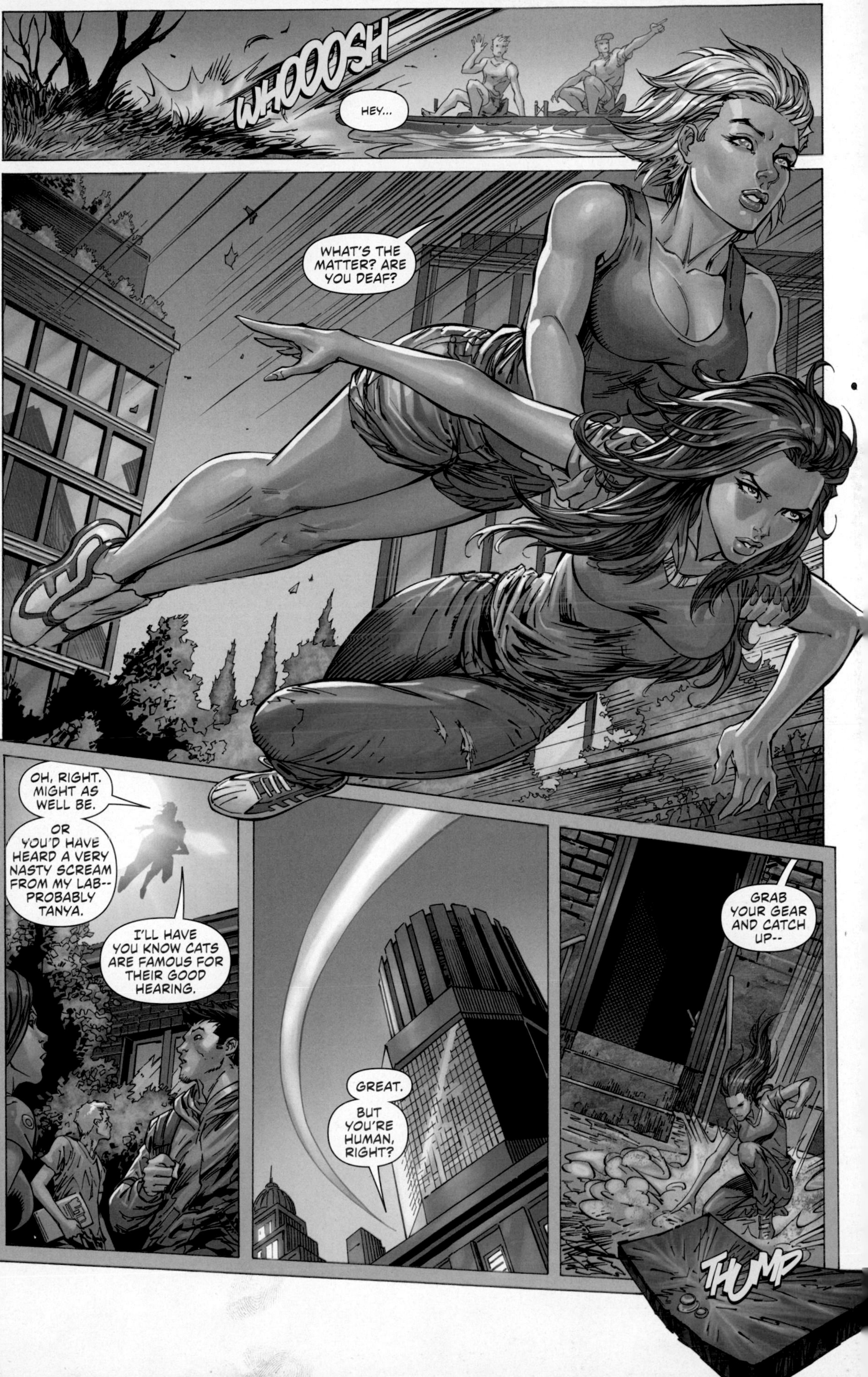
WHOOOSH
HEY...
WHAT'S THE MATTER? ARE YOU DEAF?
OH, RIGHT. MIGHT AS WELL BE.
OR YOU'D HAVE HEARD A VERY NASTY SCREAM FROM MY LAB-- PROBABLY TANYA.
I'LL HAVE YOU KNOW CATS ARE FAMOUS FOR THEIR GOOD HEARING.
GREAT.
BUT YOU'RE HUMAN, RIGHT?
GRAB YOUR GEAR AND CATCH UP--
THUMP

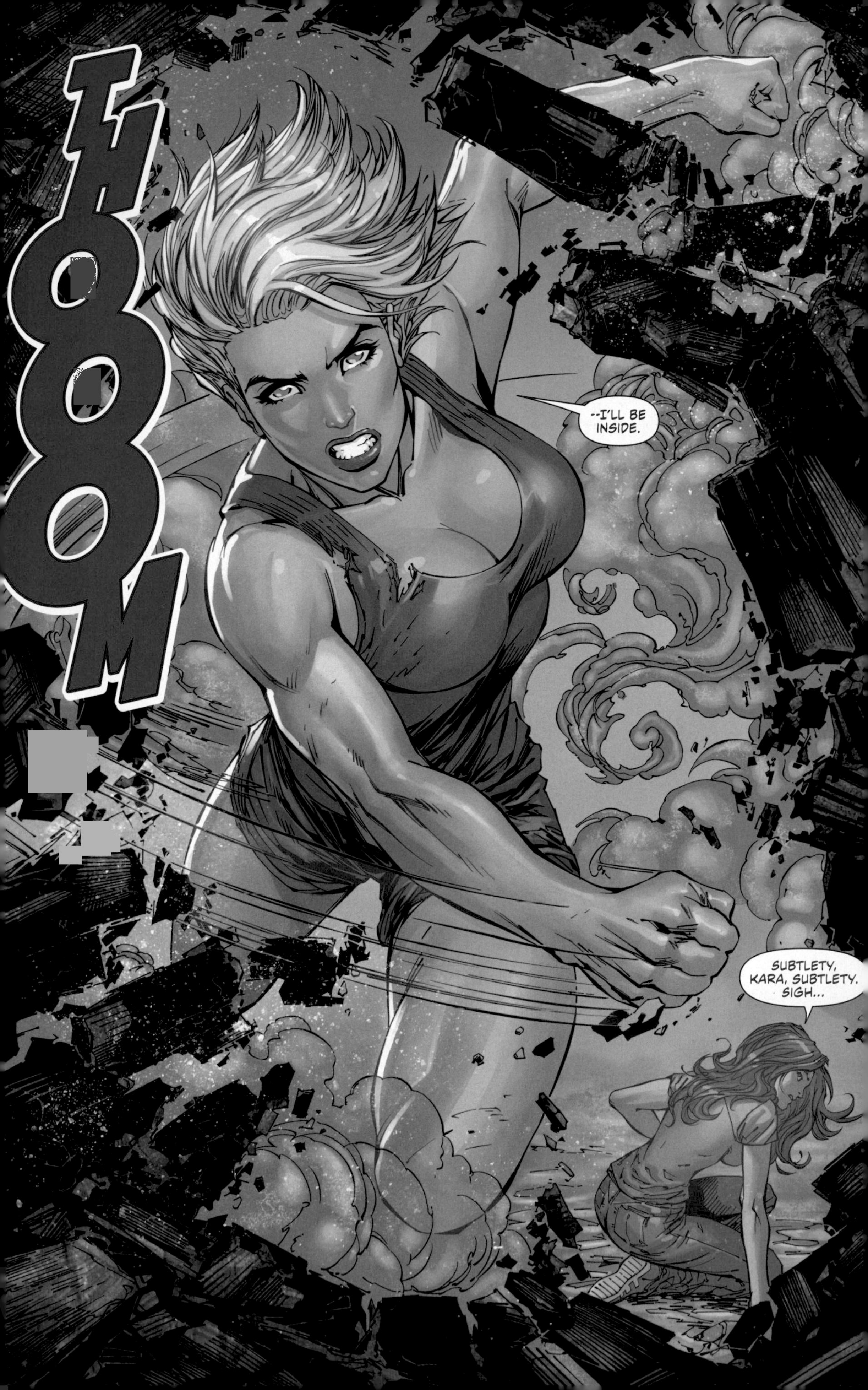
THOOM
--I'LL BE INSIDE.
SUBTLETY, KARA, SUBTLETY. SIGH...

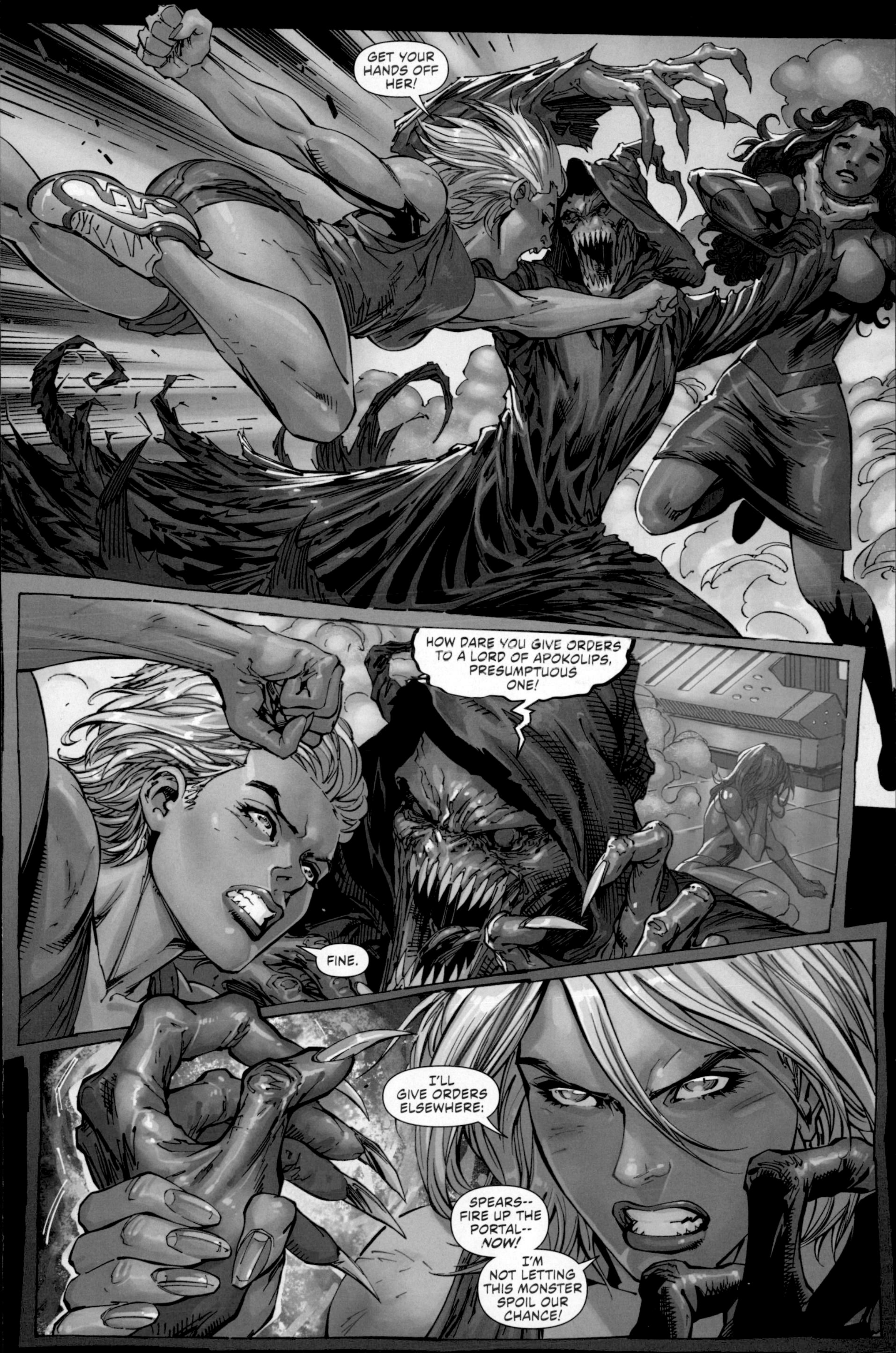
GET YOUR HANDS OFF HER!
HOW DARE YOU GIVE ORDERS TO A LORD OF APOKOLIPS, PRESUMPTUOUS ONE!
FINE.
I'LL GIVE ORDERS ELSEWHERE:
SPEARS-- FIRE UP THE PORTAL-- NOW!
I'M NOT LETTING THIS MONSTER SPOIL OUR CHANCE!

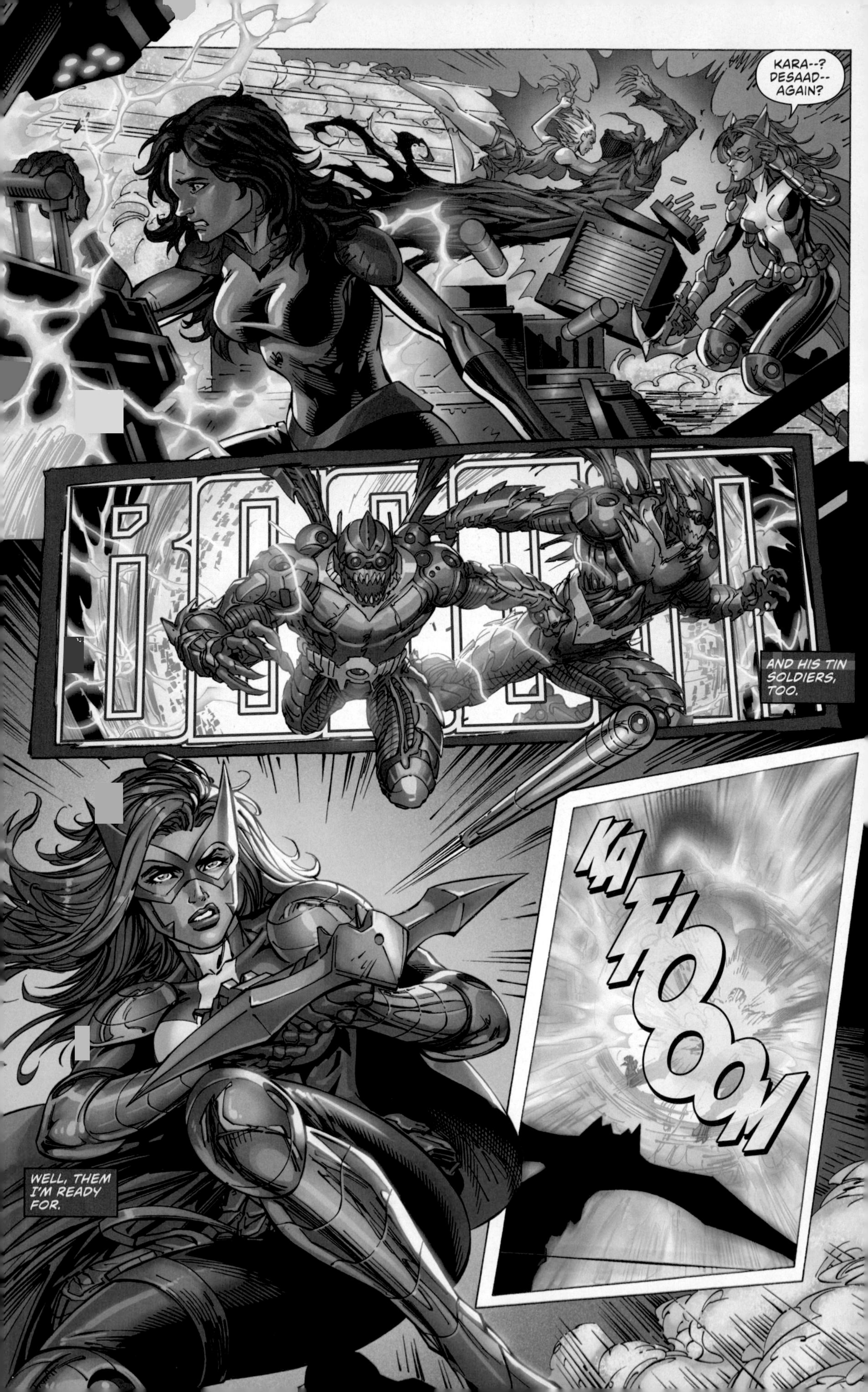
KARA--? DESAAD-- AGAIN?
AND HIS TIN SOLDIERS, TOO.
WELL, THEM I'M READY FOR.
KA-THOOOM

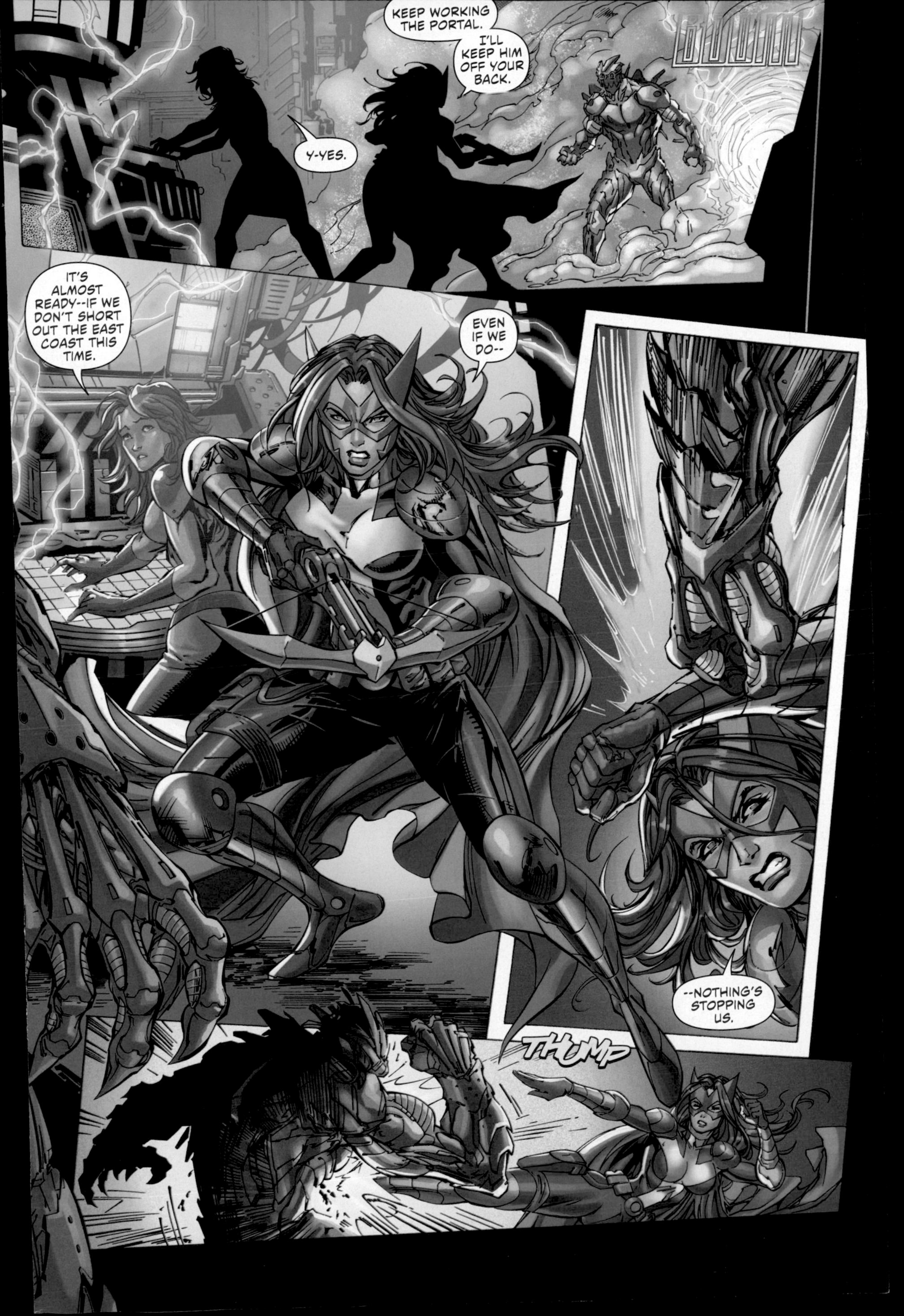

KEEP WORKING THE PORTAL.
I'LL KEEP HIM OFF YOUR BACK.
Y-YES.
IT'S ALMOST READY--IF WE DON'T SHORT OUT THE EAST COAST THIS TIME.
EVEN IF WE DO--
--NOTHING'S STOPPING US.
THUMP

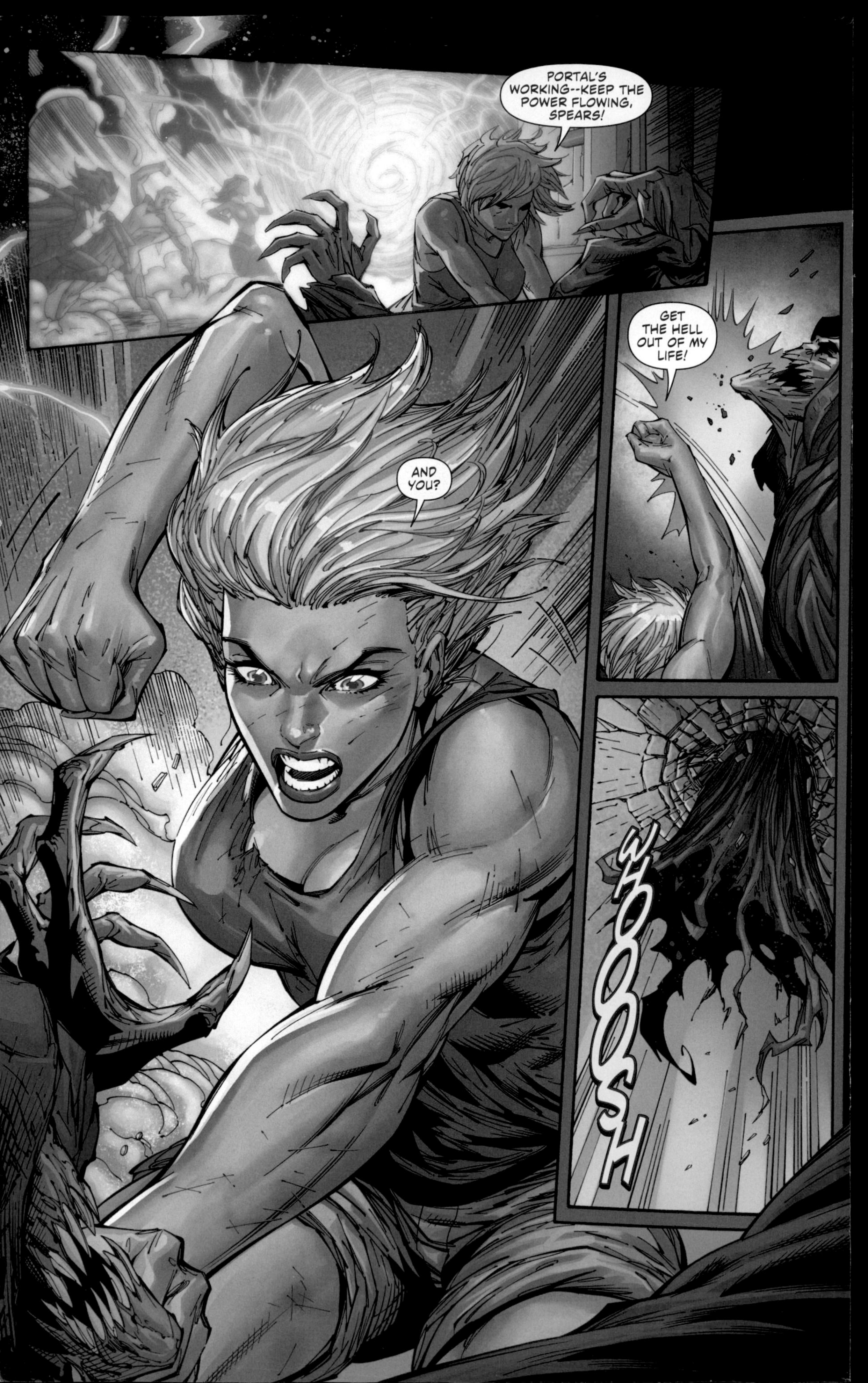
PORTAL'S WORKING--KEEP THE POWER FLOWING, SPEARS!
AND YOU?
GET THE HELL OUT OF MY LIFE!
WHOOOOSH

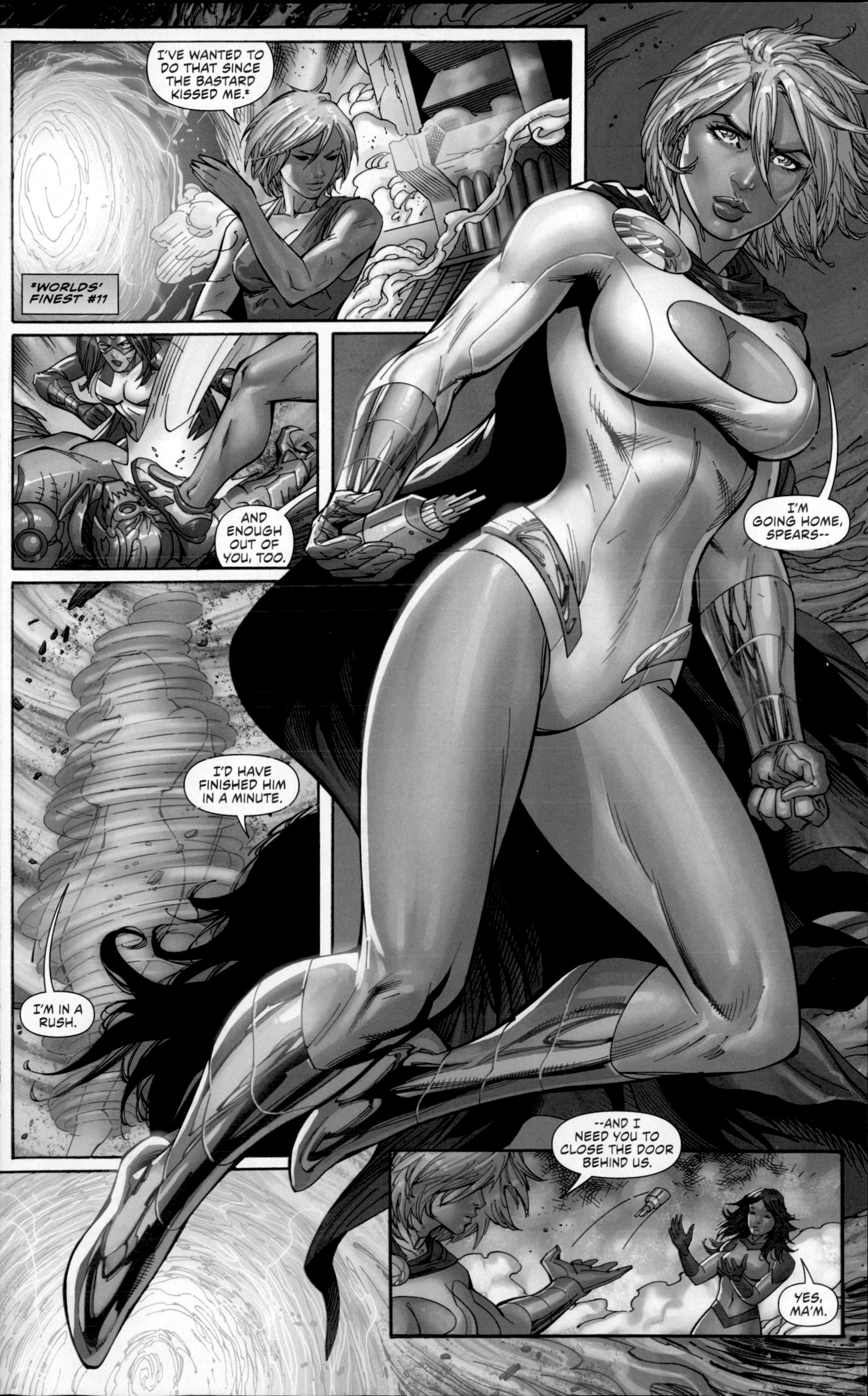
I'VE WANTED TO DO THAT SINCE THE BASTARD KISSED ME.*
*WORLDS' FINEST #11
AND ENOUGH OUT OF YOU, TOO.
I'M GOING HOME, SPEARS--
I'D HAVE FINISHED HIM IN A MINUTE.
I'M IN A RUSH.
--AND I NEED YOU TO CLOSE THE DOOR BEHIND US.
YES, MA'M.

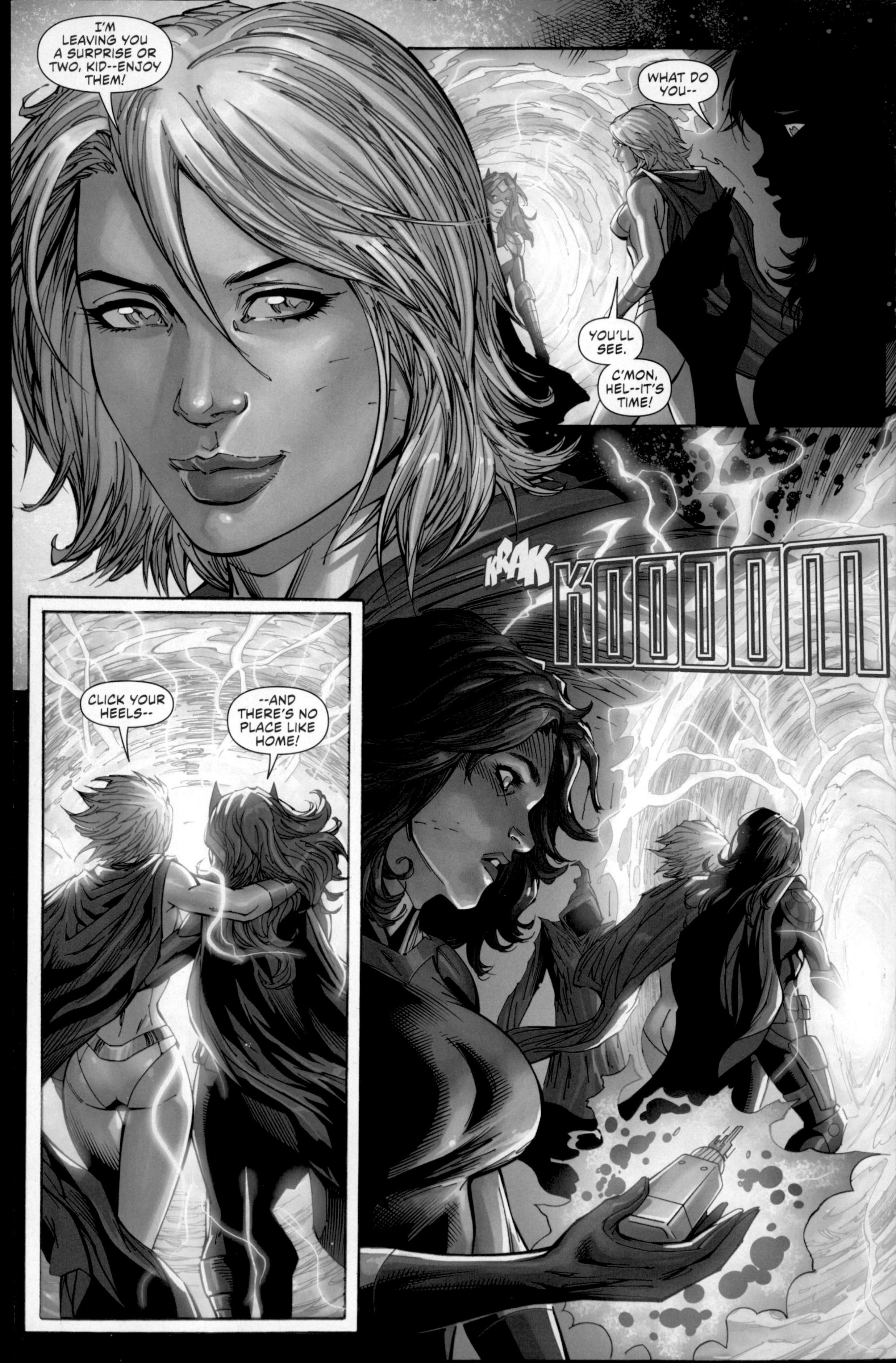
I'M LEAVING YOU A SURPRISE OR TWO, KID--ENJOY THEM!
WHAT DO YOU--
YOU'LL SEE.
C'MON, HEL--IT'S TIME!
KRAK
KOOOOM
CLICK YOUR HEELS--
--AND THERE'S NO PLACE LIKE HOME!

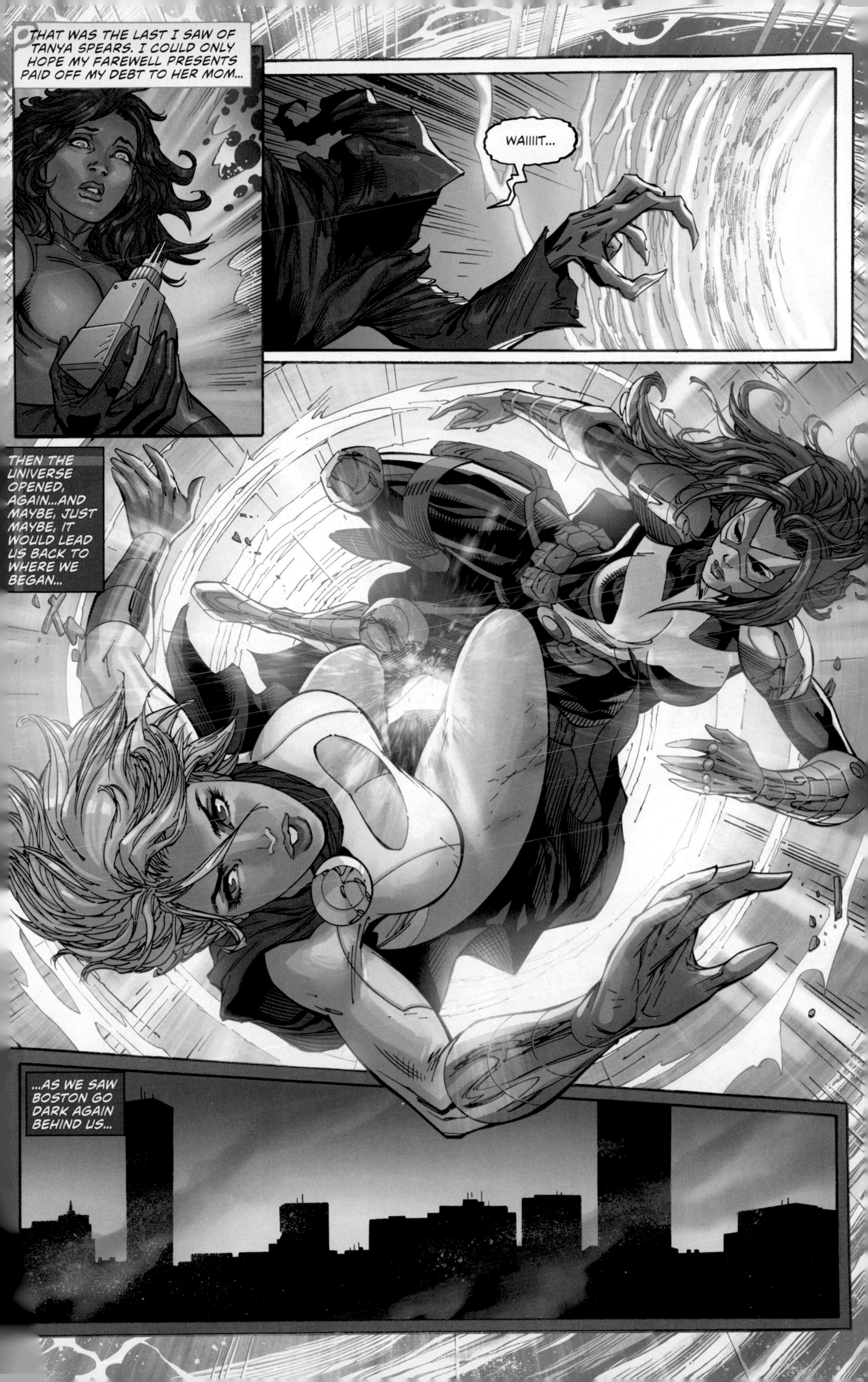
THAT WAS THE LAST I SAW OF TANYA SPEARS. I COULD ONLY HOPE MY FAREWELL PRESENTS PAID OFF MY DEBT TO HER MOM...
WAIIIIT...
THEN THE UNIVERSE OPENED, AGAIN...AND MAYBE, JUST MAYBE, IT WOULD LEAD US BACK TO WHERE WE BEGAN...
...AS WE SAW BOSTON GO DARK AGAIN BEHIND US...

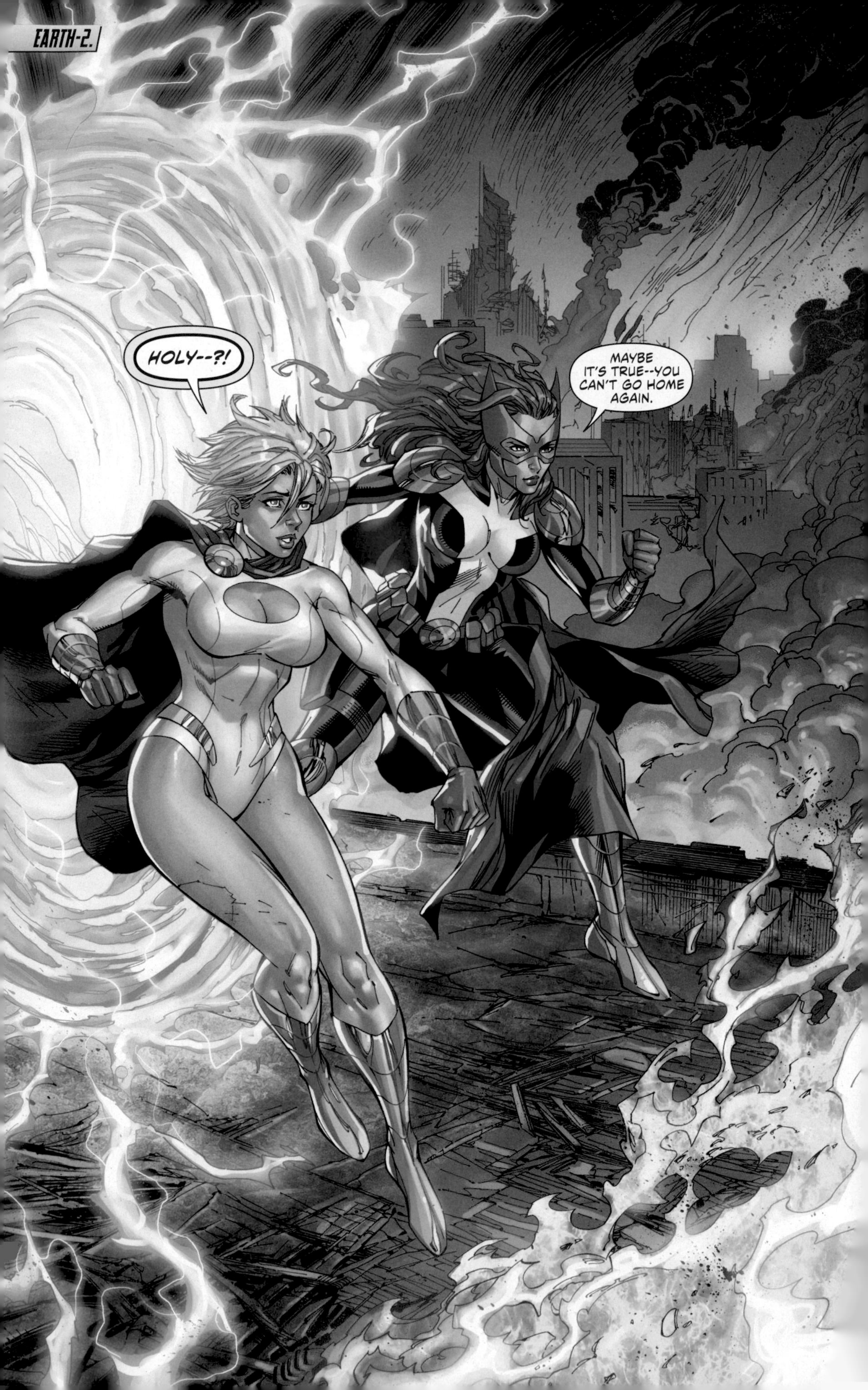
EARTH-2.
HOLY--?!
MAYBE IT'S TRUE--YOU CAN'T GO HOME AGAIN.

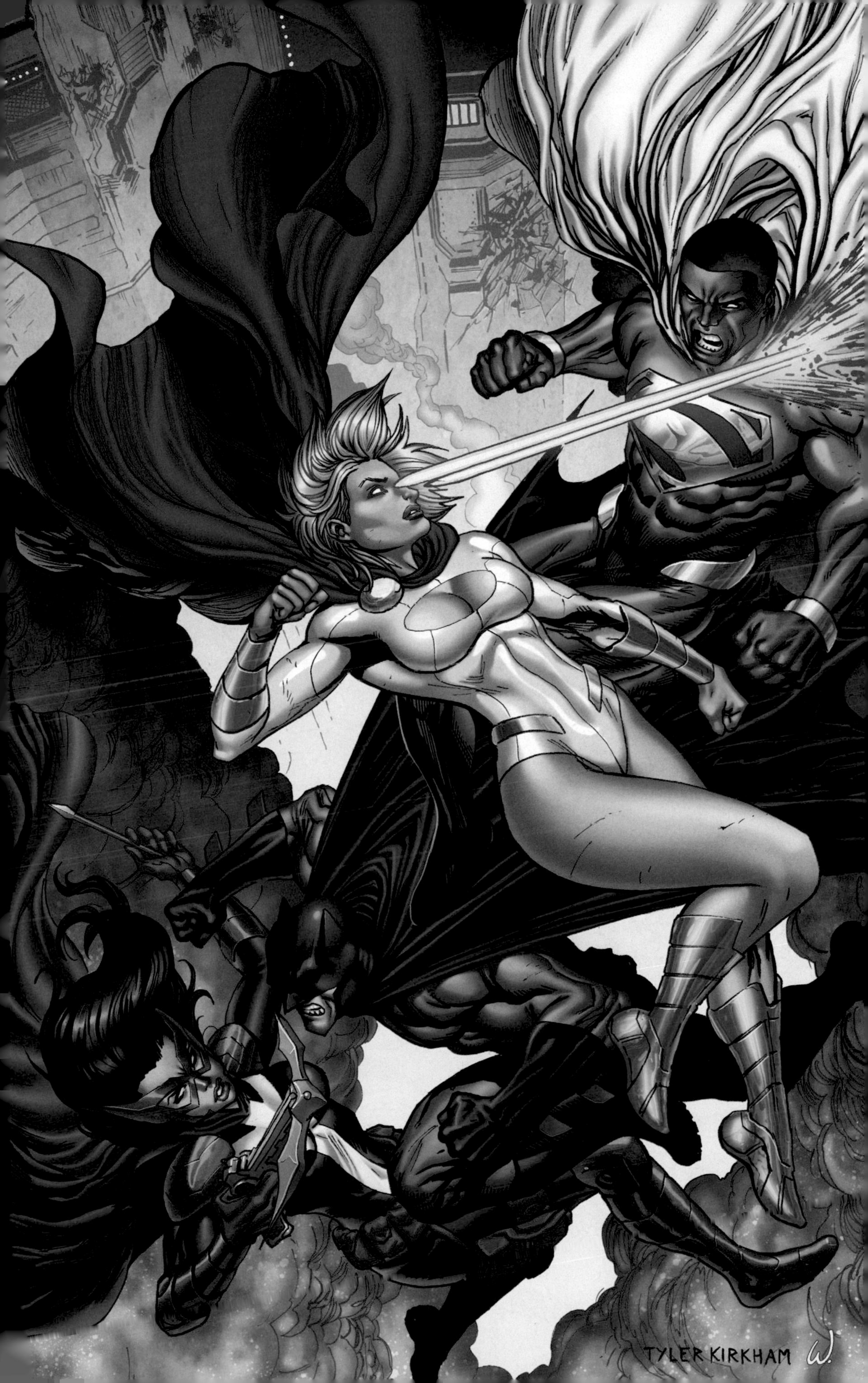
TYLER KIRKHAM

WORLD'S END?

PAUL LEVITZ writer TYLER KIRKHAM SCOTT KOLINS pencillers JOE WEEMS SCOTT KOLINS inkers
ARIF PRIANTO colorist TRAVIS LANHAM letterer cover by TYLER KIRKHAM and JASON WRIGHT

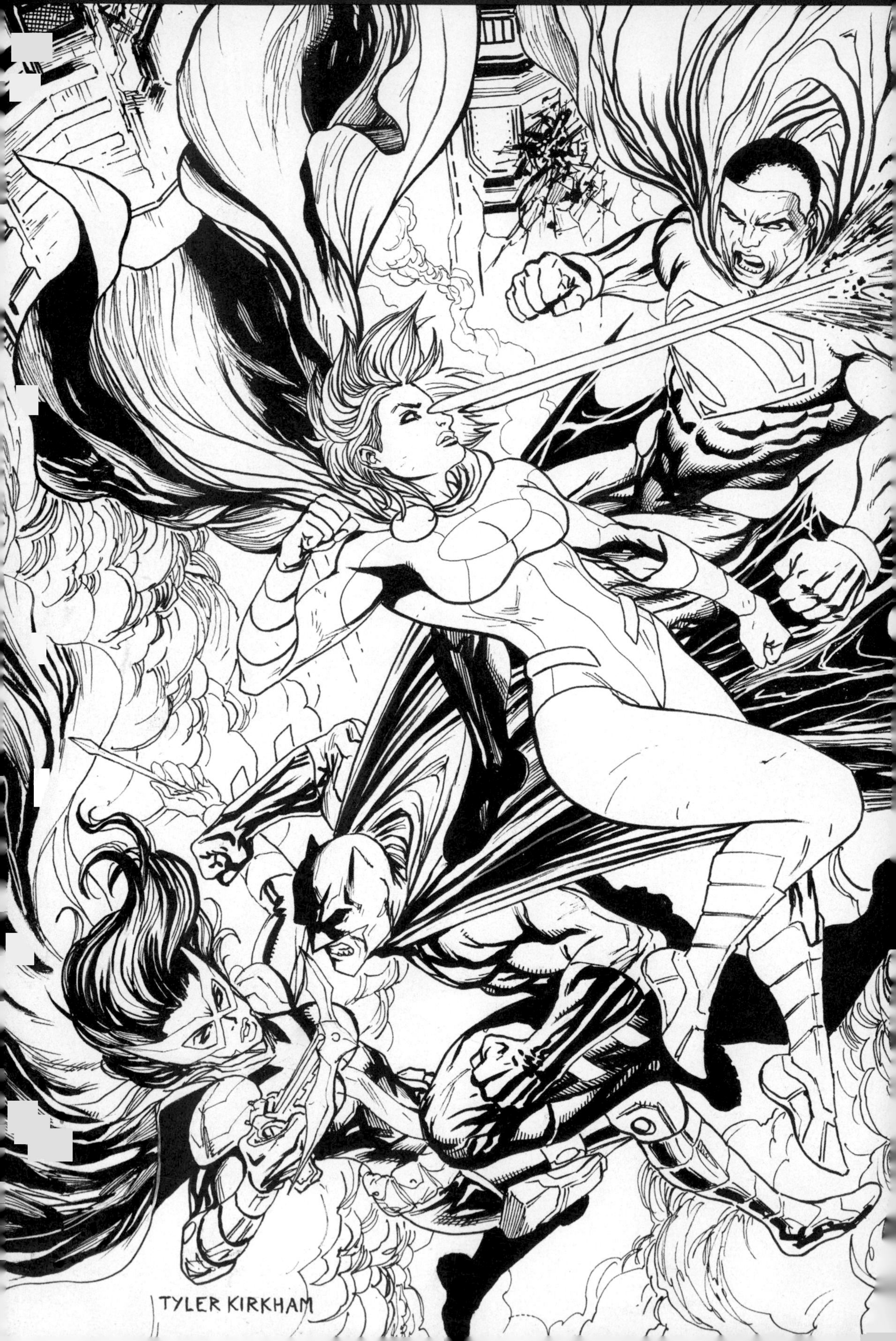
TYLER KIRKHAM

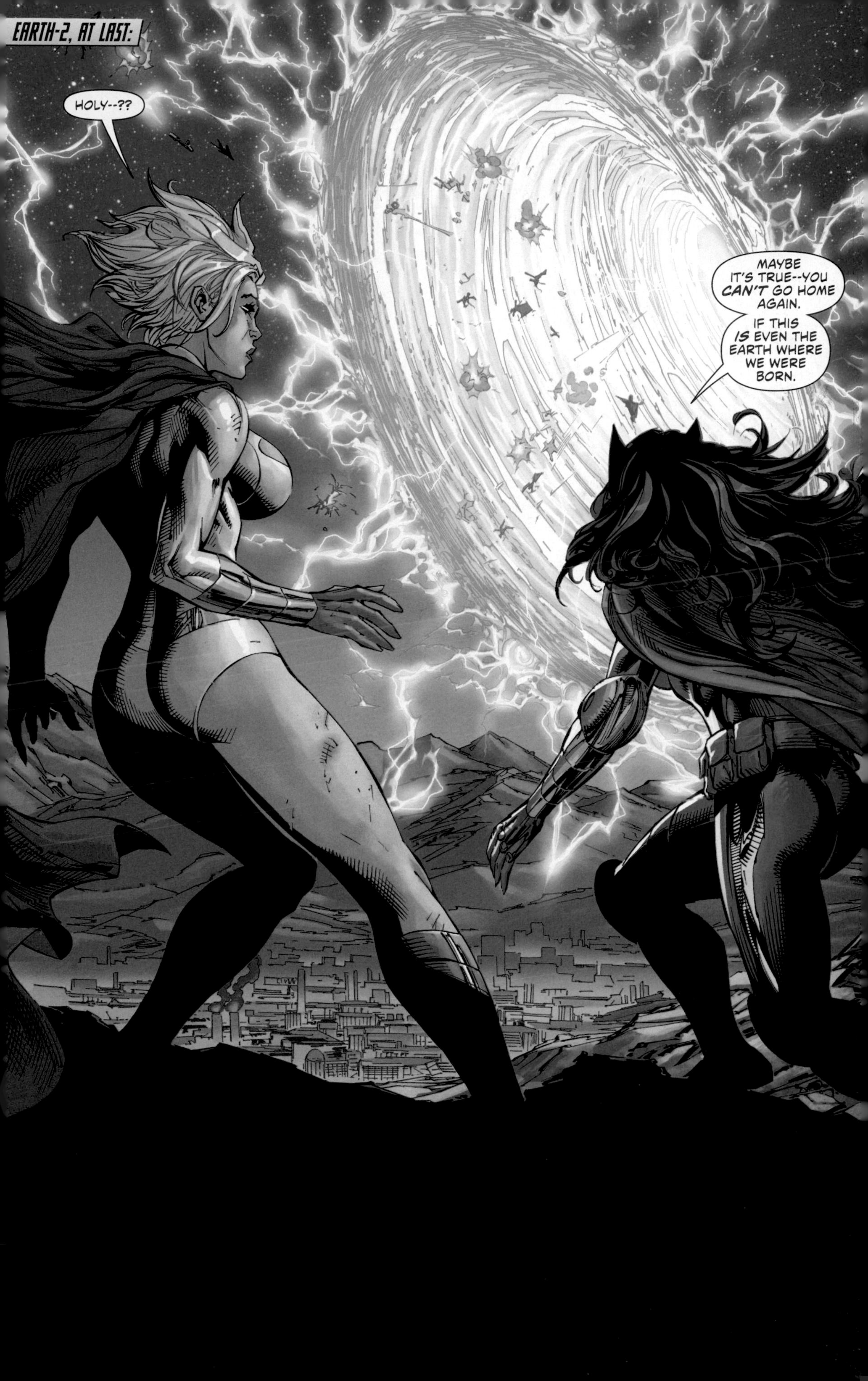
EARTH-2, AT LAST:
HOLY--??
MAYBE IT'S TRUE--YOU CAN'T GO HOME AGAIN.
IF THIS IS EVEN THE EARTH WHERE WE WERE BORN.

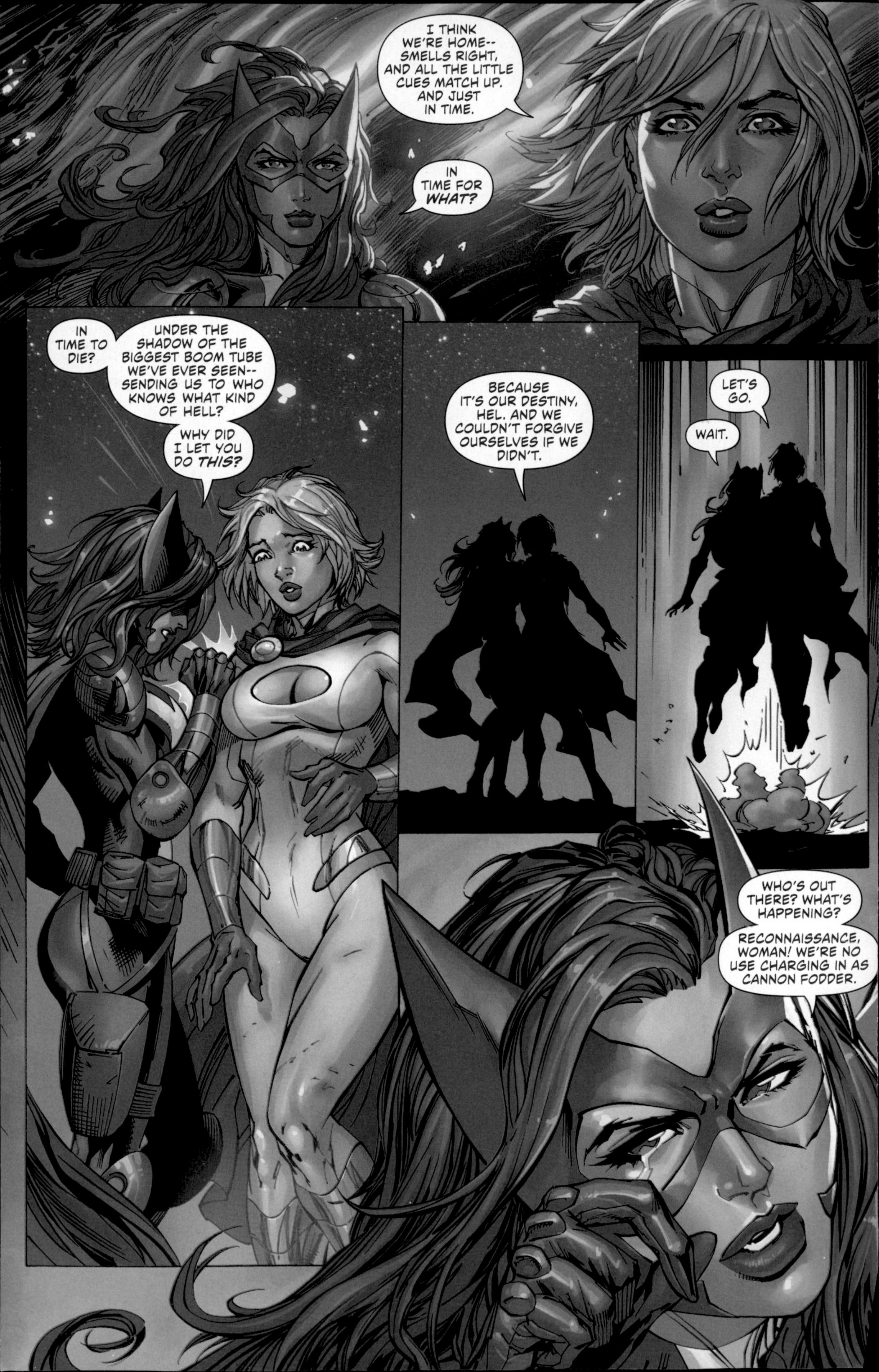
I THINK WE'RE HOME-- SMELLS RIGHT, AND ALL THE LITTLE CUES MATCH UP. AND JUST IN TIME.
IN TIME FOR *WHAT?*
IN TIME TO DIE?
UNDER THE SHADOW OF THE BIGGEST BOOM TUBE WE'VE EVER SEEN-- SENDING US TO WHO KNOWS WHAT KIND OF HELL?
WHY DID I LET YOU DO *THIS?*
BECAUSE IT'S OUR DESTINY, HEL. AND WE COULDN'T FORGIVE OURSELVES IF WE DIDN'T.
LET'S GO.
WAIT.
WHO'S OUT THERE? WHAT'S HAPPENING?
RECONNAISSANCE, WOMAN! WE'RE NO USE CHARGING IN AS CANNON FODDER.

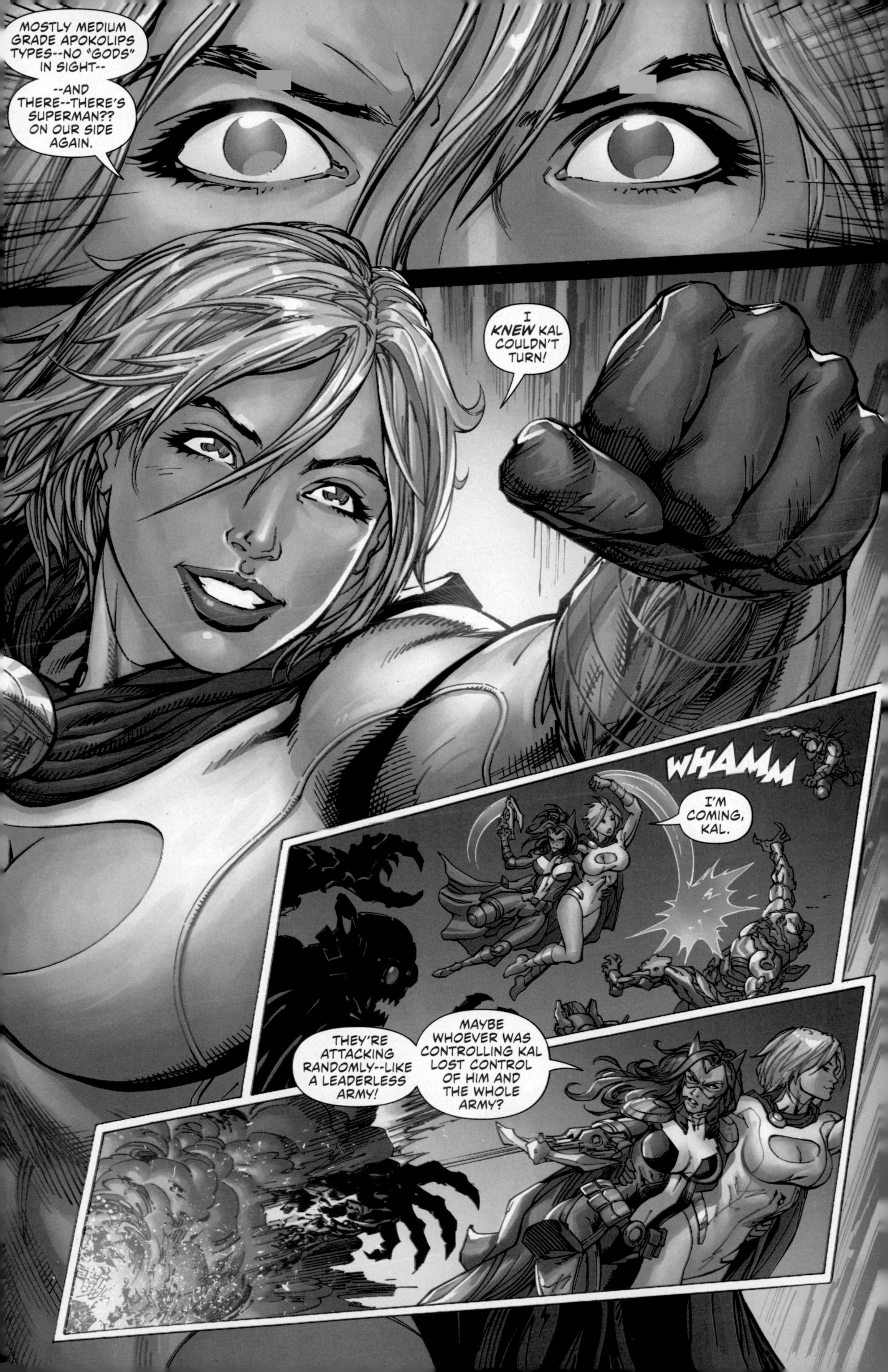
MOSTLY MEDIUM GRADE APOKOLIPS TYPES--NO "GODS" IN SIGHT--
--AND THERE--THERE'S SUPERMAN?? ON OUR SIDE AGAIN.
I KNEW KAL COULDN'T TURN!
WHAMM
I'M COMING, KAL.
THEY'RE ATTACKING RANDOMLY--LIKE A LEADERLESS ARMY!
MAYBE WHOEVER WAS CONTROLLING KAL LOST CONTROL OF HIM AND THE WHOLE ARMY?

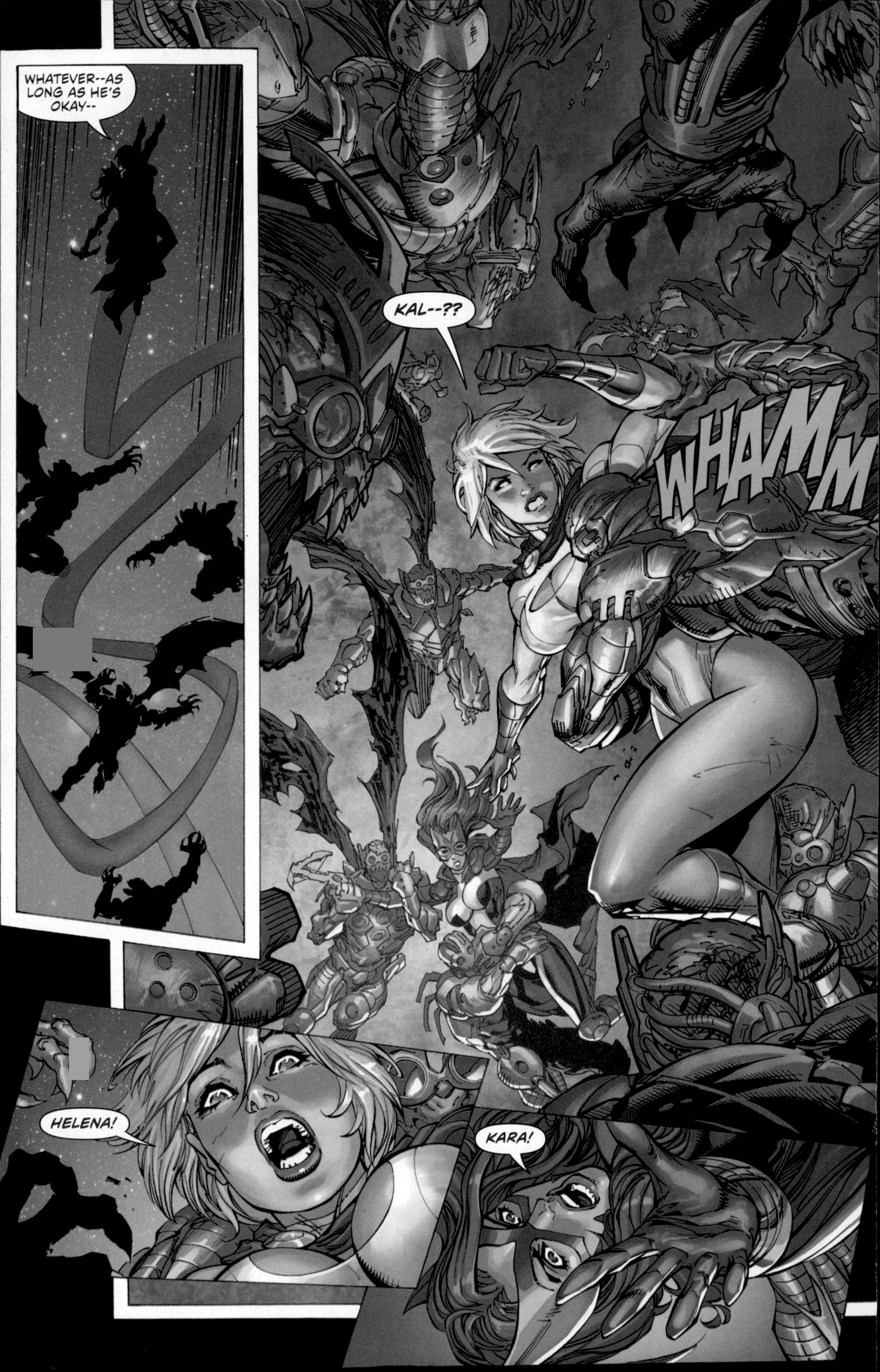
WHATEVER--AS LONG AS HE'S OKAY--
KAL--??
WHAMM
HELENA!
KARA!

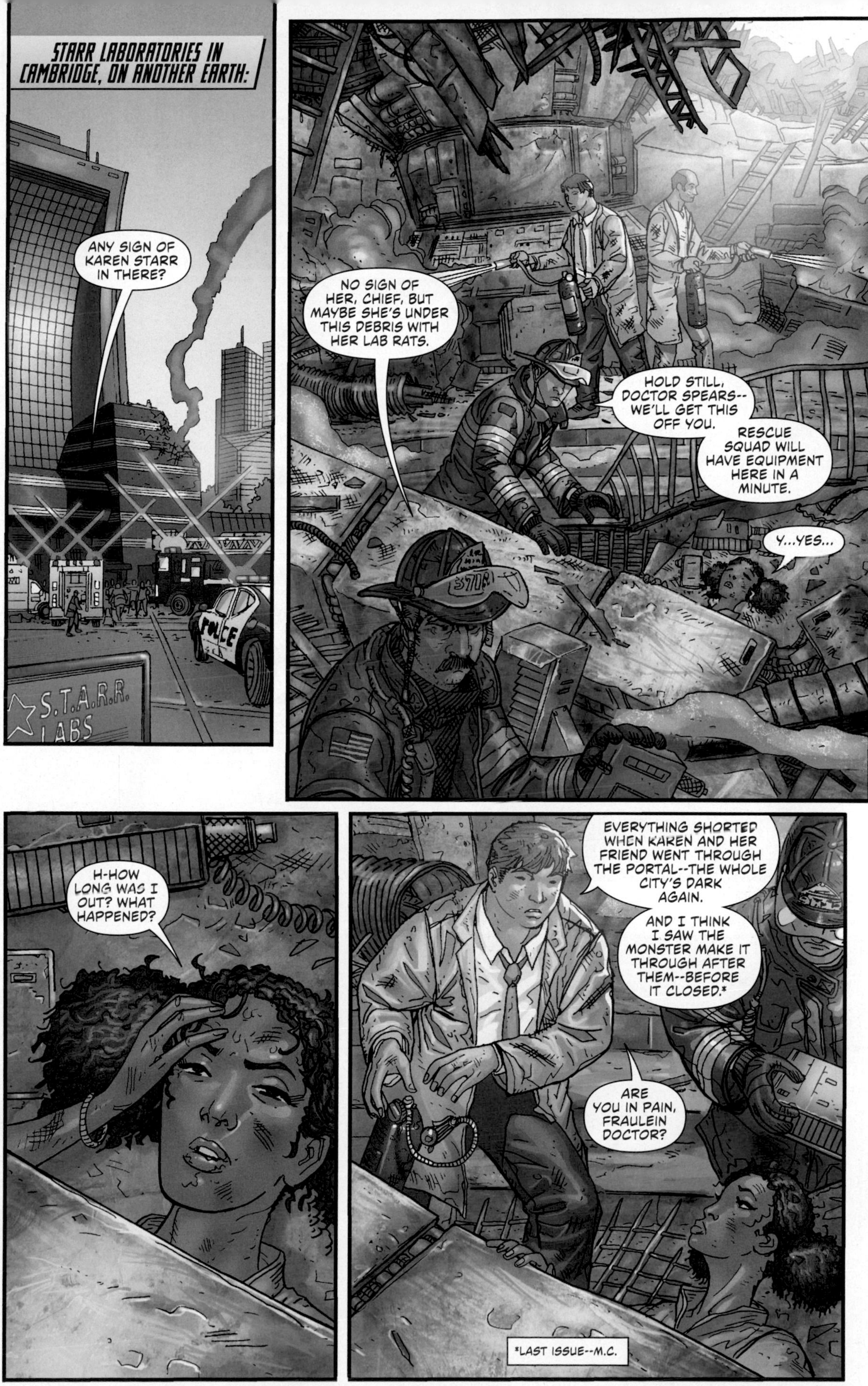
STARR LABORATORIES IN CAMBRIDGE, ON ANOTHER EARTH:
ANY SIGN OF KAREN STARR IN THERE?
S.T.A.R.R. LABS
POLICE
NO SIGN OF HER, CHIEF, BUT MAYBE SHE'S UNDER THIS DEBRIS WITH HER LAB RATS.
HOLD STILL, DOCTOR SPEARS-- WE'LL GET THIS OFF YOU.
RESCUE SQUAD WILL HAVE EQUIPMENT HERE IN A MINUTE.
Y...YES...
H-HOW LONG WAS I OUT? WHAT HAPPENED?
EVERYTHING SHORTED WHEN KAREN AND HER FRIEND WENT THROUGH THE PORTAL--THE WHOLE CITY'S DARK AGAIN.
AND I THINK I SAW THE MONSTER MAKE IT THROUGH AFTER THEM--BEFORE IT CLOSED.*
ARE YOU IN PAIN, FRAULEIN DOCTOR?
*LAST ISSUE--M.C.

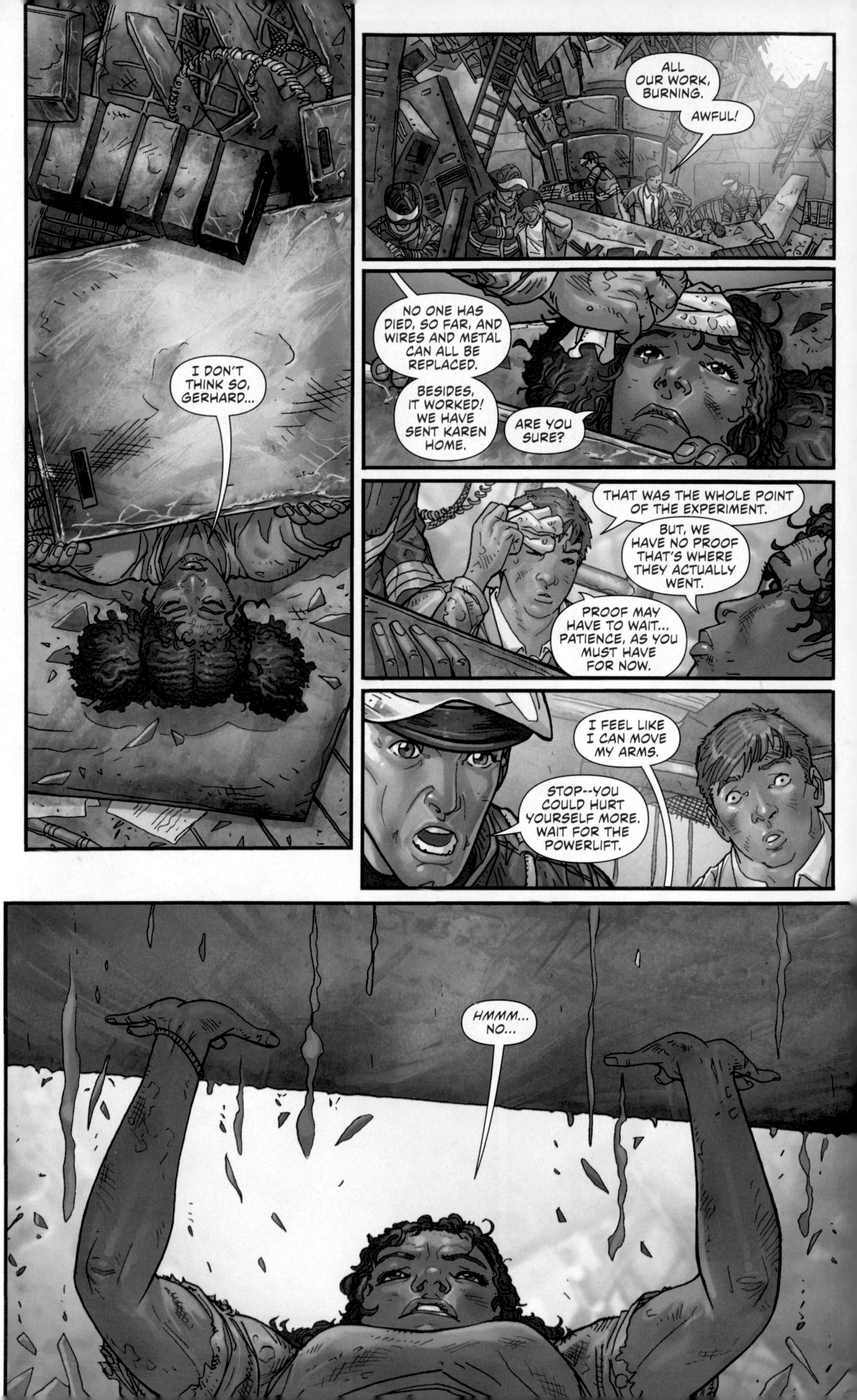

I DON'T THINK SO, GERHARD...
ALL OUR WORK, BURNING.
AWFUL!
NO ONE HAS DIED, SO FAR, AND WIRES AND METAL CAN ALL BE REPLACED.
BESIDES, IT WORKED! WE HAVE SENT KAREN HOME.
ARE YOU SURE?
THAT WAS THE WHOLE POINT OF THE EXPERIMENT.
BUT, WE HAVE NO PROOF THAT'S WHERE THEY ACTUALLY WENT.
PROOF MAY HAVE TO WAIT... PATIENCE, AS YOU MUST HAVE FOR NOW.
I FEEL LIKE I CAN MOVE MY ARMS.
STOP--YOU COULD HURT YOURSELF MORE. WAIT FOR THE POWERLIFT.
HMMM... NO...

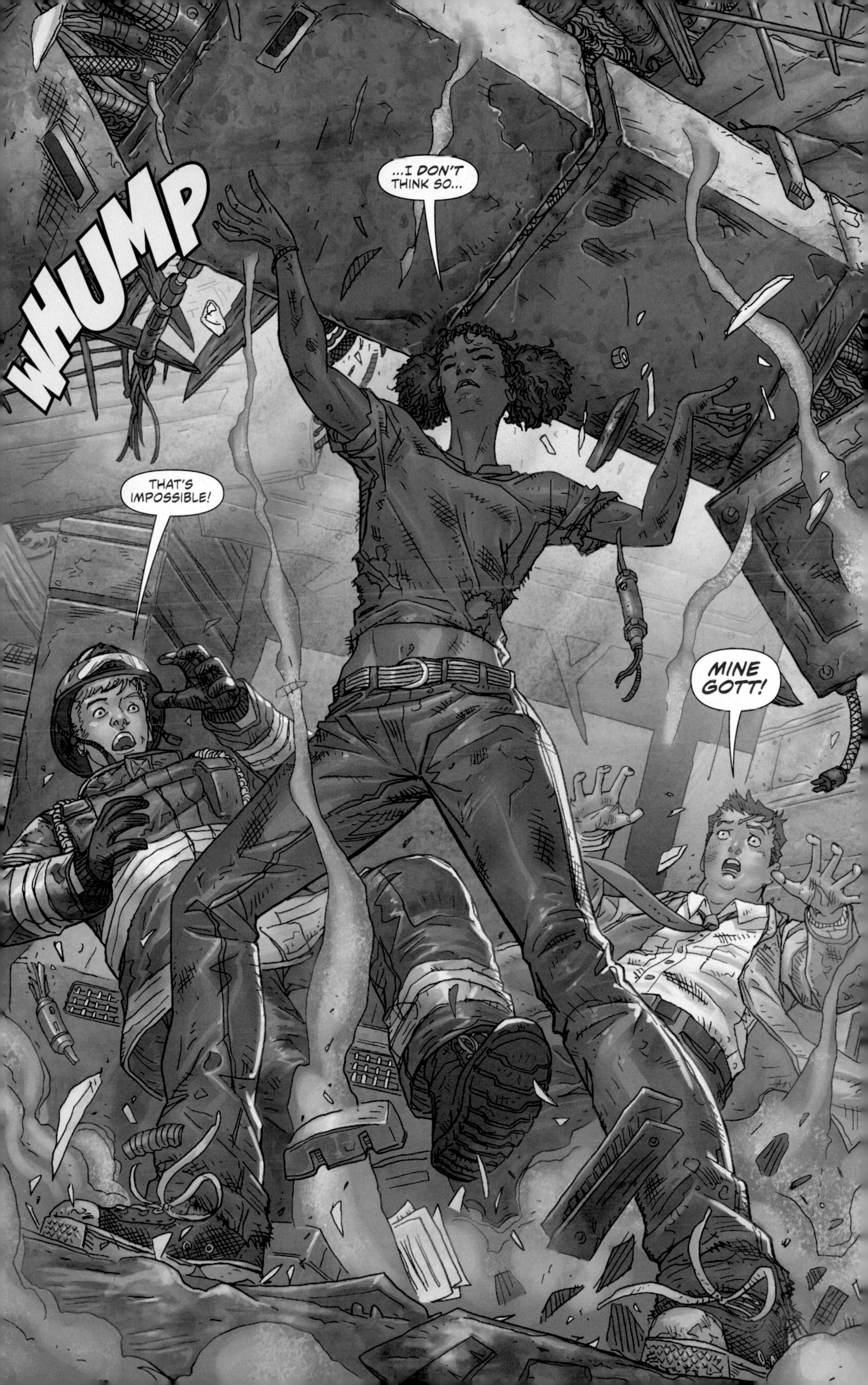
WHUMP
...I DON'T THINK SO...
THAT'S IMPOSSIBLE!
MINE GOTT!

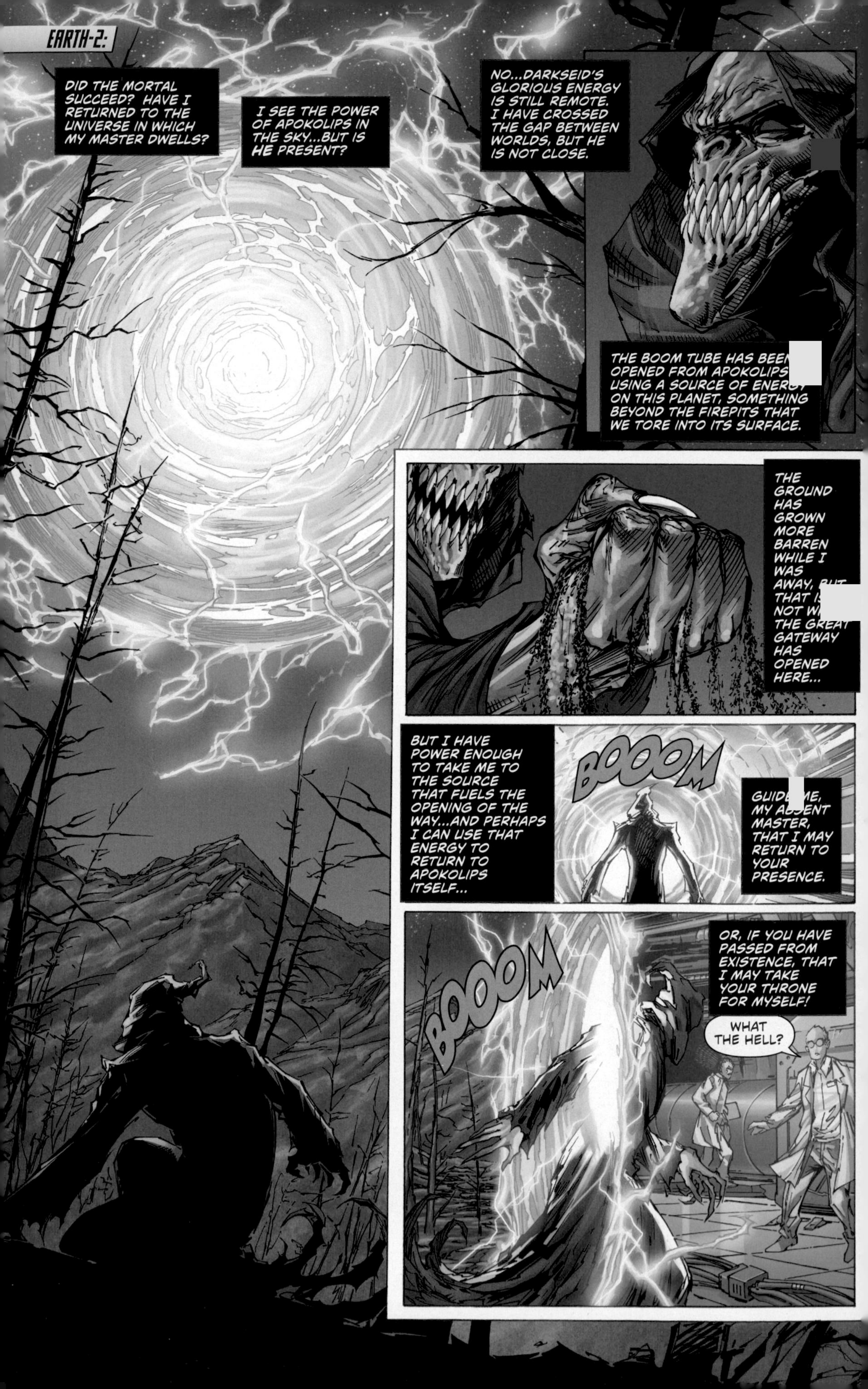

EARTH-2:
DID THE MORTAL SUCCEED? HAVE I RETURNED TO THE UNIVERSE IN WHICH MY MASTER DWELLS?
I SEE THE POWER OF APOKOLIPS IN THE SKY...BUT IS HE PRESENT?
NO...DARKSEID'S GLORIOUS ENERGY IS STILL REMOTE. I HAVE CROSSED THE GAP BETWEEN WORLDS, BUT HE IS NOT CLOSE.
THE BOOM TUBE HAS BEE OPENED FROM APOKOLIPS USING A SOURCE OF ENERG ON THIS PLANET, SOMETHING BEYOND THE FIREPITS THAT WE TORE INTO ITS SURFACE.
THE GROUND HAS GROWN MORE BARREN WHILE I WAS AWAY, BU THAT I NOT W THE GREAT GATEWAY HAS OPENED HERE...
BUT I HAVE POWER ENOUGH TO TAKE ME TO THE SOURCE THAT FUELS THE OPENING OF THE WAY...AND PERHAPS I CAN USE THAT ENERGY TO RETURN TO APOKOLIPS ITSELF...
BOOOM
GUIDE ME, MY AB ENT MASTER, THAT I MAY RETURN TO YOUR PRESENCE.
BOOOM
OR, IF YOU HAVE PASSED FROM EXISTENCE, THAT I MAY TAKE YOUR THRONE FOR MYSELF!
WHAT THE HELL?

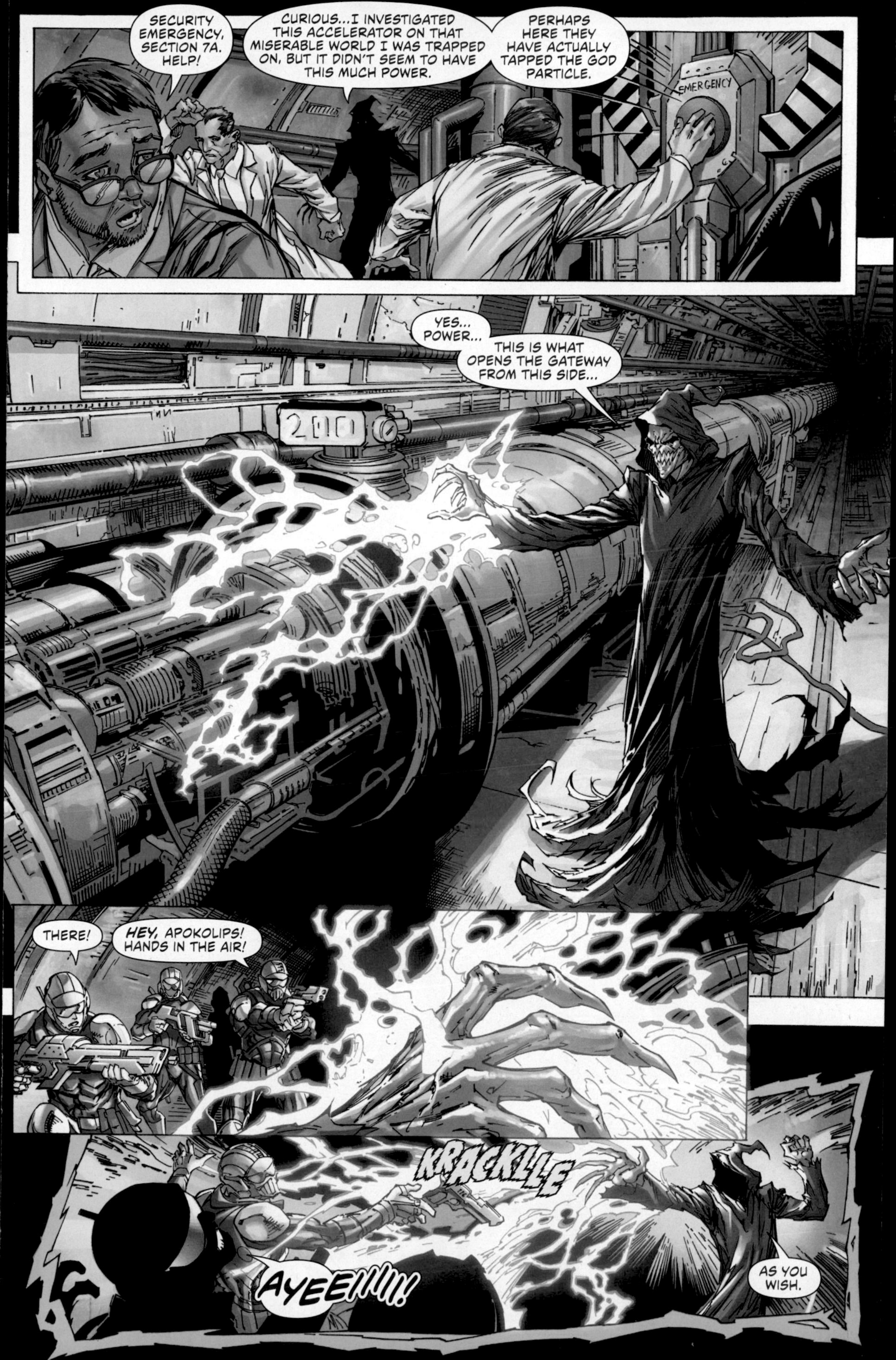
SECURITY EMERGENCY, SECTION 7A. HELP!
CURIOUS...I INVESTIGATED THIS ACCELERATOR ON THAT MISERABLE WORLD I WAS TRAPPED ON, BUT IT DIDN'T SEEM TO HAVE THIS MUCH POWER.
PERHAPS HERE THEY HAVE ACTUALLY TAPPED THE GOD PARTICLE.
EMERGENCY
YES... POWER...
THIS IS WHAT OPENS THE GATEWAY FROM THIS SIDE...
200
THERE!
HEY, APOKOLIPS! HANDS IN THE AIR!
KRACKLLE
AYEE!!!!!!
AS YOU WISH.

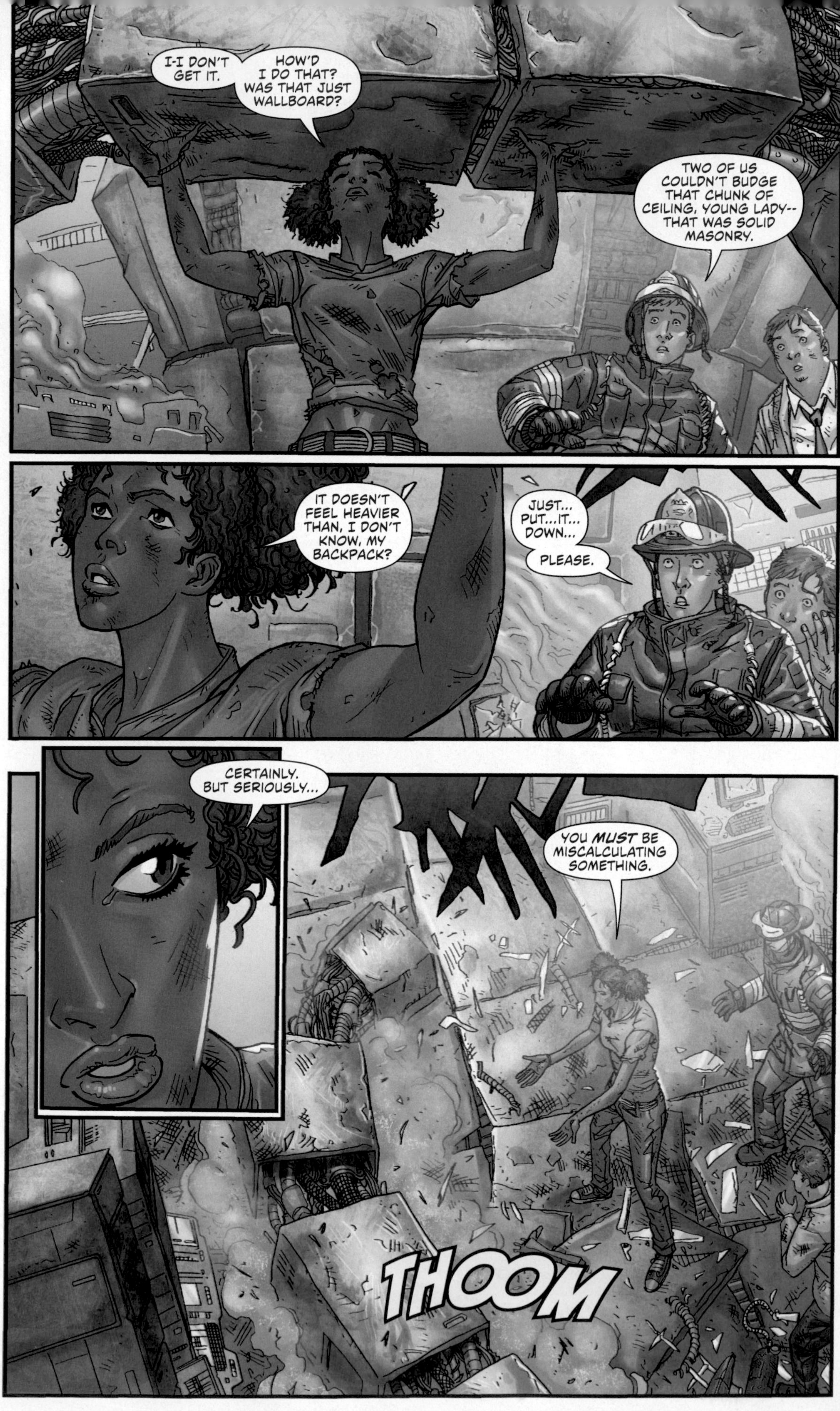
I-I DON'T GET IT.
HOW'D I DO THAT? WAS THAT JUST WALLBOARD?
TWO OF US COULDN'T BUDGE THAT CHUNK OF CEILING, YOUNG LADY--THAT WAS SOLID MASONRY.
IT DOESN'T FEEL HEAVIER THAN, I DON'T KNOW, MY BACKPACK?
JUST... PUT...IT... DOWN...
PLEASE.
CERTAINLY. BUT SERIOUSLY...
YOU *MUST* BE MISCALCULATING SOMETHING.
THOOM

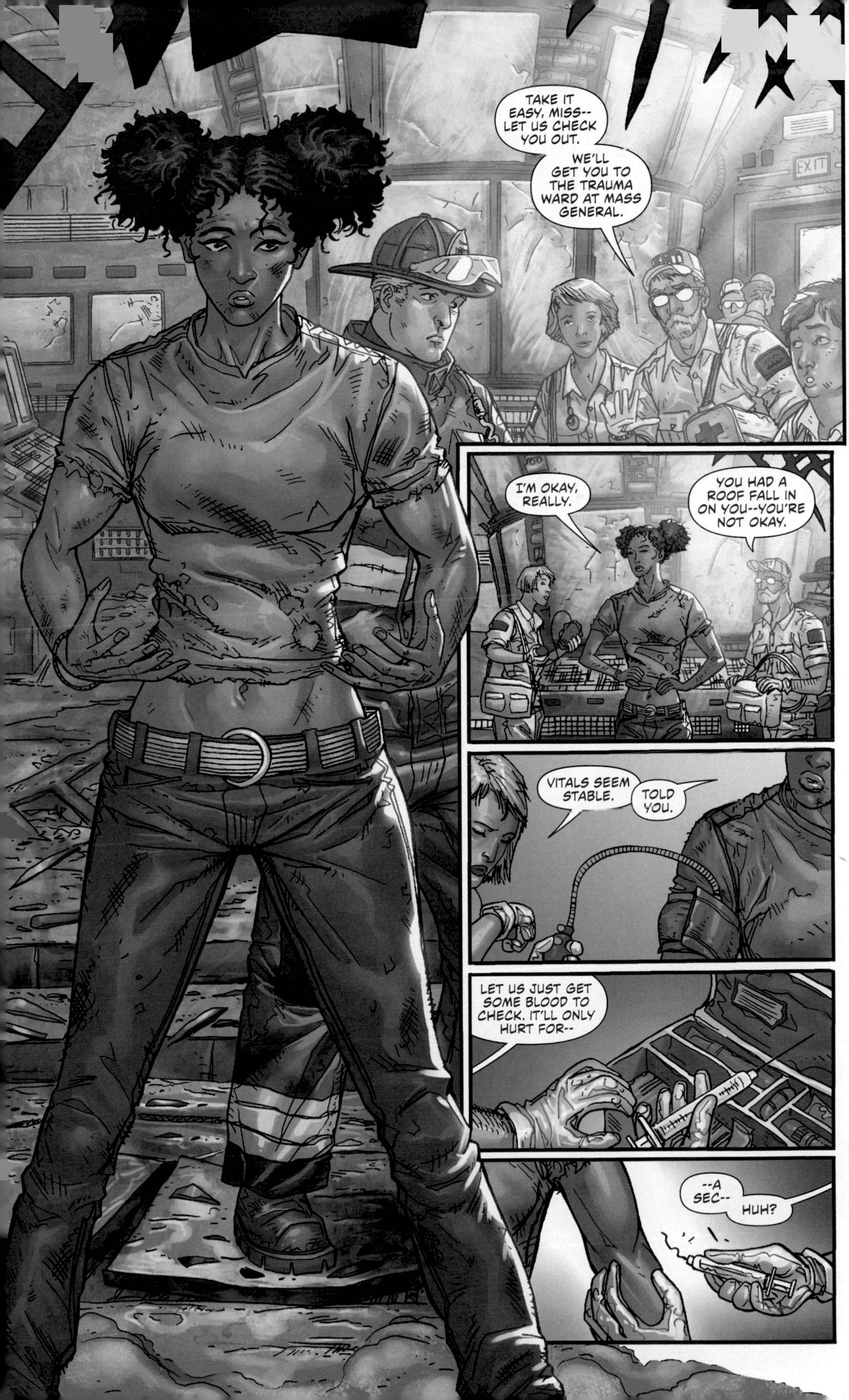
TAKE IT EASY, MISS-- LET US CHECK YOU OUT.
WE'LL GET YOU TO THE TRAUMA WARD AT MASS GENERAL.
EXIT
I'M OKAY, REALLY.
YOU HAD A ROOF FALL IN ON YOU--YOU'RE NOT OKAY.
VITALS SEEM STABLE.
TOLD YOU.
LET US JUST GET SOME BLOOD TO CHECK. IT'LL ONLY HURT FOR--
--A SEC--
HUH?

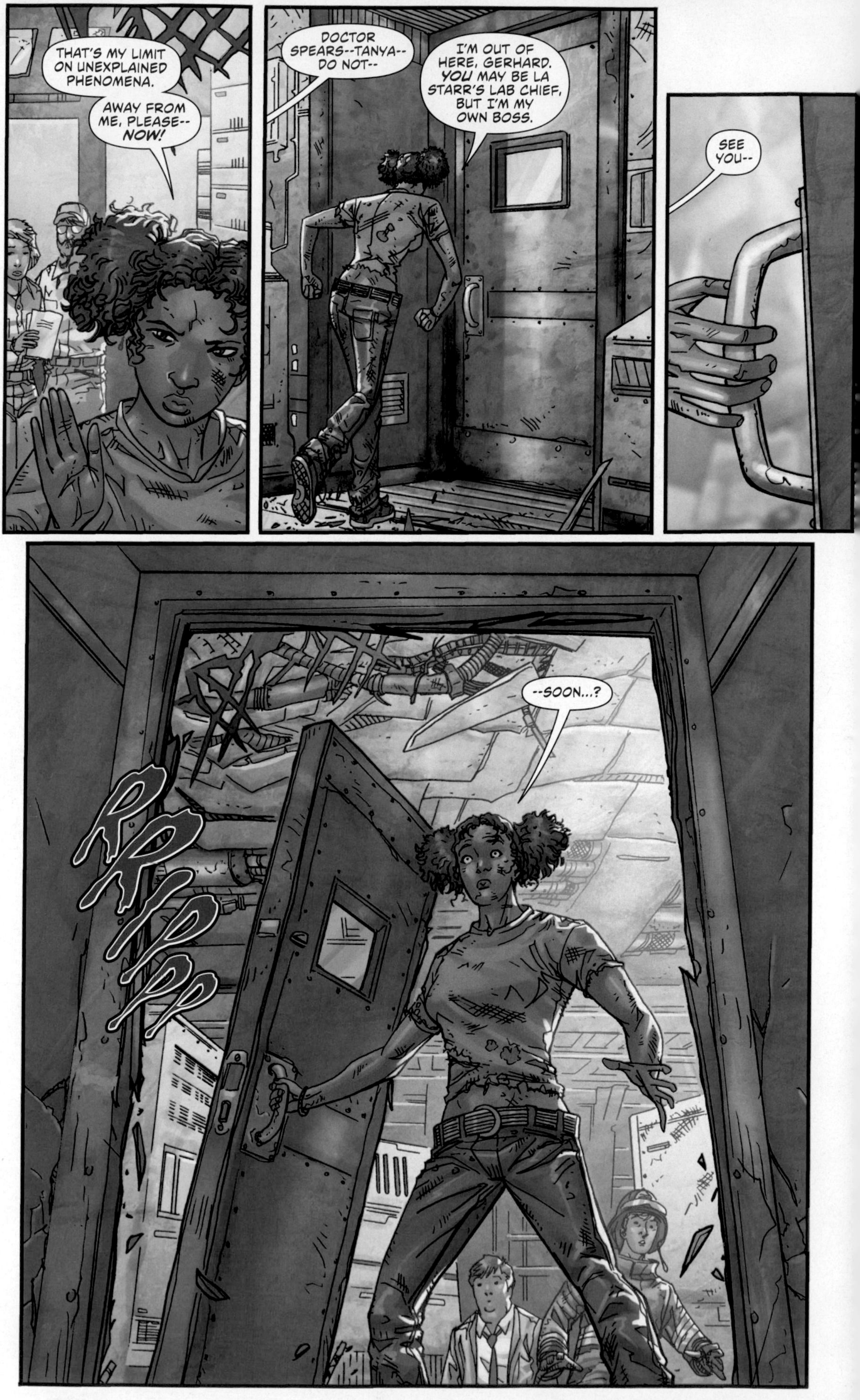
THAT'S MY LIMIT ON UNEXPLAINED PHENOMENA.
AWAY FROM ME, PLEASE-- NOW!
DOCTOR SPEARS--TANYA-- DO NOT--
I'M OUT OF HERE, GERHARD. YOU MAY BE LA STARR'S LAB CHIEF, BUT I'M MY OWN BOSS.
SEE YOU--
--SOON...?
RRIPPP

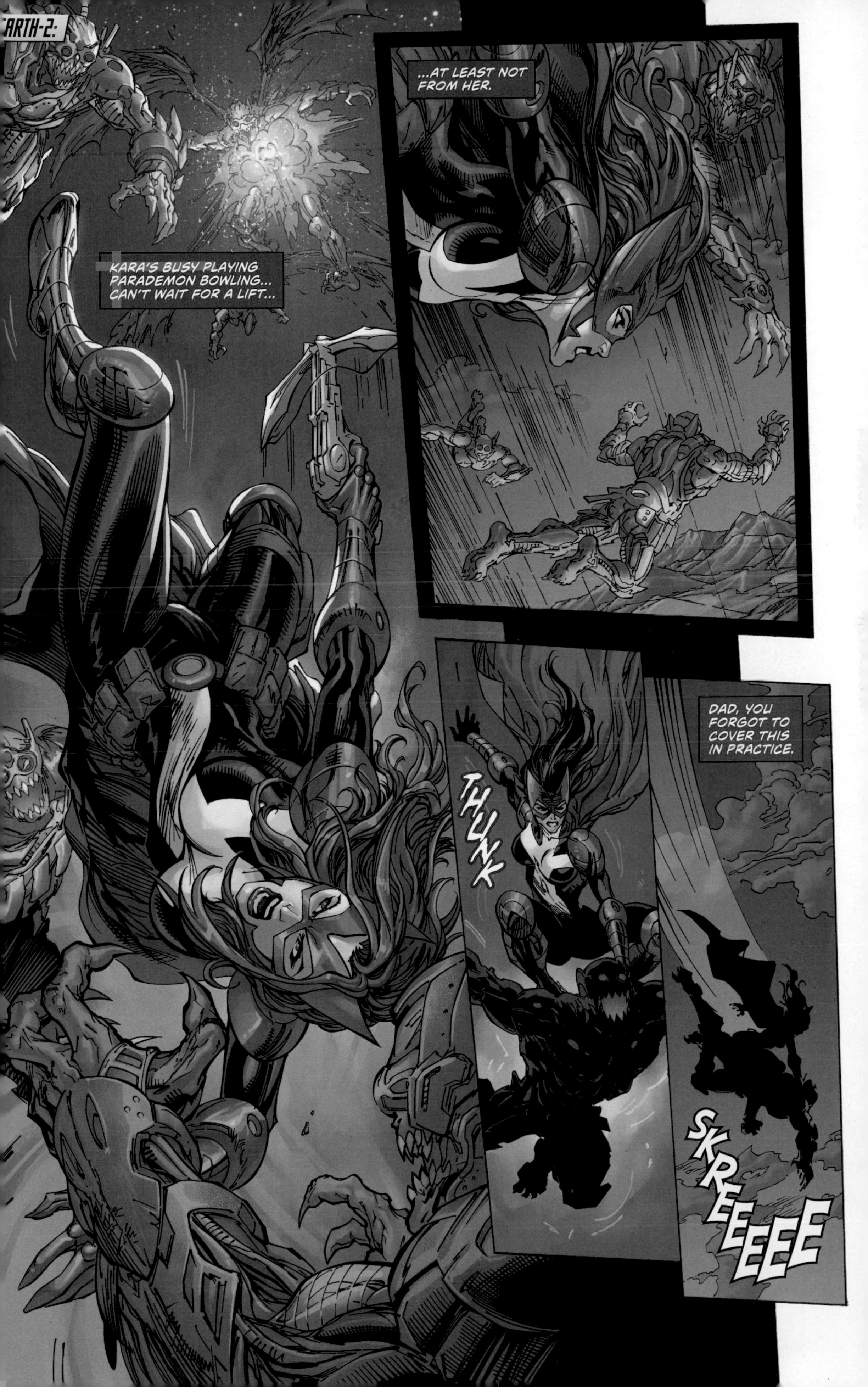
ARTH-2:
KARA'S BUSY PLAYING PARADEMON BOWLING... CAN'T WAIT FOR A LIFT...
...AT LEAST NOT FROM HER.
THUNK
DAD, YOU FORGOT TO COVER THIS IN PRACTICE.
SKREEEEEE

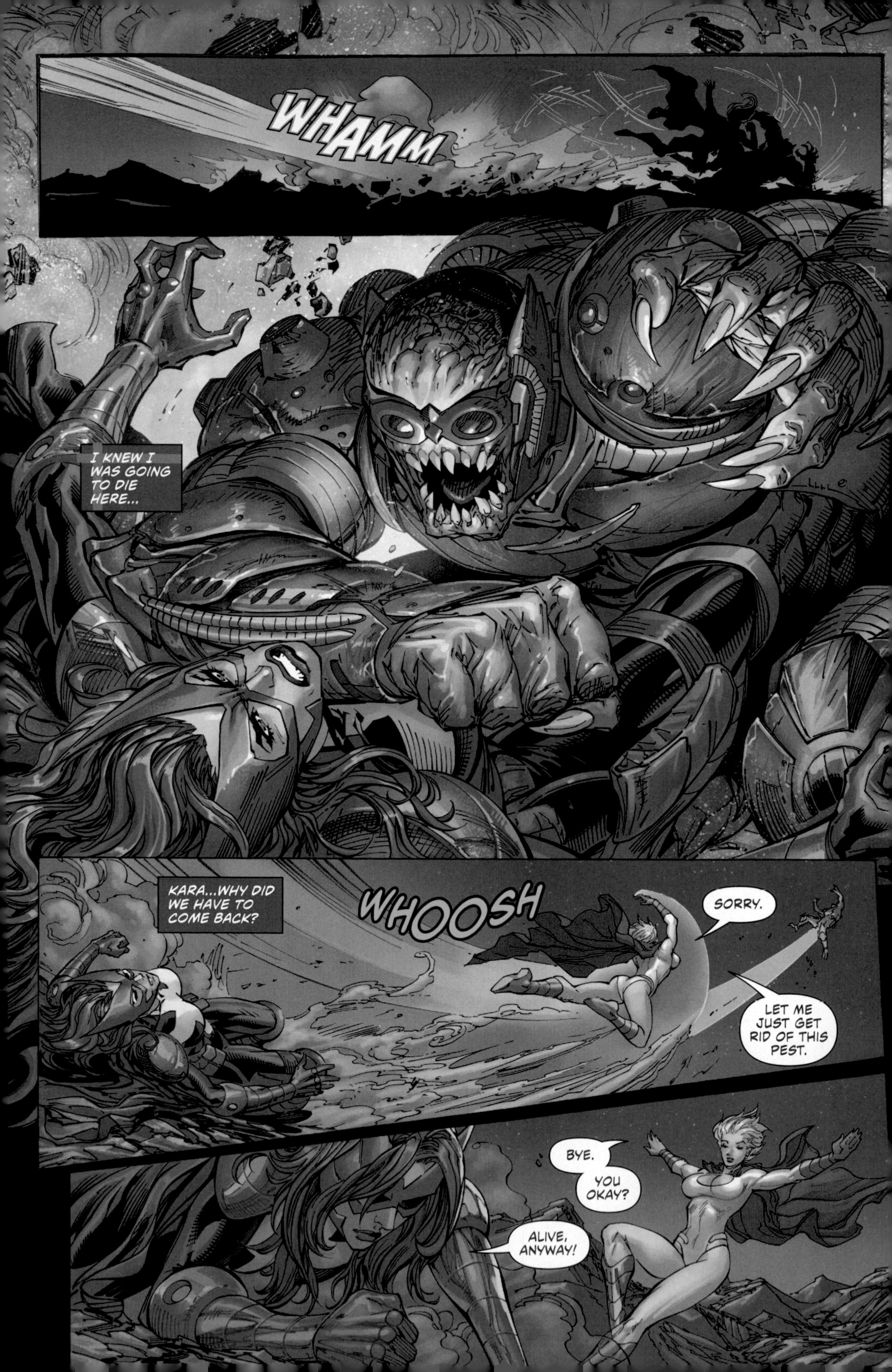
WHAMM
I KNEW I WAS GOING TO DIE HERE...
KARA...WHY DID WE HAVE TO COME BACK?
WHOOSH
SORRY.
LET ME JUST GET RID OF THIS PEST.
BYE.
YOU OKAY?
ALIVE, ANYWAY!

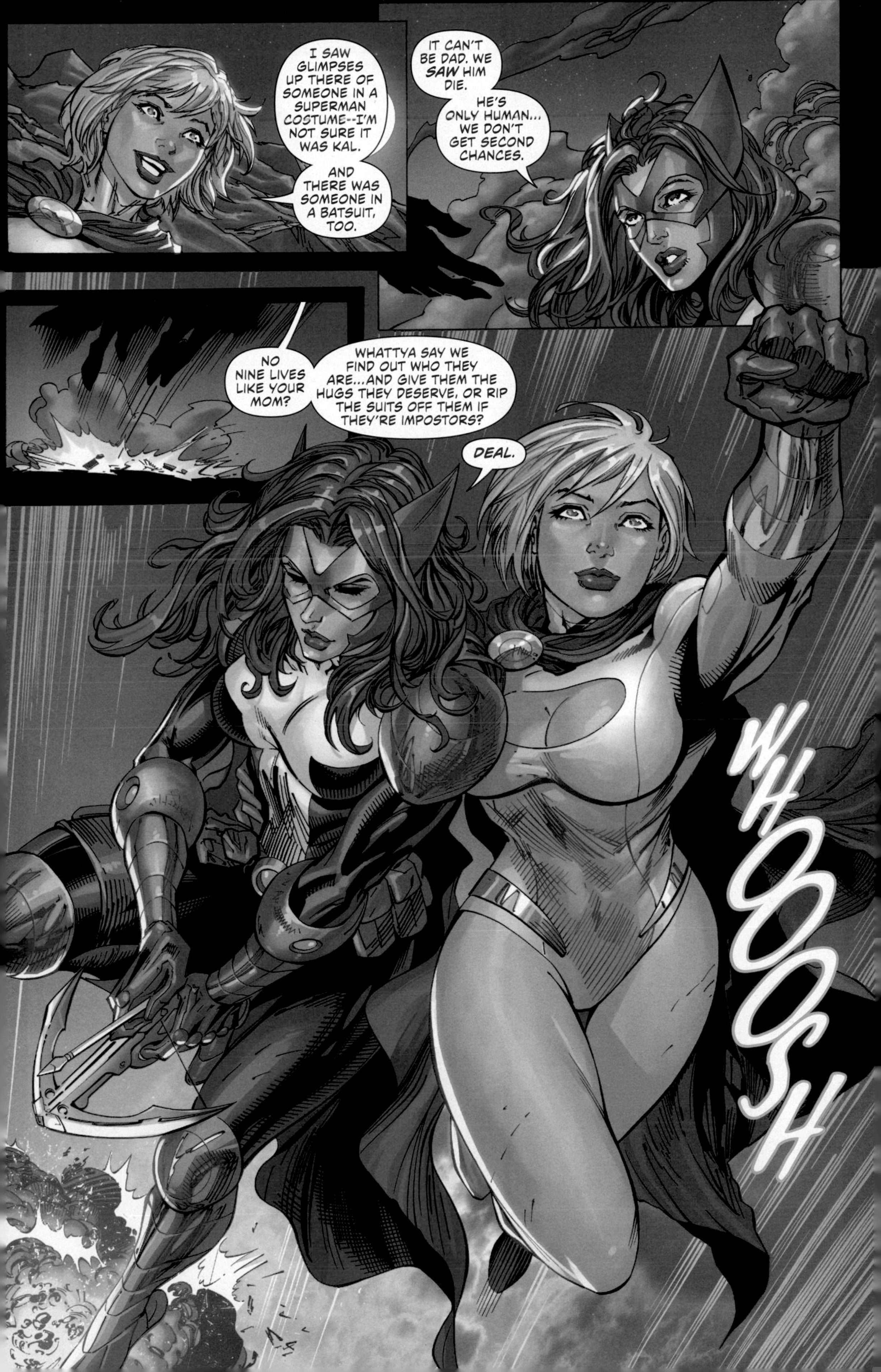
I SAW GLIMPSES UP THERE OF SOMEONE IN A SUPERMAN COSTUME--I'M NOT SURE IT WAS KAL.
AND THERE WAS SOMEONE IN A BATSUIT, TOO.
IT CAN'T BE DAD. WE SAW HIM DIE.
HE'S ONLY HUMAN... WE DON'T GET SECOND CHANCES.
NO NINE LIVES LIKE YOUR MOM?
WHATTYA SAY WE FIND OUT WHO THEY ARE...AND GIVE THEM THE HUGS THEY DESERVE, OR RIP THE SUITS OFF THEM IF THEY'RE IMPOSTORS?
DEAL.
WHOOOSH

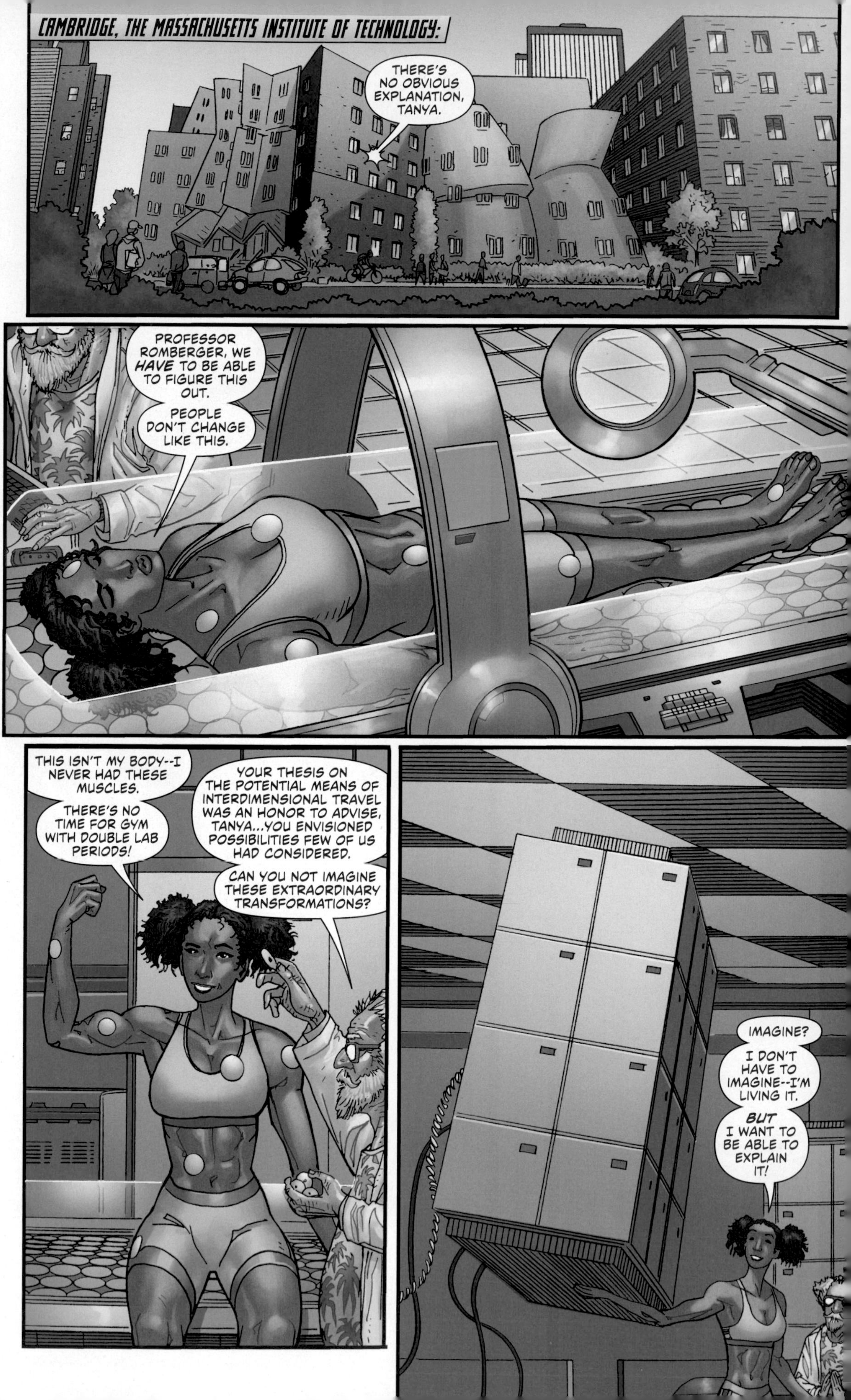
CAMBRIDGE, THE MASSACHUSETTS INSTITUTE OF TECHNOLOGY:
THERE'S NO OBVIOUS EXPLANATION, TANYA.
PROFESSOR ROMBERGER, WE *HAVE* TO BE ABLE TO FIGURE THIS OUT.
PEOPLE DON'T CHANGE LIKE THIS.
THIS ISN'T MY BODY--I NEVER HAD THESE MUSCLES.
THERE'S NO TIME FOR GYM WITH DOUBLE LAB PERIODS!
YOUR THESIS ON THE POTENTIAL MEANS OF INTERDIMENSIONAL TRAVEL WAS AN HONOR TO ADVISE, TANYA...YOU ENVISIONED POSSIBILITIES FEW OF US HAD CONSIDERED.
CAN YOU NOT IMAGINE THESE EXTRAORDINARY TRANSFORMATIONS?
IMAGINE?
I DON'T HAVE TO IMAGINE--I'M LIVING IT.
BUT I WANT TO BE ABLE TO EXPLAIN IT!

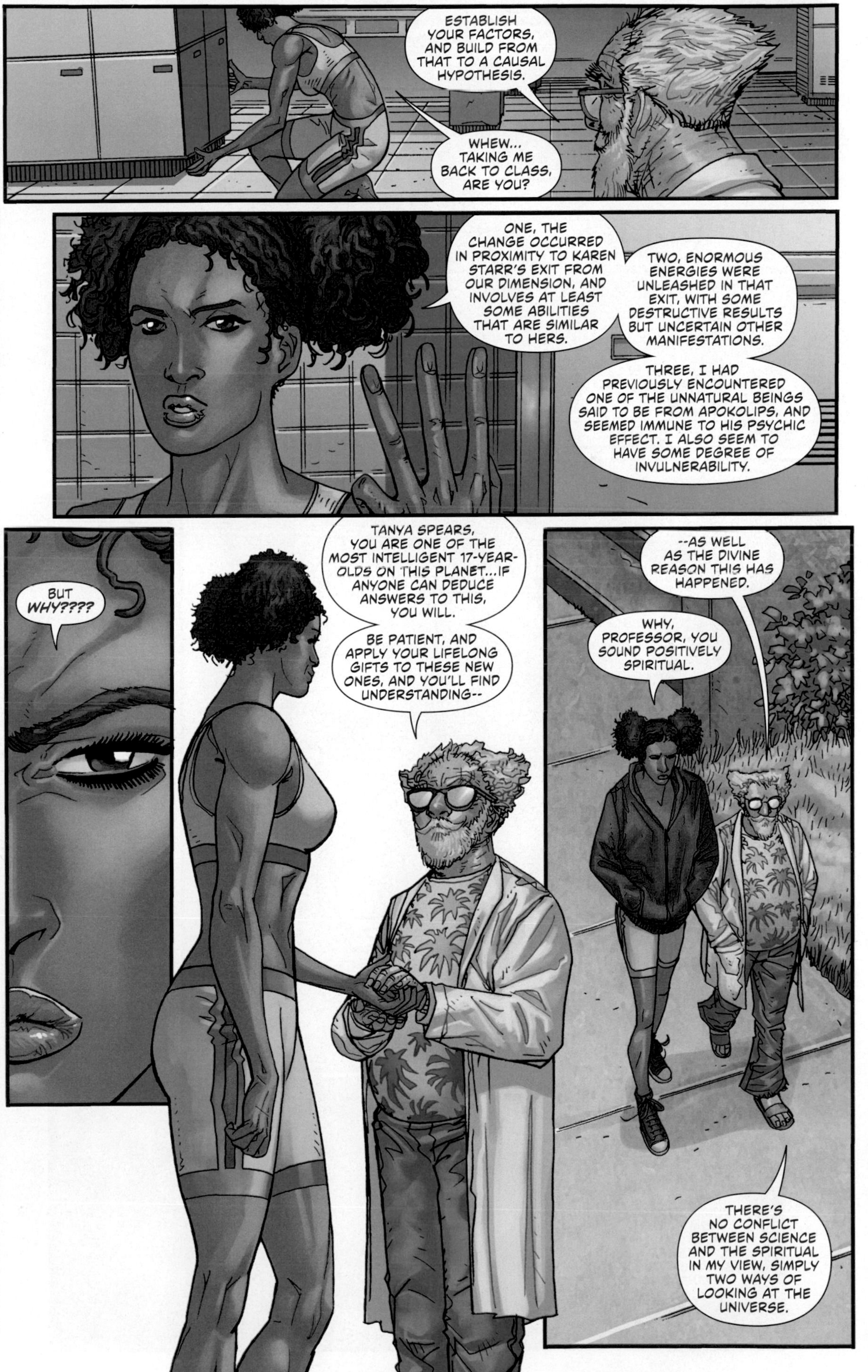
ESTABLISH YOUR FACTORS, AND BUILD FROM THAT TO A CAUSAL HYPOTHESIS.
WHEW... TAKING ME BACK TO CLASS, ARE YOU?
ONE, THE CHANGE OCCURRED IN PROXIMITY TO KAREN STARR'S EXIT FROM OUR DIMENSION, AND INVOLVES AT LEAST SOME ABILITIES THAT ARE SIMILAR TO HERS.
TWO, ENORMOUS ENERGIES WERE UNLEASHED IN THAT EXIT, WITH SOME DESTRUCTIVE RESULTS BUT UNCERTAIN OTHER MANIFESTATIONS.
THREE, I HAD PREVIOUSLY ENCOUNTERED ONE OF THE UNNATURAL BEINGS SAID TO BE FROM APOKOLIPS, AND SEEMED IMMUNE TO HIS PSYCHIC EFFECT. I ALSO SEEM TO HAVE SOME DEGREE OF INVULNERABILITY.
BUT *WHY????*
TANYA SPEARS, YOU ARE ONE OF THE MOST INTELLIGENT 17-YEAR-OLDS ON THIS PLANET...IF ANYONE CAN DEDUCE ANSWERS TO THIS, YOU WILL.
BE PATIENT, AND APPLY YOUR LIFELONG GIFTS TO THESE NEW ONES, AND YOU'LL FIND UNDERSTANDING--
--AS WELL AS THE DIVINE REASON THIS HAS HAPPENED.
WHY, PROFESSOR, YOU SOUND POSITIVELY SPIRITUAL.
THERE'S NO CONFLICT BETWEEN SCIENCE AND THE SPIRITUAL IN MY VIEW, SIMPLY TWO WAYS OF LOOKING AT THE UNIVERSE.

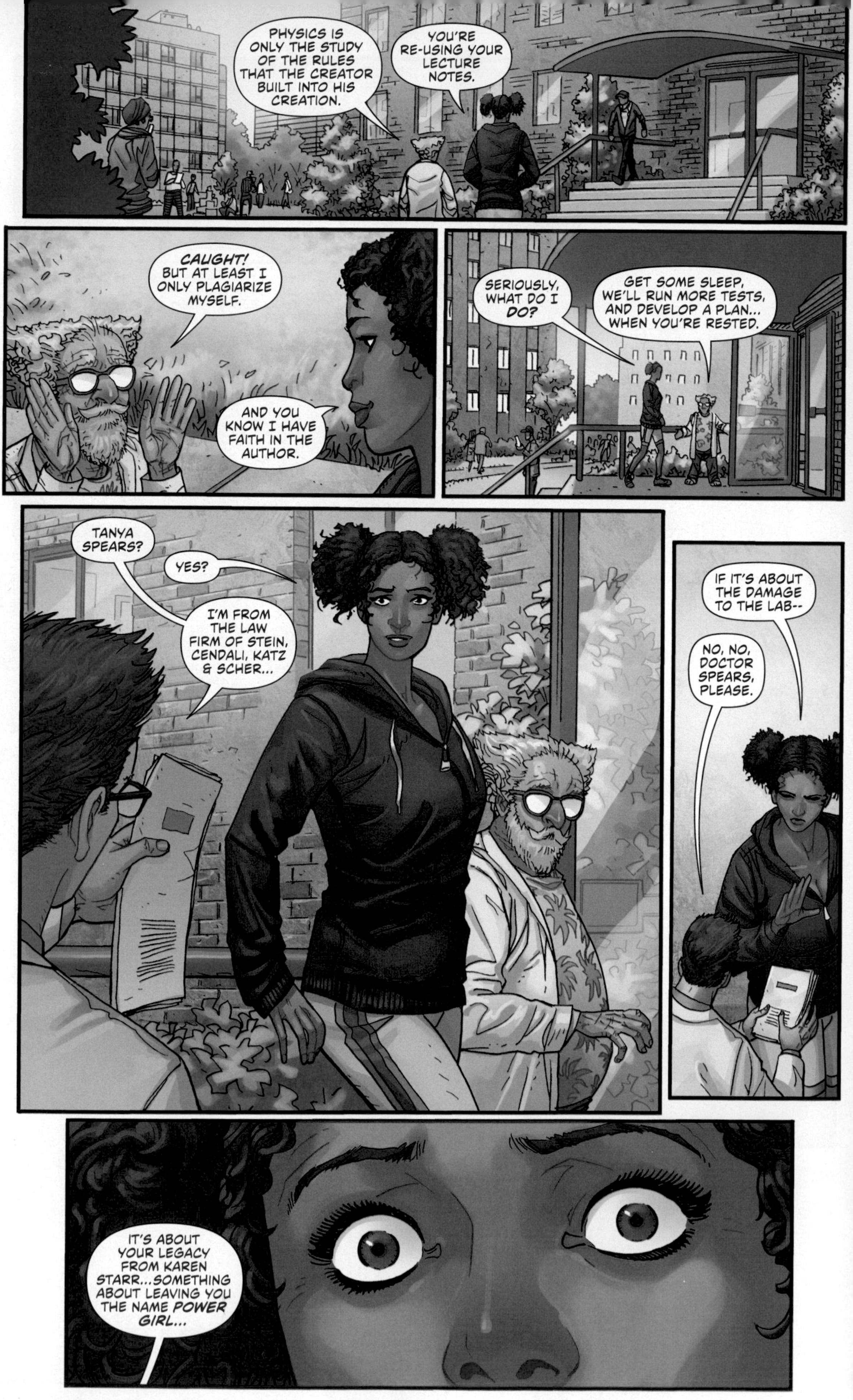
PHYSICS IS ONLY THE STUDY OF THE RULES THAT THE CREATOR BUILT INTO HIS CREATION.
YOU'RE RE-USING YOUR LECTURE NOTES.
CAUGHT! BUT AT LEAST I ONLY PLAGIARIZE MYSELF.
AND YOU KNOW I HAVE FAITH IN THE AUTHOR.
SERIOUSLY, WHAT DO I *DO?*
GET SOME SLEEP, WE'LL RUN MORE TESTS, AND DEVELOP A PLAN... WHEN YOU'RE RESTED.
TANYA SPEARS?
YES?
I'M FROM THE LAW FIRM OF STEIN, CENDALI, KATZ & SCHER...
IF IT'S ABOUT THE DAMAGE TO THE LAB--
NO, NO, DOCTOR SPEARS, PLEASE.
IT'S ABOUT YOUR LEGACY FROM KAREN STARR...SOMETHING ABOUT LEAVING YOU THE NAME *POWER GIRL*...

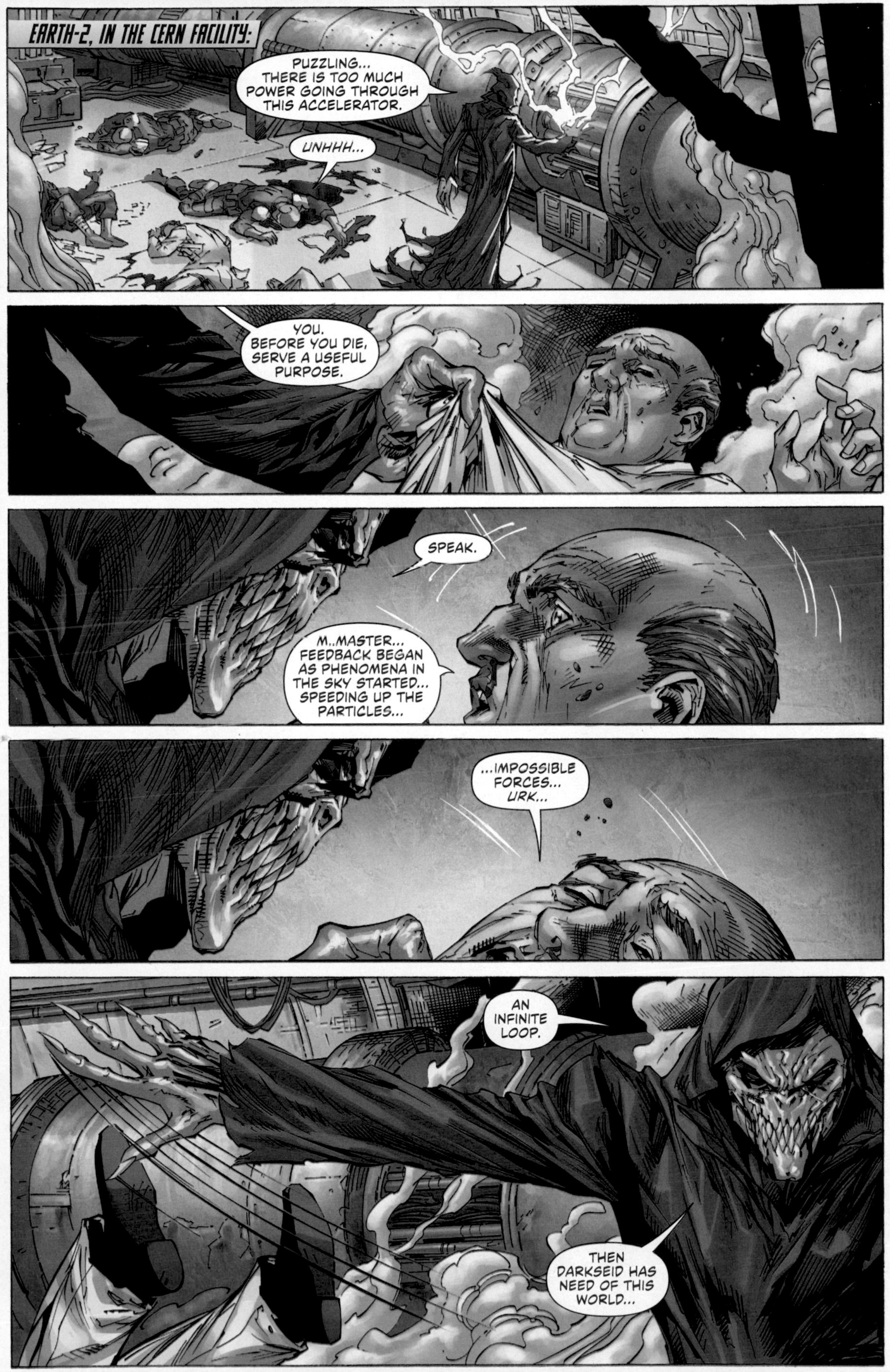
EARTH-2, IN THE CERN FACILITY:
PUZZLING... THERE IS TOO MUCH POWER GOING THROUGH THIS ACCELERATOR.
UNHHH...
YOU. BEFORE YOU DIE, SERVE A USEFUL PURPOSE.
SPEAK.
M..MASTER... FEEDBACK BEGAN AS PHENOMENA IN THE SKY STARTED... SPEEDING UP THE PARTICLES...
...IMPOSSIBLE FORCES... URK...
AN INFINITE LOOP.
THEN DARKSEID HAS NEED OF THIS WORLD...

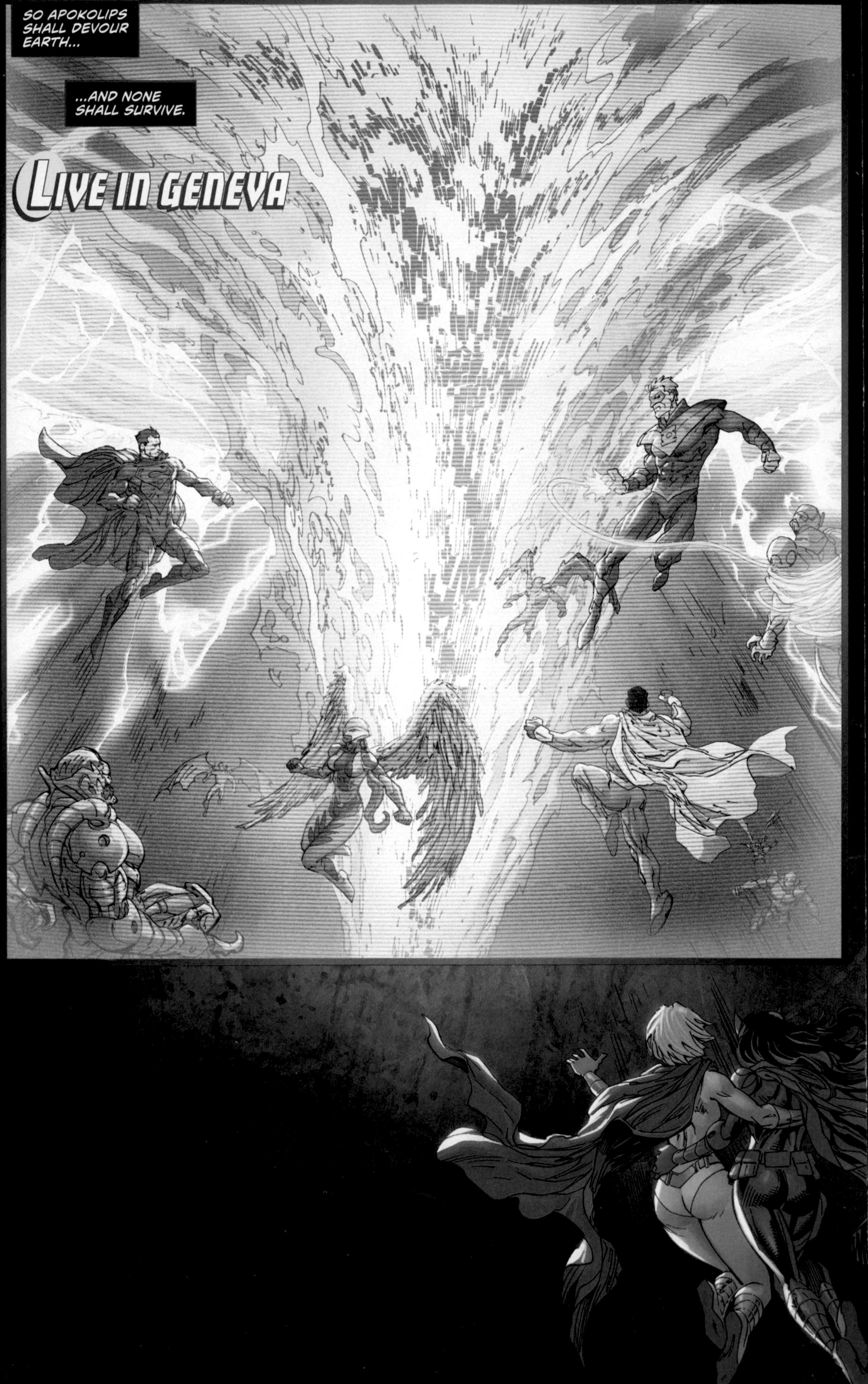
SO APOKOLIPS SHALL DEVOUR EARTH...
...AND NONE SHALL SURVIVE.
LIVE IN GENEVA

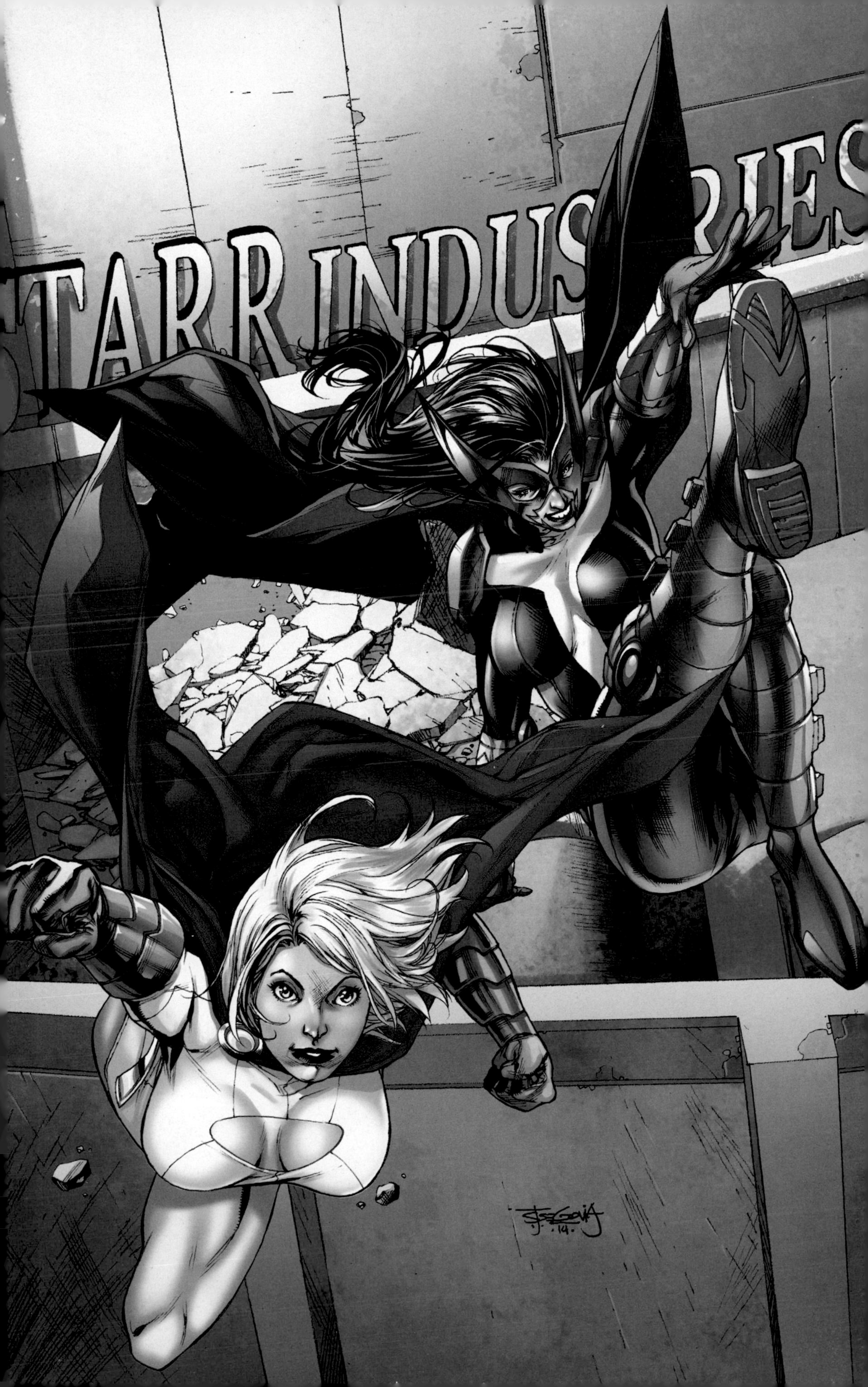
TARR INDUS RIES

BREAKING

PAUL LEVITZ writer **YILDIRAY CINAR** artist **JASON WRIGHT** colorist **CARLOS M. MANGUAL** letterer

cover by **STEPHEN SEGOVIA** and **MIKE ATIYEH**

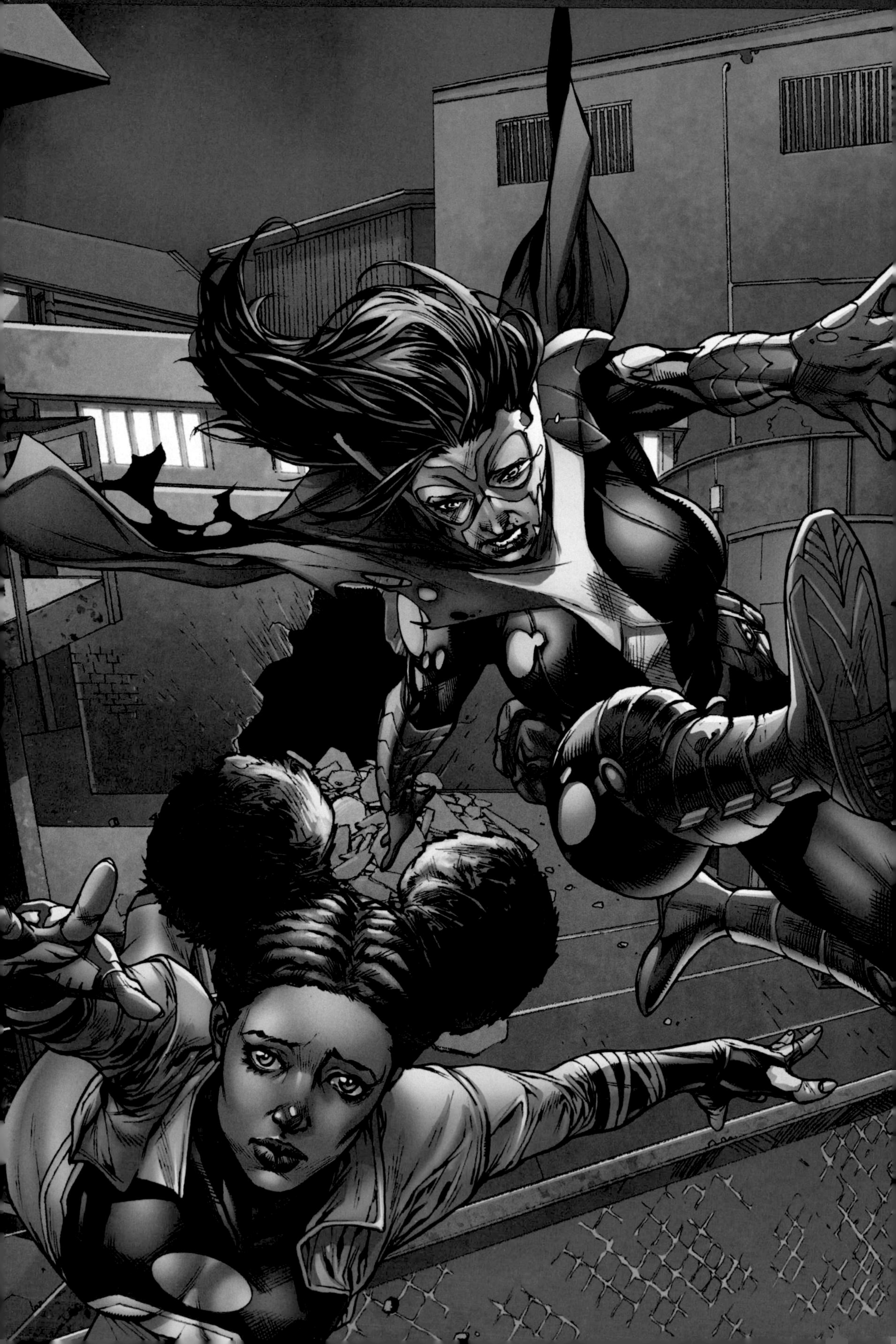

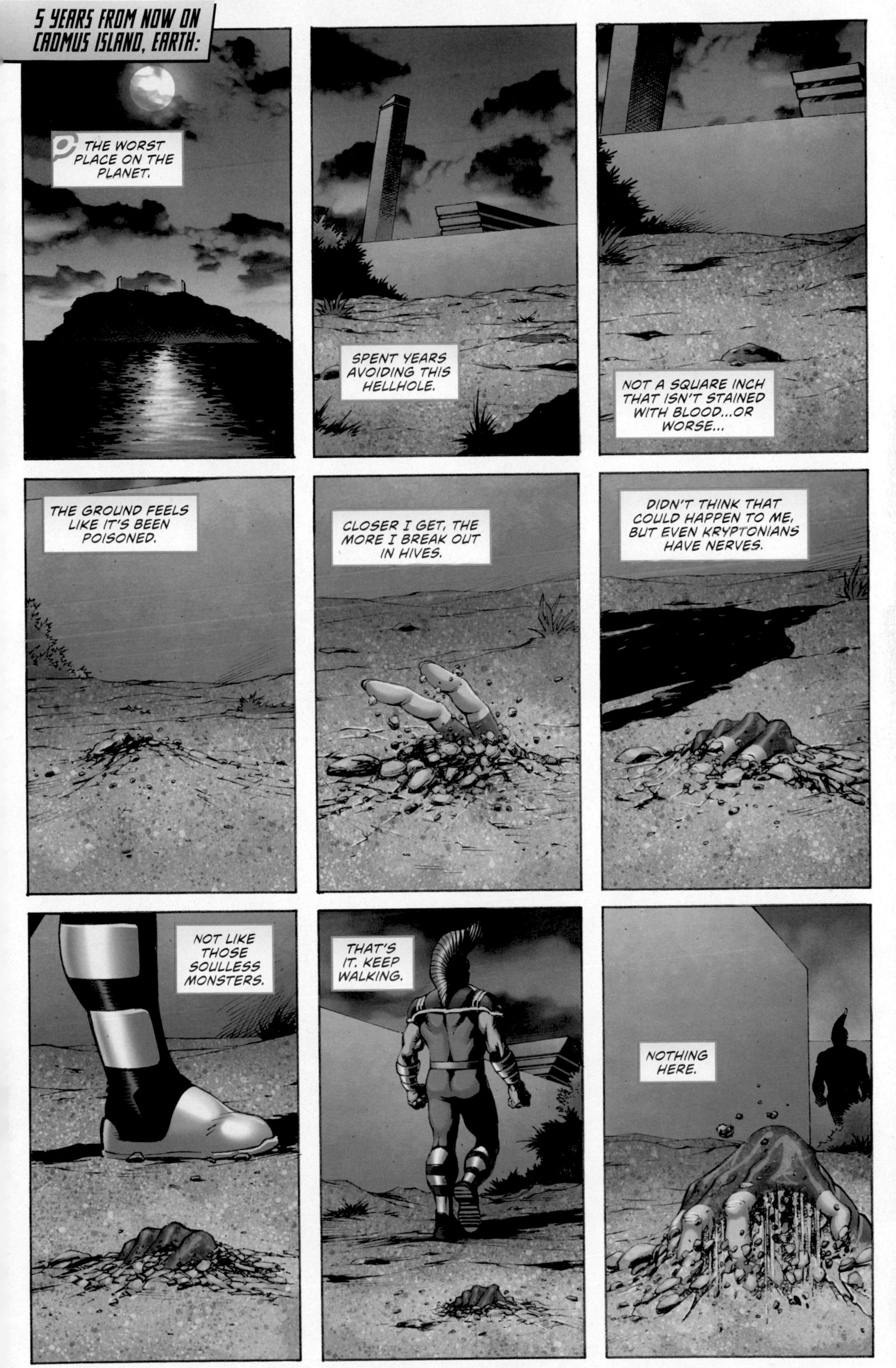
5 YEARS FROM NOW ON CADMUS ISLAND, EARTH:
THE WORST PLACE ON THE PLANET.
SPENT YEARS AVOIDING THIS HELLHOLE.
NOT A SQUARE INCH THAT ISN'T STAINED WITH BLOOD...OR WORSE...
THE GROUND FEELS LIKE IT'S BEEN POISONED.
CLOSER I GET, THE MORE I BREAK OUT IN HIVES.
DIDN'T THINK THAT COULD HAPPEN TO ME, BUT EVEN KRYPTONIANS HAVE NERVES.
NOT LIKE THOSE SOULLESS MONSTERS.
THAT'S IT. KEEP WALKING.
NOTHING HERE.

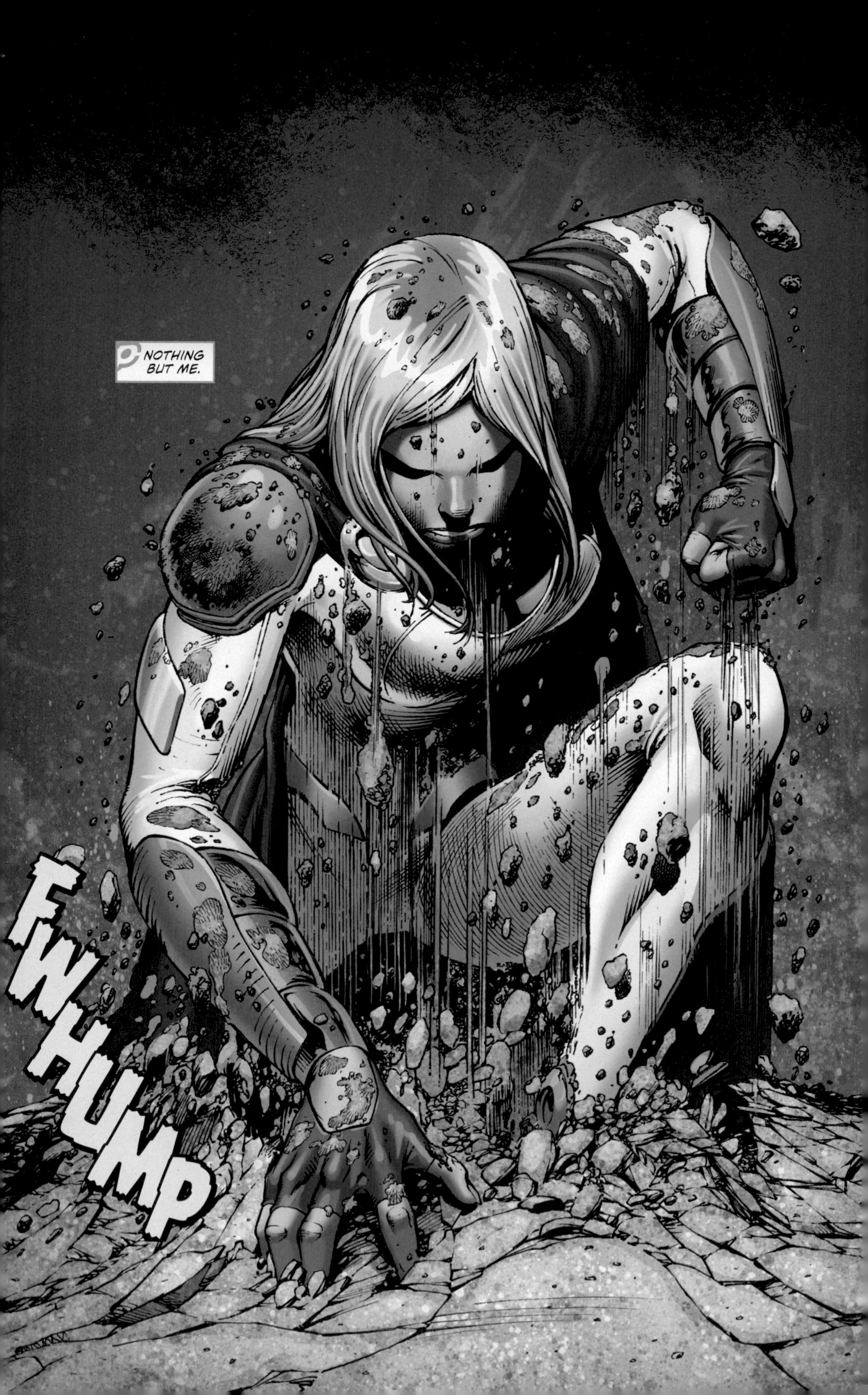
NOTHING BUT ME.
FWHUMP

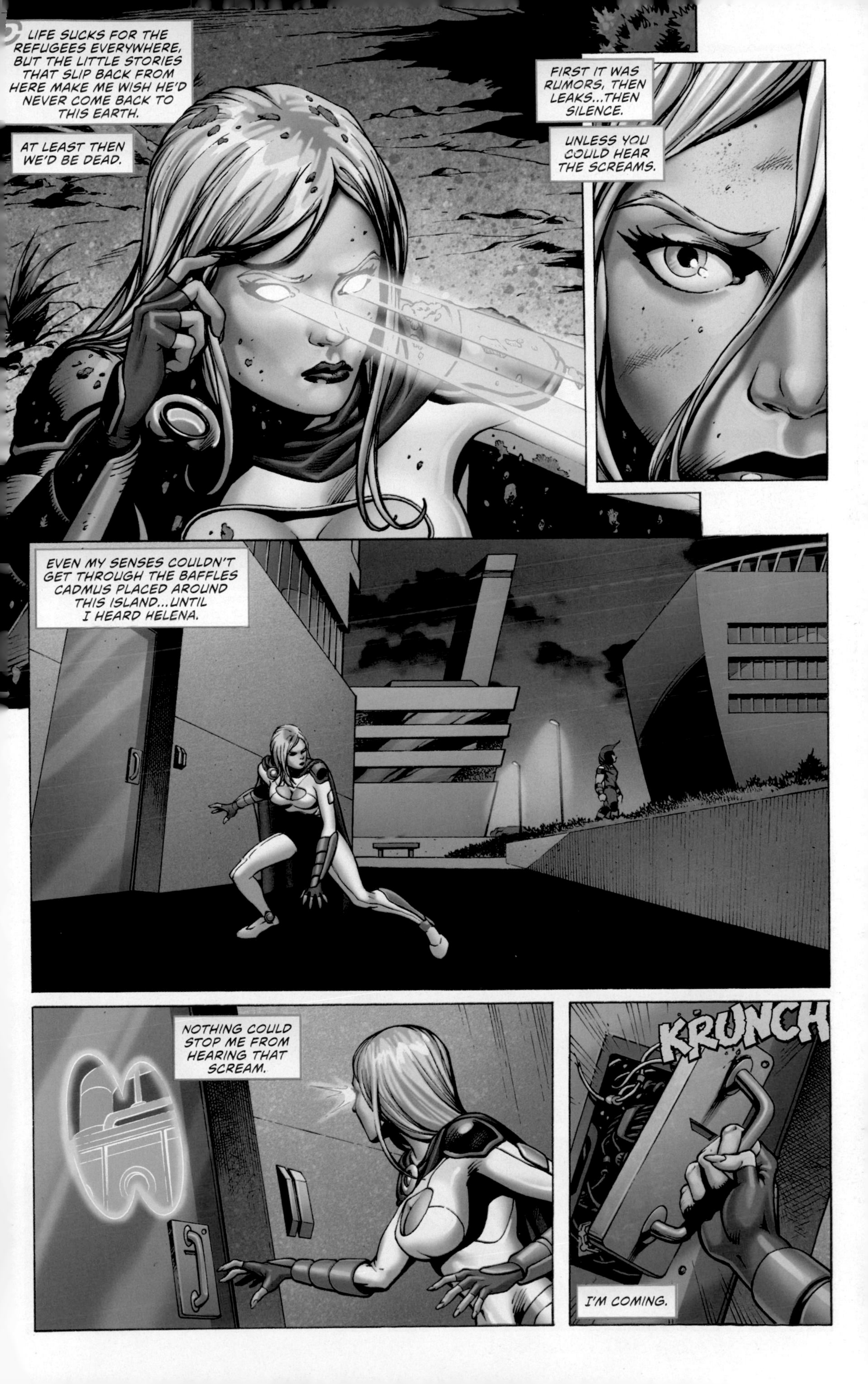
LIFE SUCKS FOR THE REFUGEES EVERYWHERE, BUT THE LITTLE STORIES THAT SLIP BACK FROM HERE MAKE ME WISH HE'D NEVER COME BACK TO THIS EARTH.
AT LEAST THEN WE'D BE DEAD.
FIRST IT WAS RUMORS, THEN LEAKS...THEN SILENCE.
UNLESS YOU COULD HEAR THE SCREAMS.
EVEN MY SENSES COULDN'T GET THROUGH THE BAFFLES CADMUS PLACED AROUND THIS ISLAND...UNTIL I HEARD HELENA.
NOTHING COULD STOP ME FROM HEARING THAT SCREAM.
KRUNCH
I'M COMING.

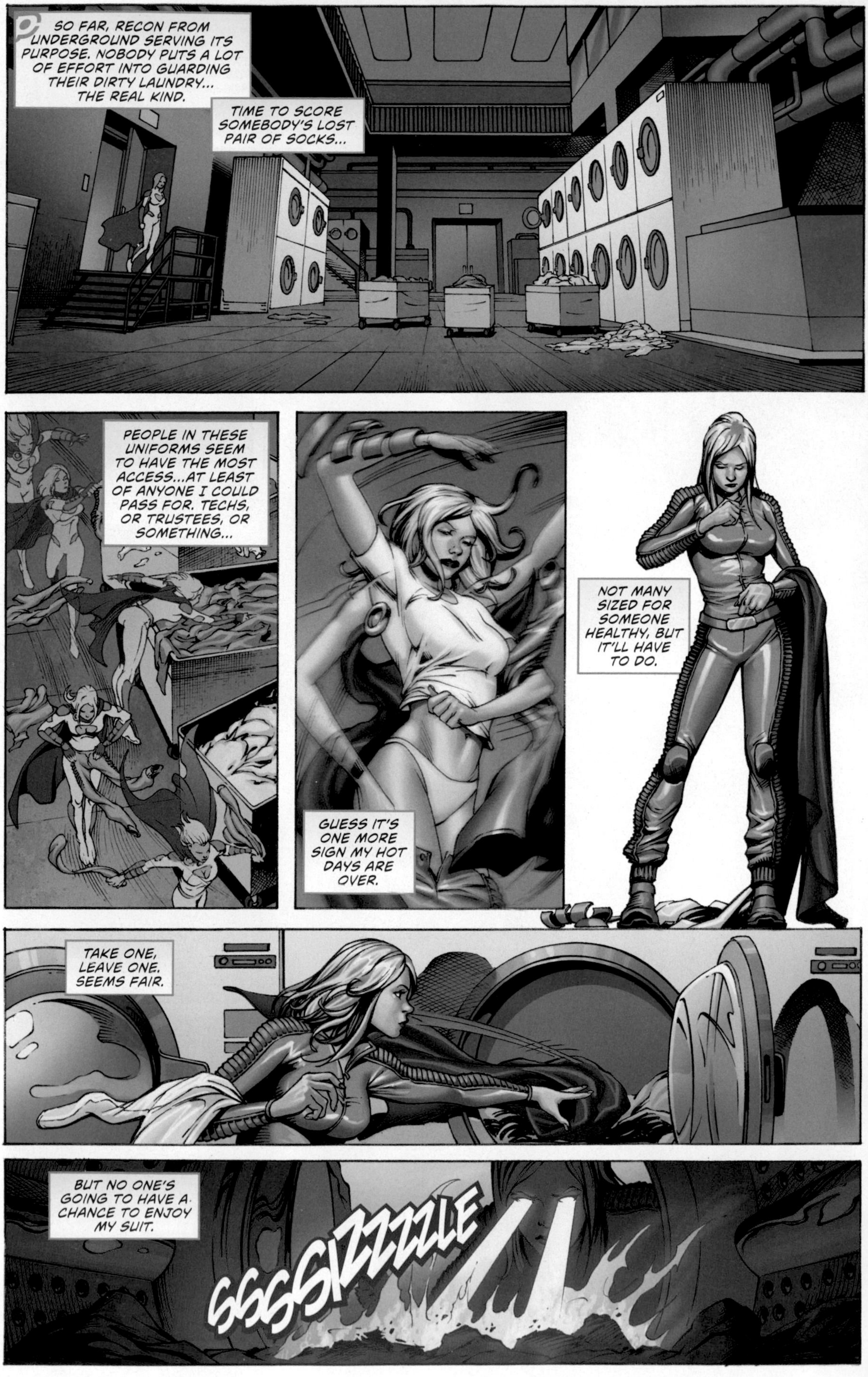
SO FAR, RECON FROM UNDERGROUND SERVING ITS PURPOSE. NOBODY PUTS A LOT OF EFFORT INTO GUARDING THEIR DIRTY LAUNDRY... THE REAL KIND.
TIME TO SCORE SOMEBODY'S LOST PAIR OF SOCKS...
PEOPLE IN THESE UNIFORMS SEEM TO HAVE THE MOST ACCESS...AT LEAST OF ANYONE I COULD PASS FOR. TECHS, OR TRUSTEES, OR SOMETHING...
GUESS IT'S ONE MORE SIGN MY HOT DAYS ARE OVER.
NOT MANY SIZED FOR SOMEONE HEALTHY, BUT IT'LL HAVE TO DO.
TAKE ONE, LEAVE ONE. SEEMS FAIR.
BUT NO ONE'S GOING TO HAVE A CHANCE TO ENJOY MY SUIT.
SSSSIZZZZZLE

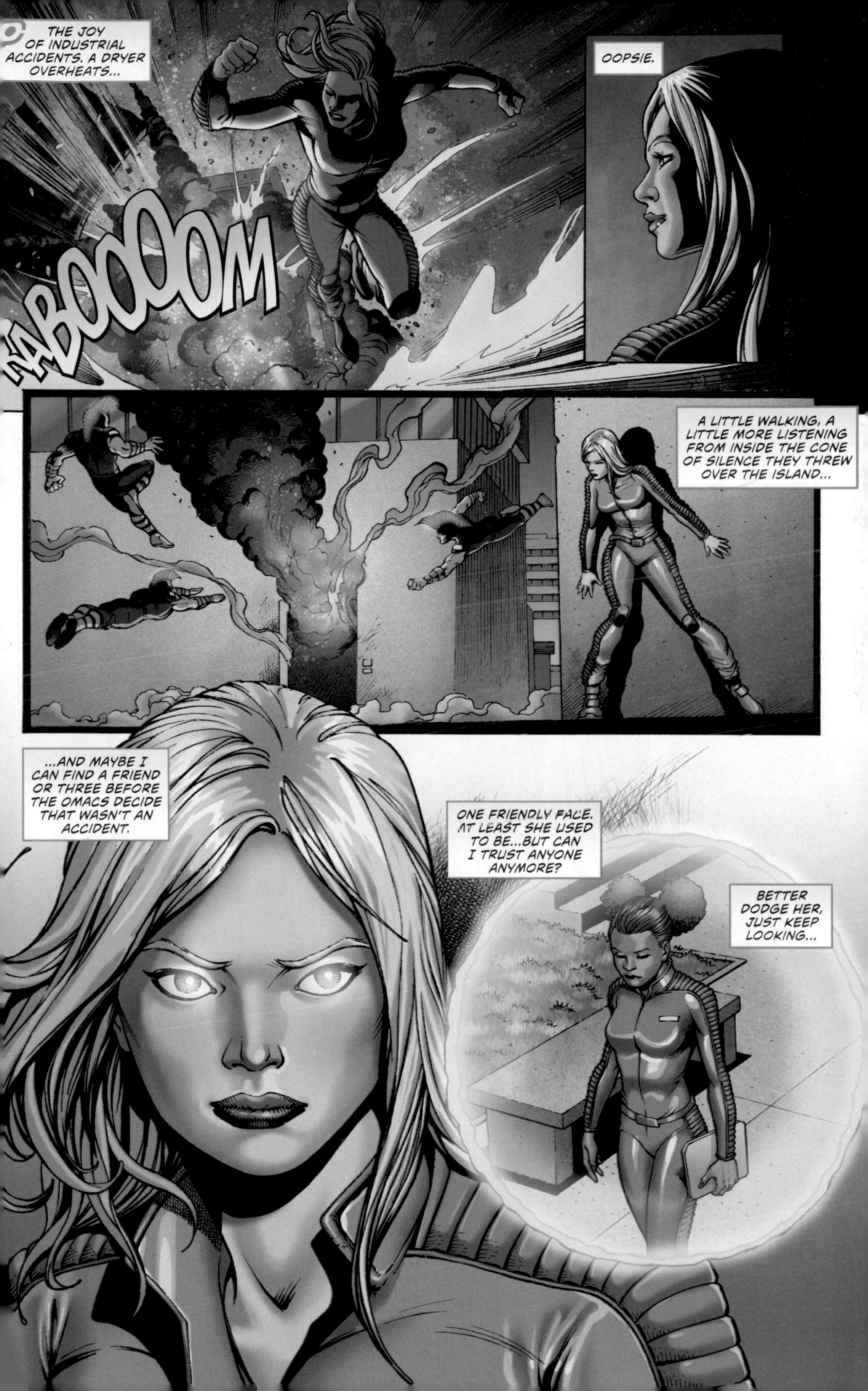
THE JOY OF INDUSTRIAL ACCIDENTS. A DRYER OVERHEATS...
KABOOOOM
OOPSIE.
A LITTLE WALKING, A LITTLE MORE LISTENING FROM INSIDE THE CONE OF SILENCE THEY THREW OVER THE ISLAND...
...AND MAYBE I CAN FIND A FRIEND OR THREE BEFORE THE OMACS DECIDE THAT WASN'T AN ACCIDENT.
ONE FRIENDLY FACE. AT LEAST SHE USED TO BE...BUT CAN I TRUST ANYONE ANYMORE?
BETTER DODGE HER, JUST KEEP LOOKING...

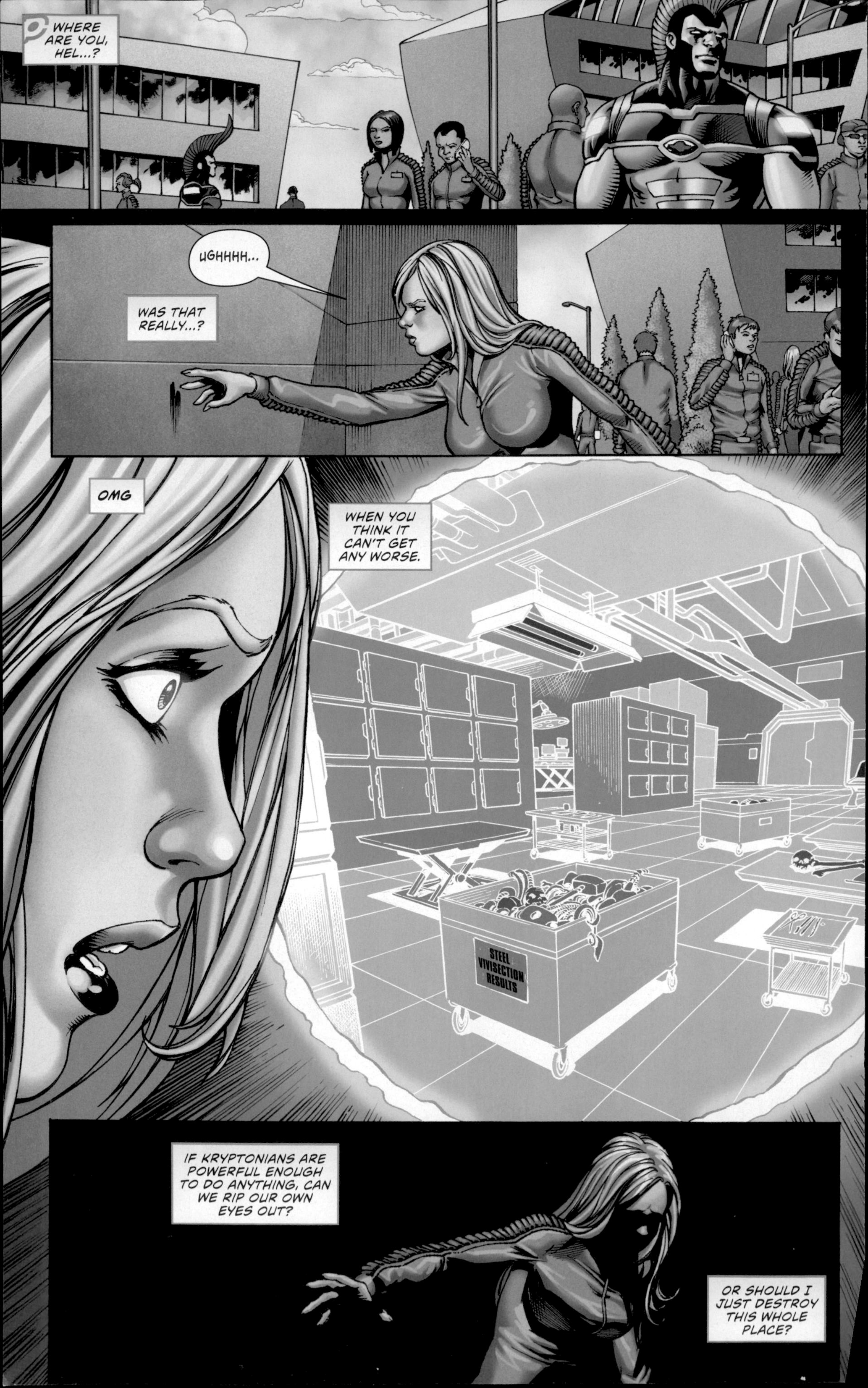
WHERE ARE YOU, HEL...?
UGHHHH...
WAS THAT REALLY...?
OMG
WHEN YOU THINK IT CAN'T GET ANY WORSE.
STEEL VIVISECTION RESULTS
IF KRYPTONIANS ARE POWERFUL ENOUGH TO DO ANYTHING, CAN WE RIP OUR OWN EYES OUT?
OR SHOULD I JUST DESTROY THIS WHOLE PLACE?

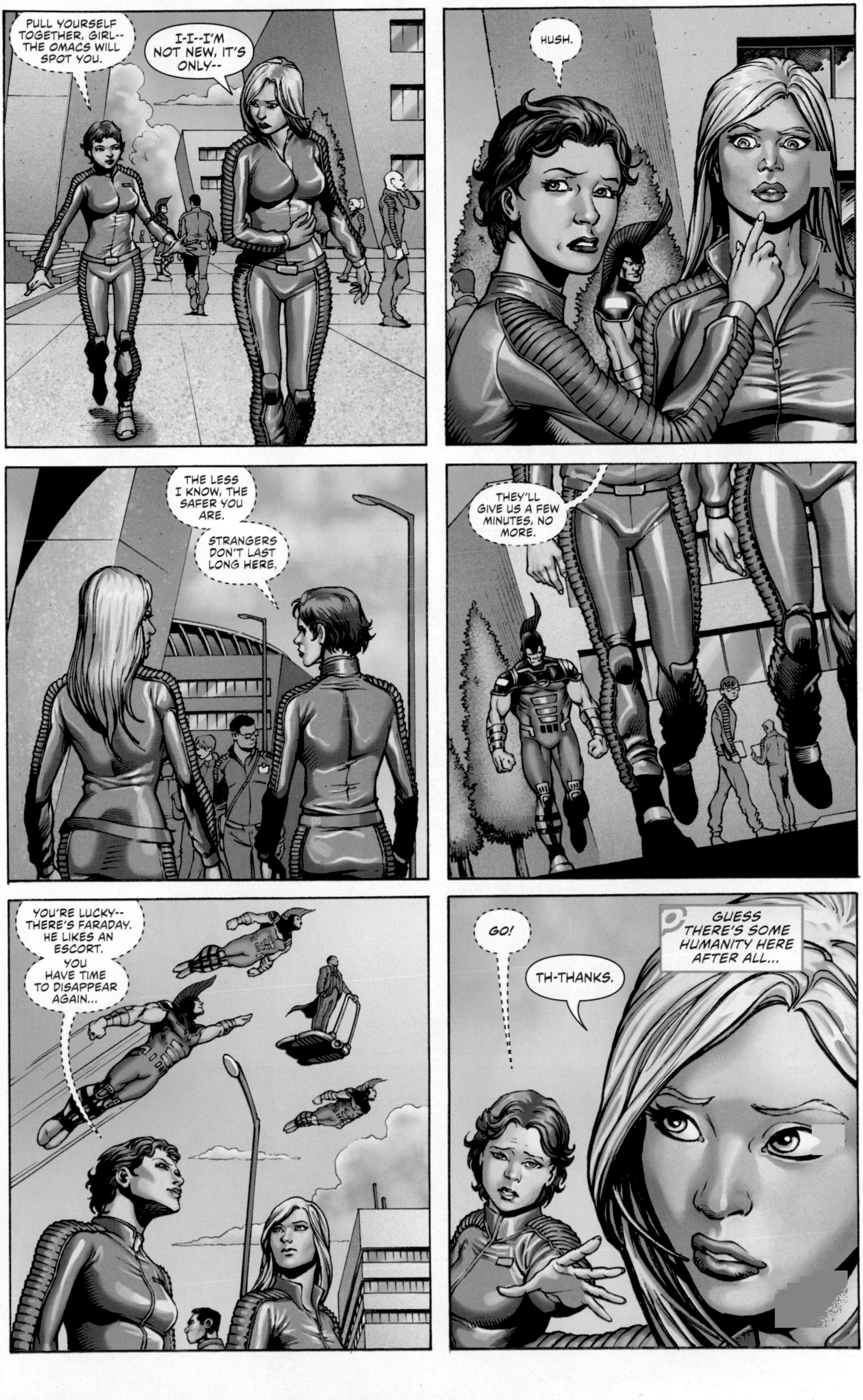
PULL YOURSELF TOGETHER, GIRL-- THE OMACS WILL SPOT YOU.
I-I--I'M NOT NEW, IT'S ONLY--
HUSH.
THE LESS I KNOW, THE SAFER YOU ARE.
STRANGERS DON'T LAST LONG HERE.
THEY'LL GIVE US A FEW MINUTES, NO MORE.
YOU'RE LUCKY-- THERE'S FARADAY. HE LIKES AN ESCORT.
YOU HAVE TIME TO DISAPPEAR AGAIN...
GO!
TH-THANKS.
GUESS THERE'S SOME HUMANITY HERE AFTER ALL...

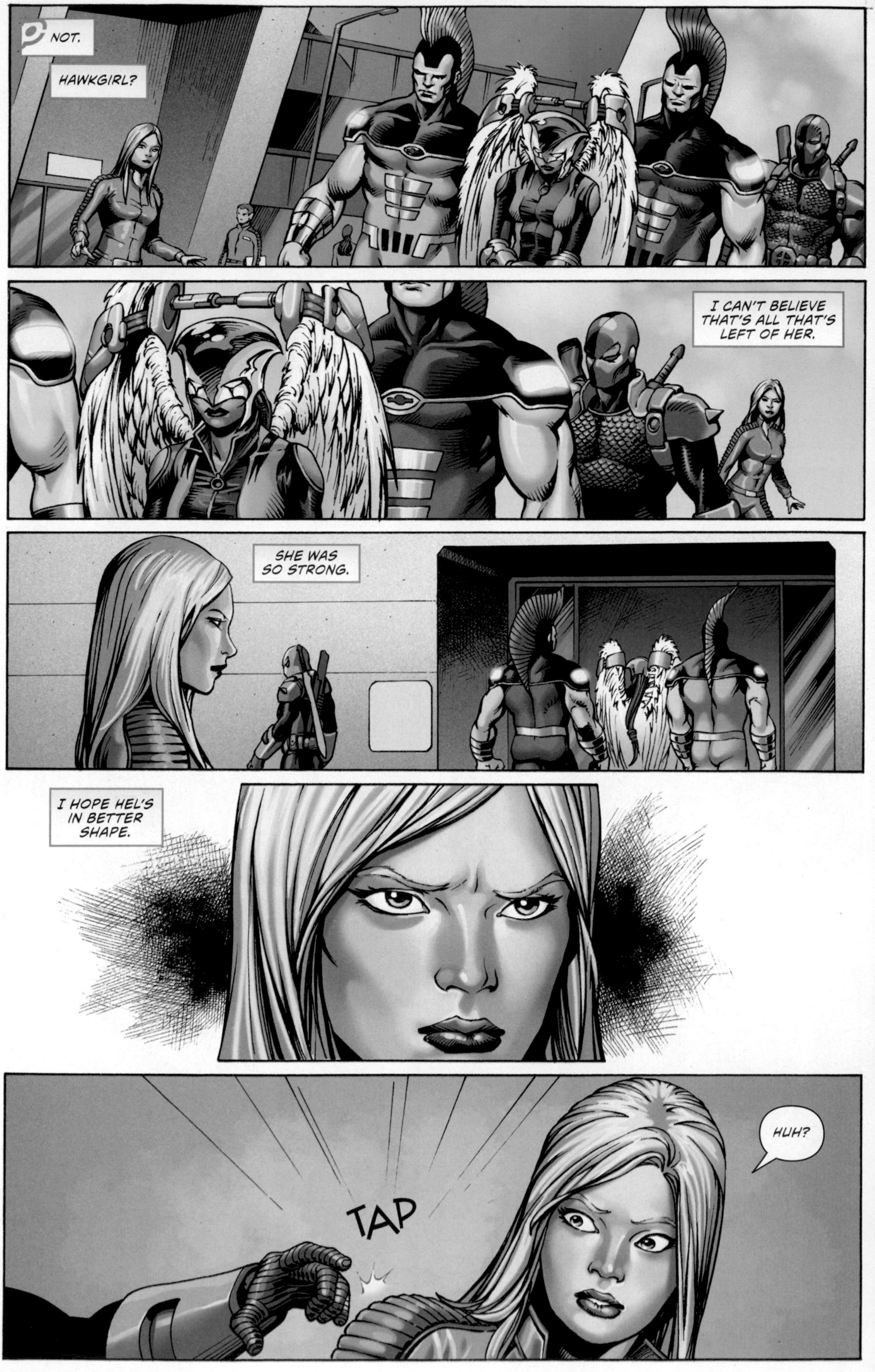
NOT.
HAWKGIRL?
I CAN'T BELIEVE THAT'S ALL THAT'S LEFT OF HER.
SHE WAS SO STRONG.
I HOPE HEL'S IN BETTER SHAPE.
TAP
HUH?

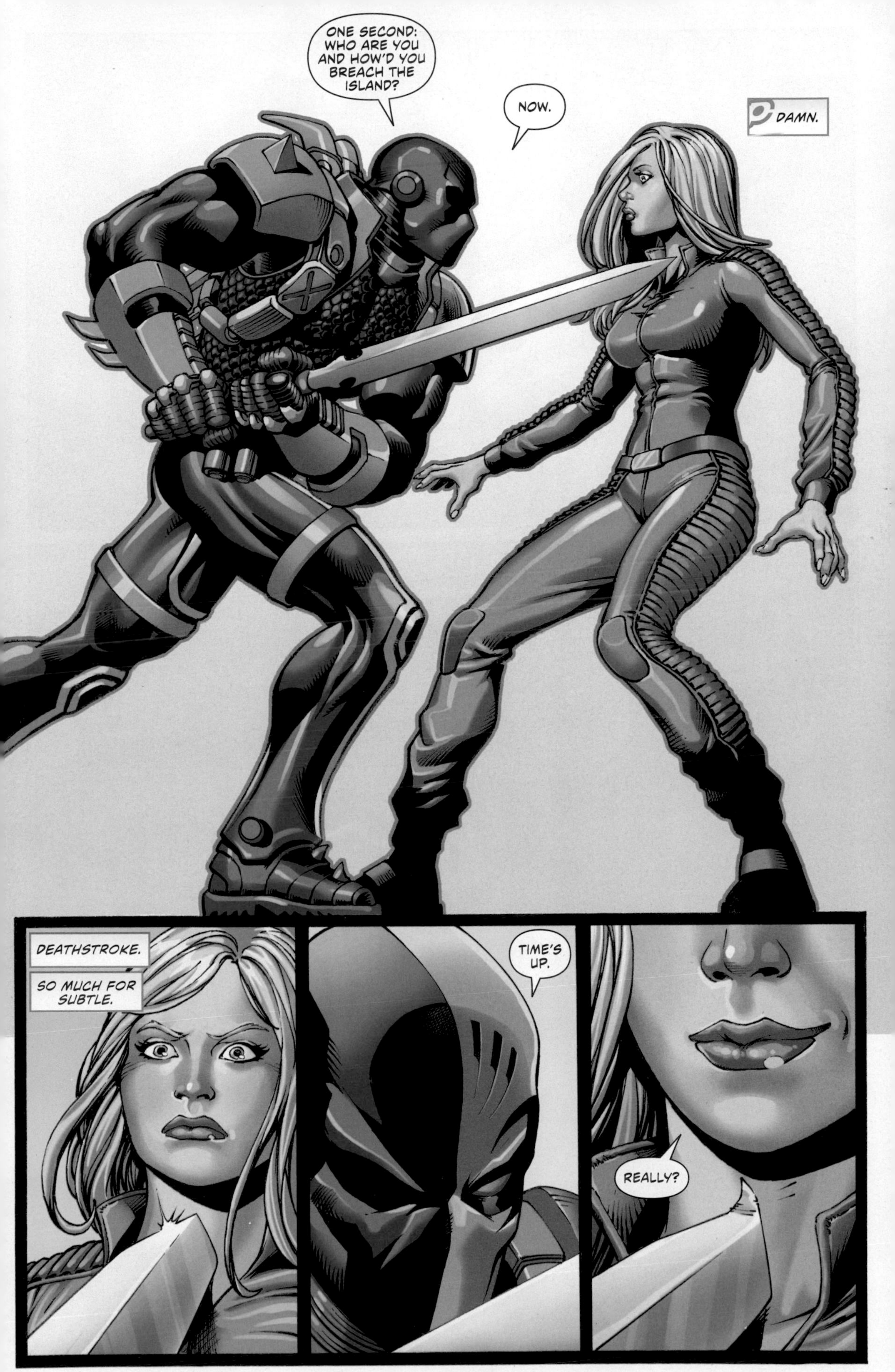
ONE SECOND: WHO ARE YOU AND HOW'D YOU BREACH THE ISLAND?
NOW.
DAMN.
DEATHSTROKE.
SO MUCH FOR SUBTLE.
TIME'S UP.
REALLY?

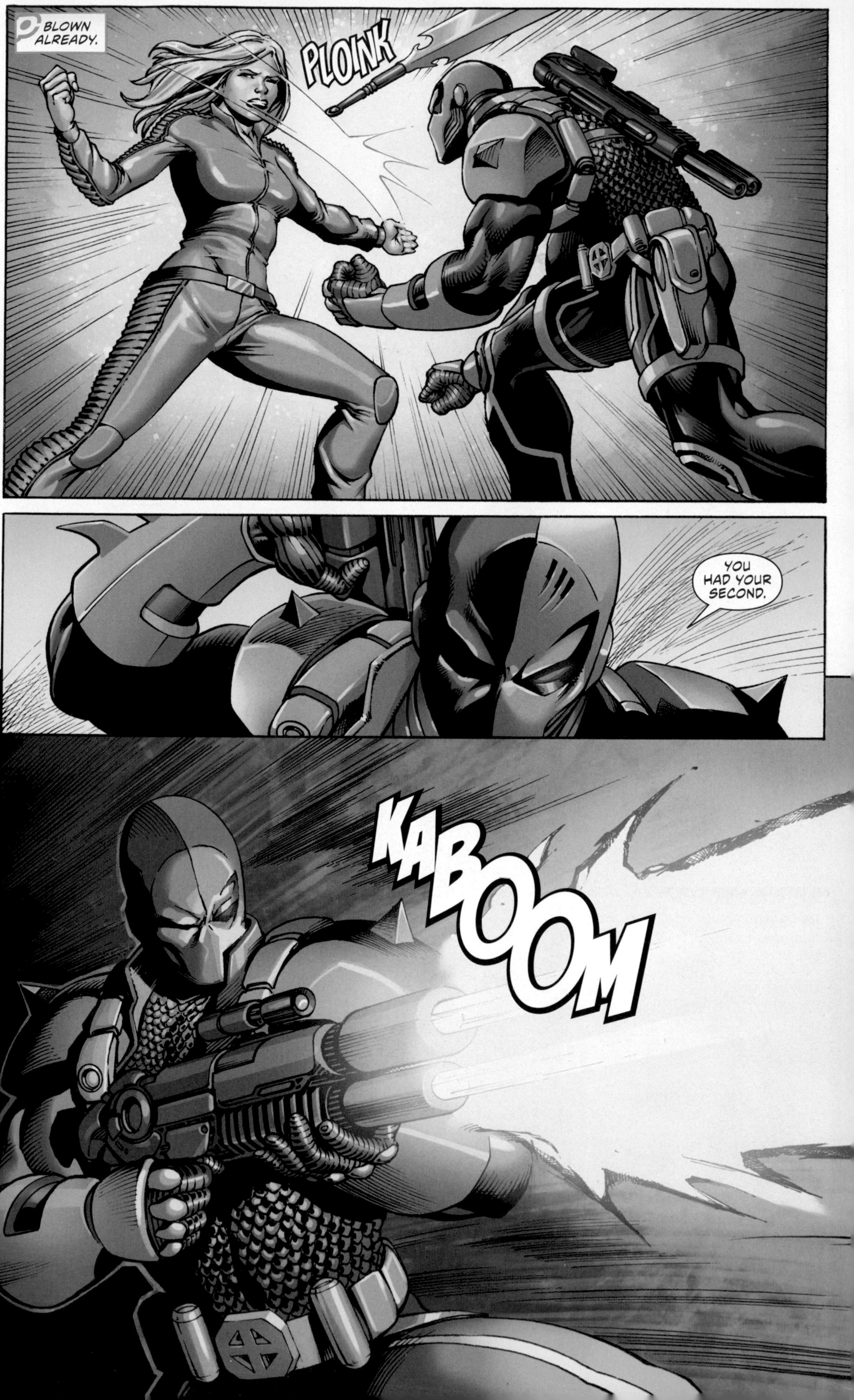

BLOWN ALREADY.
PLOINK
YOU HAD YOUR SECOND.
KABOOOM

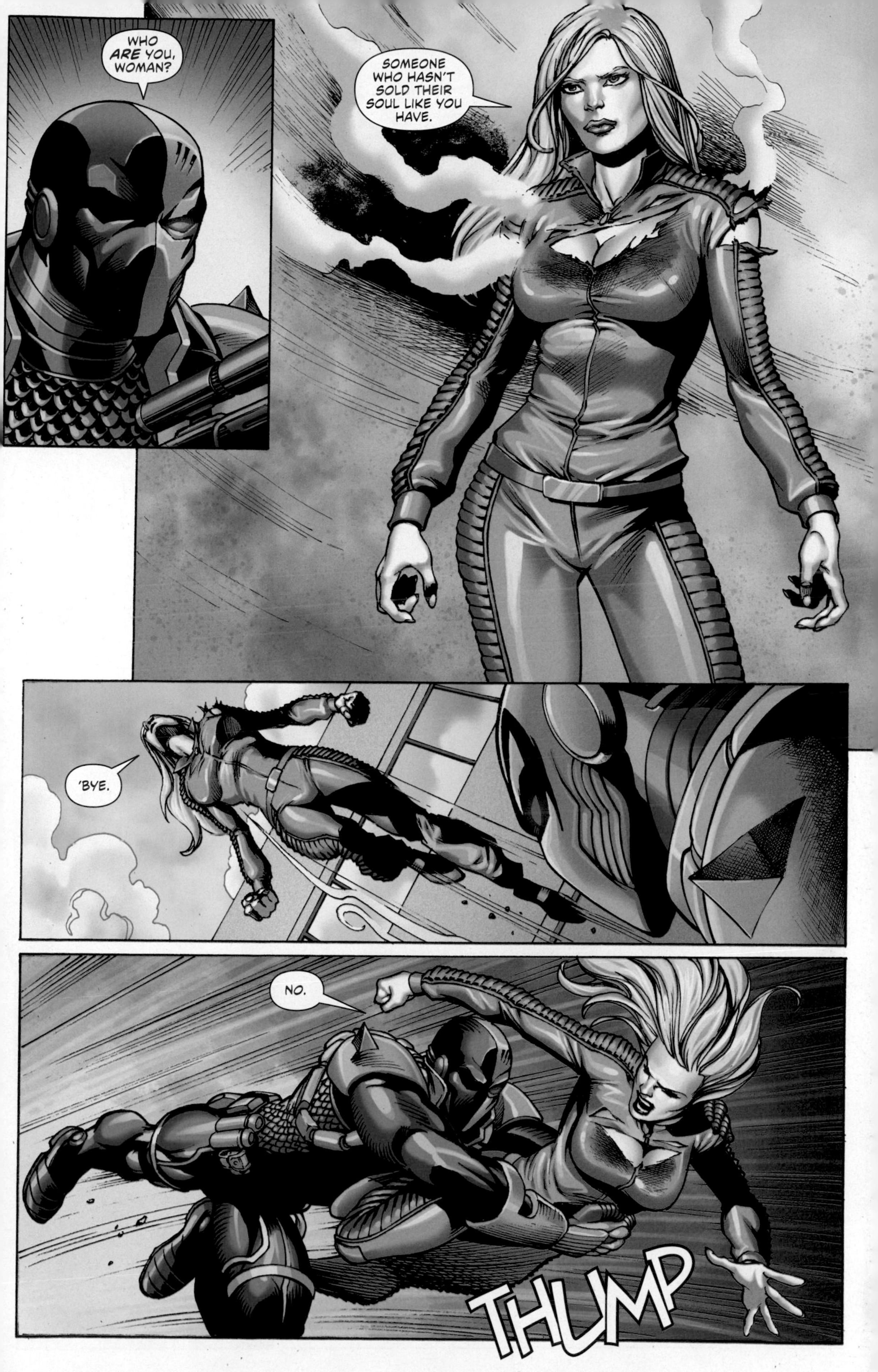
WHO ARE YOU, WOMAN?
SOMEONE WHO HASN'T SOLD THEIR SOUL LIKE YOU HAVE.
'BYE.
NO.
THUMP

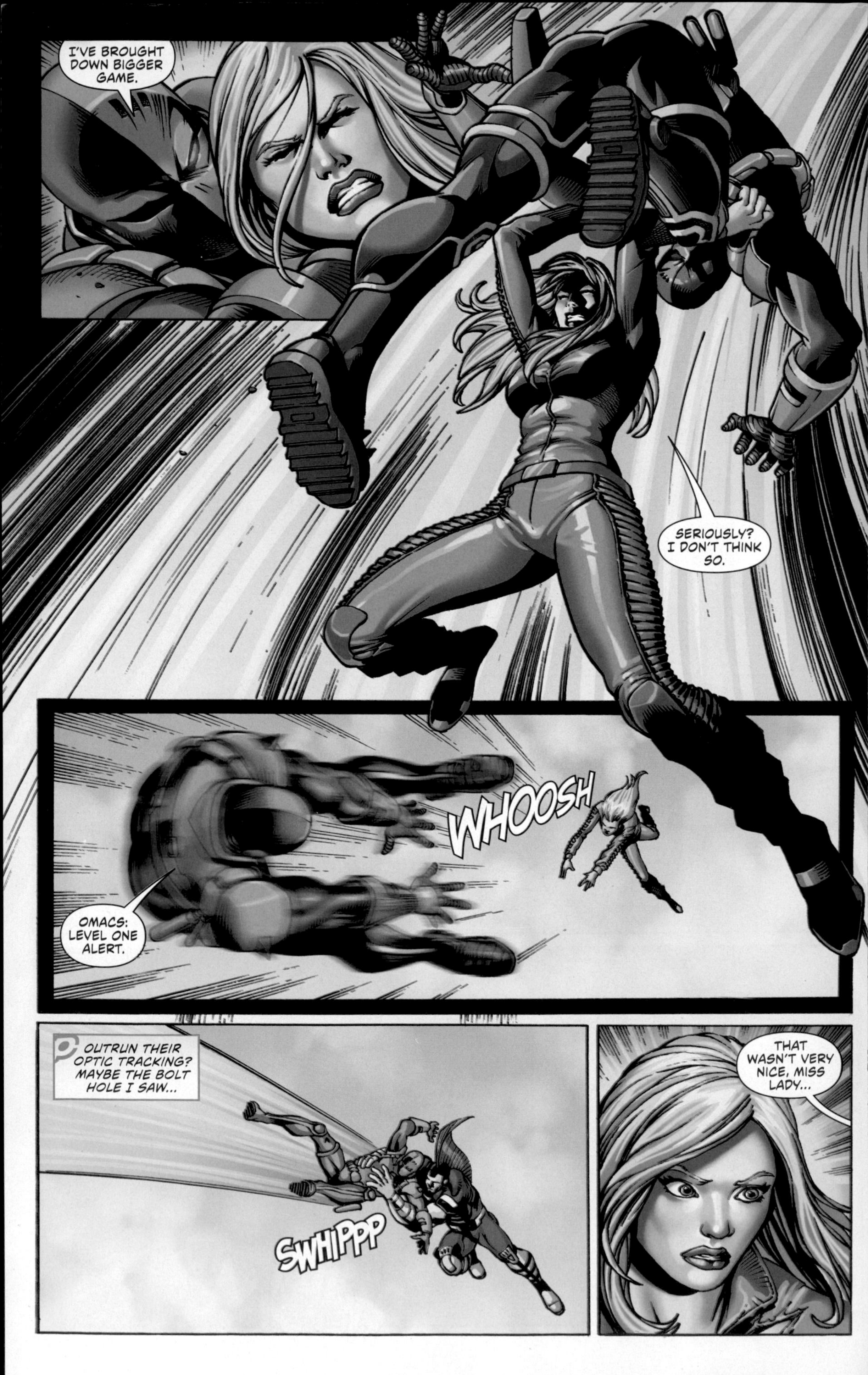
I'VE BROUGHT DOWN BIGGER GAME.
SERIOUSLY? I DON'T THINK SO.
WHOOSH
OMACS: LEVEL ONE ALERT.
OUTRUN THEIR OPTIC TRACKING? MAYBE THE BOLT HOLE I SAW...
SWHIPPP
THAT WASN'T VERY NICE, MISS LADY...

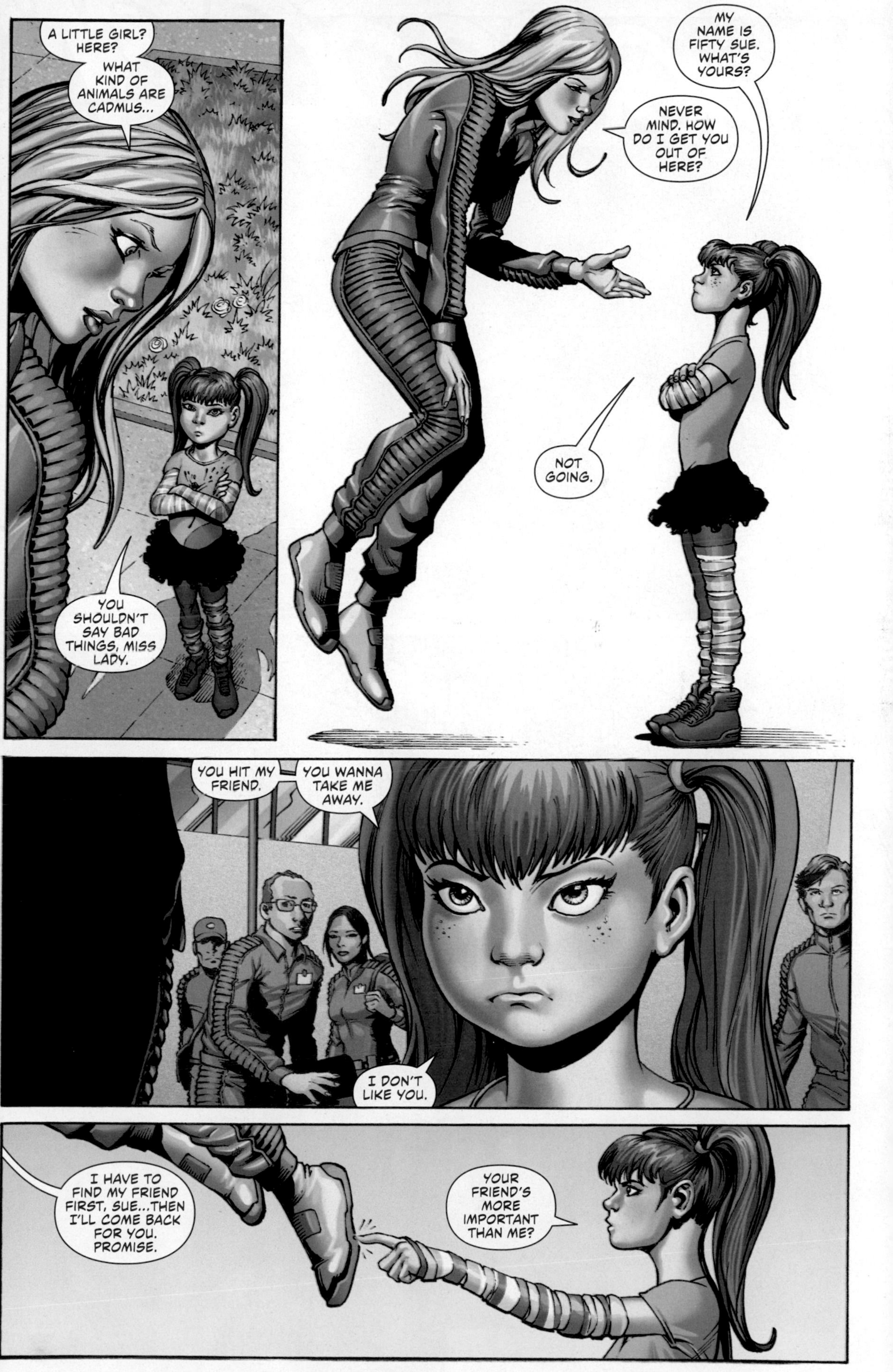

A LITTLE GIRL? HERE?
WHAT KIND OF ANIMALS ARE CADMUS...
YOU SHOULDN'T SAY BAD THINGS, MISS LADY.
MY NAME IS FIFTY SUE. WHAT'S YOURS?
NEVER MIND. HOW DO I GET YOU OUT OF HERE?
NOT GOING.
YOU HIT MY FRIEND.
YOU WANNA TAKE ME AWAY.
I DON'T LIKE YOU.
I HAVE TO FIND MY FRIEND FIRST, SUE...THEN I'LL COME BACK FOR YOU. PROMISE.
YOUR FRIEND'S MORE IMPORTANT THAN ME?

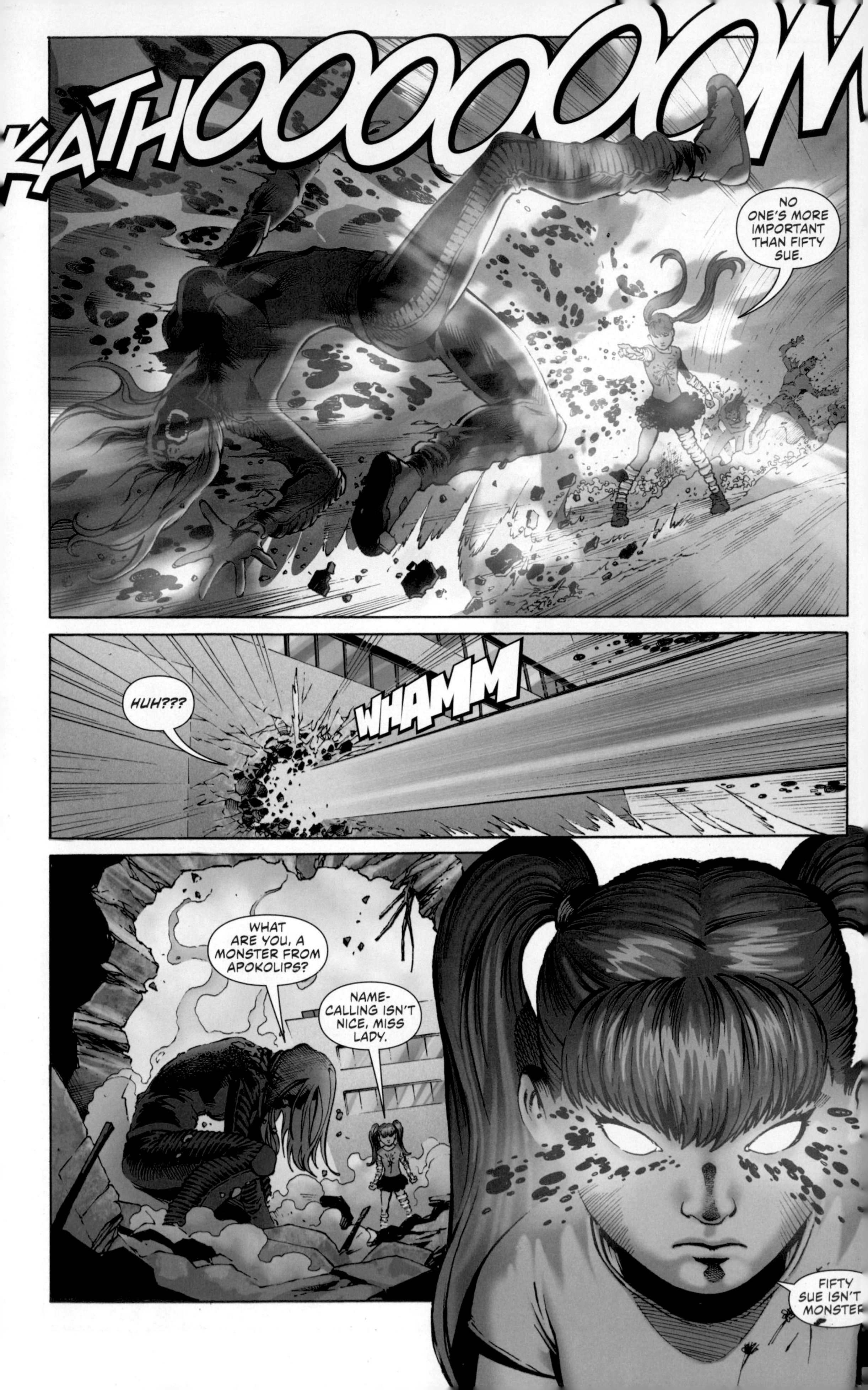
KATHOOOOOOOM
NO ONE'S MORE IMPORTANT THAN FIFTY SUE.
HUH???
WHAMM
WHAT ARE YOU, A MONSTER FROM APOKOLIPS?
NAME-CALLING ISN'T NICE, MISS LADY.
FIFTY SUE ISN'T MONSTER

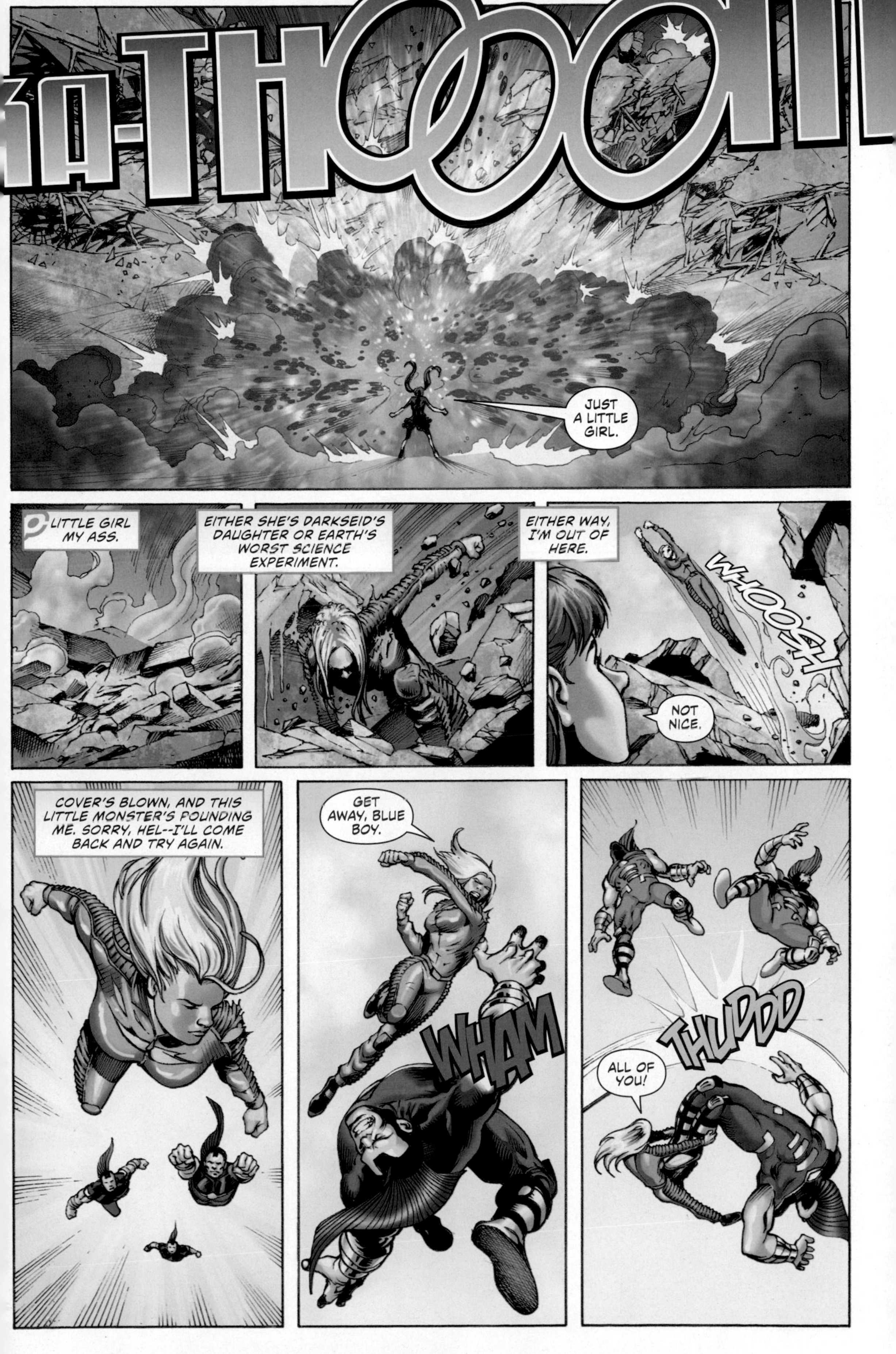
KA-THOOOM
JUST A LITTLE GIRL.
LITTLE GIRL MY ASS.
EITHER SHE'S DARKSEID'S DAUGHTER OR EARTH'S WORST SCIENCE EXPERIMENT.
EITHER WAY, I'M OUT OF HERE.
WHOOSH
NOT NICE.
COVER'S BLOWN, AND THIS LITTLE MONSTER'S POUNDING ME. SORRY, HEL--I'LL COME BACK AND TRY AGAIN.
GET AWAY, BLUE BOY.
WHAM
THUDDD
ALL OF YOU!

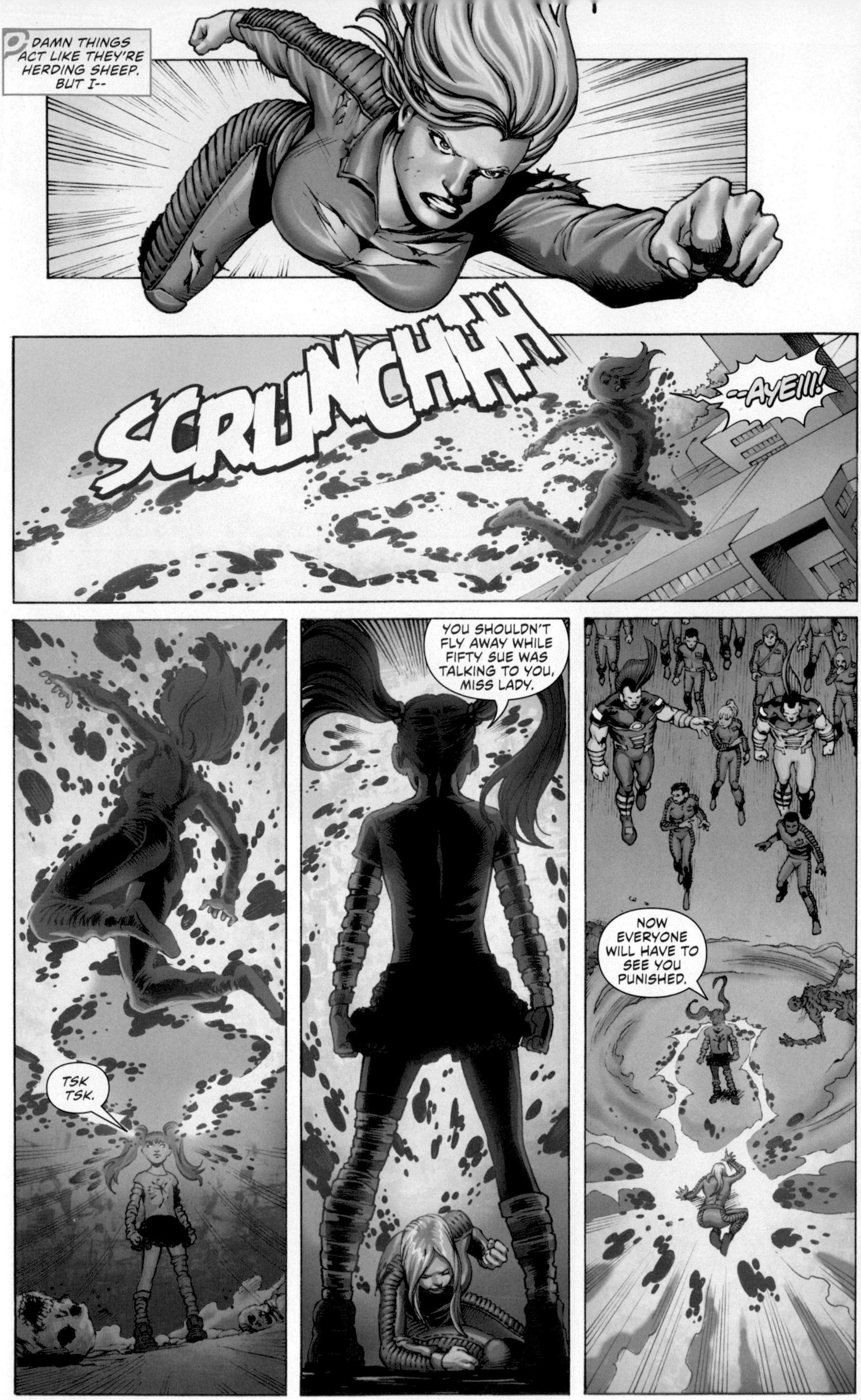
DAMN THINGS ACT LIKE THEY'RE HERDING SHEEP. BUT I--
SCRUNCHHH
--AYEIII!
TSK TSK.
YOU SHOULDN'T FLY AWAY WHILE FIFTY SUE WAS TALKING TO YOU, MISS LADY.
NOW EVERYONE WILL HAVE TO SEE YOU PUNISHED.

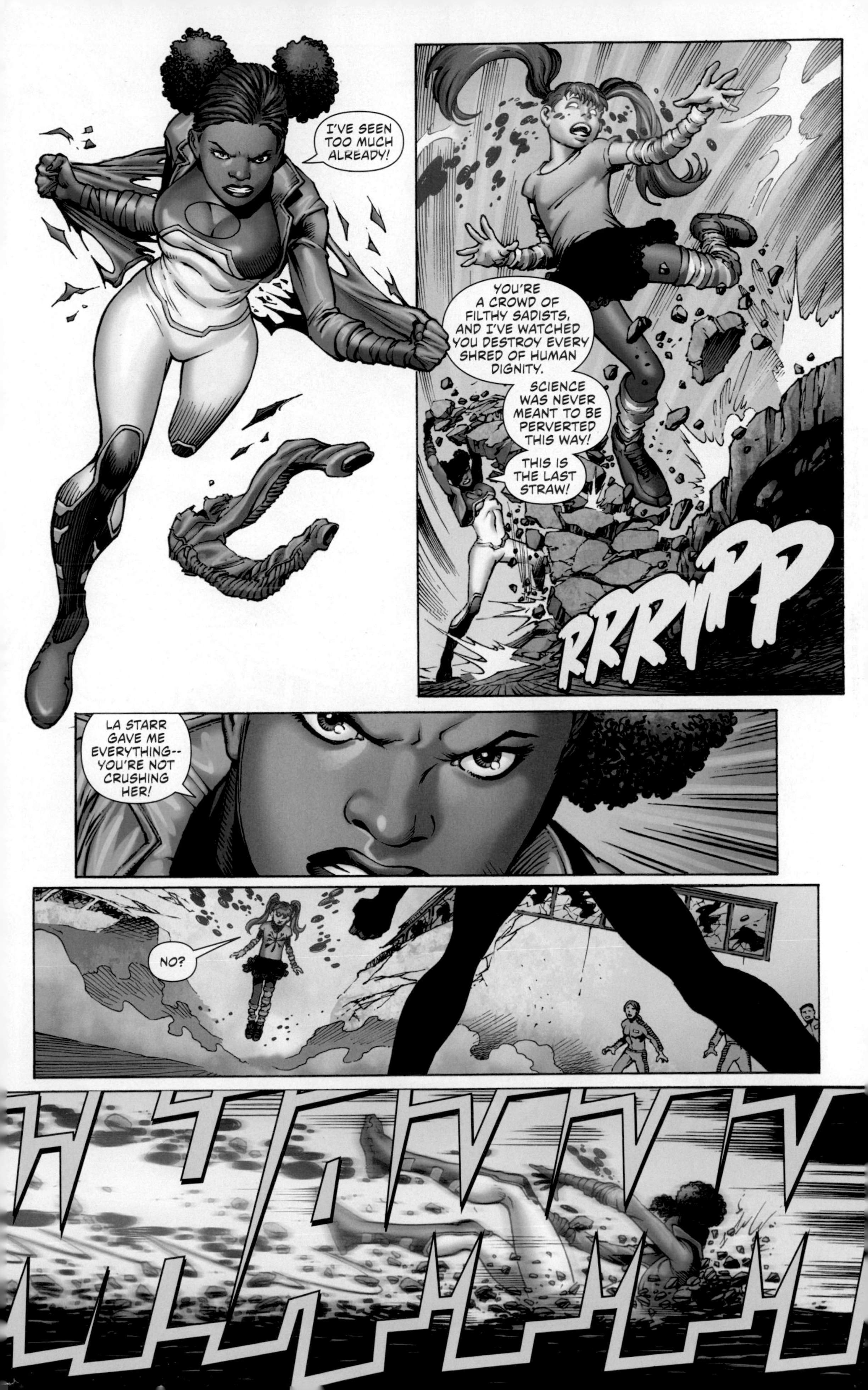
I'VE SEEN TOO MUCH ALREADY!
YOU'RE A CROWD OF FILTHY SADISTS, AND I'VE WATCHED YOU DESTROY EVERY SHRED OF HUMAN DIGNITY.
SCIENCE WAS NEVER MEANT TO BE PERVERTED THIS WAY!
THIS IS THE LAST STRAW!
RRRIPP
LA STARR GAVE ME EVERYTHING-- YOU'RE NOT CRUSHING HER!
NO?

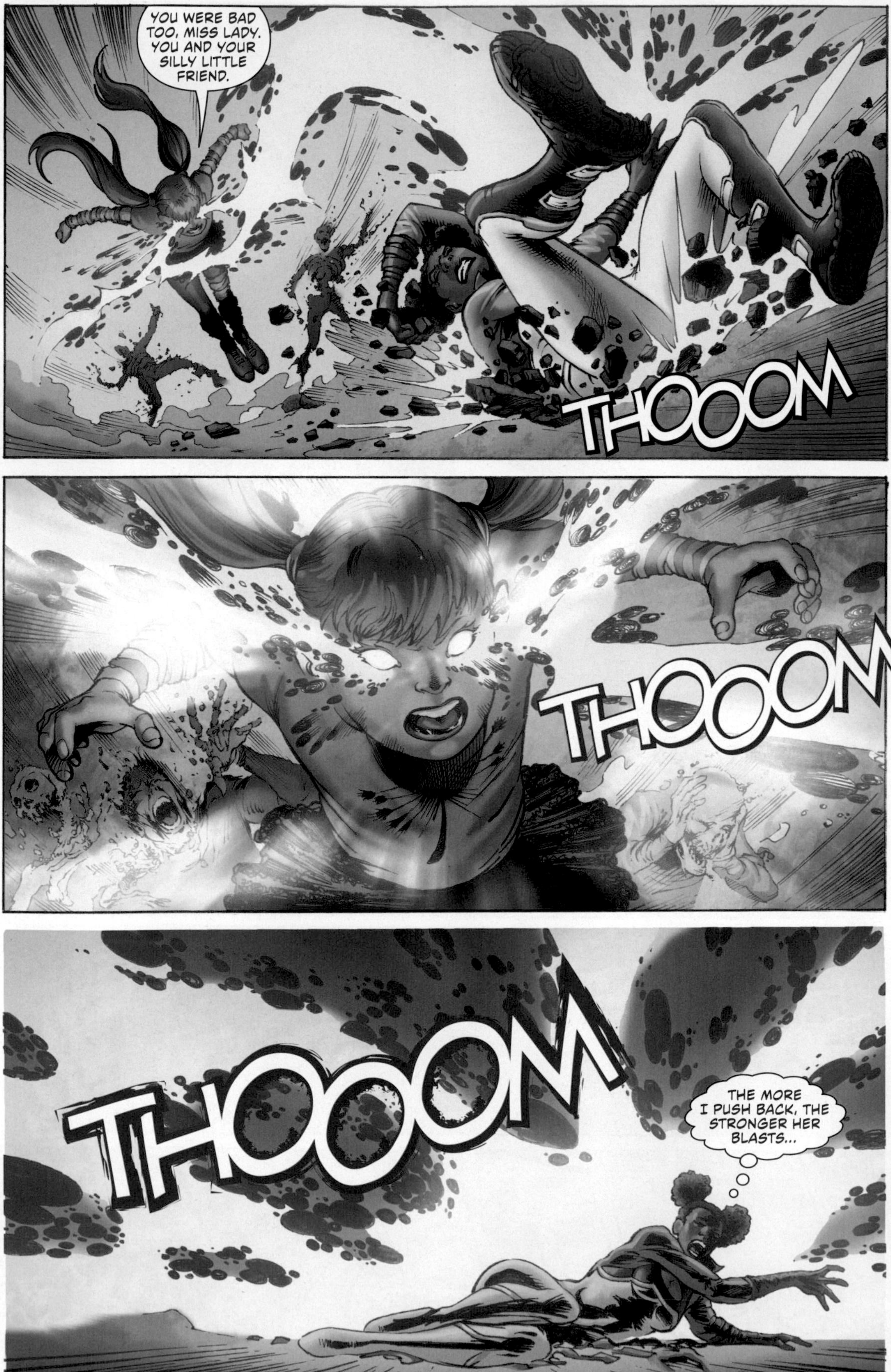
YOU WERE BAD TOO, MISS LADY. YOU AND YOUR SILLY LITTLE FRIEND.
THOOOM
THOOOM
THOOOM
THE MORE I PUSH BACK, THE STRONGER HER BLASTS...

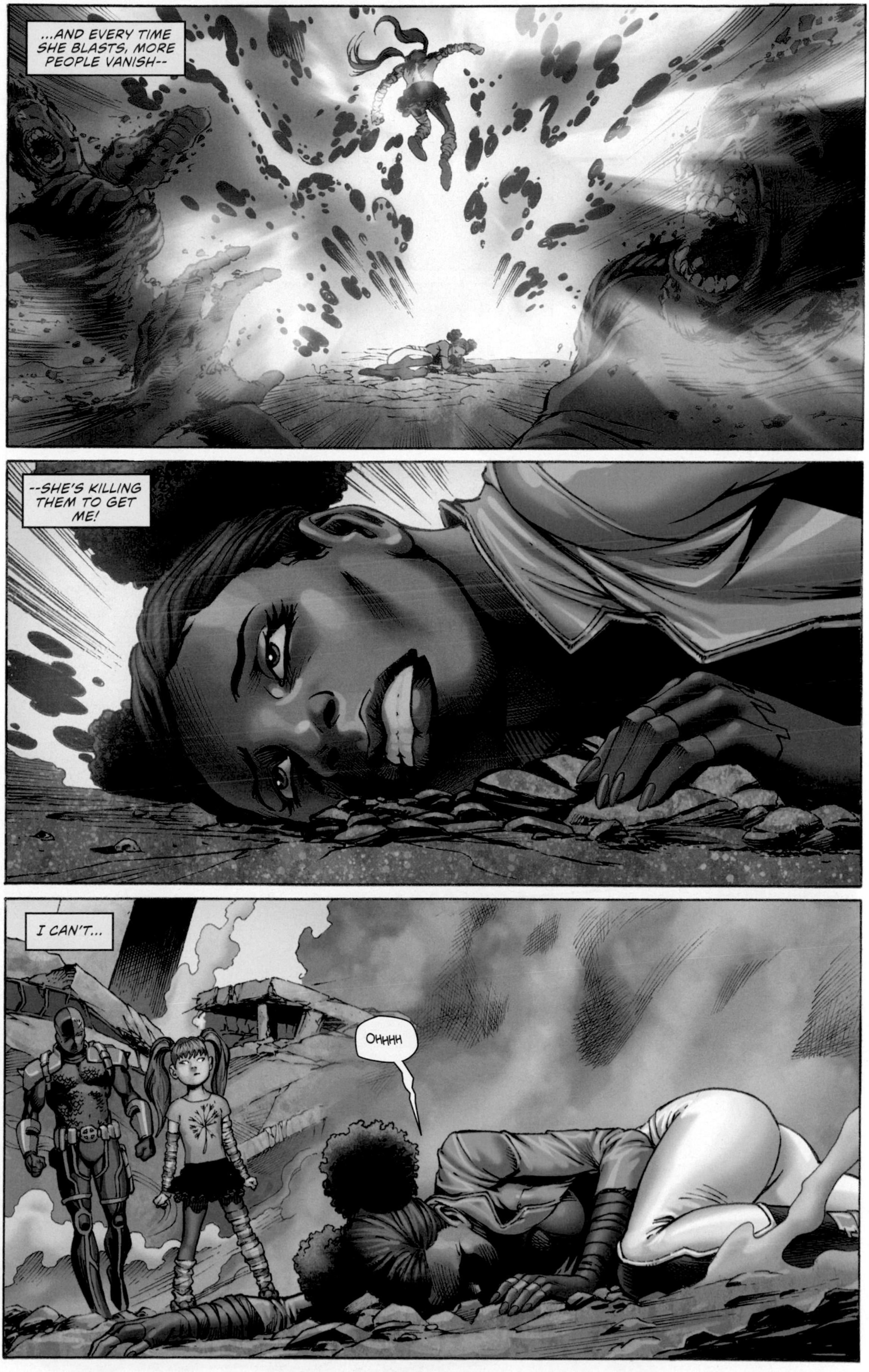
...AND EVERY TIME SHE BLASTS, MORE PEOPLE VANISH--
--SHE'S KILLING THEM TO GET ME!
I CAN'T...
OHHHH

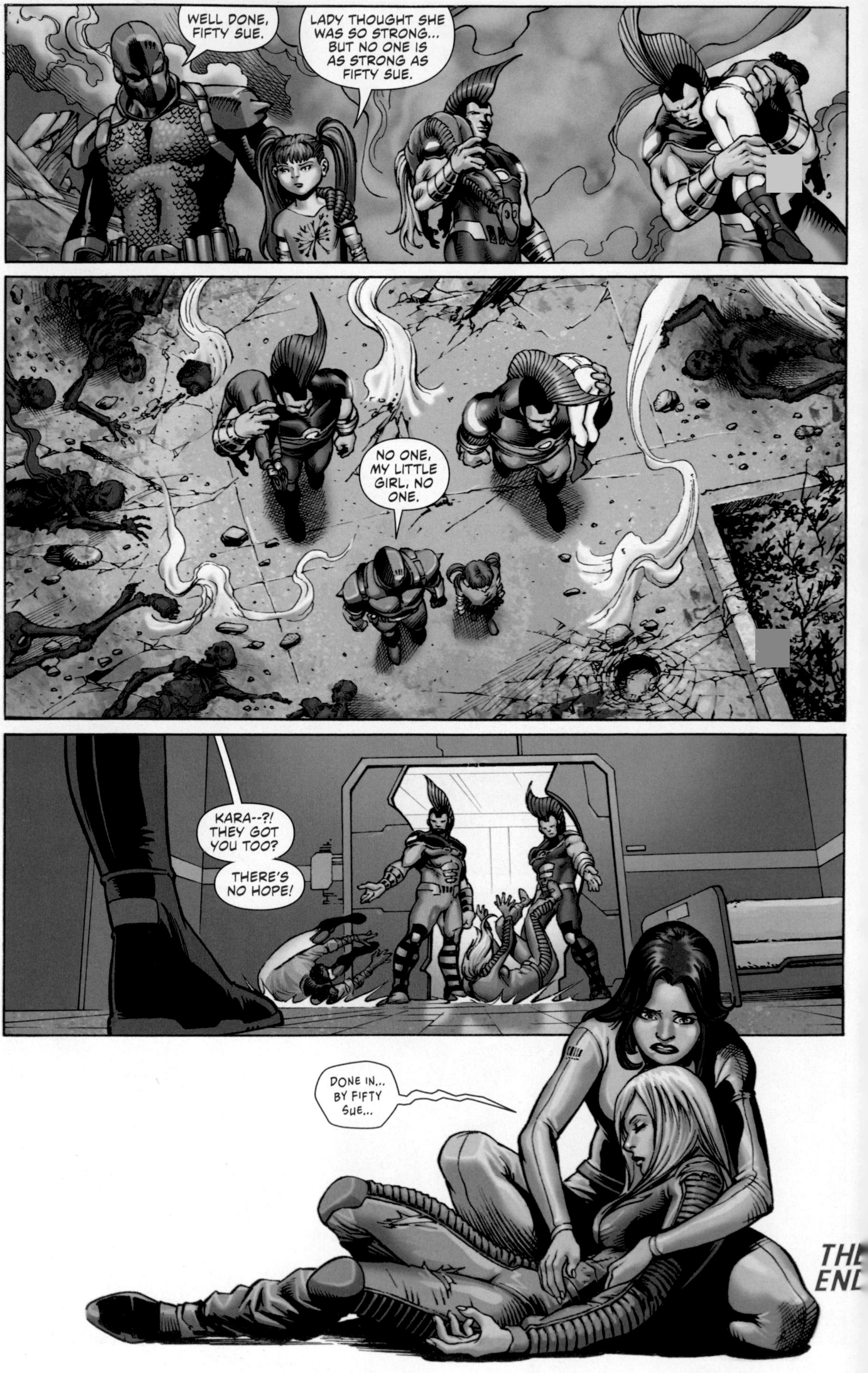
WELL DONE, FIFTY SUE.
LADY THOUGHT SHE WAS SO STRONG... BUT NO ONE IS AS STRONG AS FIFTY SUE.
NO ONE, MY LITTLE GIRL, NO ONE.
KARA--?! THEY GOT YOU TOO?
THERE'S NO HOPE!
DONE IN... BY FIFTY SUE...

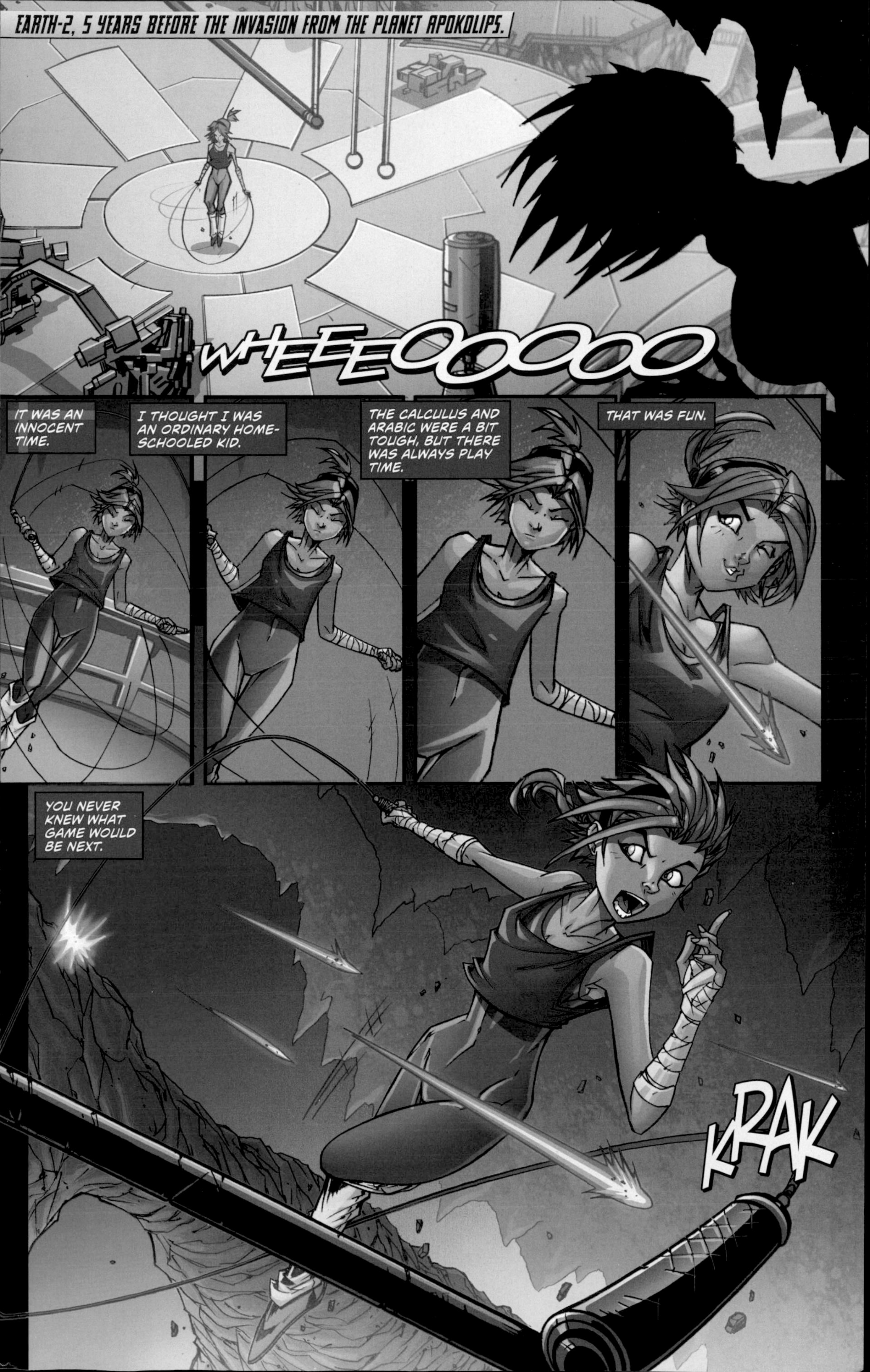
EARTH-2, 5 YEARS BEFORE THE INVASION FROM THE PLANET APOKOLIPS.
WHEEEOOOOOO
IT WAS AN INNOCENT TIME.
I THOUGHT I WAS AN ORDINARY HOME-SCHOOLED KID.
THE CALCULUS AND ARABIC WERE A BIT TOUGH, BUT THERE WAS ALWAYS PLAY TIME.
THAT WAS FUN.
YOU NEVER KNEW WHAT GAME WOULD BE NEXT.
KRAK

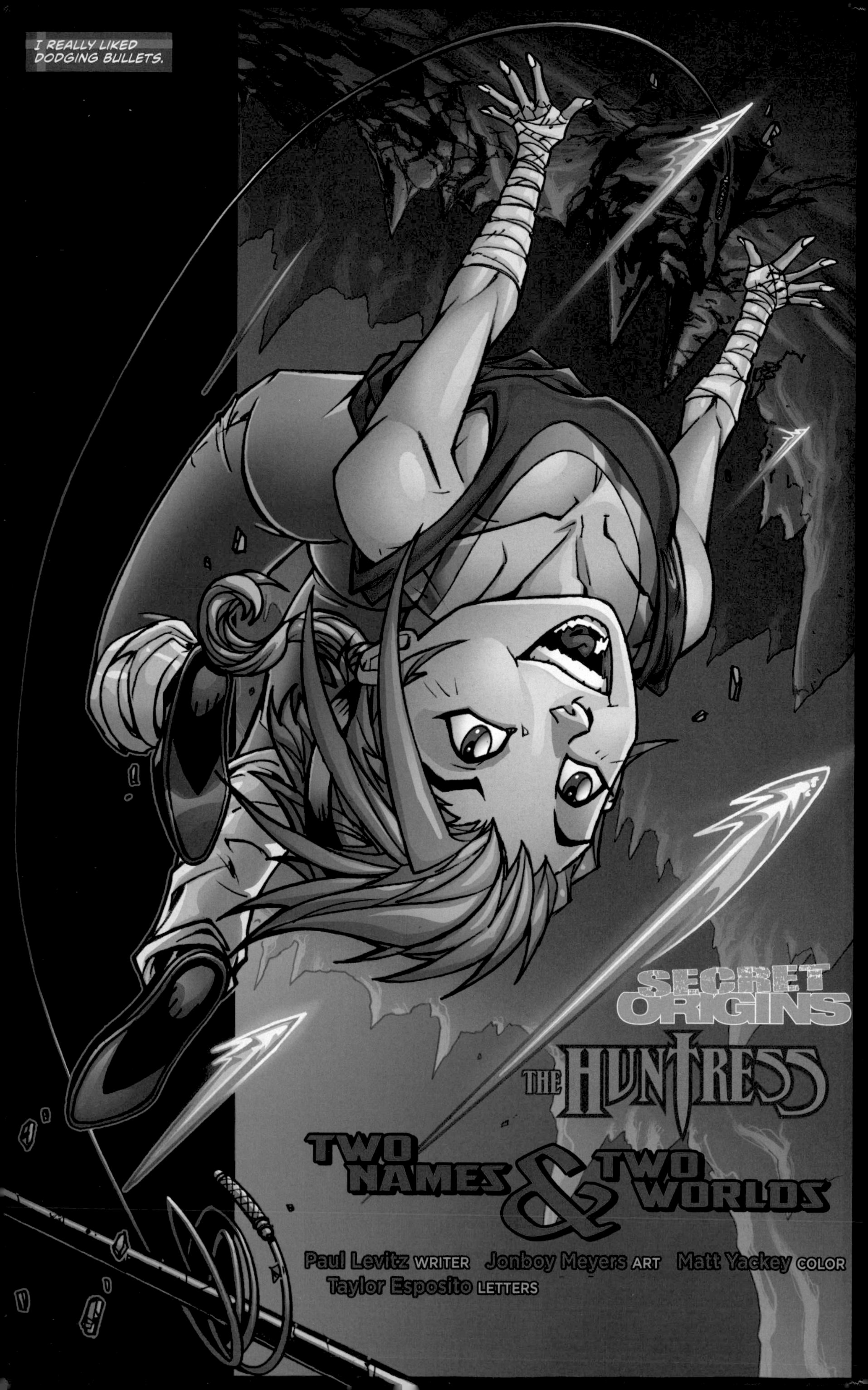
I REALLY LIKED DODGING BULLETS.
SECRET ORIGINS
THE HUNTRESS
TWO NAMES & TWO WORLDS
Paul Levitz WRITER Jonboy Meyers ART Matt Yackey COLOR
Taylor Esposito LETTERS

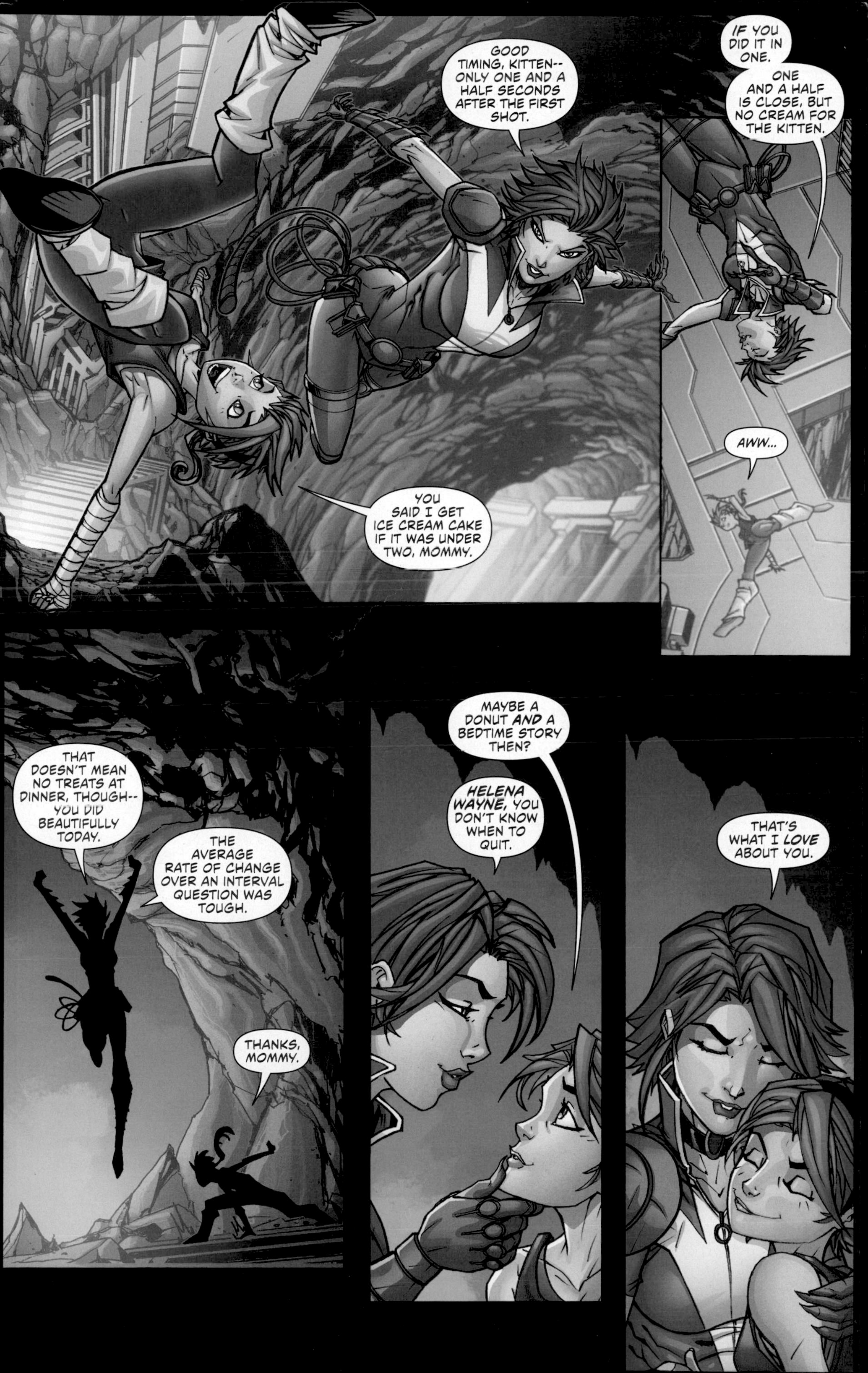
GOOD TIMING, KITTEN-- ONLY ONE AND A HALF SECONDS AFTER THE FIRST SHOT.
YOU SAID I GET ICE CREAM CAKE IF IT WAS UNDER TWO, MOMMY.
IF YOU DID IT IN ONE.
ONE AND A HALF IS CLOSE, BUT NO CREAM FOR THE KITTEN.
AWW...
THAT DOESN'T MEAN NO TREATS AT DINNER, THOUGH-- YOU DID BEAUTIFULLY TODAY.
THE AVERAGE RATE OF CHANGE OVER AN INTERVAL QUESTION WAS TOUGH.
THANKS, MOMMY.
MAYBE A DONUT AND A BEDTIME STORY THEN?
HELENA WAYNE, YOU DON'T KNOW WHEN TO QUIT.
THAT'S WHAT I LOVE ABOUT YOU.

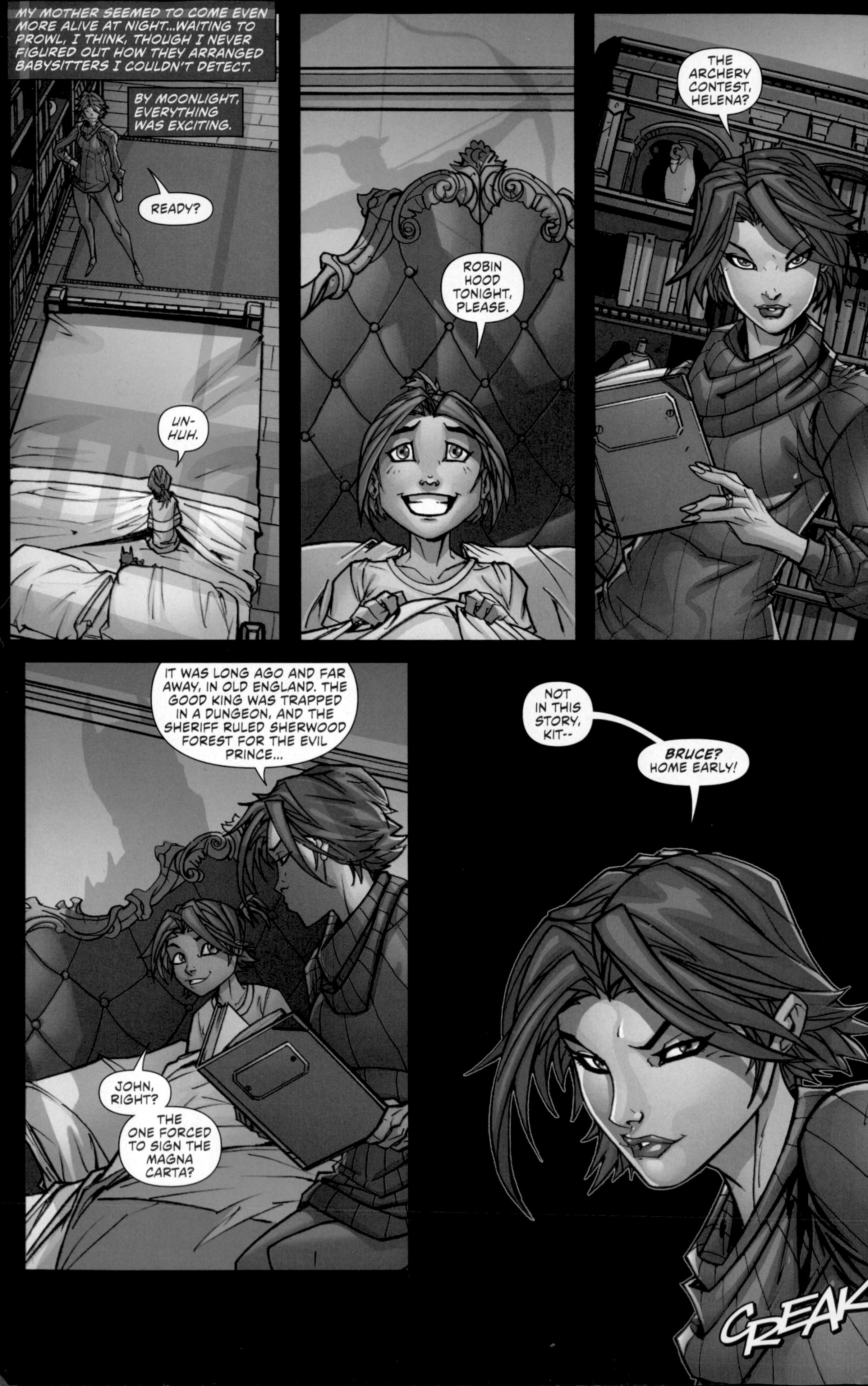
MY MOTHER SEEMED TO COME EVEN MORE ALIVE AT NIGHT...WAITING TO PROWL, I THINK, THOUGH I NEVER FIGURED OUT HOW THEY ARRANGED BABYSITTERS I COULDN'T DETECT.
BY MOONLIGHT, EVERYTHING WAS EXCITING.
READY?
UN-HUH.
ROBIN HOOD TONIGHT, PLEASE.
THE ARCHERY CONTEST, HELENA?
IT WAS LONG AGO AND FAR AWAY, IN OLD ENGLAND. THE GOOD KING WAS TRAPPED IN A DUNGEON, AND THE SHERIFF RULED SHERWOOD FOREST FOR THE EVIL PRINCE...
JOHN, RIGHT?
THE ONE FORCED TO SIGN THE MAGNA CARTA?
NOT IN THIS STORY, KIT--
BRUCE? HOME EARLY!
CREAK

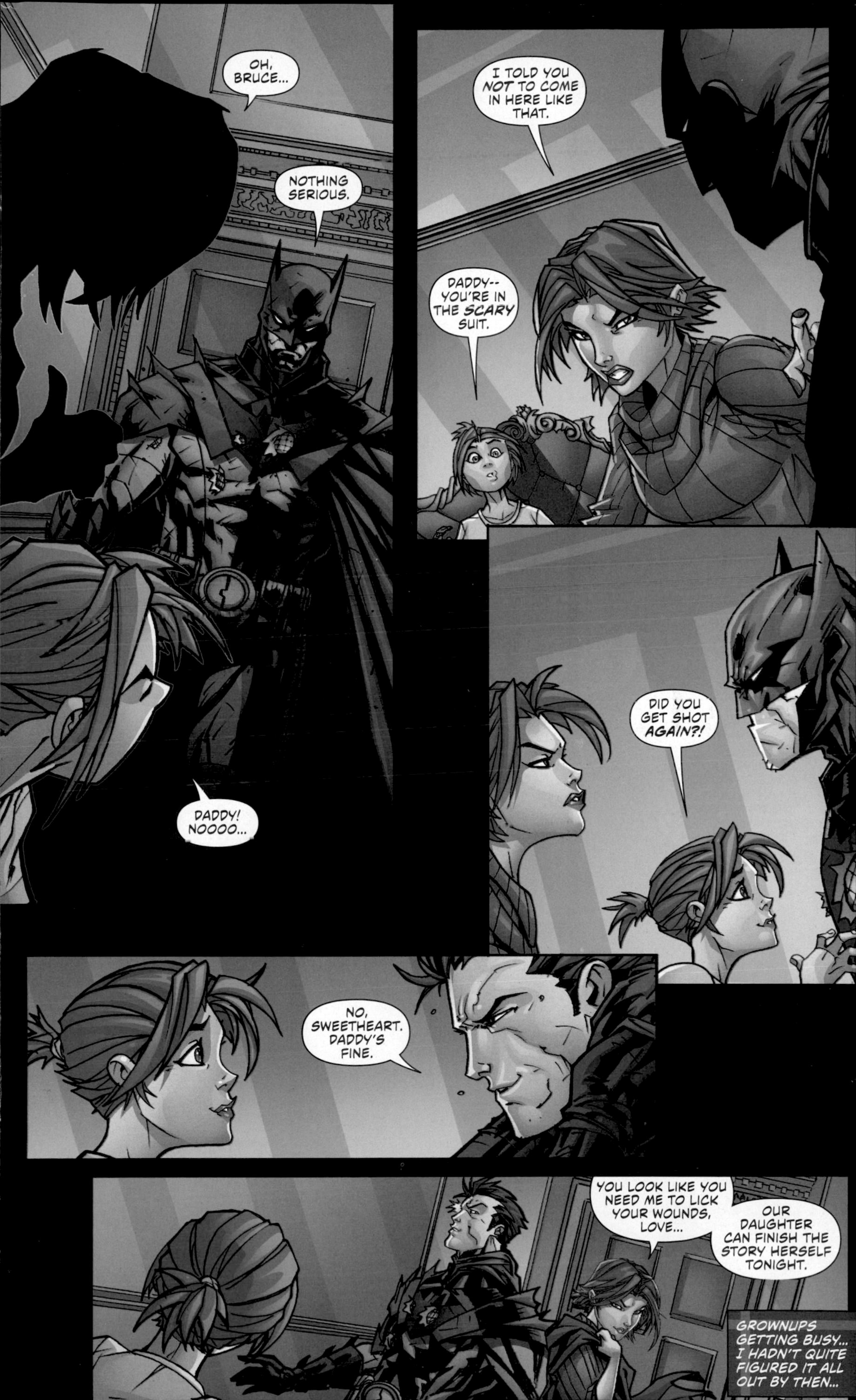
OH, BRUCE...
NOTHING SERIOUS.
DADDY! NOOOO...
I TOLD YOU *NOT* TO COME IN HERE LIKE THAT.
DADDY-- YOU'RE IN THE *SCARY* SUIT.
DID YOU GET SHOT *AGAIN?!*
NO, SWEETHEART. DADDY'S FINE.
YOU LOOK LIKE YOU NEED ME TO LICK YOUR WOUNDS, LOVE...
OUR DAUGHTER CAN FINISH THE STORY HERSELF TONIGHT.
GROWNUPS GETTING BUSY... I HADN'T QUITE FIGURED IT ALL OUT BY THEN...

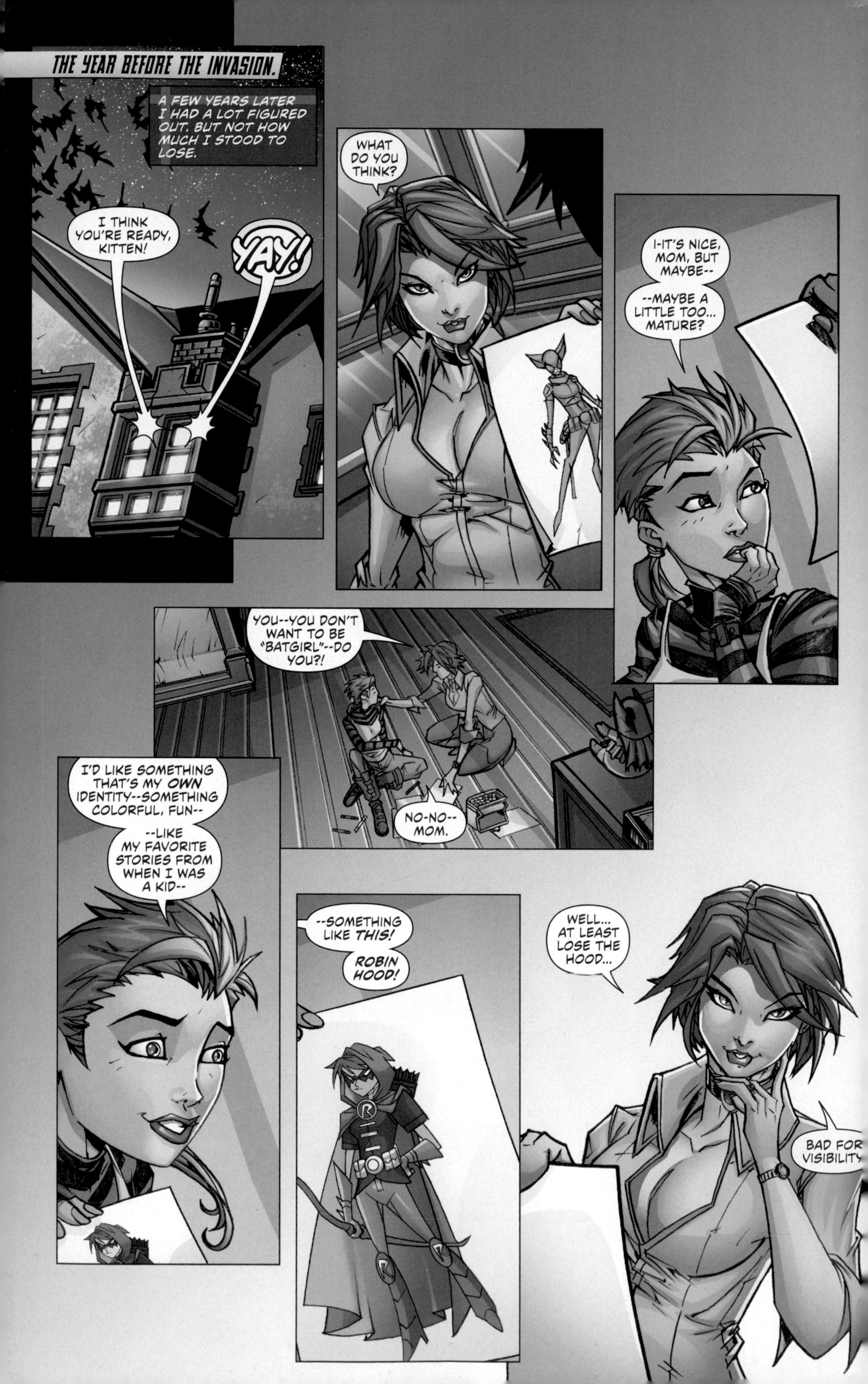
THE YEAR BEFORE THE INVASION.
A FEW YEARS LATER I HAD A LOT FIGURED OUT. BUT NOT HOW MUCH I STOOD TO LOSE.
I THINK YOU'RE READY, KITTEN!
YAY!
WHAT DO YOU THINK?
I-IT'S NICE, MOM, BUT MAYBE--
--MAYBE A LITTLE TOO... MATURE?
YOU--YOU DON'T WANT TO BE "BATGIRL"--DO YOU?!
NO-NO-- MOM.
I'D LIKE SOMETHING THAT'S MY OWN IDENTITY--SOMETHING COLORFUL, FUN--
--LIKE MY FAVORITE STORIES FROM WHEN I WAS A KID--
--SOMETHING LIKE THIS!
ROBIN HOOD!
WELL... AT LEAST LOSE THE HOOD...
BAD FOR VISIBILITY

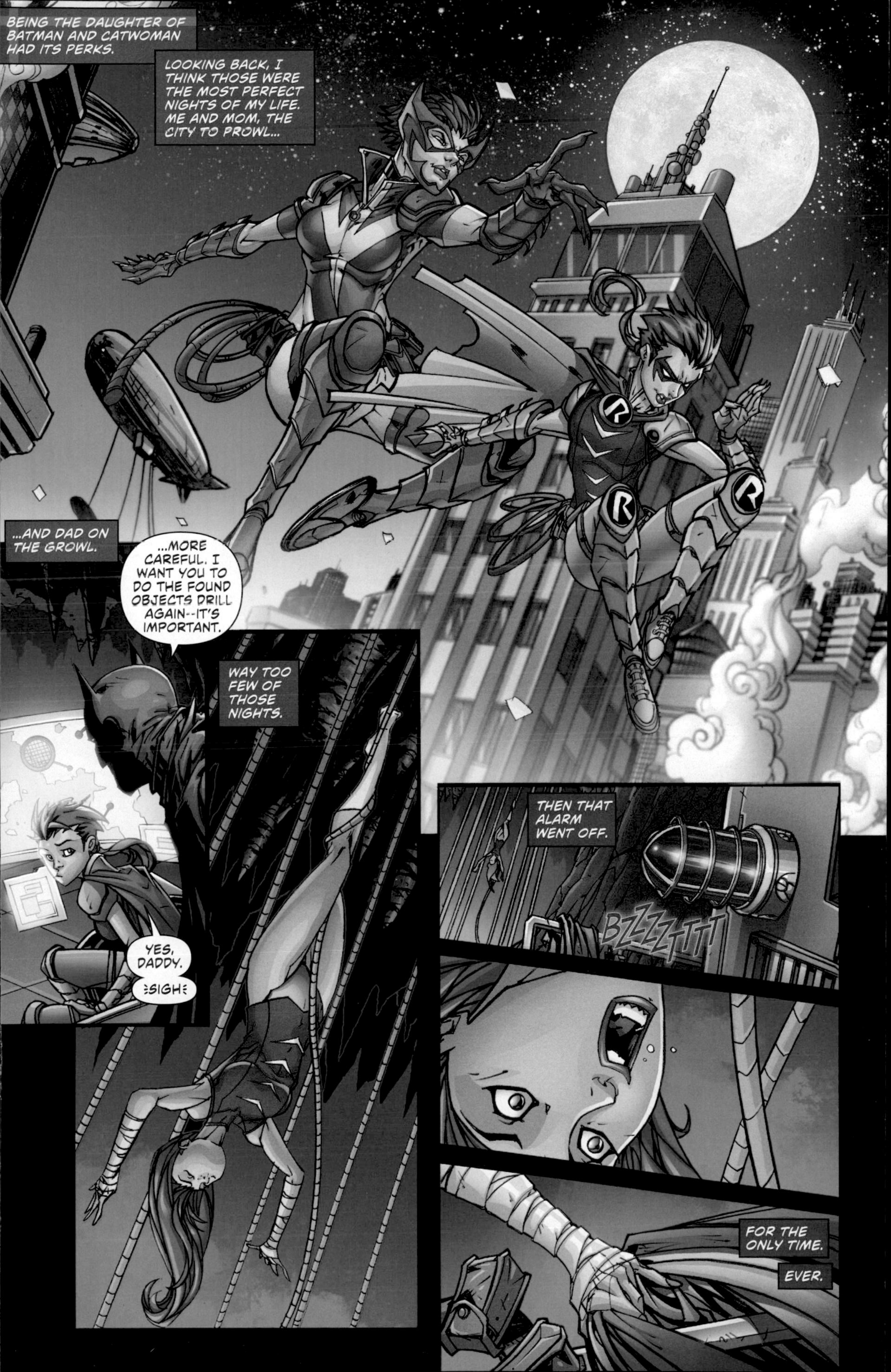
BEING THE DAUGHTER OF BATMAN AND CATWOMAN HAD ITS PERKS.
LOOKING BACK, I THINK THOSE WERE THE MOST PERFECT NIGHTS OF MY LIFE. ME AND MOM, THE CITY TO PROWL...
...AND DAD ON THE GROWL.
...MORE CAREFUL. I WANT YOU TO DO THE FOUND OBJECTS DRILL AGAIN--IT'S IMPORTANT.
YES, DADDY.
SIGH
WAY TOO FEW OF THOSE NIGHTS.
THEN THAT ALARM WENT OFF.
BZZZZTTTT
FOR THE ONLY TIME.
EVER.

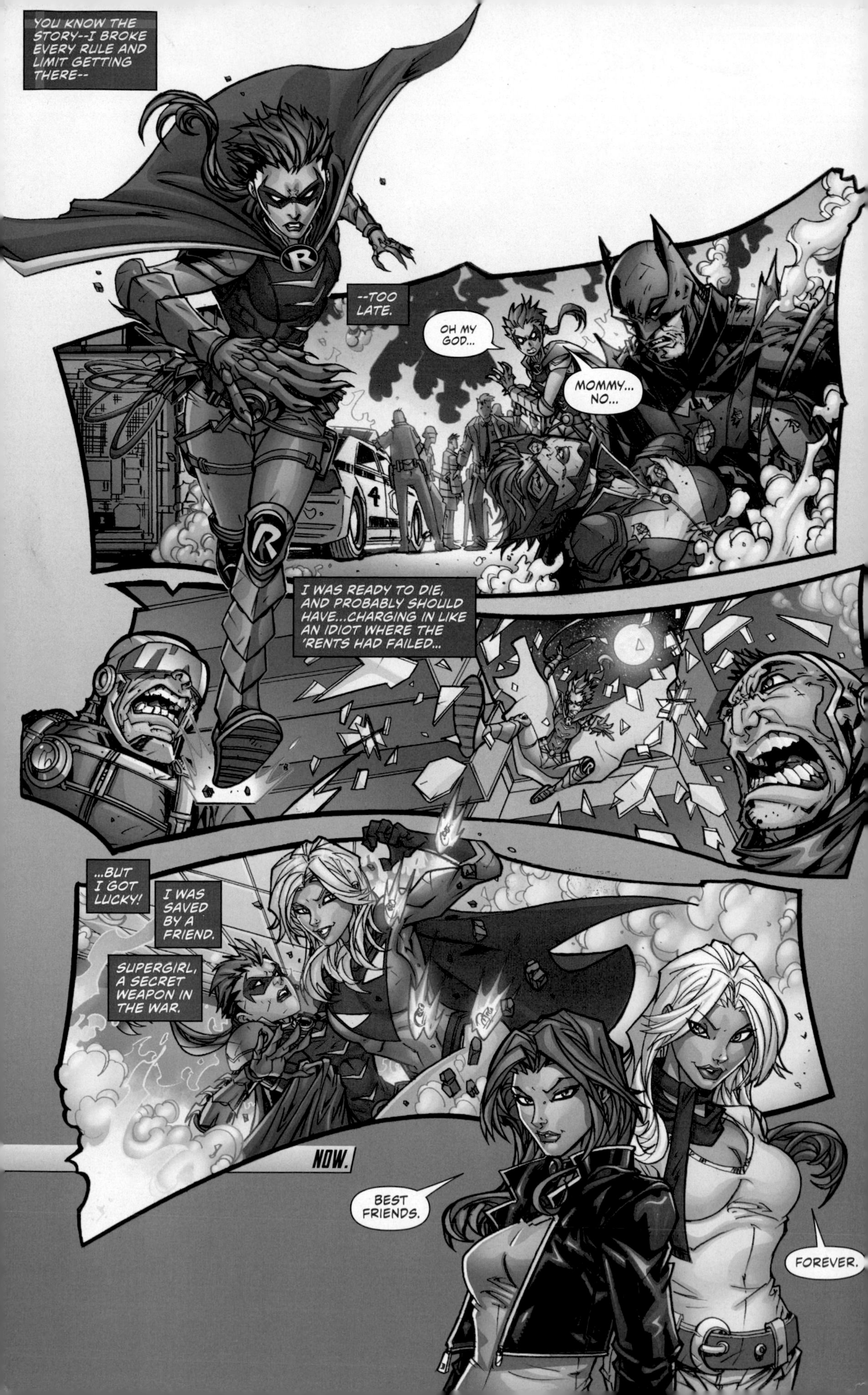
YOU KNOW THE STORY--I BROKE EVERY RULE AND LIMIT GETTING THERE--
--TOO LATE.
OH MY GOD...
MOMMY... NO...
I WAS READY TO DIE, AND PROBABLY SHOULD HAVE...CHARGING IN LIKE AN IDIOT WHERE THE 'RENTS HAD FAILED...
...BUT I GOT LUCKY!
I WAS SAVED BY A FRIEND.
SUPERGIRL, A SECRET WEAPON IN THE WAR.
NOW.
BEST FRIENDS.
FOREVER.

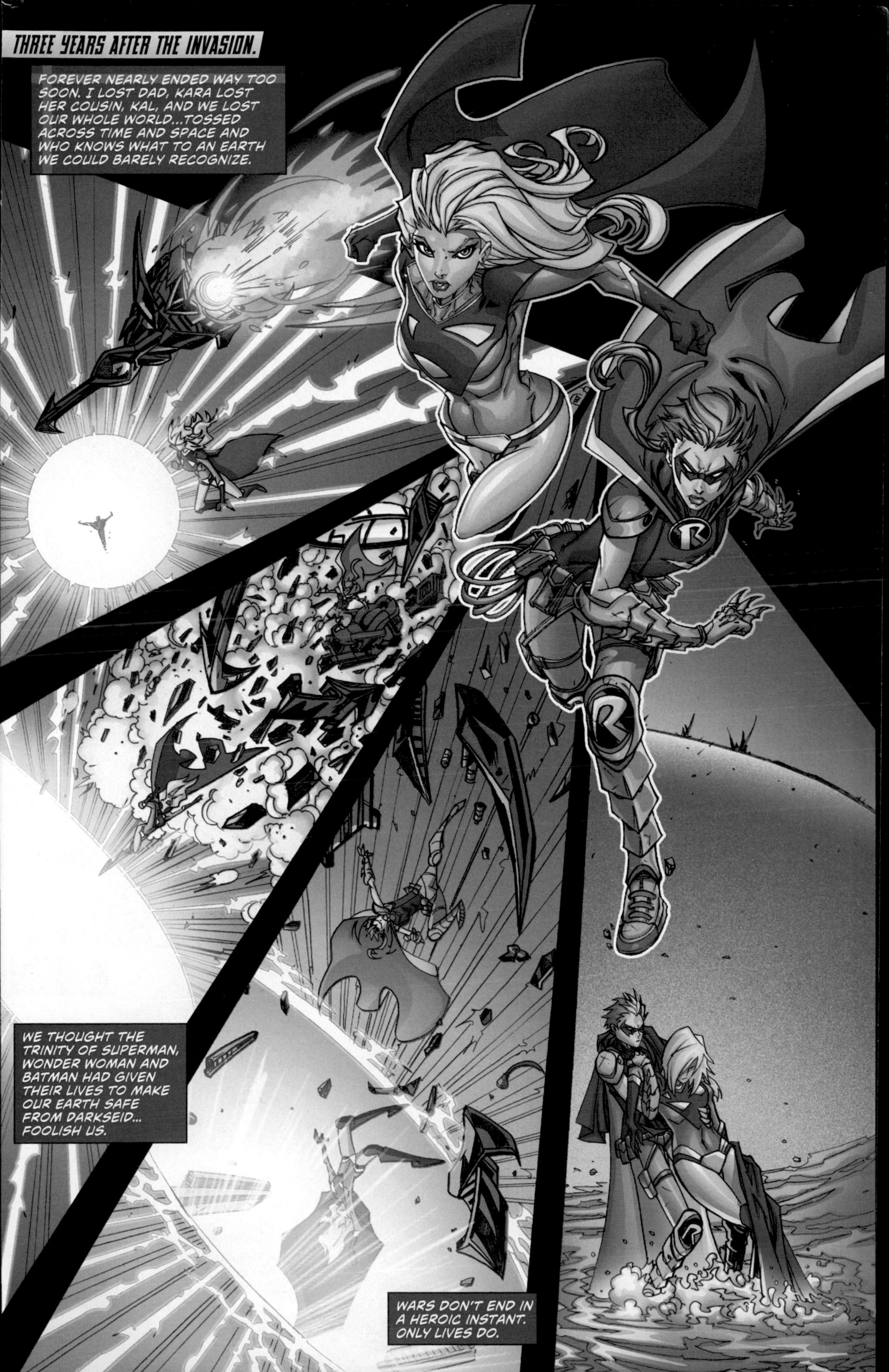
THREE YEARS AFTER THE INVASION.
FOREVER NEARLY ENDED WAY TOO SOON. I LOST DAD, KARA LOST HER COUSIN, KAL, AND WE LOST OUR WHOLE WORLD...TOSSED ACROSS TIME AND SPACE AND WHO KNOWS WHAT TO AN EARTH WE COULD BARELY RECOGNIZE.
WE THOUGHT THE TRINITY OF SUPERMAN, WONDER WOMAN AND BATMAN HAD GIVEN THEIR LIVES TO MAKE OUR EARTH SAFE FROM DARKSEID... FOOLISH US.
WARS DON'T END IN A HEROIC INSTANT. ONLY LIVES DO.

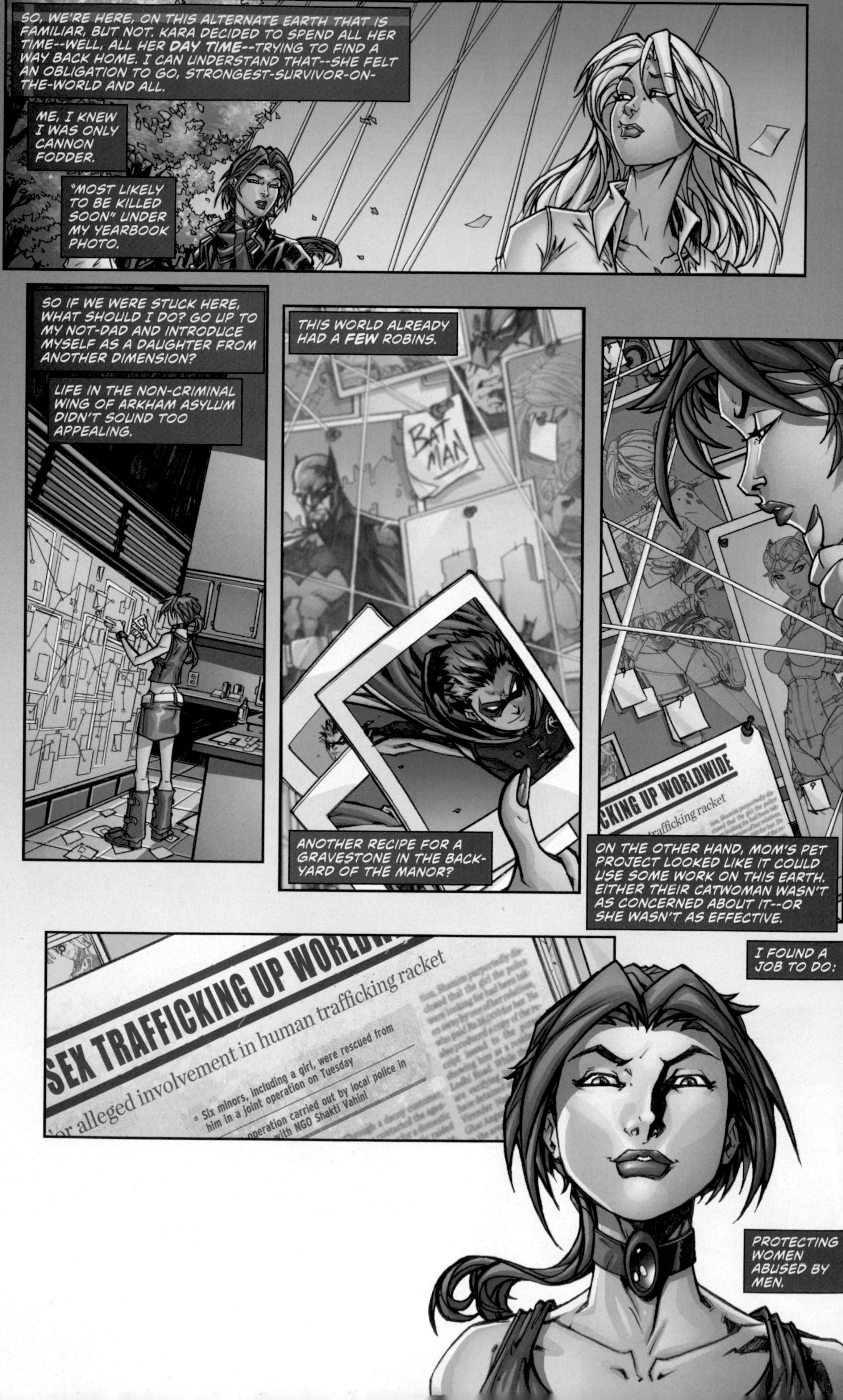
SO, WE'RE HERE, ON THIS ALTERNATE EARTH THAT IS FAMILIAR, BUT NOT. KARA DECIDED TO SPEND ALL HER TIME--WELL, ALL HER DAY TIME--TRYING TO FIND A WAY BACK HOME. I CAN UNDERSTAND THAT--SHE FELT AN OBLIGATION TO GO, STRONGEST-SURVIVOR-ON-THE-WORLD AND ALL.
ME, I KNEW I WAS ONLY CANNON FODDER.
"MOST LIKELY TO BE KILLED SOON" UNDER MY YEARBOOK PHOTO.
SO IF WE WERE STUCK HERE, WHAT SHOULD I DO? GO UP TO MY NOT-DAD AND INTRODUCE MYSELF AS A DAUGHTER FROM ANOTHER DIMENSION?
LIFE IN THE NON-CRIMINAL WING OF ARKHAM ASYLUM DIDN'T SOUND TOO APPEALING.
THIS WORLD ALREADY HAD A FEW ROBINS.
BAT MAN
ANOTHER RECIPE FOR A GRAVESTONE IN THE BACK-YARD OF THE MANOR?
CKING UP WORLDWIDE
trafficking racket
ON THE OTHER HAND, MOM'S PET PROJECT LOOKED LIKE IT COULD USE SOME WORK ON THIS EARTH. EITHER THEIR CATWOMAN WASN'T AS CONCERNED ABOUT IT--OR SHE WASN'T AS EFFECTIVE.
SEX TRAFFICKING UP WORLDW
involvement in human trafficking racket
for alleged
Six minors, including a girl, were rescued from him in a joint operation on Tuesday
operation carried out by local police in with NGO Shakti Vahini
I FOUND A JOB TO DO:
PROTECTING WOMEN ABUSED BY MEN.

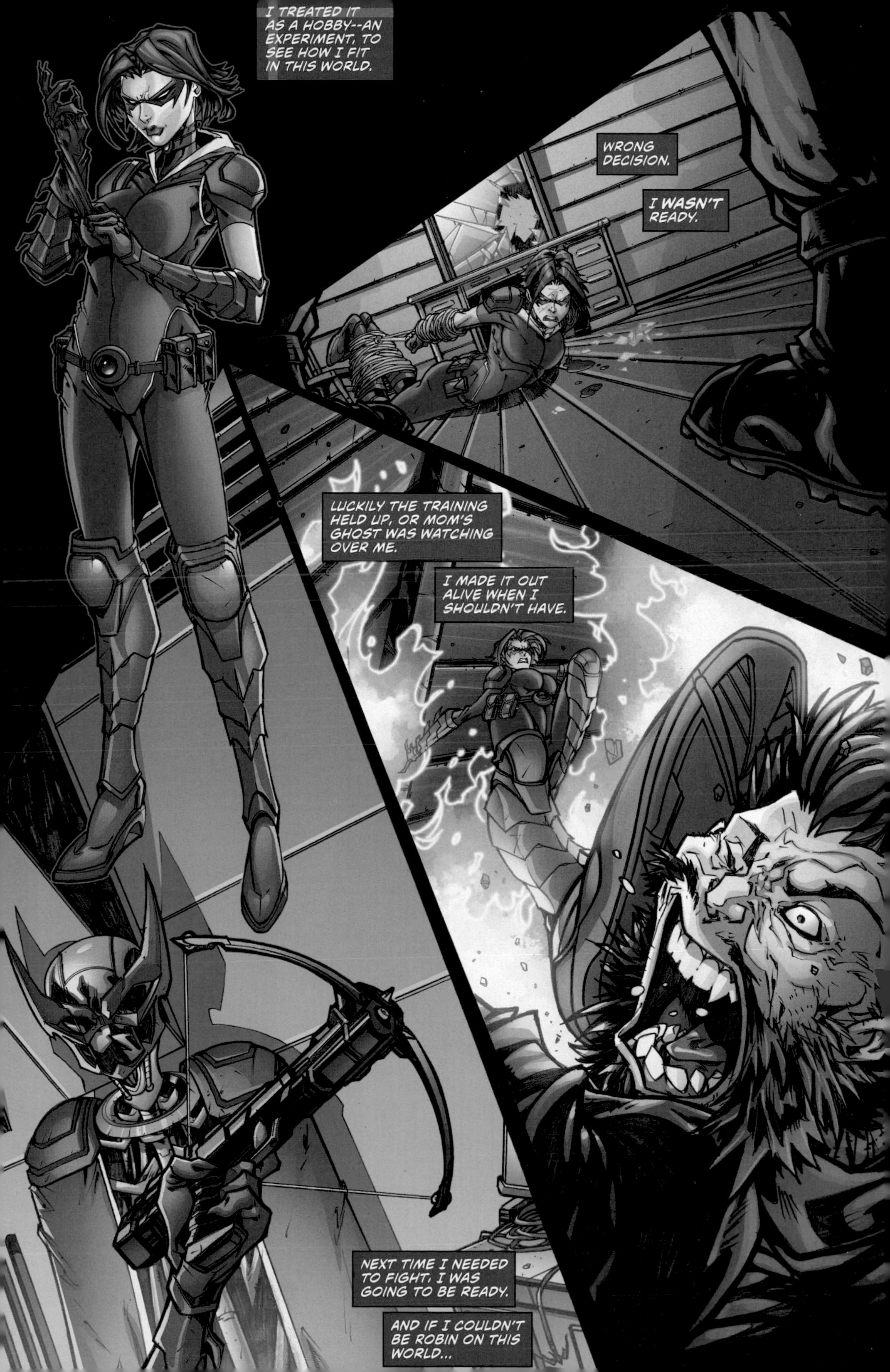

I TREATED IT AS A HOBBY--AN EXPERIMENT, TO SEE HOW I FIT IN THIS WORLD.
WRONG DECISION.
I WASN'T READY.
LUCKILY THE TRAINING HELD UP, OR MOM'S GHOST WAS WATCHING OVER ME.
I MADE IT OUT ALIVE WHEN I SHOULDN'T HAVE.
NEXT TIME I NEEDED TO FIGHT, I WAS GOING TO BE READY.
AND IF I COULDN'T BE ROBIN ON THIS WORLD...

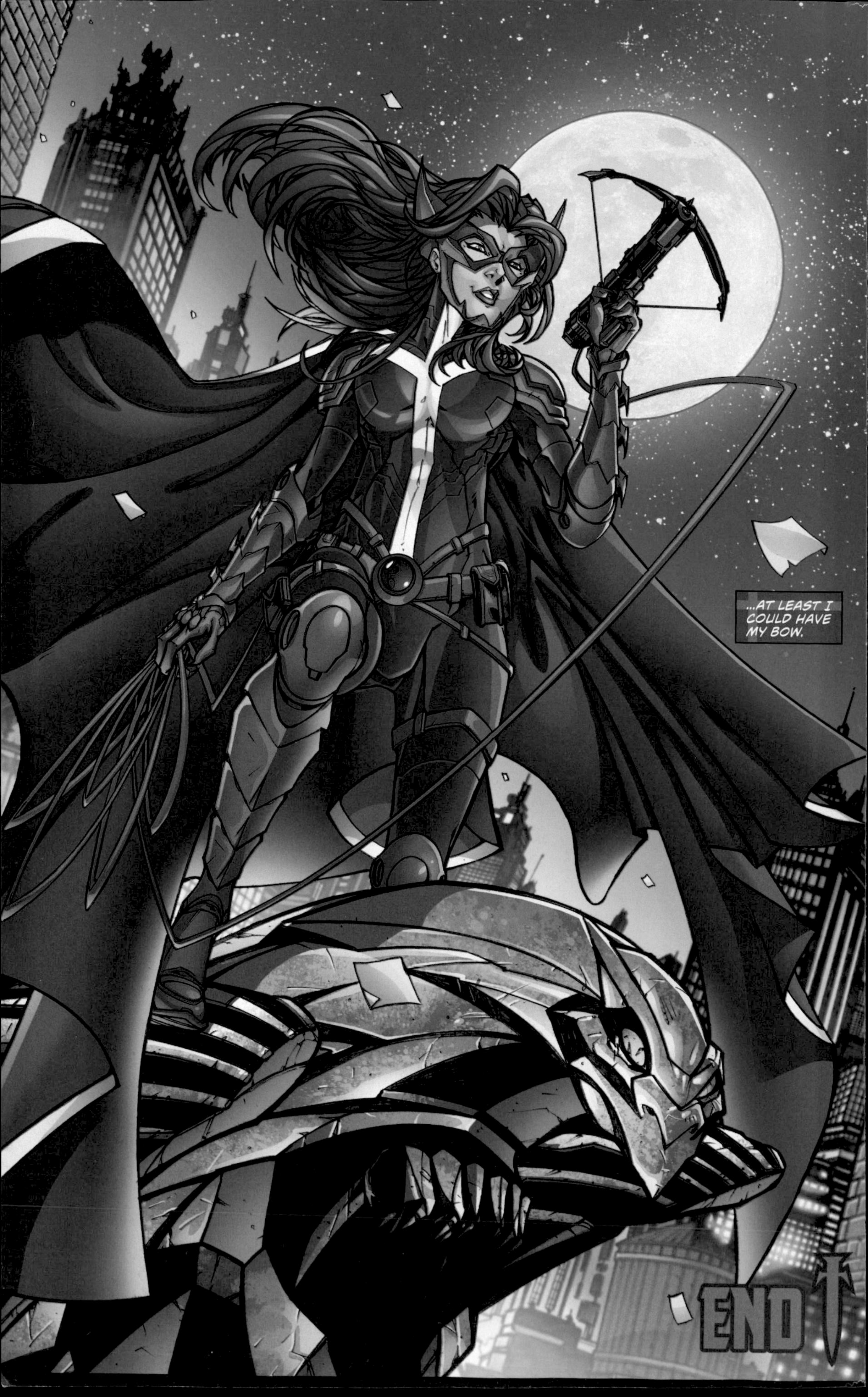
...AT LEAST I COULD HAVE MY BOW.
END

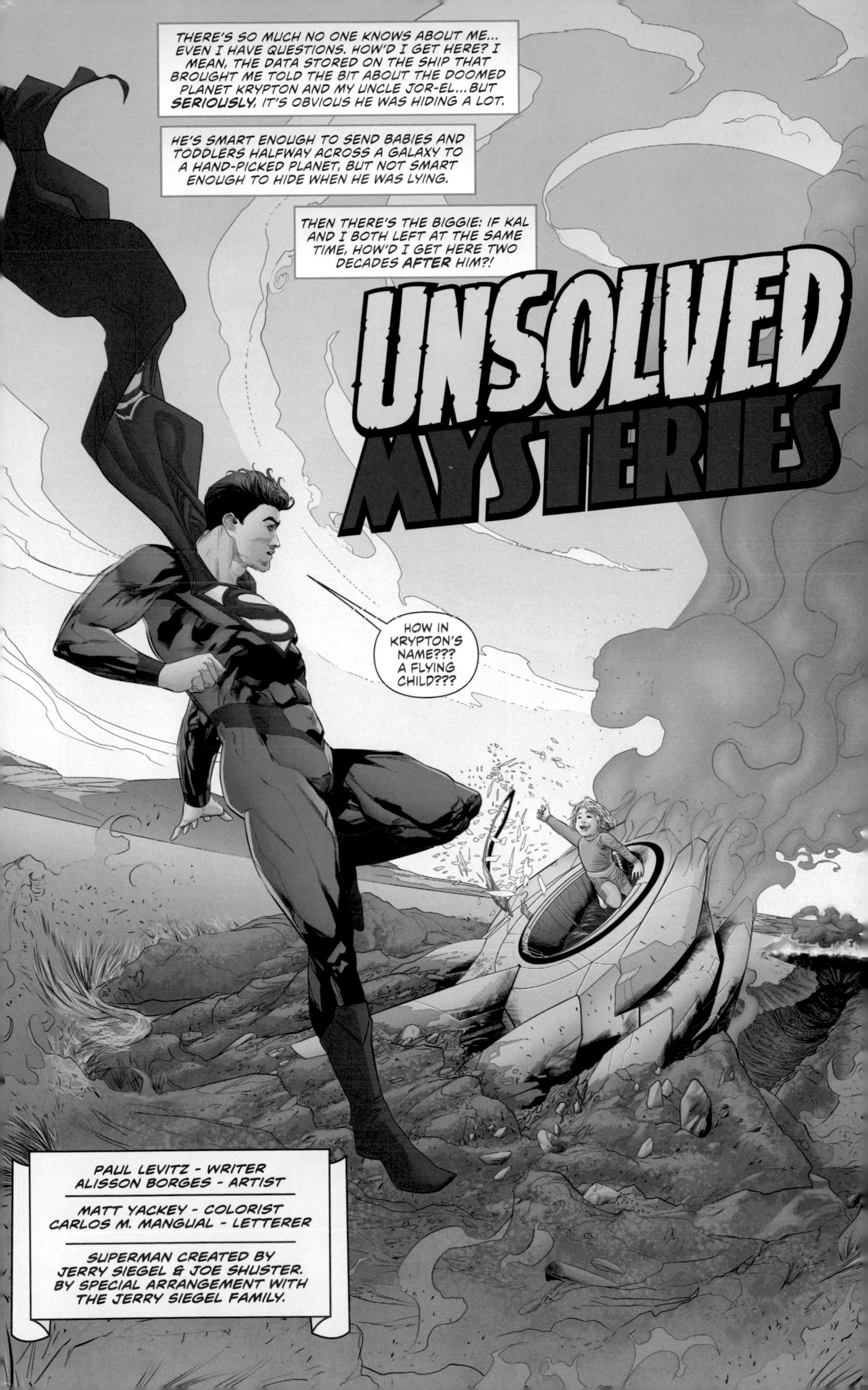
THERE'S SO MUCH NO ONE KNOWS ABOUT ME... EVEN I HAVE QUESTIONS. HOW'D I GET HERE? I MEAN, THE DATA STORED ON THE SHIP THAT BROUGHT ME TOLD THE BIT ABOUT THE DOOMED PLANET KRYPTON AND MY UNCLE JOR-EL...BUT SERIOUSLY, IT'S OBVIOUS HE WAS HIDING A LOT.
HE'S SMART ENOUGH TO SEND BABIES AND TODDLERS HALFWAY ACROSS A GALAXY TO A HAND-PICKED PLANET, BUT NOT SMART ENOUGH TO HIDE WHEN HE WAS LYING.
THEN THERE'S THE BIGGIE: IF KAL AND I BOTH LEFT AT THE SAME TIME, HOW'D I GET HERE TWO DECADES AFTER HIM?!
UNSOLVED MYSTERIES
HOW IN KRYPTON'S NAME??? A FLYING CHILD???
PAUL LEVITZ - WRITER
ALISSON BORGES - ARTIST
MATT YACKEY - COLORIST
CARLOS M. MANGUAL - LETTERER
SUPERMAN CREATED BY JERRY SIEGEL & JOE SHUSTER. BY SPECIAL ARRANGEMENT WITH THE JERRY SIEGEL FAMILY.

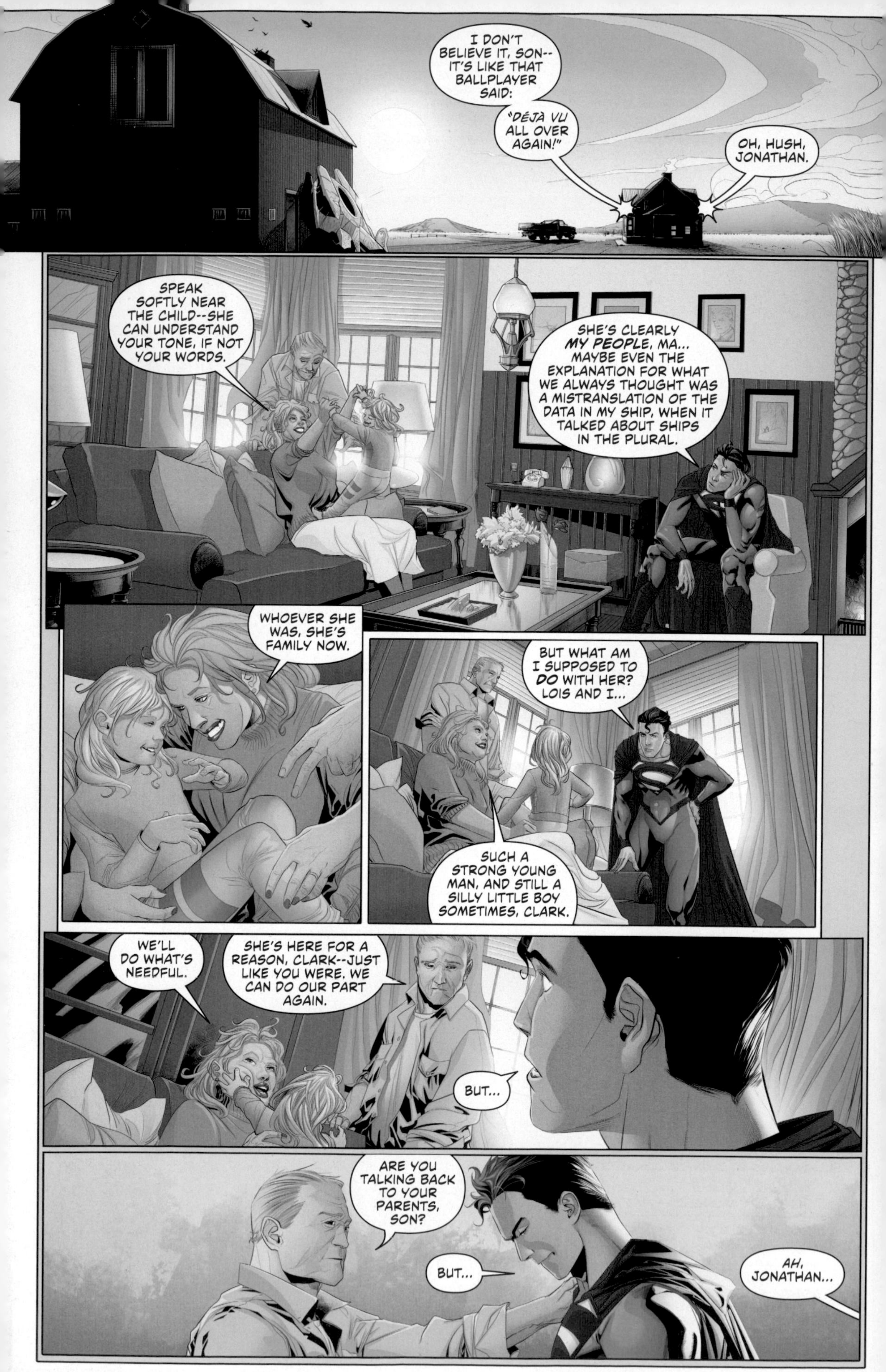
I DON'T BELIEVE IT, SON-- IT'S LIKE THAT BALLPLAYER SAID:
"DÉJÀ VU ALL OVER AGAIN!"
OH, HUSH, JONATHAN.
SPEAK SOFTLY NEAR THE CHILD--SHE CAN UNDERSTAND YOUR TONE, IF NOT YOUR WORDS.
SHE'S CLEARLY MY PEOPLE, MA... MAYBE EVEN THE EXPLANATION FOR WHAT WE ALWAYS THOUGHT WAS A MISTRANSLATION OF THE DATA IN MY SHIP, WHEN IT TALKED ABOUT SHIPS IN THE PLURAL.
WHOEVER SHE WAS, SHE'S FAMILY NOW.
BUT WHAT AM I SUPPOSED TO DO WITH HER? LOIS AND I...
SUCH A STRONG YOUNG MAN, AND STILL A SILLY LITTLE BOY SOMETIMES, CLARK.
WE'LL DO WHAT'S NEEDFUL.
SHE'S HERE FOR A REASON, CLARK--JUST LIKE YOU WERE. WE CAN DO OUR PART AGAIN.
BUT...
ARE YOU TALKING BACK TO YOUR PARENTS, SON?
BUT...
AH, JONATHAN...

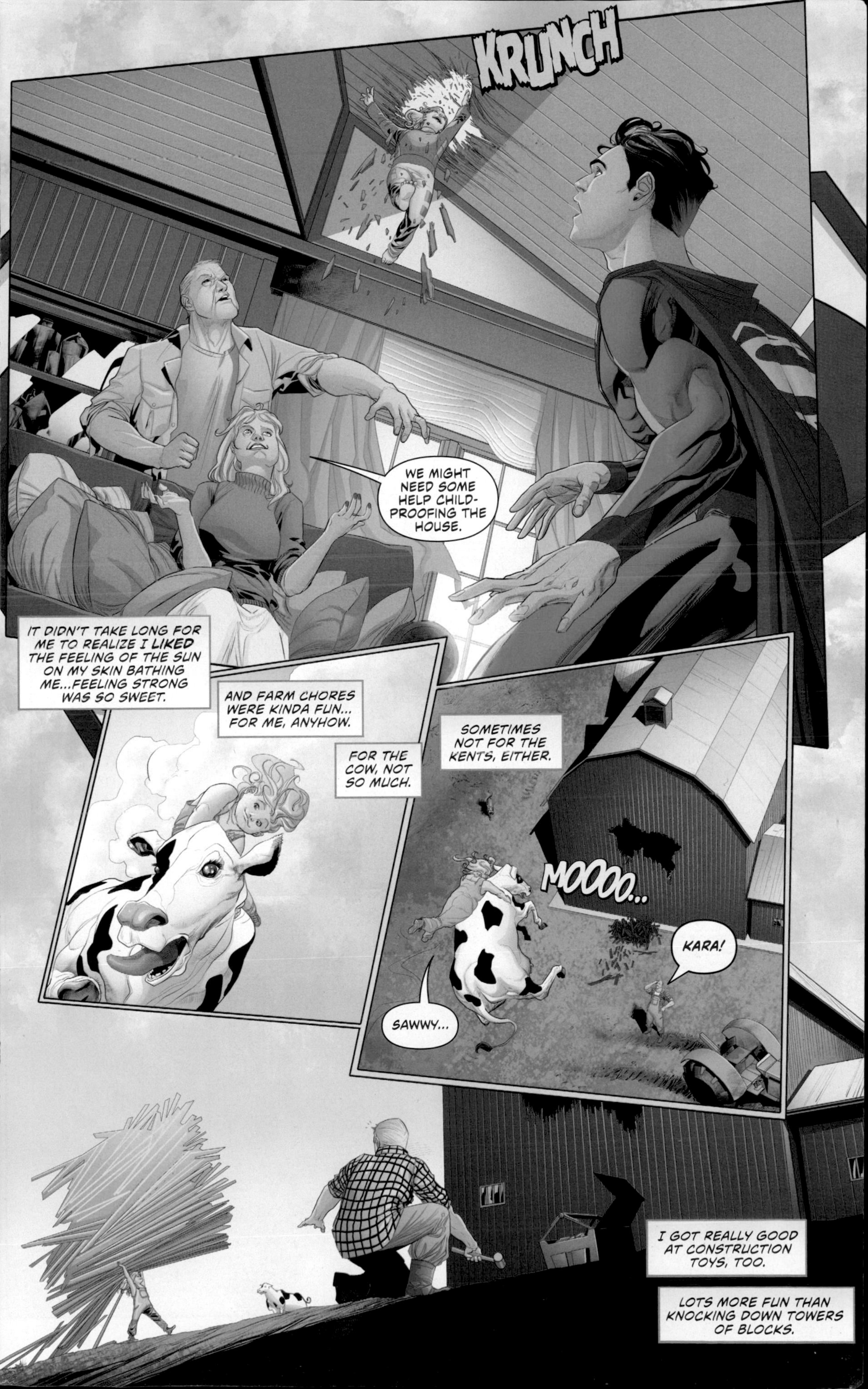
KRUNCH
WE MIGHT NEED SOME HELP CHILD-PROOFING THE HOUSE.
IT DIDN'T TAKE LONG FOR ME TO REALIZE I LIKED THE FEELING OF THE SUN ON MY SKIN BATHING ME...FEELING STRONG WAS SO SWEET.
AND FARM CHORES WERE KINDA FUN... FOR ME, ANYHOW.
FOR THE COW, NOT SO MUCH.
SOMETIMES NOT FOR THE KENTS, EITHER.
MOOOO...
KARA!
SAWWY...
I GOT REALLY GOOD AT CONSTRUCTION TOYS, TOO.
LOTS MORE FUN THAN KNOCKING DOWN TOWERS OF BLOCKS.

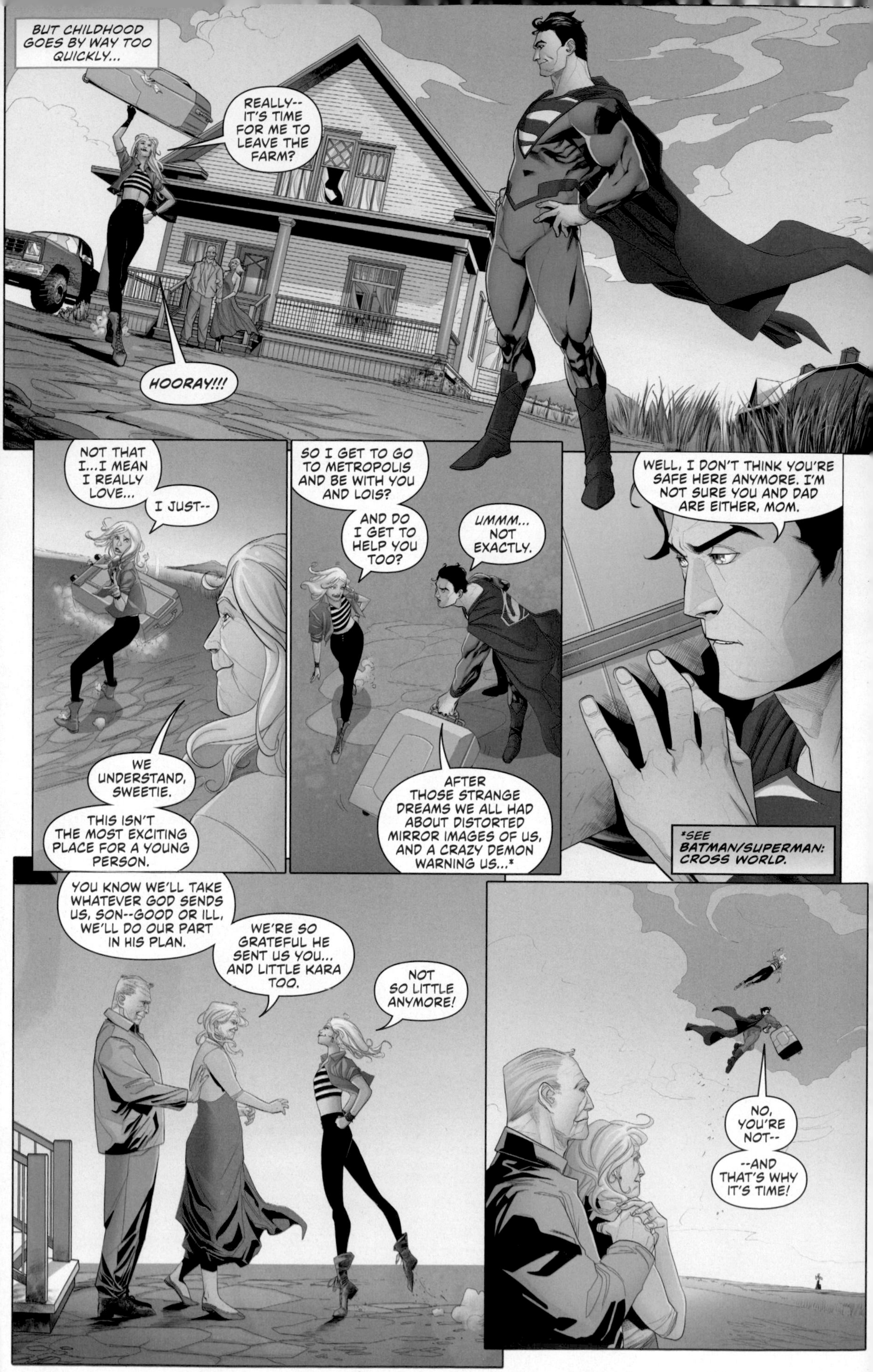

BUT CHILDHOOD GOES BY WAY TOO QUICKLY...
REALLY-- IT'S TIME FOR ME TO LEAVE THE FARM?
HOORAY!!!
NOT THAT I...I MEAN I REALLY LOVE...
I JUST--
WE UNDERSTAND, SWEETIE.
THIS ISN'T THE MOST EXCITING PLACE FOR A YOUNG PERSON.
SO I GET TO GO TO METROPOLIS AND BE WITH YOU AND LOIS?
AND DO I GET TO HELP YOU TOO?
UMMM... NOT EXACTLY.
AFTER THOSE STRANGE DREAMS WE ALL HAD ABOUT DISTORTED MIRROR IMAGES OF US, AND A CRAZY DEMON WARNING US...*
WELL, I DON'T THINK YOU'RE SAFE HERE ANYMORE. I'M NOT SURE YOU AND DAD ARE EITHER, MOM.
*SEE BATMAN/SUPERMAN: CROSS WORLD.
YOU KNOW WE'LL TAKE WHATEVER GOD SENDS US, SON--GOOD OR ILL, WE'LL DO OUR PART IN HIS PLAN.
WE'RE SO GRATEFUL HE SENT US YOU... AND LITTLE KARA TOO.
NOT SO LITTLE ANYMORE!
NO, YOU'RE NOT--
--AND THAT'S WHY IT'S TIME!

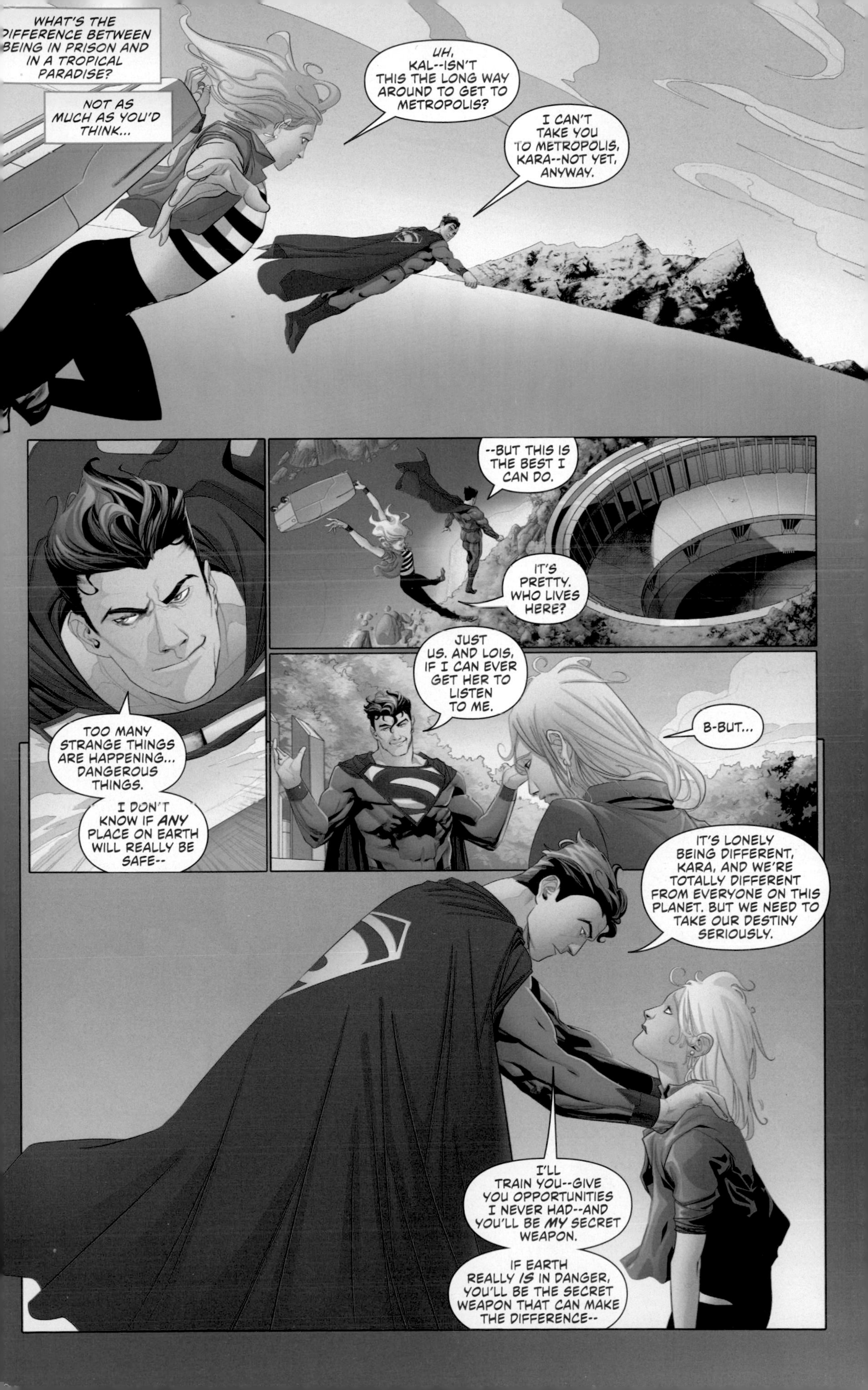
WHAT'S THE DIFFERENCE BETWEEN BEING IN PRISON AND IN A TROPICAL PARADISE?
NOT AS MUCH AS YOU'D THINK...
UH, KAL--ISN'T THIS THE LONG WAY AROUND TO GET TO METROPOLIS?
I CAN'T TAKE YOU TO METROPOLIS, KARA--NOT YET, ANYWAY.
TOO MANY STRANGE THINGS ARE HAPPENING... DANGEROUS THINGS.
I DON'T KNOW IF *ANY* PLACE ON EARTH WILL REALLY BE SAFE--
--BUT THIS IS THE BEST I CAN DO.
IT'S PRETTY. WHO LIVES HERE?
JUST US. AND LOIS, IF I CAN EVER GET HER TO LISTEN TO ME.
B-BUT...
IT'S LONELY BEING DIFFERENT, KARA, AND WE'RE TOTALLY DIFFERENT FROM EVERYONE ON THIS PLANET. BUT WE NEED TO TAKE OUR DESTINY SERIOUSLY.
I'LL TRAIN YOU--GIVE YOU OPPORTUNITIES I NEVER HAD--AND YOU'LL BE *MY* SECRET WEAPON.
IF EARTH REALLY *IS* IN DANGER, YOU'LL BE THE SECRET WEAPON THAT CAN MAKE THE DIFFERENCE--

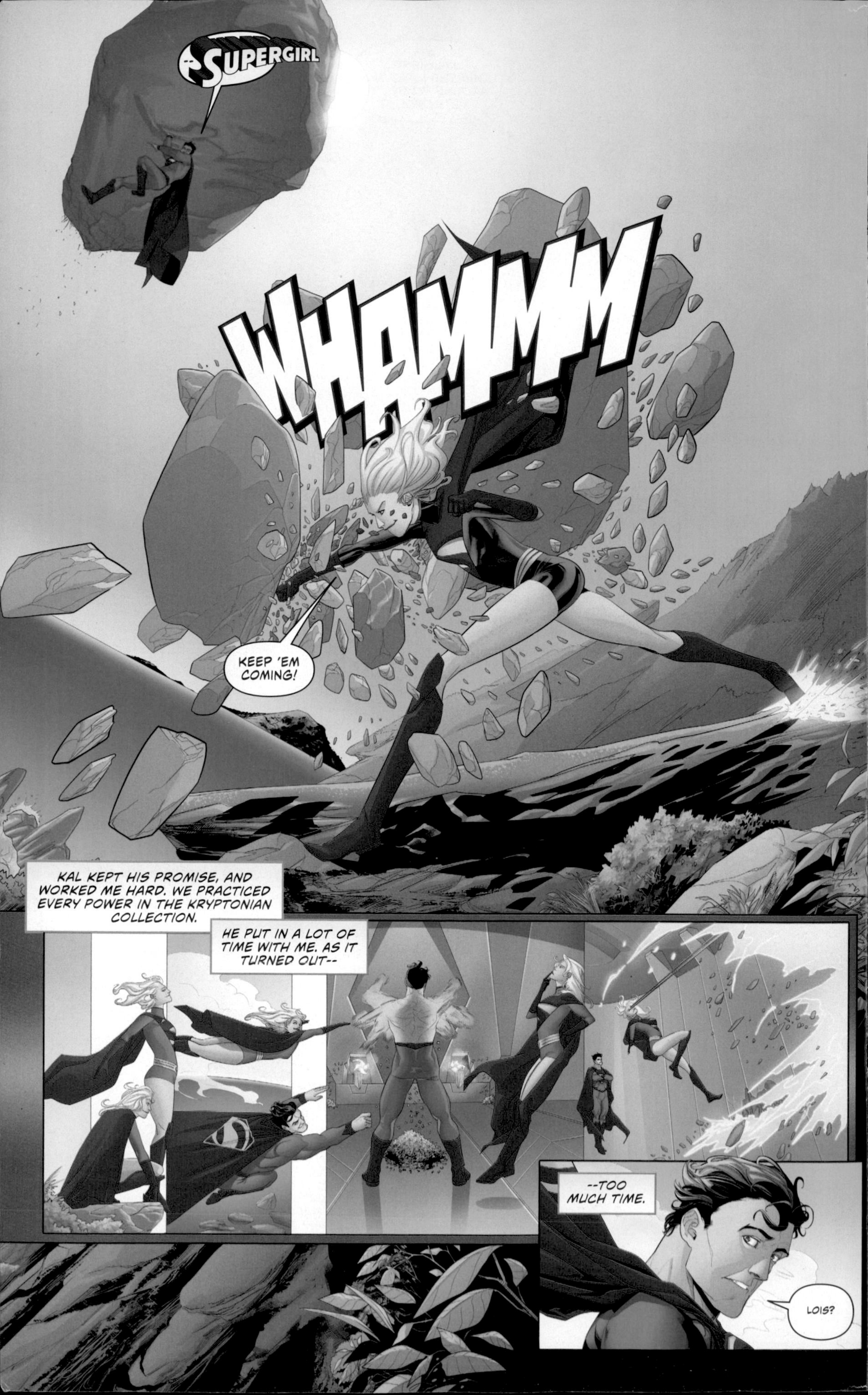
SUPERGIRL
WHAMMMM
KEEP 'EM COMING!
KAL KEPT HIS PROMISE, AND WORKED ME HARD. WE PRACTICED EVERY POWER IN THE KRYPTONIAN COLLECTION.
HE PUT IN A LOT OF TIME WITH ME. AS IT TURNED OUT--
--TOO MUCH TIME.
LOIS?

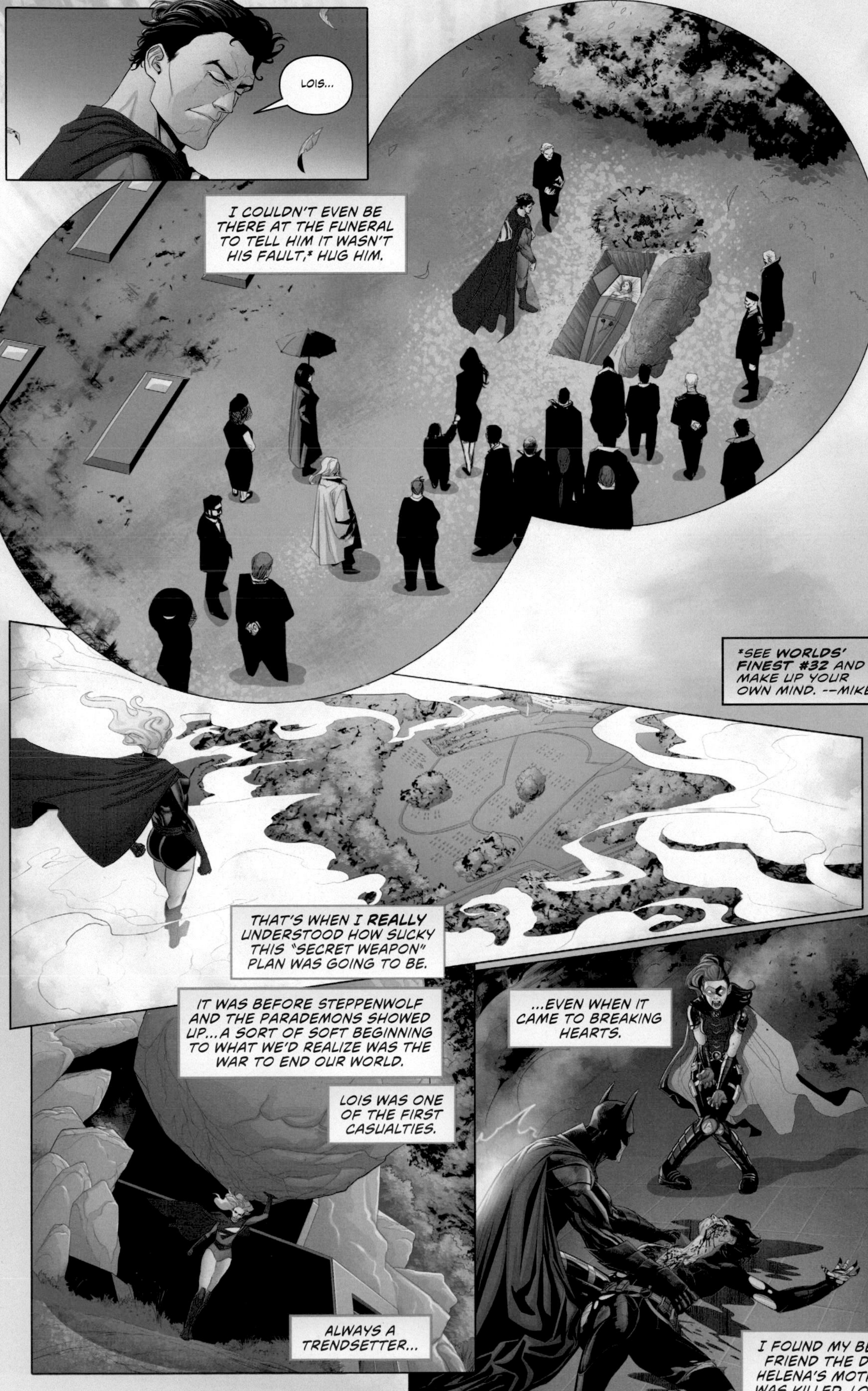
LOIS...
I COULDN'T EVEN BE THERE AT THE FUNERAL TO TELL HIM IT WASN'T HIS FAULT,* HUG HIM.
*SEE WORLDS' FINEST #32 AND MAKE UP YOUR OWN MIND. --MIKE
THAT'S WHEN I REALLY UNDERSTOOD HOW SUCKY THIS "SECRET WEAPON" PLAN WAS GOING TO BE.
IT WAS BEFORE STEPPENWOLF AND THE PARADEMONS SHOWED UP...A SORT OF SOFT BEGINNING TO WHAT WE'D REALIZE WAS THE WAR TO END OUR WORLD.
LOIS WAS ONE OF THE FIRST CASUALTIES.
ALWAYS A TRENDSETTER...
...EVEN WHEN IT CAME TO BREAKING HEARTS.
I FOUND MY BEST FRIEND THE DAY HELENA'S MOTHER WAS KILLED. LOUSY TRADE...FOR HER.

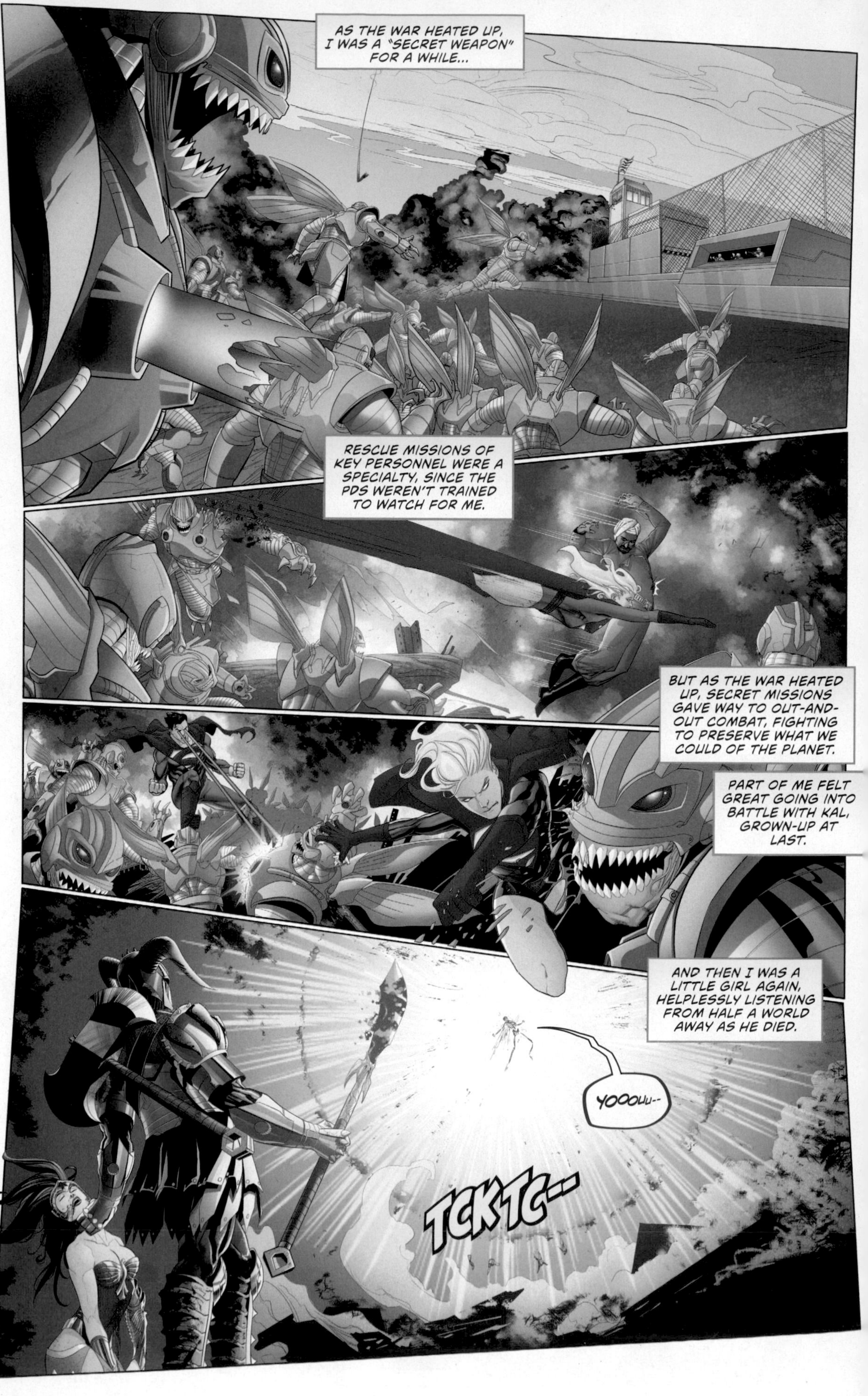
AS THE WAR HEATED UP, I WAS A "SECRET WEAPON" FOR A WHILE...
RESCUE MISSIONS OF KEY PERSONNEL WERE A SPECIALTY, SINCE THE PDS WEREN'T TRAINED TO WATCH FOR ME.
BUT AS THE WAR HEATED UP, SECRET MISSIONS GAVE WAY TO OUT-AND-OUT COMBAT, FIGHTING TO PRESERVE WHAT WE COULD OF THE PLANET.
PART OF ME FELT GREAT GOING INTO BATTLE WITH KAL, GROWN-UP AT LAST.
AND THEN I WAS A LITTLE GIRL AGAIN, HELPLESSLY LISTENING FROM HALF A WORLD AWAY AS HE DIED.
YOOOUU--
TCKTC--

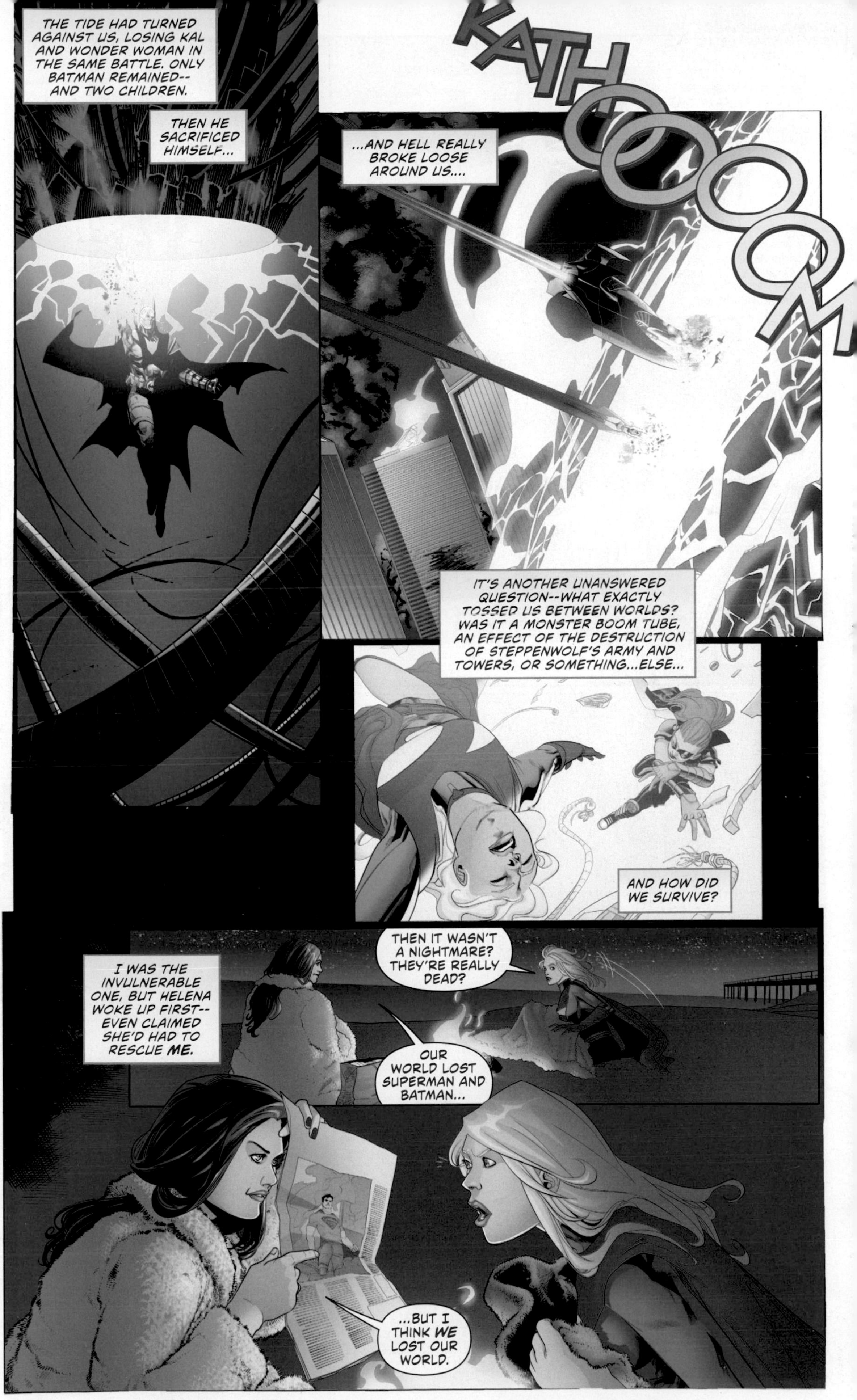
THE TIDE HAD TURNED AGAINST US, LOSING KAL AND WONDER WOMAN IN THE SAME BATTLE. ONLY BATMAN REMAINED-- AND TWO CHILDREN.
THEN HE SACRIFICED HIMSELF...
KATHOOOOOM
...AND HELL REALLY BROKE LOOSE AROUND US....
IT'S ANOTHER UNANSWERED QUESTION--WHAT EXACTLY TOSSED US BETWEEN WORLDS? WAS IT A MONSTER BOOM TUBE, AN EFFECT OF THE DESTRUCTION OF STEPPENWOLF'S ARMY AND TOWERS, OR SOMETHING...ELSE...
AND HOW DID WE SURVIVE?
I WAS THE INVULNERABLE ONE, BUT HELENA WOKE UP FIRST-- EVEN CLAIMED SHE'D HAD TO RESCUE ME.
THEN IT WASN'T A NIGHTMARE? THEY'RE REALLY DEAD?
OUR WORLD LOST SUPERMAN AND BATMAN...
...BUT I THINK WE LOST OUR WORLD.

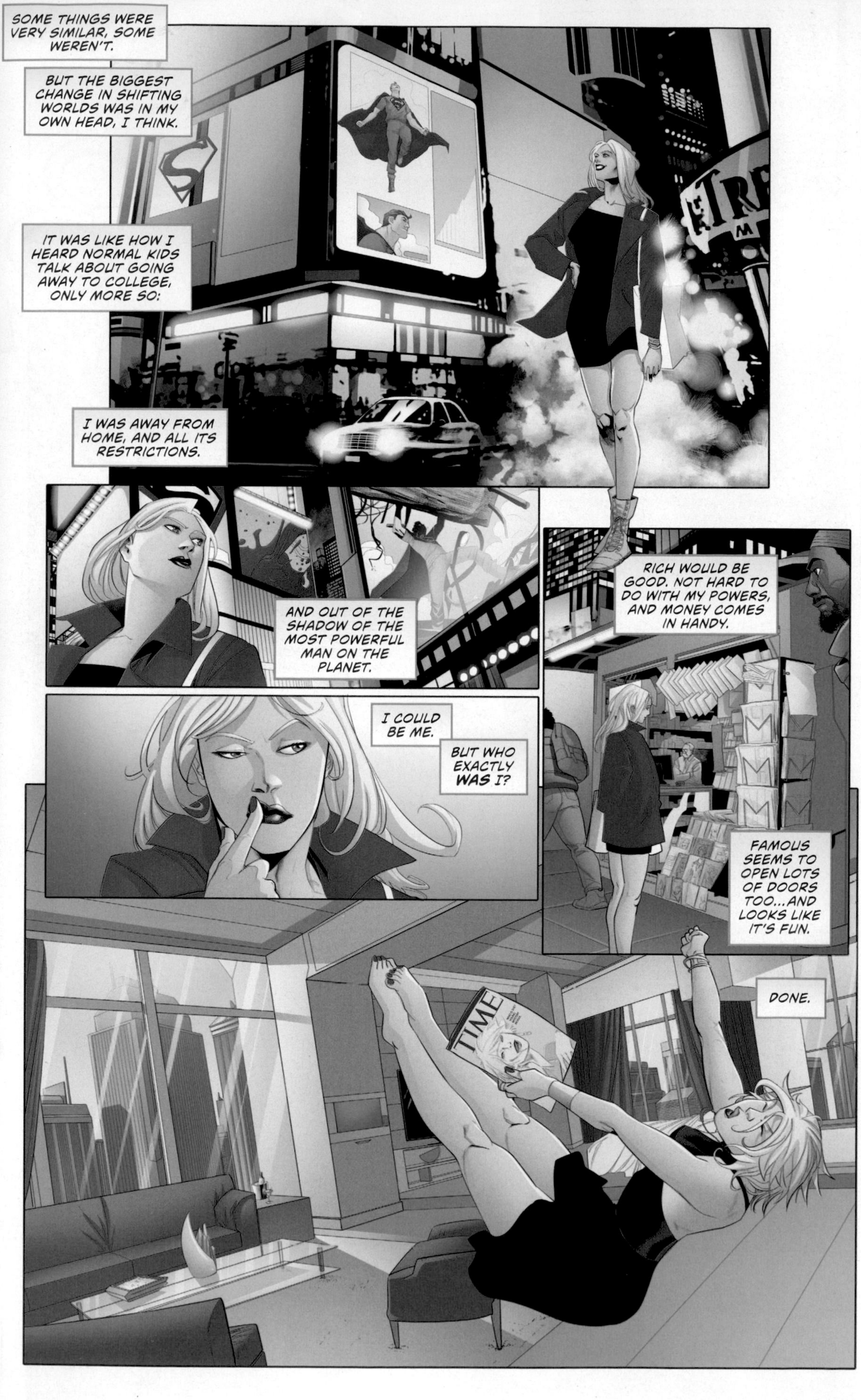
SOME THINGS WERE VERY SIMILAR, SOME WEREN'T.
BUT THE BIGGEST CHANGE IN SHIFTING WORLDS WAS IN MY OWN HEAD, I THINK.
IT WAS LIKE HOW I HEARD NORMAL KIDS TALK ABOUT GOING AWAY TO COLLEGE, ONLY MORE SO:
I WAS AWAY FROM HOME, AND ALL ITS RESTRICTIONS.
AND OUT OF THE SHADOW OF THE MOST POWERFUL MAN ON THE PLANET.
RICH WOULD BE GOOD. NOT HARD TO DO WITH MY POWERS, AND MONEY COMES IN HANDY.
I COULD BE ME.
BUT WHO EXACTLY **WAS** I?
FAMOUS SEEMS TO OPEN LOTS OF DOORS TOO...AND LOOKS LIKE IT'S FUN.
DONE.
TIME

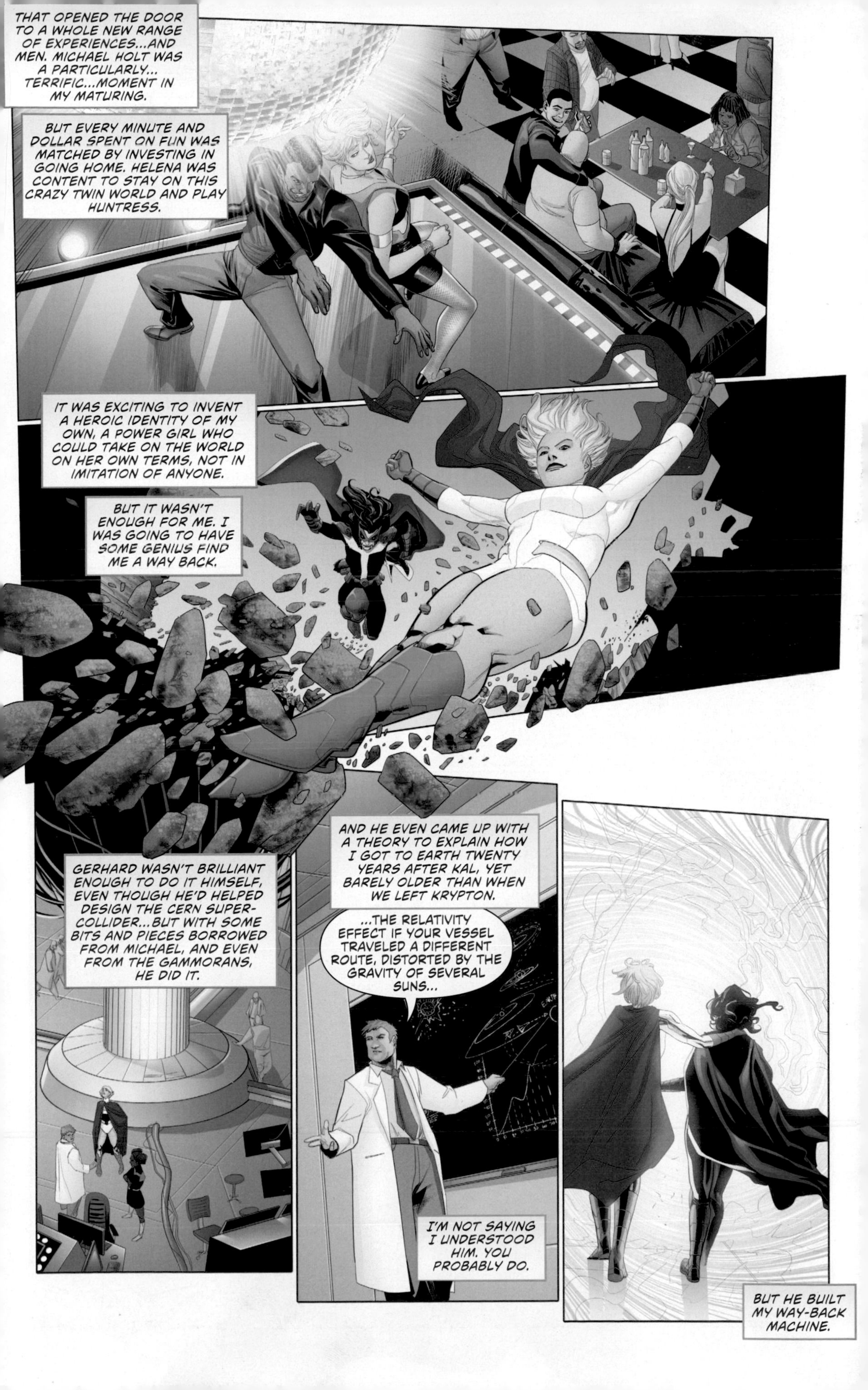
THAT OPENED THE DOOR TO A WHOLE NEW RANGE OF EXPERIENCES...AND MEN. MICHAEL HOLT WAS A PARTICULARLY... TERRIFIC...MOMENT IN MY MATURING.
BUT EVERY MINUTE AND DOLLAR SPENT ON FUN WAS MATCHED BY INVESTING IN GOING HOME. HELENA WAS CONTENT TO STAY ON THIS CRAZY TWIN WORLD AND PLAY HUNTRESS.
IT WAS EXCITING TO INVENT A HEROIC IDENTITY OF MY OWN, A POWER GIRL WHO COULD TAKE ON THE WORLD ON HER OWN TERMS, NOT IN IMITATION OF ANYONE.
BUT IT WASN'T ENOUGH FOR ME. I WAS GOING TO HAVE SOME GENIUS FIND ME A WAY BACK.
GERHARD WASN'T BRILLIANT ENOUGH TO DO IT HIMSELF, EVEN THOUGH HE'D HELPED DESIGN THE CERN SUPER-COLLIDER...BUT WITH SOME BITS AND PIECES BORROWED FROM MICHAEL, AND EVEN FROM THE GAMMORANS, HE DID IT.
AND HE EVEN CAME UP WITH A THEORY TO EXPLAIN HOW I GOT TO EARTH TWENTY YEARS AFTER KAL, YET BARELY OLDER THAN WHEN WE LEFT KRYPTON.
...THE RELATIVITY EFFECT IF YOUR VESSEL TRAVELED A DIFFERENT ROUTE, DISTORTED BY THE GRAVITY OF SEVERAL SUNS...
I'M NOT SAYING I UNDERSTOOD HIM. YOU PROBABLY DO.
BUT HE BUILT MY WAY-BACK MACHINE.

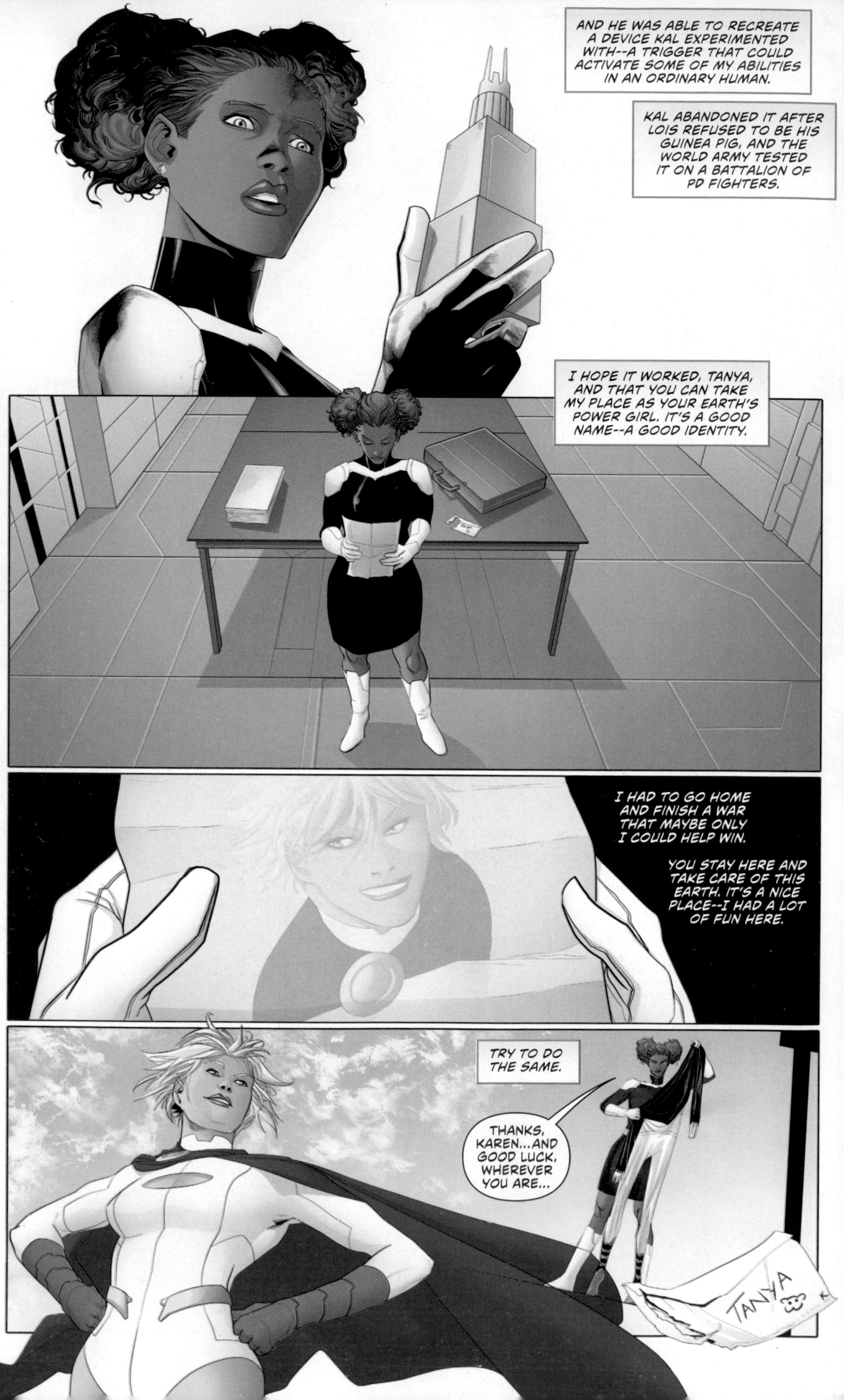
AND HE WAS ABLE TO RECREATE A DEVICE KAL EXPERIMENTED WITH--A TRIGGER THAT COULD ACTIVATE SOME OF MY ABILITIES IN AN ORDINARY HUMAN.
KAL ABANDONED IT AFTER LOIS REFUSED TO BE HIS GUINEA PIG, AND THE WORLD ARMY TESTED IT ON A BATTALION OF PD FIGHTERS.
I HOPE IT WORKED, TANYA, AND THAT YOU CAN TAKE MY PLACE AS YOUR EARTH'S POWER GIRL. IT'S A GOOD NAME--A GOOD IDENTITY.
I HAD TO GO HOME AND FINISH A WAR THAT MAYBE ONLY I COULD HELP WIN.
YOU STAY HERE AND TAKE CARE OF THIS EARTH. IT'S A NICE PLACE--I HAD A LOT OF FUN HERE.
TRY TO DO THE SAME.
THANKS, KAREN...AND GOOD LUCK, WHEREVER YOU ARE...
TANYA
K